Spirituality Matters in Social Worl

Offering a focus that is lacking (or not clearly evident) in most spirituality books, Dudley addresses specific ways of incorporating spirituality into practice and integrates many of the contributions of other writers into an overall eclectic practice approach. His approach revolves around all of the core competencies of accreditation. Special emphasis is given to ethical and professional behavior; diversity; social justice; critical thinking; and research informed practice. In addition, a major framework of the book emphasizes the practice components of engagement, assessment, intervention, and evaluation.

James (Jim) Dudley has been involved in spirituality activities and their role in social work practice for many years. Besides teaching numerous Spirituality and Social Work courses at the University of North Carolina at Charlotte, he has also conducted research and published on the topic, as well as led several retreats and workshops. He has a Master's degree in Spirituality Studies and has completed training in spiritual direction. He also has an MSW degree and a Ph.D. in Social Work, and is a licensed clinical social worker in North Carolina.

Dr. Jim Dudley's *Spirituality Matters in Social Work* is a welcome addition to the growing number of books and articles in the social work literature focused on preparing social workers to effectively engage spiritual and religious issues in the helping process when they are important to helping their clients. Dr. Dudley's book explores, in depth, key elements of ethical, spiritually sensitive social work approaches and strategies in terms of engagement, spiritual assessment, interventions and evaluation. More than most, his book pays attention to the integration of spirituality and religion at micro, mezzo, *and* macro levels of intervention, as well as the important question of how to determine the effectiveness and impact of spiritually sensitive programs and practice on the clients it serves.

Rick Chamiec-Case, *North American Association of Christians in Social Work*

There is a compelling need for clinical guidance concerning the complex issues of spirituality and religion in social work practice. Preparing students through spiritual self-exploration, engagement, assessment, intervention, and even the little considered but essential area of evaluation, this text offers valuable knowledge in an accessible format. It is both wise and wonderful.

Holly Nelson-Becker, *Loyola University Chicago*

Fantastic … Dudley not only educates social workers on the integration of clients' religion and spirituality, but also creates opportunities for the reader to explore his/her personal spiritual beliefs as they relate to practice. This balance of providing content with practicing self-awareness is critical in any helping profession. This book includes practical methods for learning about others' religious beliefs, maintaining a spiritually sensitive approach to practice, and identifying assessment tools and spiritual interventions at both the micro and macro levels. I highly recommend this text for both students and practitioners in social work and related helping professions.

Holly Oxhandler, *Baylor University*

For far too long, spirituality was neglected in social work and yet it may be a major source of strength for the clients that our students will serve. The focus on spirituality and multiple levels of practice can help students understand the place of spirituality in all levels of practice. I believe this text will benefit both BSW and MSSW students including those who consider themselves to be spiritual and those who do not.

Melody Loya, *West Texas A&M University*

Spirituality Matters in Social Work

Connecting Spirituality, Religion, and Practice

James R. Dudley

Routledge
Taylor & Francis Group

NEW YORK AND LONDON

First published 2016
by Routledge
711 Third Avenue, New York, NY 10017

and by Routledge
2 Park Square, Milton Park, Abingdon, Oxon, OX14 4RN

Routledge is an imprint of the Taylor & Francis Group, an informa business

© 2016 Taylor & Francis

The right of James R. Dudley to be identified as author of this work has been asserted by him in accordance with sections 77 and 78 of the Copyright, Designs and Patents Act 1988.

Library of Congress Cataloging in Publication Data
Names: Dudley, James R.
Title: Spirituality matters in social work : connecting spirituality, religion, and practice / by Jim Dudley.
Description: Edition one. | New York : Routledge, [2016]
Identifiers: LCCN 2015028235| ISBN 9780415747035 (hardback : alk. paper) | ISBN 9780415747042 (pbk. : alk. paper) | ISBN 9781315797144 (ebook)
Subjects: LCSH: Spirituality. | Religions. | Social service--Religious aspects.
Classification: LCC BL624 .D8325 2016 | DDC 201/.762--dc23
LC record available at http://lccn.loc.gov/2015028235

ISBN: 978-0-415-74703-5 (hbk)
ISBN: 978-0-415-74704-2 (pbk)
ISBN: 978-1-315-79714-4 (ebk)

Typeset in Warnock Pro
by Servis Filmsetting Ltd, Stockport, Cheshire

My wife, Joanna, patiently supported me throughout my writing of the book and I thank her the most for making it happen.

Contents

Foreword

You hold in your hands a gem of a book. Within its covers are many concepts, cases, methods, and questions designed to move students into greater proficiency in working with the spiritual and religious strengths or concerns that clients bring to therapeutic encounters. I have come to know Dr. Jim Dudley through the pages of this text and even though spirituality and religion (especially in gerontology) have been my primary research focus for many years, I found myself learning as you also will learn. Dr. Dudley is grounded in a faith tradition and social work; knowing both very well allows him to present important information from different vantage points in ways that are quite clearly masterful.

The human heart is vast; its depth and breadth is invisible to the human eye. Yet, it holds a power and resonance that far outstrips the ability of science to study and explain all its movements, plans, good will, artifices, and authenticity. All ancient and modern spiritual and religious traditions are founded on compassion of the heart. In fact many students enter social work and other mental health professions in order to decrease suffering of others, to continue learning and growth, and to make their own significant contribution to what is most needed in the world. This book is threaded through with ideas and methods for preserving and increasing compassionate understanding as students learn to respect all positions.

Nearly everyone carries with them at least a few of the *big questions* of living and identity: what is the nature of the universe and what is my place in it, what is the meaning and purpose of my life, how can I flourish and help others to do the same? These questions often feel intimate and hard to articulate just as they are important to consider. Individuals also need to locate anchor points in life, ideas or capacities they can hold onto when everything seems to fall apart. For many, spirituality and religion keep those questions vibrant even as they also provide answers, answers which may remain fixed or may change dynamically as life events unspool and curiosity keeps the fire of learning alive. Social work students will discover that some of their clients' questions are also their own.

However strongly we may believe in or simply be curious about the spiritual, we don't have a language for this, which by its nature and experience often lies beyond the power of the tongue to tell. There is reluctance and resistance for social workers, health, and mental health practitioners to host such conversations with clients. Nevertheless, these conversations can initiate the strength, motivation, and clarity for individuals to find their own healing, specify their questions, and move forward in faith which manifests—if not in God, a Transcendent Force, deity, deities, or nature—in the innate goodness or capacity for goodness of humankind.

A recent study presents this problem well. Ernecoff et al. (2015) explored audiotaped physician-family conversations across six medical centers over three years to see how spiritual and religious conversations fared. In 249 recorded goals of care conversations with surrogate decision makers (cases where the patients themselves were no longer capable of making their own health care decisions), spirituality and/or religion were mentioned in only 40 (16 percent) and were brought up first by family members in 26 of the 40. This ensued although 77.6 percent of family members reported that spirituality/religion were fairly important to very important. More concerning than the content of what was discussed were physician responses. When religious or spiritual statements were made, physicians often redirected the conversation to the medical plan or terminality of the patient. If empathy was shown, it was not related directly to spirituality or religion. In 11 of those 40 discussions, physicians gave closed-ended responses like "Mhmm" or "Ok." Most common where physicians did initiate the conversation, it was to ask if they should call the chaplain. Social workers can become leaders in hosting spiritual conversations.

There is a clear need for competency among all professionals in recognizing, assessing, and responding to spiritual questions and spiritual needs. Social workers, with their training in holistic biopsychosocial spiritual cultural methods, are well-poised to respond. Interspiritual and interreligious interactions are now common in work with clients: such understanding was never more needed than in our time where respect for such traditions is often censured in favor of stereotypic thinking that obfuscates the truth of the personal religious or spiritual path. Some social workers have a religious or spiritual affiliation; others come from nonspiritual and nonreligious backgrounds. Neither the former nor the latter group is innately better at assessing and working with spiritual strengths or spiritual struggles. Both groups require more knowledge and skills. They will find them here.

Spirituality needs to take its place fully on the biopsychosocial spiritual cultural assessment spectrum. On many occasions it is absent from this list or much diminished, on the roster but without direction, if any at all, on how to approach it. Why this marginalization? There are many reasons: the dismissal of the right to self-determination of clients or patients through religious evangelization that crosses boundaries, loss of belief when harm is done to others through religious leaders, but most of all, discomfort and lack of perceived competence as well as professional confidence. This text, with its emphasis on methods, will help social workers build their competence and confidence in addressing this area.

In this book you will find a number of important features addressed from constructing a spiritually sensitive approach, to engagement, spiritual assessment, working with spiritual interventions, and evaluation. Evaluation is a critical, but oft-neglected, component that provides feedback and evidence for effectiveness. Finally the self-care of the practitioner is also included. Social workers are healers of the heart. They work with time, families and communities, and the mind. They employ the learned tools of their trade to heal where that is possible, or to kindle hope for healing. Let Jim Dudley be your guide to working with spiritual matters in this remarkable text on spirituality, religion, and social work practice.

Holly Nelson-Becker
Loyola University Chicago

Reference

Ernecoff, N. C., Curlin, F. A., Buddadhumaruk, P., & White, D. B. (2015). Health Care Professionals' Responses to Religious or Spiritual Statements by Surrogate Decision Makers During Goals-of-Care Discussions, *JAMA*, published online August 31, 2015.

Preface

Spiritual and religious diversity currently flourish in the United States and trends suggest even greater diversity in the future. Not only is diversity evident in the growing numbers of Muslims, Buddhists, and Hindus, but especially within Christianity where over a hundred denominations are said to exist (Canda & Furman, 2010). Some people are devout in their religious beliefs and others are not. While most Americans identify as Christians, many do not: They could be devoted to Judaism, Buddhism, Hinduism or Islam or another less well known or smaller religious group. One group may be growing faster than any other: young people raised in religious families but now identifying as "nones," or spiritual but not religious (Pew Research Center, Religion and Public Life, 2015).

The topics of spirituality and religion are important for social workers because they are a major source of identity and meaning for our clients. It's important to always remember that our clients are the primary focus in this practice book, and a focus on us as social workers is only to prepare us to be effective practitioners. For many, the topics of spirituality and religion are controversial. These are sensitive topics that are difficult to discuss with people with whom we disagree. It seems likely that when people come in contact with others of a different religious orientation, discomfort and defensiveness emerge more often than curiosity and desire to learn. This is unfortunate since we have so much we can learn from each other on these topics. So I hope everyone who reads this book will try to be as open, curious, and invigorated as possible regarding the diversity of views that await you. Some material you will find familiar, affirming, and maybe gratifying, while it's possible that other material will be unfamiliar, different from what you believe, and perhaps unsettling. My hope is that this book will help us all become better prepared to engage in dialogue on these topics and more appreciative of each other.

As the author, I have my own spirituality and religious affiliations that I bring to the book and I share them upfront so that you will understand my personal preferences and likely biases. I hope my own background and interests, being a reflection of my personal life, are kept separate from what our clients need. That is a major theme throughout the book; it is about our clients, not us. I have mostly been affiliated with Mainline Protestant Christian churches throughout my life and currently tend to gravitate toward churches that emphasize the mystical and heart-felt side of Christianity. Some are modeled after the Eastern Orthodox Church and its religious practices. I also have always chosen religious affiliations that are committed to social justice, and that is largely why I chose to be a social worker over 45 years ago. In addition, I have a growing interest in the teachings of Buddhism as they are practiced in North America. Concepts like mindfulness, meditation, and stilling the mind are important to me personally. Because I believe that these and other Buddhist concepts also have important contributions to make to social work practice, they are often highlighted. I have been a social work educator for over 40 years. During most of my career, I took the position, as many other social work educators do, that spirituality and religion were important but outside the spectrum of a social worker's professional domain. Other professionals, I thought, were more equipped to address these issues. But what led me to pursue this book project over three years ago was a growing conviction that social workers do have an important role to play in addressing these issues; the clients' spirituality can often be a central domain for empowering them.

Views about spirituality are different than religion unless you consider your religion to be the sole source of your spirituality, which seems unlikely. When spirituality is expressed in other than religious terms, ambiguity can become apparent as many people do not have a good grasp of what spirituality actually means in non-religious areas. The exploration of spirituality can be exciting because it is so open-ended, individualized, familiar at a deeper level, and often inspiring. While a definition of spirituality is provided in chapter 1, it may be more important to understand the multitude of ways that this concept is defined by different people. Indeed, it seems that there could be as many descriptors of spirituality as there are people who define it.

Religion, perhaps the more controversial concept of the two, can only be covered in an introductory way in the book with references and websites offered for readers who want more information. If you are religious, you may find that your religious group is not given enough attention or the description doesn't emphasize what you would choose to highlight. On the other hand, if you are non-religious, you may feel that too much attention is given to religious groups generally. However, since religious groups are a major source for the spirituality of many people, it is an important area to emphasize in the book.

If you are not a Christian, you may question, for example, why Christianity seems to be given more attention than other religions, even though the other major religions are covered quite extensively. About seventy percent of Americans claim to be affiliated with Christianity (Pew Research Center, Religion and Public Life, 2015). Christianity is examined in several of its variations as expressed by many of our clients. For example, many recent immigrants from Mexico and Central America are frequently our clients and bring their affiliation with the Catholic Church across the border with them. This is a cultural and religious tradition to many of them. In addition, large numbers of other immigrants from the South of the United States are also joining Pentecostal and other evangelical Protestant churches; to them, these churches bring new life and hope as they settle in their new home in the U.S.

While I identify as a Christian, this is not the reason why I am focusing on Christianity more than other groups. The sole intent and purpose of the book is to help prepare you to practice social work in a spiritually sensitive way. The other major religions of the world, Judaism, Islam, Buddhism, and Hinduism, are also highlighted, even though they are practiced by less than 10 percent of the U.S. population. These groups are often the most likely ones that our non-Christian religious clients are affiliated with.

Spiritually sensitive practice naturally begins with understanding the concepts of spirituality and religion. The first two chapters highlight these two concepts and unpack much of what they mean that is important to social workers. Numerous terms are introduced, such as the importance of meaning, inner peace, a moral and ethical code, sin and forgiveness, sacred texts, transcendence, a Higher Power, and others. Readers are invited to reflect on several questions in chapter 2 intended to help you articulate your own understanding of spirituality and any preferences you have for spiritual beliefs and practices. You are also helped to delve into identifying your religious or non-religious beliefs and affiliations and what they mean to you. Readers are encouraged to engage these questions early on because a spiritually sensitive approach needs to begin with ourselves and what we understand and believe. This important foundation helps prepare us to effectively engage the spirituality of our clients.

Chapters 3 and 4 move beyond your beliefs to the many spiritual and religious beliefs and practices that others, especially our clients, are committed to. The readers are especially encouraged to become more acquainted with many of the beliefs and practices different from your own. These may be instances when your clients' spirituality can bring the most challenge to you as you attempt to get into their shoes and imagine how their beliefs and practices shape their lives and daily functioning. The readers are encouraged in chapters 3 and 4 to go out and meet people of different faith groups and participate with them in their services, study groups, celebrations, and powwows. Guidelines and specific suggestions for how to visit these groups along with several experiences of students are highlighted in chapters 3 and 4.

These early steps of the first four chapters are an important foundation for spiritually sensitive practice as we prepare ourselves to provide services to our clients. Chapter 5 goes on to build a spiritually sensitive approach that brings together different elements of practice. A crucial issue that continues to be debated in the profession is under what circumstances the client's spiritual issues are to be discussed, if any. Drawing from the literature, the different positions on this question are discussed. In addition, several features of the approach proposed by the author are described. They include being proactive in engaging the spiritual issues of clients and not underestimating religion's importance to many clients, among others. Spiritually sensitive social work practice is a process of several distinct phases, including engagement, assessment, intervention, and evaluation (CSWE, 2015, p.6) that are preceded by an important phase of preparation. In actuality this helping process usually is like a spiral that moves forward to a new phase and then possibly back to a previous one. These phases are emphasized in several later chapters in the book.

Moral and ethical issues are always important to social workers and they are particularly important in the realm of work with the clients' spiritual issues. This is the focus of chapter 6. Several ethical issues are examined, including whether spirituality should be included in the social work curriculum, the ethics of when to use spiritual interventions and when not to, and the ethical challenges that some faith-based agencies have in focusing on the clients' needs. Also, the chapter has a section on ethical conflicts that social workers have with some religious positions and how they can be addressed.

Chapter 7 covers the initial engagement of clients, the first phase of the approach. The engagement phase is highlighted as a pivotal one for setting the stage to discuss the clients' spiritual issues. Often the clients' spirituality and related concerns are revealed overtly or covertly in the initial sessions. The chapter offers suggestions that help to identify spiritual cues. The chapter also discusses how a spiritually sensitive relationship can be developed with clients, some of the obstacles, and deeper explorations into the clients' spiritual concerns. Chapter 8 focuses on the second phase of the spiritually sensitive approach: assessment. Topics covered include what spiritual assessment questions to ask, spiritual questions that are both religious and non-religious, and specific assessment questions to ask different client groups such as LGBT, people with health care needs, those with mental illness, and older adults.

The next three chapters cover a range of spiritual interventions that can be used and how they fit with the general approaches social workers use. Chapter 9 focuses on several interventions that usually are most relevant at the micro and mezzo levels of practice. This is not an exhaustive list but covers some of the most popular and relevant interventions for clients. They include mindfulness, meditation, prayers, metaphors and guided imagery, and altars. In each of these cases, several variations are offered on how they can be used. For example, meditation is described to include a basic approach and a more complicated American Buddhist approach. Meditation also can be experienced as walking meditation, walking the labyrinth, and creating mandalas.

Chapter 10 covers more spiritual interventions, in this case macro interventions. Spiritually sensitive practice at the macro level is unfortunately under-covered in the social work literature. This chapter explores some of these deficiencies. The chapter looks at agency organizational work that is important to do. It begins with the question of what a spiritually sensitive human service organization should look like. Some of the important organizational tasks are to prepare practitioners to be effective in engaging this work. Also, agency policies and guidelines are encouraged on how to implement spiritual practices, along with procedures for conducting spiritual assessments and introducing relevant spiritual interventions. The chapter also examines the special case of faith-based agencies and the opportunities and challenges that they face in implementing a spiritually sensitive approach that is client-centered. The importance of spirituality and religion in social movements is also shared, along with how spirituality can play a role in community practice.

Another chapter on interventions describes how spiritually focused practice can be woven into the general practice approaches that social workers use. Chapter 11 begins by identifying several "spiritual bridges" that can help practitioners infuse this practice area into general approaches. The spiritual bridges that are proposed include spiritual relationship-building and ways to communicate spiritual empathy. Other bridges are working with the clients' spiritual messaging in both positive and faulty ways of thinking, facilitating the clients' spiritual development, and giving attention to spiritual strengths and resources of clients. Seven general practice approaches are then introduced and the chapter illustrates how these spiritual bridges can infuse these approaches with spiritually sensitive elements.

Chapter 12 spotlights the fourth phase of practice, evaluation. Evaluation of spiritual practice is another neglected area that the book addresses. The chapter discusses how the complexity of the concepts of spirituality and religion complicate measurement and evaluation. Qualitative methods of evaluation are introduced along with quantitative ones. Use of multiple methods are encouraged. Evaluation is proposed, in part, as an empowering process that encourages agencies to give priority to the benefits of an evaluation for clients. Then three important evaluation topics are discussed and research questions are identified under each topic for future research. Topic one focuses on how to determine when an agency is prepared to offer a spiritually sensitive approach. Topic two considers what practitioner competencies are needed in delivering spiritually sensitive practice. Topic three discusses the need to evaluate the impact of spiritual practices on clients and how this can be done.

Finally, chapter 13 is titled Tools for Your Journey. This chapter returns to the needs of practitioners to help them deliver effective spiritual practices. Topics and tools are the focus. The reader is first encouraged to face the challenges of the workplace in today's world. Stress, compassion fatigue, burnout, and vicarious traumatization are among the problems to be faced. Self-care is paramount to succeeding and spiritual and positive psychology tools are offered to assist in self-care. Finally, a spiritual practice is encouraged for social workers.

References

Canda, E. R., & Furman, L. D. (2010). *Spiritual diversity in social work practice: The heart of healing.* 2nd edition. New York: Free Press.

CSWE (Council on Social Work Education) (2015). *2015 Educational Policy and Accreditation Standards for Baccalaureate and Master's Social Work Programs.* Educational Policy Approved by the CSWE Board of Directors on March 20, 2015; Accreditation Standards approved by the CSWE Commission on Accreditation on June 11, 2015. Alexandria, VA: Author.

Pew Research Center, Religion and Public Life (2015). America's changing religious landscape. Pew Research Center, Religion and Public Life, Washington, DC, May 12. 2015. Available online at http://www.pewforum.org/2015/05/12/americas-changing-religious-landscape.

Acknowledgments

This book was by no means a single-person effort. I have so many people and organizations to thank. Among them are my social work students who were enrolled in several Spirituality and Social Work courses that I taught. A few of them are identified in their journal entries describing their experiences with faith groups in some of the chapters. Also I have had very enthusiastic and talented graduate assistants who were invaluable in assisting me with reviewing and interpreting the literature, conducting community research, and participating with me in some valuable discussions about what students will and will not need to become spiritually sensitive. Students in recent years are Michelle Davis, Alexandria Elmore, and Heather Rikli Semmens.

Organizations were also very supportive in various aspects of my work. The School of Social Work at University of North Carolina at Charlotte provided me with graduate assistants and assigned me courses on Spirituality and Social Work that were used to explore some of my ideas for the book with students. Many community leaders and organizations were also invaluable and have become good colleagues and friends in the process. They include Thackor Topiwala and Rashmi Pandey-Eddins of the Charlotte Hindu Center; Rose Hamid and others at Mecklenburg Ministries; Charlene Hoover; Dr. Rodney Sadler; and Dr. Andrew Kille and Rev. Bill Dols of the Bible Workbench.

My publisher, Routledge (Taylor & Francis), was also vital to my success in completing the book. They were very patient and flexible with me. They provided me the time that I needed and were responsive to many of my requests. The editor assigned to me, Samantha Barbaro, was particularly helpful. She surveyed several schools of social work to find out what was happening in Spirituality courses and what kinds of course assistance faculty and students needed. She also supported me throughout the process and was very collaborative and responsive to my efforts to figure things out as we proceeded.

I am also grateful to several other people who helped with the final stages of the book's preparation. They included Drew Acuff who assisted with numerous issues,

Cinqué Hicks and Bookbright Media for their professional copyediting services, Kaye Tencgo for her thoughtful and creative initiatives in marketing the book, Carrie Bell at Routledge, and the proofreader Mike Hamilton.

Dr. Michael Sheridan and the administrative staff of the *Journal of Religion and Spirituality in Social Work: Social Thought* made available the entire library of their past journals as well as access to other pertinent journals; this opportunity provided me with easy access to much of the pertinent literature that I needed. That was a special gift that I did not anticipate, and made things go much more smoothly and easy.

My reviewers were especially encouraging as I explored how useful the book would be to social work programs and they also gave me many helpful suggestions that greatly strengthen the book. These reviewers included:

Rick Chamiec-Case of the North American Association of Christians in Social Work
Holly Oxhandler of Baylor University
Richard E. Hennicke of Saint Louis University
Margo Heydt of Xavier University
Kathleen Belanger of Stephen F. Austin State University
Holly Nelson-Becker of Loyola University Chicago
Tatsushi Hirono of Austin Peay State University
Melody Aye Loya of West Texas A&M University

INTRODUCING SPIRITUALITY AND RELIGION

Listen to your life. See it for the fathomless mystery that it is. In the boredom and pain of it no less than in the excitement and gladness; touch, taste, smell your way to the holy and hidden heart of it because in the last analysis all moments are key moments, and life itself is grace.

(Buechner, 1992, p. 2)

What is my gift to the world?

(Walsh, 1999, p. 122)

A spiritually sensitive practice approach is the primary focus of the book. Being spiritually sensitive means *being prepared to effectively engage spiritual and religious issues in the helping process whenever they are important to helping clients.* The purpose of the book is to help you develop this approach. It involves multiple ways of preparing as well as some challenges you will have to face. Spiritually sensitive practice is not something easy to implement. It requires a commitment to being sensitive to and compassionate about our clients' spiritual and religious needs. Also having extensive knowledge about these two concepts and how they are relevant and important to many of our clients. In addition, you will need skills in knowing if, when, and how to address the spiritual issues of your clients.

Before delving in to discuss this approach, it is important to begin with the two key concepts, spirituality and religion. They are different and yet related to each other in many ways. Spirituality is an inner personal quality. Everyone has a spirituality and has the potential of developing it whether they are religious or not. Religion, in contrast, exists as an external entity. Religion refers to institutional groups like the Southern Baptist Church, the Roman Catholic Church, and Islam; these and other institutional groups promulgate doctrine, beliefs, and practices important to many people. Religion is important to spirituality because it is a major source for how many people express their spirituality. In the United States, the vast majority of the clients of social work services are likely to be religious in some way (Ellor, Netting, & Thibault, 1999; Hodge, 2003; Pew Research Center, Religion and Public Life, 2015). It is also important to note that many of our clients are non-religious and their spirituality is equally important and finds expression in other ways.

These two concepts are abstract, not easily understood, and sometimes controversial. So the first step is to explore what they mean. Religion is easier to describe even though most of us know surprisingly little about religious groups different from our own. Spirituality, in contrast, is more difficult to define as it is broader, more elusive, and could possibly be expressed in as many forms and variations as there are people to express it.

Discovering Spirituality

Defining Spirituality

Let's begin with some of the definitions of spirituality in the literature. Canda and Furman (2010, pp. 59, 74–75) refer to spirituality as a complex concept that has both shared aspects of the human experience and unique aspects that fit some people and not others. They go on to say that spirituality refers to a universal and fundamental human quality involving the search for a sense of meaning, purpose, morality, well-being, and profundity in relationships with ourselves, others, and ultimate reality. They point out that while some aspects of a person's spirituality can be observed and measured, other aspects like the mystical and sacred may be beyond the limits of language and reason to express. They may also be beyond scientific efforts to prove. Canda and Furman add that spirituality can be expressed in religious or non-religious forms. They describe attributes of spirituality to include being inherently sacred, and being connected to such virtues as compassion, love, a sense of justice, forgiveness, and humility. Canda conducted his own research on how people in the United States, United Kingdom, Norway, Australia, and New Zealand defined spirituality and found six descriptors most associated with spirituality in all of these countries. They include meaning, personal, purpose, values, belief, and ethics. People in the United States, unlike the other countries, also selected personal relationship with a Higher Power and meditation among their most frequent selections.

Caroll (2001) suggests that spirituality can be viewed and expressed in three different ways. It can be a reflection of the whole person, the central core of a person, or in a more limited way, one aspect of the person. Rothman (2009) offers a slightly different definition that emphasized transcendence. She defines spirituality as an awareness of transcendence or a connection beyond self to something greater. This greater entity could be understood as a Higher Power, such as Yahweh, God, Allah, or another entity depending on who defines it. Spirituality is a source of meaning and purpose in life and a guide for action and choice. Spirituality helps us by providing the ground for connectedness among people and communities.

Gardner (2011, p. 77) introduces the concept of "critical spirituality." According to her, critical spirituality suggests a "new way" of thinking about spirituality that is beyond any specific traditions or expression; it affirms that there is no one true path but a diversity of spiritual and religious expressions. She refers to the use of this term from a perspective of viewing people holistically, seeking to understand where they are coming from and what matters to them at a fundamental level. Her concept aims to move beyond a spirituality that is linked to a particular religious

What Spirituality Means to a Group of BSW Students

- Spirituality is the feeling of wholeness and total peace with oneself.

- Spirituality is who we really are on the inside. It is what we believe to be true and therefore live by.

- Spirituality is the essence of life where your spirit of good, bad, right or wrong flow. It is where you know who you are.

- Spirituality is the essence of myself and finding out the meaning of my life. It gives me personal comfort and support.

- I define it as who God created me to be. It's the foundation of who I am as a person and how I reflect on others.

- Spirituality means to me my beliefs and what I as a person may do.

- To me my spirituality is like a magical child inside my heart that is the child of God/Jesus who he loves. The most important part of my spirituality is LOVE. To me it is the highest of all powers.

- Spirituality to me is that inner strength and comfort of knowing that I'm not alone. I'm trying to figure out exactly what I believe in but I do believe in a Higher Power that gives me strength and an inner peace.

- Spirituality means motivation, hope, and future. It stands for a dream that will one day become real because of spirits within you.

tradition, but can include those who have such traditions. Life is lived from a place of values of openness, acceptance of pluralism, the ability to live with contradictions and uncertainty, and not to be coercive. She describes three groups of people: those with no affiliation with a religious group, those who have an affiliation with a religious group to varying degrees, and those who choose to express their spirituality within a religious group.

Bachelor of Social Work (BSW) students in a class on spirituality and social work illustrate how varied and personal this term can be. Examples of some of their comments are evident in the above box. Some of their comments center on wholeness, peace, and comfort. Others allude to it as a direction for their future. Many of them reflect on it as their essence, what is most meaningful, or a foundation for them. Some mention a Higher Power and other religious notions while others do not. Some also reflect on spirituality as involving morality and what is right and wrong.

In addition, quotes from colleagues of the author share their perspective on what spirituality means. They are a Latina, an American Indian, and a Hindu, all of whom live in the United States.

- **A Latina who is a humanist:** Spirituality is the path towards your inner thoughts and feelings. It is when you wonder about life and the meaning of it. It is different from religion because it does not adhere to anyone else but me. I don't follow any rites, practices, schedules, doctrines, etc. It is when you are finally open to all possibilities and you shed off any prior beliefs. You relinquish your fears and embrace your own words. Spirituality means to me to be open to the unknown or to the known that was silent inside of you. . . . I am you and you are I. In others I can witness the expression of myself as I can witness it in all creation.

- **American Indian:** Spirituality is the way we live. We live spirituality every day. It is everywhere . . . in trees, the ground, animals, people, and all around us. The Spirit is freeing me to do my best for each day. It's knowing how to do something without training.

- **A Hindu:** By Nature my identity is spiritual but being affected by material modes of the Earthly planet my spiritual Identity is not visible. A central belief (of mine) is that because of our actions and reactions (karma) we are affected by happiness and distress. So by our humble efforts we should try to create good karma to improve our spiritual welfare. Hindus describe the Higher Power as the supreme controller, full of knowledge, full of Joy and eternal. We can realize GOD based on individual sincerity and faith in the existence of GOD. Hindus also believe in reincarnation. All of these beliefs are based on the Vedas, the original Hindu scriptures written approximately 5000 years ago.

As these definitions and numerous others suggest, spirituality is defined in many ways and each definition seems to be somewhat unique and personal. Several authors in the human services field have offered operational definitions of spirituality. A consensus on a definition is a search for purpose and meaning in life; a sense of being connected with self, others, and the universe; and an ability to transcend one's immediate experience to something larger known by many to be a Higher Power beyond human power (Canda & Furman, 2010; Chandler, Holden, & Kolander, 1992; Hill & Pargament, 2003; Kvarfordt & Sheridan, 2007; Lindgren & Coursey, 1995; Pargament, 2007). These authors add that spirituality may or may not be expressed through religion. If it is, there is likely to be an adherence to specific creeds, doctrines, and beliefs associated with particular religious denominations, sects, or groups. In light of all of these definitions and expressions, the book adopts the following definition of spirituality as its definition as well.

A search for purpose and meaning in life, a sense of being connected with self, others, and the universe, and an ability to transcend our immediate experience to something larger known by many to be a Higher Power beyond human power.

Manifestations of Spirituality

Spirituality is a broad, multifaceted concept much like the terms psychology and sociology. Because of this, spirituality may be easier to understand as an umbrella term under which many subareas can be explored, studied, and practiced. In other words, a definition of spirituality can only be a broad, general statement and a *starting point* from which most of its particulars can be illuminated. Unpacking the term spirituality is a helpful way to begin to operationalize it and to clarify why it is so important to social work practice. Specific manifestations of spirituality important to practice are numerous. Let's consider some of the commonly known ones (e.g. Canda & Furman, 2010; Scales & Kelly, 2012; Walsh, 1999).

- **Seeking Meaning for Our Lives:** People often need to explore and understand what they are feeling and experiencing at a deeper level. Meaning can be important with bigger questions in our lives like, "Am I doing what I want to do in my job or career?", "Would I be more true to myself if I got married, had children, or ended a long term partnership?", "Am I overlooking another direction that I need to take before it may be too late in my life?". Other types of questions could be more basic: "What is my life about?", "Why am I here?", "Why did this (e.g. an accident) happen to me?", "Why am I suffering from this disease or disability?". Meaning can also be important to explore in smaller, specific circumstances like having a profound experience in a dialogue with someone, a challenging encounter with a boss, unusual difficulties coping for a period of time, or any number of other things.
- **Finding Purpose:** As people discover meaning about something, they often want to act upon it, and that can lead to needing a purpose. Most people seek to have a purpose for what they are doing in the present or what they want to do in the future. Purpose provides a direction and goals; also it seeks an action.
- **Pursuing Hope:** Many people, including most of our clients, need hope to survive. Otherwise it may be easy to give up or back away from taking steps to improve our lives. Hope comes from our spirituality in that we have, at a deeper level, a capacity to transcend hopelessness and develop hopefulness. We draw on energy from within, from others, and sometimes from a Higher Power to generate hope. For many, religious groups are a substantial source of help for instilling more hope in their lives.
- **Embracing Love:** Maybe the most important descriptor of spirituality, love, is the ultimate goal of most people in their relationships. Our spirituality offers many ways to more fully experience love based on engaging concepts like forgiveness, transcendence, gratitude, other-centeredness, and fulfillment. Virtually all religions claim love as a core aspect of their beliefs.

- **Seeking an Inner Source of Peace:** Related to hope, we have the capacity to both overcome and manage anxiety, inner turmoil, and personal losses by drawing from our spirituality. It helps comfort us in the face of pain, suffering, despair, loss, and anticipation of death. Spirituality also helps us to adapt to pain and suffering as we come to view it to have deeper meaning to us.

- **Experiencing Wonder:** This is a human emotion that helps us come to realize, at a deeper level, the gift and amazement of being human, the miracles that exist and appear every moment in our lives, and the overwhelming beauty and vastness of our immediate environment and the larger universe. Some believe that wonder is a defining element of spirituality (e.g. Fuller, 2006). We experience wonder when we no longer take for granted the countless blessings that we have. As we grow older, we can lose our connection with a sense of wonder. Children can help us rediscover wonder as we observe all that amazes them, simple and profound.

- **Openness to Mystery:** Mystery is an important concept of our spirituality as it addresses questions without answers from scientific evidence. Where did our world come from? Where do we go after death? What is the power of prayer in healing someone? How do we know something in a deeper intuitive sense? Mystery is usually associated with such questions and our beliefs in a Higher Power.

- **A Personal Relationship with a Higher Power:** Most people's spirituality encompasses a Higher Power or Supreme Being whom we can turn to especially when nothing else exists within our reach or capacity to survive. This Higher Power is called many different names like God, Allah, Yahweh, Lord, Divinity, and The Light. Spirituality offers many different paths for communicating with our Higher Power such as prayer, meditation, chanting, and various forms of worship.

- **Morality and Ethics:** As we mature, most people develop a deeper sense of what they feel is right or wrong, fair or unfair, just or unjust. Our moral code, while not often as clear to us as we would like, derives from our spiritual self. Our morality and ethics as social workers, for example, involve commitments to social justice for those who are downtrodden, rejected, poor, sick, and otherwise disadvantaged. This is a central tenet of the National Association of Social Workers (NASW) Code of Ethics (2008). Often people depend upon their religious group to inform their moral code.

- **Personal Beliefs:** People have beliefs that they abide by to varying degrees that are part of their spirituality. Some of these beliefs relate to positions that we take on moral and ethical issues. Some beliefs may come from a religious group to which people belong, a political party, or other social group. While many beliefs of people are strongly held, they are often views about what people favor or oppose when science cannot prove them to be right or wrong.

- **A Capacity for Connectedness, Transcendence, and Oneness with Others:** Our spirituality can help us transcend ourselves to experience others in a more heart-felt, empathetic way. In transcendence, we may be able to imagine and thus feel ourselves in "another person's shoes", feeling as they feel. This tendency can even sometimes be felt toward everyone around us or even all human beings. Some people have an easier time experiencing transcendence than others, and we can learn a lot from such people.

It is important to note that religion is not readily apparent in most of these manifestations of spirituality as they are described above. These manifestations are important qualities of numerous non-religious people as well as those who are religious. Religious groups in particular have a significant influence over how many people understand and express their spirituality. Religious groups, for example, are a source of beliefs and practices that have profound meaning and purpose in the lives of many of their followers. Love, inner peace, and mystery are central concepts taught and practiced by religious groups. And perhaps most important, a relationship with a Higher Power and rules of morality and ethics are central to many of their teachings.

Engaging Spirituality at Different Levels of Intervention

Social work is a profession that is concerned with three overall levels of intervention: micro, mezzo, and macro. Spirituality can be experienced at each of these levels. For example, various aspects of spirituality can be important at the:

- micro level, such as hope, wonder, joy, belief, and coping with deeper suffering;
- mezzo level, as intimacy, connectedness, and I-Thou relationships (Buber & Kaufmann, 1971);
- macro level, as justice, unity, empowerment, oneness, and cooperation with others.

These aspects of spirituality are not meant to be solely at one level of practice. For example, a community can celebrate joy and experience deeper suffering, while notions of cooperation and social justice are evident not just in macro entities but also in dyads, families, and small groups.

Defining Spirituality for Yourself

Spirituality is a phenomenon that tends to resist definition and consensus as it is an intangible, much like the terms "soul" or "a compassionate heart". However,

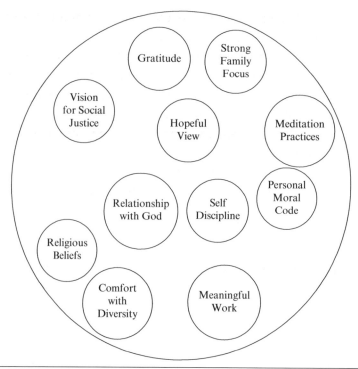

Figure 1.1   An Example of One Social Worker's Spirituality

spirituality has a mixture of ingredients like wonder, joy, love, belief in a higher being, and the capacity for suffering. As Figure 1.1 indicates, spirituality may have a different meaning for each of us that potentially includes all or some of the characteristics described so far and others. The characteristics that make up each person's definition of spirituality can be located in a circle like Figure 1.1 as a collection of interacting entities of importance to them at any particular point in time.

A consensus on a specific definition of spirituality may be less important to provide to others than encouragement for them to define spirituality for themselves.

Exercise: How would you define what spirituality means to you if you were asked?

1. How would you define spirituality overall?

2. What manifestations of spirituality, mentioned above, are most important to you?

3. In what ways is your spirituality important to you?

4. What role does a religious group play in your definition, if any?

Gotterer (2001) describes a social constructivist approach that may be helpful when we do not have agreement with a client on what spirituality is. We may need to remember that our reality is subjective and determined by our culture; as social workers, we cannot become completely free of our own beliefs and values. If we are to truly hear our clients, Gotterer recommends that we take the stance of "not knowing," as long as we do not lose sight of our general purpose in helping. To arrive at an understanding of the problem, we need to remember that the client's own understanding is central.

Actually it would be helpful, when initially discussing spirituality with clients, to ask them in an open-ended way to define what it means to them. If they are having difficulty describing their definition, that may be a time to mention a common definition or examples of what it has meant to other clients. Mentioning manifestations of spirituality of particular importance to a client could be highlighted as well. For example, if clients seem to have lost their way after losing a partner, helping them find meaning for their life may be a concept to consider.

The Spirit World

A relatively small segment of the population in the United States has reported experiencing spirituality in deeper more unusual ways and this can be relevant to practice with some clients. Most people in the Western world do not believe in a spirit world existing outside the material world while many in other parts of the world and many Native American (or First Nation) people do (Ingerman, 2008). The spirit world can be made up of people who have died and return in some form. A shaman is a spiritual leader of believers in such a world who interacts directly with spirits for many purposes. Among them, a shaman provides people with divine information from the spirit world, helps the spirits of deceased people to cross over, and performs a variety of ceremonies for their communities. A shaman provides many other roles to communities including a healer, doctor, priest, social worker, and mystic (Voss, Douville, Soldier, & Twiss, 1999).

Some immigrants from the Far East and other regions of the world and others who are Americans may believe in such spirits. This can be a challenge to many social workers who are expected to listen to these experiences and explore what they may mean to these clients in a non-judgmental way. An example is a Native American colleague as she and the author were having a conversation over lunch. She said that she visualized a grandmother figure hanging behind the author's left shoulder appearing to be protective of him as he talked to this new acquaintance. As we discussed this vision, she went on to explain that since being a small child she has had these visions of beloved people who have passed away and returned in a form that she can visualize. While the author was somewhat skeptical of what his Native American colleague was saying, he openly listened as she told her story about her life and the mixed feelings she has had about her unusual propensity to visualize people who are no longer alive.

The field of parapsychology investigates some of these areas, including telepathy, precognition, clairvoyance, near-death experiences, reincarnation, and apparitional experiences (Irwin & Watt, 2007; Hagerty, 2009). While mainstream psychology and science in general do not recognize these spiritual experiences because they cannot be observed in measureable ways, they are spiritual to some. Parapsychological concepts refer to such things as communicating with others without using any known sensory channels or physical interaction, spiritual experiences in which someone receives information about a person or event from unknown sources, or obtains information about the future from sources unavailable to others. Another area studied by parapsychologists are near-death experiences reported by people who have died for a brief time and returned to life, usually after being revived by a medical intervention. In these brief death experiences, these people have reported having a variety of unexplainable, unusual, and often blissful sensory experiences. Reincarnation is another area of study in which a person dies and then begins a new life in another body. Also, studies have been conducted of people who survive death in some form that is perceptible to people who are alive. All of these areas are relevant to spirituality but mostly are beyond the scope of the book.

Understanding Religion

Religion, the other central concept of this book, is also important to spiritually sensitive social work practice. Most people in the United States are affiliated with a religious group and these groups tend to have a major influence on their spirituality (e.g. Pew Research Center, Religion and Public Life, 2015; Smith, 1991). Like spirituality, the concept of religion is complex and has many ambiguities; it is also often controversial to discuss. Religion usually refers to institutional groups like Christianity, Islam, and smaller religious groups.

Sacred Doctrines

Each of the world religions and other smaller religious groups have sacred doctrines that their members believe are a form of "truth" for them (Smith, 1991). These truths are often associated with one or more spiritual figures whom they hold in high esteem and reverence such as Buddha, Moses, Jesus Christ, or Muhammad. Often the major sources of their sacred doctrines consist of the words reported to be spoken by this spiritual figure and the teachings about this spiritual figure by others. For example, the Torah is the most sacred text of Judaism and reflects, among other things, the life and teachings of Moses, a central figure in the history of Judaism. The Torah describes the miraculous story of the Exodus in which Moses led his people out of Egyptian slavery and into a Promised Land provided by Yahweh. In Christianity the Bible is the most sacred text and includes the Old Testament describing Jewish teachings and history and a New Testament describing the life, crucifixion, and resurrection of Jesus and the spreading of his Gospel that followed. Islam has the Quran as its sacred book, which records the actual words of Muhammad that he received from Allah.

Religious Beliefs

These sacred doctrines are a major source of the religious and spiritual beliefs held by people belonging in these groups (Smith, 1991). These beliefs can often become rules or guidelines for people and prescribe how people are to live their daily lives. For example, a religious group may prescribe how men and women are to interact in public and private, how children are to be raised, how older people are to be treated when they become dependent on others, a variety of end-of-life issues, and what people should eat and not eat. In essences, these beliefs become, in many instances, customs or practices that people follow without often being consciously aware of them.

If you are not familiar with any of these sacred doctrines, I encourage you to pick up and read one of these sacred texts. For example, if any of your clients are Muslims, or of the Islamic faith, it could be informative to review portions of the Quran. Do you know, for example, that the Quran views Jesus Christ as a great prophet and it frequently mentions him as part of Islamic history? The Quran also emphasizes that Muhammad is the supreme and final prophet of importance to Muslims. Islam, Judaism and Christianity have common histories, to an extent, as all three trace their beginnings back to Abraham, the father of all of three religions.

Examples of Important Passages and Beliefs in Sacred Texts

The Hebrew (Jewish) Bible (Psalm 51:1–2): Have mercy on me, O God . . . blot out my transgressions, wash me thoroughly from my iniquity, and cleanse me from my sin. (Importance of confession of sin and repentance.)

The New Testament of Christianity (Matthew 5:43–44): You have heard people say, "Love your neighbors and hate your enemies." But I tell you to love your enemies and pray for anyone who mistreats you. Then you will be acting like your Father in heaven. (Belief in love of enemy.)

The Quran (verse 284): Lay not on us a burden greater than we have strength to bear. Blot out our sins and grant us forgiveness. Have mercy on us. You are our Protector; help us against those who stand against Faith. (Importance of dependence on Allah.)

The Bhagavad-Gita (text 13): As the embodied soul continually passes, in this body, from boyhood to youth to old age, the soul similarly passes into another body at death. The self-realized soul is not bewildered by such a change. (Explanation of reincarnation.)

Example of a Religious Ritual

Enjoy a short excerpt of music and liturgical ritual of the Russian Orthodox Church views. Beliefs and views involving the mind are set aside so that all of a person's senses can be experienced in the service. Go to www.youtube.com and search "Russian Orthodox Music"

Religious and Spiritual Practices

Religious groups are also known to have important religious practices that are presented when members meet as a community and sometimes when they are alone (Smith, 1991). Prayer, reading religious material, meditating, rituals, worship, chanting, confession, education classes, and sacred music are among their practices. Some of these religious practices may be mentioned by clients, especially if they find them helpful. For example, the Bible is sometimes a companion carried openly by clients who are homeless; mentioning their Bible could prompt a beginning discussion about their spiritual practices and some of the hopes important to them.

The Importance of Spirituality and Religion to Social Work

Spirituality and religion are very important in the history of social work (Ellor, Netting, & Thibault, 1999; Loewenberg, 1988). Religion was a key factor in social work's early history and development at the turn of the 20th century. The settlement house movement and charity organization societies were openly affiliated with religious volunteers, groups, and purposes. Their sponsors were Christians and many of their messages involved helping people become or return to a Christian way of living as the way to resolve their problems.

Later, social work began to openly distance itself from the religious tenets that formerly gave it shape, inspiration, and energy. With a growing emphasis on becoming a profession and having a body of knowledge and a scientific base of operation, conflicts with many Christian teachings and churches became an increasing problem for their identity (Ellor, Netting, & Thibault, 1999; Loewenberg, 1988). Further, the religious fervor and efforts to proselytize clients became increasingly problematic and fell out of favor. This became particularly problematic with social workers employed in governmental agencies because of the constitutional doctrine of separation of church and state. Also, growing numbers of immigrants increasingly came with other religious affiliations—Islam, Buddhism, Hinduism, and other smaller religious groups such as the Baha'i faith, Sikhism, Taoism, and modern paganism, and this began to pose problems for social work approaches that emphasized Christianity.

Based on the educational policy and accreditation standards of the Council on Social Work Education, religion is one of the dimensions of diversity that social workers are now expected to engage as a competency (CSWE, 2015). Most people still express much of their spirituality through a religious group. As our clients are increasingly sharing a variety of religious and cultural connections, social workers are also becoming more aware that they lack the preparation they need to help them. We are realizing that both our personal ignorance and a lack of attention given in social work degree programs are factors that need to be addressed (Canda & Furman, 2010; Furman & Chandy, 1994; Rothman, 2009; Sheridan, 2009). This text gives considerable attention to the influences of religion for these reasons.

Meanwhile, the topic of spirituality has consistently made inroads into the social work community, especially in recent decades. Since its early history, social workers are expected to be holistic in their perspective. We have been expected to view people as biological, psychological, social, intellectual, and cultural beings; a spiritual dimension has become an important addition to this long list. Based on the new accreditation standards in 2015, spirituality is also now one of several dimensions of diversity that social workers are expected to engage (CSWE, 2015).

Spirituality has been received in social work somewhat differently than religion. Early on in social work, Towle (1965) assumed that a complete understanding of a person involved their spiritual aspects. These aspects included a sense of meaning and purpose in life, the use of church-based resources, the formation of a value framework, and an expectation of social responsibility for others. Siporin (1985), more recently, referred to the spiritual as a moral aspect of a person, called the soul. This soul strives for relatedness with other people and a Higher Power, seeks knowledge of ultimate reality, and forms value frameworks. Numerous others in social work and related fields have also defined spirituality as mentioned earlier.

Changing Landscape of Religious Affiliations

The Pew Forum on Religion and Public Life collects valuable data about the religious affiliation of the population in the United States. The Pew Forum also conducts a wide variety of smaller studies of specific religious groups, different segments of the population, and some religious figures like Pope Francis (www.pewforum.org). The Pew Forum provides fairly up-to-date statistics on the religious affiliation of United States citizens 18 years of age and older and the shifts or changes occurring over time (Pew Research Center, Religion and Public Life, 2015). Based on a representative sample of more than 35,000 Americans age 18 and older, the U.S. Religious Landscape Survey found that religious affiliation in the U.S. is both very diverse and fluid. The religious affiliations of interviewees were based on how the interviewees identified themselves.

As Table 1.1 indicates, it's no surprise that Christians made up 70.6 percent of the population in the United States in 2014 (Pew Research Center, Religion and Public Life, 2015). However, Christians as a group decreased by 7.8 percent from

Table 1.1   Religious Affiliations of U.S. Citizens in 2007 and 2014

CHRISTIANS DECLINE AS SHARE OF U.S. POPULATION; OTHER FAITHS AND THE
UNAFFILIATED ARE GROWING

	2007 %	2014 %	CHANGE* %
Christian	**78.4**	**70.6**	**−7.8**
Protestant	51.3	46.5	−4.8
Evangelical	*26.3*	*25.4*	*−0.9*
Mainline	*18.1*	*14.7*	*−3.4*
Historically black	*6.9*	*6.5*	*–*
Catholic	23.9	20.8	−3.1
Orthodox Christian	0.6	0.5	–
Mormon	1.7	1.6	–
Jehovah's Witness	0.7	0.8	–
Other Christian	0.3	0.4	–
Non-Christian faiths	**4.7**	**5.9**	**+1.2**
Jewish	1.7	1.9	–
Muslim	0.4	0.9	+0.5
Buddhist	0.7	0.7	–
Hindu	0.4	0.7	+0.3
Other world religions**	<0.3	0.3	–
Other faiths**	1.2	1.5	+0.3
Unaffiliated	**16.1**	**22.8**	**+6.7**
Atheist	1.6	3.1	+1.5
Agnostic	2.4	4.0	+1.6
Nothing in particular	12.1	15.8	+3.7
Don't know/refused	**0.8**	**0.6**	**−0.2**
	100.0	**100.0**	

Notes: * The "change" column displays only statistically significant changes; blank cells indicate that the difference between 2007 and 2014 is within the margin of error.
** The "other world religions" category includes Sikhs, Baha'is, Taoists, Jains and a variety of other world religions. The "other faiths" category includes Unitarians, New Age religions, Native American religious and a number of other non-Christian faiths.
Source: 2014 Religious Landscape Study, conducted June 4-Sept. 30, 2014. Figures may not add to 100% and nested figures may not add to subtotals indicated due to rounding.

2007 to 2014. Those who are Christians primarily break down into four major groups: Evangelical Protestants, Catholics, Mainline Protestants, and historically Black Churches. Christians also include Mormons, Jehovah's Witnesses, Orthodox, and other Christian groups. This leaves a relatively large 22.8 percent that are unaffiliated; they are atheists, agnostics, and the unaffiliated for other reasons. Other major religions, including Judaism, Islam, Buddhism, and Hinduism, make up a total of 5.9 percent.

The subgroups in the unaffiliated category are interesting in that the majority of them are not atheists or agnostics (Pew Research Center, Religion and Public Life, 2015). They were unaffiliated with any religious group and made up 15.8 percent of the U.S. adult population in 2014. This group, in turn, is fairly evenly divided between the "secular unaffiliated," that is, those who say that religion is not important in their lives, and the "religious unaffiliated," that is, those who say that religion is either somewhat important or very important in their lives. An interesting finding is the shift in affiliation that has been occurring in recent times in the unaffiliated category overall. The unaffiliated made up 16.1 percent in 2007 and increased to 22.8 percent by 2014. Related to this, 35 percent of young adults (ages 18 to 29 years) reported they were not currently affiliated in 2014. Most of the unaffiliated adult population comprises people who simply describe their religion as "nothing in particular" or "none."

About one-fourth of the unaffiliated describe themselves as either atheist or agnostic. As Table 1.1 indicates, atheists and agnostics made up about 7 percent of the population in 2014 and should be included in any discussion of spirituality (Pew Research Center, Religion and Public Life, 2015). By the author's definition, they may reject any form of religion and religious beliefs, but they do have a spirituality. Like everyone else they seek meaning in their lives, hope for the future, and see the value of transcending themselves to connect with others. Atheists usually seem certain that God or a Higher Power does not and could not exist. Agnostics have more complicated beliefs. Krasny (2010), an agnostic himself, serves as one example. He identifies agnostics as doubters. He suggests they are somewhere in the middle between those with faith and those with disbelief, or they vacillate between the two. He described his many efforts to pray to God for security during various times of crises hoping God was available to help, but he also doubted that such a God exists.

Taking the discussion of the "spiritual but not religious" group a step further, Bass (2012) a religious writer, suggests that this trend of the unaffiliated is likely to continue to grow. Further, this trend may be a time of cultural revitalization and reorientation for our society, perhaps similar to previous awakenings in earlier centuries. She thinks it reflects a "Great Awakening" in the United States toward a more experiential, pluralistic, holistic, and environmentally concerned type of American religion and politics. She cites several indicators of the discontent and breakdown including a boredom by many in existing church services, too much emphasis by churches on self-preservation, and a rejection of the imposition of conformity and control. She adds that churches have created a culture of their own that merely skims over what Jesus said and stood for. Some of the unaffiliated prefer a direct embrace of a relationship with Jesus rather than to be wedded to an institutional church. Bass suggests that this discontent and breakdown are beginning to result in a new vision and the creation of new spiritual practices and communities. She also suggests that these changes are occurring within the other major religions in the United States as well.

Other Important Findings from the Pew Study

(Pew Research Center, Religion and Public Life, 2015)

- While the Mainline Protestants' share of the population was significantly smaller in 2014 than it was in 2007, the Evangelical Protestants' share of the population has remained comparatively stable. As a result, Evangelicals constituted about one-quarter of all Christians in 2014.

- The share of the public identifying with religions other than Christianity has grown from 4.7 percent in 2007 to 5.9 percent in 2014. Gains were most pronounced among Muslims (who accounted for 0.4 percent of respondents in 2007 and 0.9 percent in 2014) and Hindus (0.4 percent in 2007 vs. 0.7 percent in 2014).

- Whites continue to be more likely than both blacks and Hispanics to identify as religiously unaffiliated; 24 percent of whites said they have no religion, compared with 20 percent of Hispanics and 18 percent of blacks in 2014. But the religiously unaffiliated have grown as a share of the population within all three of these racial and ethnic groups.

- More than a quarter of men (27 percent) in 2014 described themselves as religiously unaffiliated, up from 20 percent in 2007. Fewer women are religious "nones," but the religiously unaffiliated are growing among women at about the same rate as among men.

Recent Immigrants

Among recent immigrants, Catholics outnumber Protestants by nearly a two-to-one margin, while native-born Americans reflect the opposite; Protestants outnumber Catholics by an even larger margin (Pew Research Center, Religion and Public Life, 2014). While Latinos account for about one-in-three adult Catholics overall, their ages suggest a major shift over time. About one-in-eight U.S. Catholics age 70 and older are Latinos, and nearly half of all Catholics ages 18 to 29 are Latinos. The Pew Research Center's Survey found that a majority (55 percent) of the estimated 35.4 million Latino adults in the U.S.—or about 19.6 million Latinos—identify as Catholic today. About 22 percent are Protestant (including 16 percent who describe themselves as born-again or Evangelical) and 18 percent are religiously unaffiliated. The trend of Hispanics in the United States who are Catholic has been declining in recent years.

Distinguishing Spirituality from Other Fields of Study

You may be thinking that such qualities as being hopeful, having compassion, or experiencing inner peace and strength are not unique to the field of spirituality. Actually, other fields of study beyond spirituality and religious studies also claim them as concepts relevant to their body of knowledge (e.g. Koenig & Spano, 2007). Many psychologists, for example, refer to some of the above qualities as psychological concepts; to them compassion, hopefulness, and self-confidence are desired outcomes of psychological interventions and qualities of a psychologically well-adjusted person.

Cultural studies may also be thought of as a home for many of the concepts. When we explore a person's culture, we may find that meaning in life is provided, directly or indirectly, by culture. For example, the African adage, "It takes a village to raise a child," offers profound meaning to many African American parents struggling to raise children by themselves. In many ways, our cultural and spiritual identities overlap and it may not make sense to emphasize how they are different. Martin and Martin (2002) provide an example of how they view spirituality from a cultural perspective as African American social workers. To them it involves being communally oriented, being caregivers, and having a hopeful, positive, and optimistic outlook on life even in the midst of oppression and despair. Spirituality also means feeling an emphatic sense of belonging to their group, having an inner sense of responsibility for themselves and others, and experiencing an unshakable sense of human dignity and self-worth. Martin and Martin also add that spirituality, to them, means having a cool head and a warm heart and experiencing a keen sense of the sacredness of life. All members of their group are sacred, families, parents, elders and children; actually they believe that Black life itself is sacred.

Spirituality is often embedded in how people in some cultural groups behave in response to the challenges of their lives. For example, a group of African American women in a job readiness program revealed, in a theme analysis study, their views about the importance of spirituality in response to challenges of poverty and welfare reform (Banerjee, M. M., & Canda, 2009). They repeatedly stated that spirituality is a source of their strength. Their definitions of spirituality were expressed as religious practices. It is infused in their daily lives and in spiritual dreams and visions of life directions. It is also evident in the ways in which they cope with poverty, welfare, and welfare reform.

In another study, Westbrooks (2008) describes how the spirituality of fifty low income families was a strength in their family processes. She stated that their spirituality "emerges from a well-spring of deep culture that is reflected in roles, rules, and patterns of families that contribute to their functioning and actual survival. Some LGBT (lesbian, gay, bisexual, or transsexual) groups also have identified spirituality as a strength in their cultural groups. Some of these groups have evolved their definition of spirituality as a reflection of their efforts to cling to something meaningful to them in an environment in which they are sometimes faced with persecution and rejection, especially within some religious communities.

Muslims provide another example of how culture and spirituality are closely connected. While American Muslims are a diverse group in terms of country of origin and how long they have been in the U.S., their spirituality has a strong tendency to be expressed through the key elements of the Islamic worldview. This worldview is deeply embedded in the culture in which they were raised, especially in the Middle Eastern, African, or Asian worlds (Ibrahim & Dykeman, 2011). In these cultures, Muslims understand the Quran as the ultimate and only truth that reveals guidance for mankind. Allah is at the center of that universe and peace is achieved through submission to Allah's will, and the five pillars of Islam provide the basic rules for how Muslims are to live their lives.

It seems impossible to extract religion and spirituality from the culture of most groups. Cultural competence, further developed in the NASW Code of Ethics, is central to this discussion (NASW Code of Ethics, 2008). The Code recognizes the importance of spirituality and religion in the lives of people by suggesting that these concepts may be as important in shaping a person's culture as ethnicity, national origin, and other social factors (e.g. Canda & Furman, 2010; Hodge, 2007). According the NASW Code, cultural competence is "the process by which individuals and systems respond respectfully and effectively to people of all cultures, languages, classes, races, ethnic backgrounds, religions, and other diversity factors in a manner that recognizes, affirms, and values [their worth and dignity]."

Practice Implications of Spirituality and Religion

This book is devoted to explaining how spirituality and religion may play a role, sometimes a primary and central one, in helping our clients. Examples are noted so far only in an introductory way. All of the manifestations of spirituality covered earlier open up numerous opportunities to explore this realm in the lives of our clients when they see its relevance and wish to engage it. In brief, spirituality is a human quality present in everyone. A few examples of how these concepts can become part of the helping process are described next.

Meaning in the Lives of Clients

Meaning has enormous potential as a topic in helping clients. Can you imagine living in a world without any meaning? Our spiritual selves are where questions of meaning primarily emerge within us. Who am I? Why are we here? What is my life about and what is it supposed to be in the future? Helping clients search for deeper meaning in their lives can be important at times. Clients usually need to know that there is more meaning in their everyday lives than merely struggling to survive or exist. Meaning may be important to consider, for example, when a client cannot seem to partake in another boring, monotonous day of employment in a factory. Or when a parent is ready to give up on raising a child with a disability who doesn't seem to be getting any better. Or when a couple in a troubled marriage seem to be at the end of their ropes with their unproductive arguments. With more meaning, many clients may be able to shift their thinking from the dull or chaotic aspects of their lives to more meaningful thoughts and actions that can be uplifting and encouraging. There is actually a specific therapeutic approach used by some social workers called Meaning Therapy that is discussed in chapter 11 (Wong, 2010).

Clients' Beliefs

Clients' beliefs are another concept that is pertinent to helping them. Religion often plays a role in forming our beliefs about our families and neighbors, how to get along, and knowing what's right and wrong. These beliefs can help clients strengthen their families, promote the well-being of their children, and encourage positive interactions with neighbors, others at work, and even their adversaries. That is why it is important for social workers to be aware of and reinforce the healthy and productive religious beliefs of their clients. If these religious beliefs pose problems for clients they also need to be taken seriously—for example, when a religious group appears to be discouraging a woman from seeking help to get out of an abusive relationship with a spouse or other family member.

Clients and Mystery

Mystery, another manifestation of spirituality, can be important to some clients and easily overlooked by many practitioners. Mystery is a phenomenon that many clients may find helpful in the absence of knowing what will happen with certainty in the future. An example could be a woman in an early stage of breast cancer who is fearful of what her future holds. Mystery is a concept that may offer comfort and reassurance when clients are filled with doubt, fear, or confusion. Related to mystery, a Higher Power is another central spiritual concept important to many people. To what extent do clients depend upon a Higher Power when answers are not forthcoming? What do clients believe happens, for example, after they die? How much importance do they place on the next life as opposed to their present one? If clients believe that they can communicate with a Higher Power, how important is prayer or meditation in helping them to cope with and bring change to their lives for the better?

Clients and Transcendence

Transcendence is another spiritual concept. A dictionary definition of transcendence is to exceed or surpass the limits of ordinary experiences; it is also a spiritual

Exercise: Exploring transcendence in our lives

How well can you transcend beyond where you are as a person (e.g. your ego, preoccupations, anxieties, possessions) to experience a greater sense of oneness in your relationship with others? How well can you do this with . . .

- A significant other (e.g. spouse, partner)
- Your parents
- Your children
- Spiritual or religious groups to which you belong
- Neighbors
- Strangers
- Homeless and hungry people on the streets
- Adversaries

What are some of the difficulties that you have in attempting to transcend yourself? What personal changes can you make to help you become more present to others?

condition of moving beyond physical needs and realities. Clients may wish to seek changes in their lives, and especially change aspects of themselves. In such cases, they could be helped to explore ways of transcending their limitations. For example, if they are religious and participate in prayer, perhaps they could be helped to manage their worries or other disturbing chatter through their prayer life. Similarly, they could be introduced to mindfulness techniques that can help them more fully experience the present moment without the interference of external and internal distractions. Transcendence is an important concept that tends to be unfamiliar to many people when their personal lives are being considered. Please stop for a moment and complete the above exercise on transcendence in relationships with others to gain more familiarity with the possible applicability of this concept to you.

All of the manifestations of spirituality and religion described above are potentially valuable in helping clients. These concepts and others can be crucial in instances when clients need such things as comfort, improved coping capacity, insight, a calming effect, a way to face sorrow, and courage to act in ways that benefit themselves and others? The concept of spirituality may often seem too abstract, obscure, or controversial to comprehend and use with confidence, but efforts are made throughout the book to view it in a more tangible, concrete way that can be pertinent to practice.

Conclusion

The chapter introduces two important concepts pertinent to social work practice: spirituality and religion. Many definitions are offered for each of them by authors in social work and other human services. Spirituality is differentiated from religion in that it is a personal quality inherent in all of us, while religion is viewed as an external entity that is manifested primarily in religious groups and their creeds, beliefs, and practices. The spirituality of many who are affiliated with religious groups can be and often is shaped by the beliefs and practices of these groups. Religion was at one time central to the history of social work as a profession. The settlement movement and charity organization societies were openly affiliated with Christian groups and purposes. Then religion fell out of favor because of the changing demands on the profession. In recent years, spirituality and religion have returned to have more favor in social work practice. Understanding both concepts is now required in professional social work programs and social work practice based on the NASW Code of Ethics and social work accreditation standards. Spirituality is manifested in concepts such as meaning, purpose, ethics, and transcendence, which can be readily applied to helping many social work clients.

Discussion Questions and Exercises

1. How would you define your own spirituality? What aspects or manifestations of spirituality mentioned in the chapter (e.g. meaning, purpose, etc.) are most helpful in describing your spirituality? How is your spirituality important in your personal life? In what ways, if any, is it important in your professional life?

2. The chapter points out that the social work profession is concerned with three overall levels of intervention—micro, mezzo, and macro—and that spirituality and religion can be relevant at each of these levels. Select one of the levels of your practice and identify three ways that spirituality and religion can be relevant to your work with clients. Identify one problem that you might anticipate in introducing either of these concepts at this level of practice.

3. Transcendence is viewed by many people as one aspect of spirituality. How well can you transcend yourselves (e.g. your comforts, preoccupations, anxieties, possessions, ego) to be more fully present with clients? With what types of clients and client circumstances might transcendence be easier for you and with what types might it be more difficult? Why do you think this is so?

References

Banerjee, M. M., & Canda, (2009). Spirituality as a strength of African-American women affected by welfare reform. *Journal of Religion and Spirituality in Social Work, 28*(3), 239–262.

Bass, D. B. (2012). *Christianity after religion: The end of church and the birth of a new spiritual awakening.* New York: HarperCollins.

Buber, M., & Kaufmann, W. (1971). *I and Thou.* New York: Touchstone.

Buechner, F. (1992). *Listening to your life. Daily meditations with Frederick Buechner.* New York: HarperCollins.

Canda, E. R., & Furman, L. D. (2010). *Spiritual diversity in social work practice.* 2nd edition. New York: Oxford University Press.

Caroll, M. (2001). Conceptual models of spirituality. *Social Thought, 20,* 5–22.

Chandler, C. K., Holden, J. M., & Kolander, C. A. (1992). Counseling for spiritual wellness: Theory and practice. *Journal of Counseling & Development, 71*(2), 168–175.

CSWE (Council on Social Work Education) (2015). *2015 Educational Policy and Accreditation Standards for Baccalaureate and Master's Social Work Programs.* Educational Policy Approved by the CSWE Board of Directors on March 20, 2015; Accreditation Standards approved by the CSWE Commission on Accreditation on June 11, 2015. Alexandria, VA: Author.

Ellor, J. W., Netting, F. E., & Thibault, J. M. (1999). *Religious and spiritual aspects of human service practice.* Columbia, SC: University of South Carolina Press.

Fuller, R. C. (2006). *Wonder: From emotion to spirituality.* Chapel Hill: NC: University of North Carolina Press.

Furman, L. D., & Chandy, L. M. (1994). Religion and spirituality: A long neglected cultural component of rural social work practice. *Human Services in the Rural Environment, 17* (3/4), 21–26.

Gardner, F. (2011). *Critical spirituality: A holistic approach to contemporary practice.* Burlington, VT: Ashgate.

Gotterer, R. (2001). The spiritual dimension in clinical social work practice: A client perspective. *Families in Society: The Journal of Contemporary Human Services, 82*(2), 187–193.

Hagerty, B. B. (2009). *Fingerprints of God: The search for the science of spirituality.* New York: Riverhead Books.

Hill, P., & Pargament, K. I. (2003). Advances in the conceptualization and measurement of religion and spirituality. *American Psychologist, 58*(1), 64–74.

Hodge, D. R. (2003). Hodge responds. *Social Work, 48*(3), 431–432.

Hodge, D. R. (2007). The spiritual competence scale: A new instrument for assessing spiritual competence at the programmatic level. *Research on Social Work Practice, 17*(2), 287–295.

Ibrahim, F. A., & Dykeman, C. (2011). Counseling Muslim Americans: Cultural and spiritual assessments. *Journal of Counseling & Development, 89,* 387–394.

Ingerman, S. (2008). *Shamanic journeying: A beginner's guide.* Boulder, CO: Sounds True.

Irwin, H. J., & Watt, C. A. (2007). *An introduction to parapsychology.* 5th ed. Jefferson, NC: McFarland.

Koenig, T., & Spano, R. (2007). The cultivation of social workers' hope in personal life and professional practice. *Journal of Religion & Spirituality in Social Work: Social Thought, 26*(3), 45–61.

Krasny, M. (2010). *Spiritual envy: An agnostic's quest.* Novato, CA: New World Library.

Kvarfordt, C. L., & Sheridan, M. J. (2007). The role of religion and spirituality in working with children and adolescents. *Journal of Religion & Spirituality in Social Work: Social Thought, 26*(3), 1–23.

Lindgren, K. N., & Coursey, R. D. (1995). Spirituality and mental illness: A two-part study. *Psychosocial Rehabilitation Journal, 18*, 93–111.

Loewenberg, F. (1988). *Religion and social work practice in contemporary American society.* New York: Columbia University Press.

Martin, E. P., & Martin, J. M. (2002). *Spirituality and the Black helping tradition in social work.* Washington, DC: NASW Press.

NASW (National Association of Social Workers) (2008). Code of Ethics of the National Association of Social Workers. Washington, DC: National Association of Social Workers. Approved by the 1996 NASW Delegate Assembly and revised by the 2008 NASW Delegate Assembly. Available online at http://www.socialworkers.org/pubs/code/default.asp.

Pargament, K. I. (2007). *Spiritually integrated psychotherapy: Understanding and addressing the sacred.* New York: Guilford Press.

Pew Research [Center] [...] [r]eligious identity of Latinos in the U[nited States ...] [Pew Research] Center, Washington, DC., Ma[...] [...] [pe]wforum.org/2014/05/07/the-shiftin[...]

Pew Research [Center ...] changing religious landscape. Pe[w Research Center, Wa]shington, DC, May 12, 2015. Ava[ilable ...] [...][5]/12/americas-changing-religious-l[...]

Rothman, J. (20[...] [...] can teach it. *Journal of Religion an[d ...]* [...]), 161–184.

Scales, T. L. & [...] [...] *dings on the integration of Christia[n ...]* [...]d, CT: North American Association [...]

Sheridan, M. (20[...] [...] [inter]ventions in social work practice: W[...] [...] [Spir]ituality in Social Work, 28(1/2), 99–[...]

Siporin, M. (1985[...] [...] [...]e. *Clinical Social Work Journal, 13*([...]

Smith, H. (1991). *The World Religions.* New York: HarperCollins.

Towle, C. (1965). *Common Human Needs.* Revised edition. Washington, DC: National Association of Social Workers.

Voss, R. W., Douville, V., Soldier, A. L., & Twiss, G. (1999). Tribal and shamanic-based social work practice: A Lakota perspective. *Social Work, 44*(3), 228–241.

Walsh, R. (1999). *Essential spirituality: The seven central practices to awaken heart and mind.* New York: John Wiley & Sons.

Westbrooks, K. L. (2008). Spirituality as a form of functional diversity: Activating unconventional family strengths. *Journal of Family Social Work, 2*(4), 77–87.

Wong, P.T.P. (2010). Meaning therapy: An integrative and positive existential psychotherapy. *Journal of Contemporary Psychotherapy, 40*, 85–93.

2

Affirming Your Own Spirituality

Life usually offers so much more than our biases and preferences will allow us to have. Beyond comfort lie grace, mystery, and adventure. We may need to let go of our beliefs and ideas about life in order to have life.

(Remen, 1996, p. 75)

Wisdom is a living stream, not an icon preserved in a museum. Only when we find the spring of wisdom in our own life can it flow to future generations.

(Nhat Hanh, 2011)

Let's begin a spiritual exploration, not with our clients, but with ourselves. Who are we spiritually? If we want to be fully tuned in to the spiritual and religious aspects of our clients, we need to know who we are spiritually, where we have come from, and where we think we may be going on our spiritual path. This helps us become more deeply conscious of who we are in a spiritual sense. It also helps us realize the importance of our own spirituality, what we believe, and how spirituality affects us in both positive and negative ways. If we know and appreciate who we are spiritually, we will be better prepared to begin to engage our clients' spirituality. Further, as we explore our own spirituality, we can reflect on how authentic we really are. Are each of us actually the person we are supposed to be and become? The more authentic we are, the more effective we can be as social workers.

People can learn more about themselves if they have opportunities to explore their beliefs and other spiritual qualities with others, including their colleagues. Explorations may occur quite naturally and meaningfully when we explore what we believe with others who belong to the same or a similar religious or spiritual group. When we are with people whose beliefs are noticeably different or are unknown to us, we are more hesitant and guarded. Yet, we may learn the most about ourselves with people with beliefs different from ours. Students in social work programs are likely to have additional barriers in exploring their spiritual beliefs because academia often discourages such explorations, especially when these conversations can be politically incorrect (Hodge, 2002; Reamer, 2003). Therefore, I suggest that opportunities be arranged in academic programs for students to openly discuss their varied spiritual and religious beliefs with each other, preferably in small groups. The intent would be to learn more about each other without any attempt to judge, influence, or control what others might believe. Actually, this can be a good exercise as we prepare to hear our clients' comments about their spiritual and religious beliefs without judging them. In these student groups, it would be beneficial to end these conversations by having each person share what they learned about other people's beliefs and any difficulties they had in hearing what others shared.

Understanding and claiming our own spirituality can prepare us to help our clients discover, understand, and affirm their own spirituality. How can we do this? We do not encourage our clients to be like us spiritually or religiously. The NASW Code of Ethics (2008) reminds us that this is unacceptable. We are to continually encourage our clients to be self-determining and to become more fully the person they are supposed to be. The specific content of our spirituality is not important to our clients. Actually, we must be continually vigilant in not introducing our own spiritual issues or biases, consciously or subconsciously, into the clients' work (Gardner, 2011). Instead, the value we place on this aspect of who we are helps us to recognize how important it can potentially be to our clients as well. Assisting our clients in understanding, claiming, and engaging their own spiritual energies is a principle of the spiritually sensitive practice approach described in the book.

One way we can learn more about our own spirituality is by exploring a range of spiritual and religious questions for ourselves (Canda & Furman, 2010). Some of these questions are similar to the ones that are also asked of clients, particularly during the assessment phase. This will become evident in later chapters as we examine the questions we can ask our clients about their spirituality. Chapter 8 on the assessment phase, in particular, describes a wide range of questions that can be asked of clients about their spirituality and religion.

As we discussed in chapter 1, spirituality is a complex and challenging concept to put into words, let alone define. Because of this, questions that are intended to help someone describe their spirituality are likely to touch on several different topics that fall under the rubric of spirituality. These topics include manifestations of spirituality introduced in chapter 1. Some include religion and religious issues that may influence a person's spirituality and others do not. Canda and Furman (2010, pp. 379–383), for example, offer several topics for organizing questions about spirituality including our religious and spiritual beliefs, our moral and ethical positions, our well-being as spiritual people, our spiritual group memberships and activities, how our spirituality has developed over time, and our experiences with spiritual transformation. This chapter draws on many of their helpful questions. Other topics are also pertinent in this exploration, such as our views about our purpose in life, our views and relationships with our Higher Power, and how we describe an afterlife or reincarnation. Let's begin with our beliefs.

Your Spiritual and Religious Beliefs

Our beliefs are a logical place to begin. Our most important beliefs are likely to evolve from the things we hold as important. Thus, answering questions of importance to us personally can be a good place to begin. Please answer the questions in Personal Exercise 1 (Walsh, 1999).

Beliefs are positions that we take and we sometimes embrace deeply. What do you believe that is important to you? How are these beliefs an expression of your spirituality and religion? We should keep in mind that our beliefs can be at many levels of certainty. They can be something we believe without question, things about which we believe but could change our mind, or beliefs we may have strongly agreed with in the past but are not so sure about now. Beliefs about a Higher Power and a spirit world, for example, cannot be verified using scientific methods, so doubts about religious and spiritual beliefs can be very common.

Religious beliefs may be easier to identify or detect than non-religious spiritual ones. Here are some religious and spiritual questions to consider that can be central in defining part of your belief system. Please reflect on and answer the questions in Personal Exercise 2 before proceeding.

Are there religious doctrines that you follow? What is the source of these doctrines? Who are its authors or from where does a religious group's tradition claim it comes? Is it considered a divinely inspired source? Do you believe in a Higher

---

Personal Exercise 1: What is most important to you?

1. What is really important in your life?

2. What would you like to do more often?

3. What would you like to do less often?

Personal Exercise 2: What are your spiritual and religious beliefs?

1. What are your most important spiritual and religious beliefs? Please describe at least two or three of each if you can.

2. How are your spiritual and religious beliefs similar to each other? How are they different?

3. Do you believe in God, a Higher Power with a different name, or some other sacred force? If so, please describe it. If not, describe what you do believe.

4. What religious beliefs do you question, struggle with, find upsetting, or outright reject?

5. How are your responses to these questions similar to what you answered in the previous exercise?

Power such as "God" or "Allah?" What kind of Higher Power is it? Is it a distant being far removed from conversation or is it a personal being that you can interact with in a close intimate relationship? What does this Higher Power offer or provide to you, if anything, tangible or intangible? Does this Higher Power give you support and comfort or answer some of your questions? Is it a power to be reckoned with if you have committed a sin? Is this force largely a friendly and supportive being or one that poses strict demands and can overwhelm you with fear and retribution? Or are you largely indifferent to what God might mean in your life most of the time?

If you are a Christian, how do you view the person of Jesus Christ and how does that impact your life? To some he is their Lord and Savior. To some he is actually God. To others, he may be a significant prophet or possibly a model for how they wish to live their lives. When Christians are asked about Christ, people seem to have varying views on what he means to them (Borg & Wright, 1999; McLaren, 2010; Spangler & Tverberg, 2009). Also, Christians of different sects give varying emphases to what Christ's life, death, and resurrection mean to them. Some—for example many fundamentalists and Evangelical Christians—believe that giving a personal testimony about their belief in Christ (e.g. "Christ died on the cross to save me from my sins") is key to their belief system and evidence of their claim to be Christians. Others, many affiliated with Catholicism and Mainline Protestantism, tend to believe that their deeds are more important.

Views about Muhammad among Muslims could be similarly varied in nature and importance. One of the five pillars of the "straight path" is a declaration by Muslims of their belief with the statement, "There is no God but God and Muhammad is His Prophet." This declaration is repeated in the five daily prayers that Muslims recite each day. However, the actual prayers of each believer may be somewhat different from each other. In a similar way, Buddha, Moses, Elijah, and Hari Krishna, for example, are incorporated into the beliefs of their respective religious groups. Also groups like American Indians have strong spiritual figures that symbolize for them what they believe and what is most important in life. Examples include Chief Seattle, who is partially known for his speeches on the environment, and warriors such as Crazy Horse and Sitting Bull, who have stood up for the rights of Indians in their struggles with Euro-Americans over issues of land (Eastman, 1997).

Another set of beliefs important to human behavior focus on such concepts as sin, remorse, forgiveness, good and evil, and karma. How do members of a particular religion define sin or evil? Very different definitions of these terms are evident in the sacred writings of most religious groups. Sin can refer to specific behaviors such as murder, stealing, and adultery, that are forbidden by some religious groups; it can also be, at times, defined more abstractly as a set of principles, leaving it up to the individual to decide (Borg & Wright, 1999). Other religious groups, such as Buddhists and Hindus, refer to the term karma instead of sin. Karma refers to all of the actions, good and bad, of someone, which are viewed as determining the fate of the person in their future and in reincarnated form.

Also many sacred writings offer different ways to overcome such things as sin or evil in a person's life. For example, what religious supports are available to help someone to forgive or be forgiven? Catholics have traditionally emphasized confession of sins in a semi-private exchange with a priest. Other groups offer pastoral counseling, spiritual direction, and educational groups. What do your religious or non-religious beliefs say about what sin and evil are? Are these terms useful to you in your personal life? How do you know when you have committed a sin and how does it affect you emotionally, socially, or physically? Or possibly, is karma an important term for you? Any of these questions may be pertinent to explore with clients if they are struggling with issues revolving around any of them.

On a related topic, how do we explain why people suffer? Is it a consequence of something we or someone close to us may have done wrong? In some cases, religious beliefs are taught that explain an association between a hardship or loss and a reason for it, such as punishment. Yet in contrast, other religions make clear that there is no connection. Buddhists, for example, view suffering as a state of existence that is common to all people and not to be feared or resisted (Chodron, 2012). Suffering is caused by "ego clinging" or resisting the continual changes in our lives that threaten our ego. Buddhists also refer to the spiritual path as a process of shedding the "armor" of our ego and suffering.

What happens after we die is another very important topic that draws on the religious beliefs of many people (Borg & Wright, 1999). Is there another life in the hereafter? If so, what is it like? Most religions give considerable attention to an afterlife and its meaning to us while we are still living. Some groups teach that the afterlife is more important than what is going on with us now. According to the Hebrew Bible, some Jewish groups believed in an afterlife thousands of years ago, while most contemporary Jews stress the importance of living this life as fully as we can. Most Christians continue to believe in an afterlife or resurrection where they hope to meet Jesus Christ. Some Christian denominations emphasize a heaven and a hell and give considerable attention to what each place or experience looks like and who deserves to go where. Muslims also believe in an afterlife. Instead of an afterlife, Buddhists believe in reincarnation. They believe that when people die they are born again as another person or as another living creature. Hindus also believe in some form of reincarnation. The connections between a person's current life and an afterlife are also important to consider according to some religious groups. For some, the degree to which one sins or is disobedient to God or a religious doctrine determines what happens after they die. Other sects teach that when we sin, our Higher Power will forgive us, permitting us to start over again with the caveat to sin no more. Any of these topics may also be relevant to issues our clients are working on with us.

The topic of an afterlife is often given inadequate attention by most agencies, with the possible exception of hospice. Instead, agencies tend to refer such clients to a clergy person without engaging in any meaningful discussion about it. Many questions could be explored in various forms about the afterlife and these questions may be important for readers to consider for themselves. Attempt to answer the questions in Personal Exercise 3 about the afterlife.

Others believe in reincarnation. Reincarnation refers to becoming a new life in a new body after we die. This belief is prevalent in Hinduism, Buddhism, Sikhism, and other religions originating in India. Some of the same questions asked about an afterlife could also be asked about reincarnation. For example, how would you describe reincarnation if you believe in it? How important is reincarnation to you? How do you think it will be determined who you will become after you die?

What Is Your Worldview?

Beliefs about a worldview are also important. They can be religious or non-religious. Kelly (2012) offers three questions for defining our worldview. How do we view the world in terms of how we think it is supposed to be? What are the main problems

---

Personal Exercise 3: What do you believe about an afterlife?

1. Do you believe in an afterlife?

2. How have you learned about the afterlife? (Religious group, significant person, readings, etc.)

3. How would you describe this afterlife if you believe in it? Do you view it in terms of a heaven and hell?

4. How important is an afterlife to you, if at all, in comparison to your life now?

5. How do you think it will be determined where you will go after you die? What types and severities of sin, if any, may determine where you go?

6. What images of heaven do you have or do you wish to explore?

7. What images and ideas might be stirred up in you about hell? What glooms or fears do you imagine about this? What do you believe about hell?

8. Is there a chasm between heaven and hell for you? Or is there a pathway between them such that you can move from one to the other? What might be satisfying or unsatisfying in this vision of reality?

9. Where do you think you currently stand in terms of where you will eventually end up? How important is this to you? How much attention do you give in your consciousness to this matter? How does it affect you in your daily life? How does it influence what you do or think?

with things as they are? What are the solutions and how can they be realized? How would you answer these questions? After answering this question, reflect on how likely your religious and spiritual beliefs are imbedded in your answers.

Cox and Steiner (2013), in their book on self-care, studied "global assumptions" about ourselves, others, and the world. Their formulation of a worldview is somewhat different from Kelly's and can be understood and measured using the statements that follow:

- People are basically good.
- I have a purpose in life.
- Life is predictable.
- Life is fair.
- The world makes sense.
- There is order in the world.

Cox and Steiner ask people to respond to these statements using a 5-point Likert scale of never, rarely, sometimes, usually, or always. Using questions by Kelly (2012) and Cox and Steiner (2013), attempt to put together your own worldview and reflect on whether it is complete enough to reflect your views. If you feel that something is missing, add more information to complete it.

Do you find that your spiritual and religious beliefs are evident in your worldview? In what ways are these beliefs evident? Our spiritual beliefs could largely coincide or overlap with our religious beliefs if we are religious and actively involved with a religious group. For many, spirituality is mostly expressed in the form of religious doctrine and practices determined by a religious group. Others identify themselves as spiritual but not very or at all religious. Increasing numbers—as many as one in three young people in the United States, for example—take this position (Pew Research Center, Religion and Public Life, 2015).

What are the spiritual beliefs of people that are not derived from or dependent upon a religious organization? These beliefs are more likely inherent in an individual's personal background and experiences rather than coming from an external source such as a religious group. In addition, they are often more difficult to articulate spontaneously. Sometimes people may need assistance in defining what is meant by spiritual before they can respond to their spiritual identity. Spiritual beliefs often evolve from definitions of spirituality described in chapter 1, such as concerns revolving around meaning, hope, mystery, and transcendence. Some examples of our spiritual beliefs revolve around our concerns for ourselves and other people:

- Do unto others as you would have them do unto you (the Golden Rule).
- When we focus on the needs of others instead of ourselves, we find greater joy for ourselves.
- It is important to do what is in one's own best self-interest (ethical egoism).

- We need to take care of ourselves in order to be able to help others.
- I am my brother's (or sister's) keeper.

Other examples of spiritual beliefs are:

- (I am a social worker because) I want to help other people.
- I experience the divine while walking in the woods.
- I trust that I will live a long, healthy life.
- Because I believe in the mystery and unpredictability of life, I want to be willing to face whatever challenges me in my future.

McLaren (2011) found that when people said that they were spiritual but not religious, they usually gave one of four explanations for what spirituality meant to them. These explanations describe, in part, their beliefs. McLaren added that the

---

"I'm Spiritual but not Religious."

1. Secular sciences, politics, and economics don't have all of the answers for them.

2. Organized religion doesn't have all of the answers for them either.

3. Spiritual means aliveness, meaning, and sacredness in the entire universe – including as part of our bodies, sexuality, our work, animals, plants, the earth, daily life and history along with the so-called sacred – God, meaning, values, souls, worship, afterlife, etc.

4. They seek practical ways as a substitute for organized religion such as meditating, hiking, volunteering, doing yoga, attending art galleries and festivals, and going on pilgrimages.

Listening to the "Wrong Voice"

(Buechner, 1969)

So many people may have listened to the "wrong voice" earlier in their lives and now are engaged in a life in which they do not find purpose or pleasure. They may come to suddenly realize that they have spent their entire adult life in a way that could not matter less to them and is irrelevant to the human needs of others. The moral of the story is that our lives are very precious and what we do with them matters enormously. Maybe we need to be told this stark reality more than once because there is always the temptation to think that we have all the time in the world when we don't. Eventually, there comes a time when we no longer have enough life left to go back and start all over again.

truth is that all four of these responses are at the heart of what he refers to as "true" religion.

Exploring questions about what is meaningful in our personal lives is another way of discovering our worldview. What is meaningful about our lives as family members—as fathers, mothers, spouses, partners, grandparents, and children? What is most meaningful about our jobs? Do we experience a special sense of meaning in our relationships with other employees? Or is the end product of our work particularly meaningful (e.g. growing and harvesting food, serving people in health care, protecting the public as a police officer)? How we use our leisure time may be where some of our most meaningful activities occur. For example, we may find considerable meaning in camping in a national park, growing vegetables or flowers in our backyard, repairing clocks or other household items, exercising, shopping, reading, taking care of children, chopping wood for the fireplace, or visiting with a friend.

Your Moral and Ethical Positions

The moral and ethical positions that people hold often derive from their religious beliefs. These positions can be distinguished from other positions that we take in that they are expressions of what we hope for or prefer. They are views about what "should be," what we want for ourselves, for others, and for our world. These positions are likely to vary widely from one person or group to the next; they may change for us over time and in reaction to experiences we have in our own lives. These positions are also so important to us that they can bring us in conflict with others holding contrary views. Examples of a variety of moral or ethical positions held about different people are:

- Everyone should be treated with dignity and worth.
- People must work for what they get; handouts are harmful and foster dependency and laziness.
- We are all God's children.
- Some people are good and others are evil.
- More is expected of those who have more wealth and talent.
- Do unto others as you would have them do unto you.
- People must pull themselves up by their bootstraps. Welfare only interferes with this process.
- People with wealth have received it as a blessing from God (prosperity gospel).
- When people contract a disease, they deserve what they get because of past wrongdoings.
- I am my brother's keeper.
- Everyone has within them the potential to do good or evil.

As these positions suggest, our views about people can vary widely and may have little in common with the views of others. Some are considered ethical principles of the social work profession while others draw from sacred passages of religious groups. Still others reflect the views of different political groups. Many have been handed down to us from our ancestors. Please reflect on and answer the questions in Personal Exercise 4 before proceeding.

Your Spiritual Well-Being

Spiritual well-being is an important concept to a spiritually sensitive social worker! A healthy spirituality reminds us that we need to be continually concerned with our own well-being. We can only be helpful in promoting the well-being of our clients if we are also committed to ourselves. Please answer the questions in Personal Exercise 5 on p. 35 before proceeding.

What do we need to do to work on enhancing a healthy spirituality? Numerous spiritual and religious writings of Christians, Jews, Buddhists, Muslims, humanists, and others offer suggestions of healthy traits associated with our spirituality (Aria & Gon, 1992; McLaren, 2011; Svoboda, 2005). The list of healthy spiritual traits in Figure 2.1 is not an exhaustive one, but it does provide us with a wide and varied collection of characteristics to consider. As an exercise, select two or three of these traits that you believe you have as personal strengths. Then select two or three traits that need further development. Discuss these selections with someone who also participates in this exercise.

While many of these spiritual qualities reach across virtually every religion and population of the world, some are emphasized more in some cultural groups and not others. Examples are some of the qualities considered spiritual in the Chinese character that may be overlooked in other cultures (Aria & Gon, 1992); they include enlightenment, energy, eternity, loyalty, melancholy, destiny, ambition, virtue, and honor. Qualities more likely to be valued in the Western world, in some contrast, are happiness, friendships, benevolence, perseverance, risk taker, and restlessness.

Personal Exercise 4: Your moral and ethical positions

1. What are the key moral and ethical principles that guide your life?

2. What is the source(s) for these principles?

3. What role does religion play in choosing these principles, if any?

4. How do these principles influence your life?

5. What moral and ethical principles do you reject or struggle with accepting?

Personal Exercise 5: How is your spiritual well-being doing?

1. What is most meaningful to you? Please explain how your spirituality and religion relate to this, if at all.

2. How often do you feel like life is worthwhile? Please explain how your spirituality or religion relate to this, if at all.

3. How strongly do you feel a connection with something inspiring that is greater than yourself, like God, nature, or sacredness? Please explain this connection and what it means to you.

Self-esteem	Ambition	Eternity
Self-awareness	Thankfulness	Humility
Authenticity	Justice	Acceptance
Wonder	Love	Joy
Friendships	Creative doubt	Perseverance
Courage	Mindful	Freedom
Self-love	Present now	Generativity
Commitment	Personal balance	Prayerful or meditative
Hope	Harmony with others	Forgiveness
Restlessness	Harmony with self	Gratitude
Faith	Compassion	Playfulness
Humility	Self-transcendence	Trust
Inner freedom	Open to learning	Reverence
Patience	Risk taker	Enlightenment
Grace	Tolerance	Unity
Virtue	Benevolence	Tranquility
Wisdom	Honesty	Honor
Clarity	Happiness	
Energy	Melancholy	

Figure 2.1   Healthy Spiritual Traits

Spirituality is a phenomenon that is both alive and changes in people throughout the life cycle. It exists in people of all ages and can become evident by exploring, in a selective way, some of the spiritual qualities most evident in each of the life stages. For example, spirituality begins to form at a young age (Crompton, 1998). For children, spiritual qualities that may be most evident are wonder, inquisitiveness, being in the moment, and being playful. Children tend to be spontaneous and activity-driven starting at a young age. Wonder, for example, is a quality that they often express. They are often in wonder about exciting new things that appear around them such as new people, unusual play objects, and animated scenes. They may be enamored or amazed about something that adults may take for granted.

Examples of this can be interacting with a funny clown, riding on a carousel, watching a puppet show or cartoons, observing a train go by, playing in the snow, smelling the fragrance of flowers, climbing a tree, or seeing a mountain for the first time.

Adolescents may reveal their spirituality with other qualities such as restlessness with themselves or their surroundings, the lure and excitement of freedom, an openness to learning something new, or a heightened awareness of their enjoyment and attractions in relationships with others. Questions of meaning are also important as they struggle with finding their own identity, differentiating themselves from their parents, and individuating. Adults at different stages will have a tendency to emphasize still other qualities such as self-awareness, authenticity, valuing friendships, courage, self-love, commitment, faith, grace, justice, love, compassion, and self-transcendence. Older adults, for example, may be faced with finding courage as they physically decline, developing their faith in response to losses, experiencing grace and gratitude for what they have, sharing wisdom with younger people, and experiencing a new inner freedom to be who they want to be.

Taking care of ourselves is important to our spiritual development. As we will be exploring later, our spirituality is not static but ever changing and evolving. Developing a healthy spirituality helps us to become more fully the person we are supposed to be. Thus, one way to explore whether our spirituality is healthy is to consider whether it is authentic to the person we are and are becoming, and the more authentic we are, the more effective we can become in helping others.

Going a step further, some spiritual qualities may become disciplines that are spiritual in nature. While they may overlap with some of the spiritual qualities mentioned above, they also go further as actions some people regularly take to strengthen their spirituality. Willard (1988) refers to the disciplines of abstinence and engagement. Some of the disciplines of abstinence, like solitude and silence, are similar to some of the qualities mentioned above. Others are disciplines that could be more challenging to many people, such as fasting, frugality, chastity, and sacrifice. Disciplines of engagement, including study, worship, celebration, service, prayer, fellowship, confession, and submission, also overlap with some of the above spiritual qualities while going further as regular actions.

Your Spiritual and Religious Group Memberships and Involvements

When researchers and agency personnel are interested in finding out if a person is spiritual or religious, they often ask some basic questions. They usually begin by asking a person if they are affiliated with or have a membership in a church, mosque, synagogue, or other house of worship. Typical questions are: Do you belong to a church, mosque, or synagogue? If so, how often do you attend services? Often this question is followed by a set of response categories like: weekly, two or three times a month, monthly or less often, once or twice a year, almost never.

Ellor, Netting, and Thibault (1999) developed a model describing the various types of functions that groups within church and synagogues have. It is based on the classic work of Warren (1978), who developed a construct of community as a system of subsystems, each of which having a function. Ellor and colleagues came up with seven functions for such groups:

1. production, distribution, and consumption—goods and services are exchanged;
2. socialization—learning the customs and norms of the group;
3. social control—rules and laws exist to keep people within acceptable boundaries;
4. social placement—associations and ceremonies for members' acceptance and recognition;
5. mutual support—help provided to members when they have special needs or emergencies;
6. defense—protection from harm;
7. communication—shared language, symbols, and other forms of expression.

This model may help readers who are unfamiliar with many of these religious groups to understand their purposes better. Some of these seven functions are more likely to be evident in religious groups than others. *Socialization*, for example, is import-ant in all religious groups in the form of educational programs for children and adults, retreats, revivals, and in parts of worship services such as sermons. *Social placement* is evident in ceremonies like baptism, liturgies, and corporate worship generally. *Mutual support*, a function of most interest to social workers, is evident in visitations to those who are home bound, prayer groups, funerals and memorial services, and often many community outreach efforts to others with special needs such as the homeless. *Communication* as a function of a religious group involves using terms that may be important to members but not well understood by out-siders such as "being saved," "speaking in tongues," and washing each other's feet. *Defense* may be an important function for religious minorities in countries with a national religion such as in many Islamic countries. The Anti-Defamation League is an example of a defense organization in the United States whose purpose is to oppose anti-Semitism and other forms of bigotry against Jewish people. Defense may also be relevant sometimes in Muslim communities in the United States when Muslims feel threatened by protesters responding to terrorist attacks against Westerners in the Middle East or terrorist attacks in the Homeland.

Religious groups can often be a center or maybe even *the* center for social sup-ports of some of our clients. These groups often offer worship experiences daily or weekly. Child and adult education are usually offered once a week or sometimes on weekdays and weekday evenings. Other activities could include socials, study groups exploring their sacred texts, women's and men's support groups, choir and other singing groups, prayer groups, meditation groups, senior social groups, retreats, outreach efforts to help people in need, consumer or self-help groups like wellness clubs, yoga and Reiki classes, 12-step programs, book clubs, and other activities unique to a religious group.

Religious-sponsored human service organizations can also be valuable supports for a wide range of professional services. Examples of organizations include Catholic Charities and Catholic Social Services, Jewish Family and Children Services, and Lutheran Children and Family Services located in many larger cities. Immigration and refugee services and food relief and temporary shelters to homeless people are examples of services that could be offered. Community and professionally based aids such as spiritual directors, shamans, faith healers, pastoral counselors, chaplains in hospitals, and parish nurses are also important resources to consider (Harr & Yancey, 2014).

Environmental resources are also available in developing the spirituality of religious and non-religious people alike. Many geographical areas offer resources that can be natural for praying or meditating, relieving stress, biking, fishing, boating, or taking a relaxing walk. Geographical areas can be parks, forests, mountains or beaches; planting in a garden, or playing with beloved animals in the backyard. Activities involving interactions with other people can also be helpful, especially

---

Conducting an Information Interview with a Spiritual Provider

Find out more about a spiritual or religious provider with an unfamiliar title to you. Interview someone with the title of spiritual director, pastoral counselor, hospital chaplain, shaman, faith healer, or parish nurse. How is their job similar and different from yours as a social worker? In what ways would you consider such a person as a referral for your clients? What reservations, if any, would you have in making such a referral?

Personal Exercise 6: What are your spiritual and religious memberships and supports?

1. Do you belong to any spiritual or religious groups? If so, please describe them. How often do you meet with them?

2. What kinds of spiritual or religious activities do you participate in (e.g. prayer, meditation, ritual, reading a sacred text, music, support group, etc.)? Please describe them and indicate how often you do them.

3. When you have been in times of crisis or serious need, what spiritual or religious groups or other supports have been useful to you? Please describe them and how they have helped you.

for people who tend to be isolated, withdrawn, or depressed and often without positive relationships with other people. These interventions can occur at churches, recreation or senior centers, at ball games, on picnics, or simply sitting on a front porch talking to people going by. Finally, non-physical beings can be meaningful resources to some, including a figure of Buddha, Christ, icons of the Madonna and baby Jesus, Hindu idols, and symbols of ancestors, angels, or various types of altars. Take a moment and consider a few personal questions about your current spiritual and religious memberships and supports and answer or reflect on the questions in Exercise 6 on p. 38.

The services provided by houses of worship vary considerably across different religious groups and even among different denominations of Christianity. A brief introduction to some of the services that could be offered by many synagogues, churches, mosques, tribes, and temples follows. This section offers examples of services and is not intended to be a complete list of such services.

Synagogues typically offer Friday evening or Saturday worship services, educational experiences for all age groups, prayer experiences, social activities, outreach and social action activities, women's and men's groups, senior social clubs, and other charitable efforts. Groups are available that focus on charitable acts. For example, a Hadassah ladies' group could cook meals for a food pantry. A Mitzvah Wagon group could provide assistance to children and adolescents such as sponsoring a visit to a senior center. Groups often focus on social activities and holidays, for example, lunches, dinners, hayrides, art events, film showings, and parties for Jewish holidays such as Chanukah. Groups are also offered that focus on education, for example, learning Hebrew, or interfaith trips to Israel. Sometimes synagogues have Hebrew schools available for Jewish children and adolescents that teach Jewish history, customs, and values as well as prepares them for their bar and bat mitzvahs.

Churches offer a variety of spiritual and religious activities. Worship services occur on Sunday mornings and sometimes on Saturday or Sunday night. Bible study groups and support groups for all ages and both genders are examples. Choir and other singing groups, potluck dinners, Sunday school programs, and excursions to relevant sites are also offered. Larger Christian churches, sometimes referred to as mega-churches, offer additional services such as nursery school and day care during the week, private schools, and parish nurses who provide initial nursing screenings and other medical services; these churches could also offer senior centers and social clubs for seniors, and symposiums and other educational programs that sometimes involve nationally known speakers and key leaders of the community.

Mosques typically offer prayer services on Fridays at noon or early afternoon. Mosques can often offer a range of other activities for members. Three different mosques that were consulted, for example, offer Muslim Scouts, Young Ladies' Study of Islam, Young Brothers' Study of Islam, and summer camp. Other activities include Arabic classes, Women's Study of Islam, Brothers and Sisters Classes,

Committee for the Enhancement of Women in Society Retreats, and outreach to feed the homeless.

Tribes of Native People can offer a variety of activities. One tribe, the Lumbees, for example, offers community service opportunities for teens, cultural enrichment classes, Boys and Girls Clubs, Native Daughters Empowerment Walk (for domestic violence survivors), Tribal Council Meetings, Dance of the Spring Moon Powwow, Sacred Fire Ceremonies, Summer Elders Gatherings, and Lumbee Homecoming.

Hindu Temples offer daily worship practices, yoga that involves healing and stress management practices rooted in Indian culture, other types of meditation, assistance from religious teachers and temple priests, community celebrations, educational programs for young people on a range of topics, and assistance to senior citizens. Religious education groups are usually available for children and adults. Groups focus on teaching sacred Hindu verses (Shlokas), learning Hindi, and learning Gujarati. Temples also may sponsor senior citizens groups and leisure activities such as table tennis.

Your Spiritual Development

Spirituality is in no way static for the vast majority of people. Canda and Furman (2010) refer to spirituality as a developmental process of searching and moving toward a sense of wholeness and connectedness, within oneself and with others. Our spirituality increasingly helps us to engage in beliefs and behaviors that support our growth toward wholeness and contact with the sacred in both religious and non-religious contexts. As mentioned earlier, our spirituality appears soon after birth and gradually evolves to the present time and beyond. Spirituality is part of our overall developmental nature. As we evolve spiritually, we also develop biologically, psychologically, socially, cognitively, and culturally.

Our spirituality emerges and changes throughout the life cycle. As children's bio-psychosocial-cultural aspects evolve and develop, so does their spirituality. Spirituality is most successfully manifested for children in a context where a search for positive meaning can easily occur, reliable and nurturing adult relationships are available, hope for the future is possible, and mystery can be introduced and supported (Crompton, 1998). The developmental theories of Piaget, Oser, Erikson, and Fowler are summarized next.

Piaget's Theory

Since spirituality is tied to one's cognition, it can be helpful to mention Piaget's theory of cognitive development (Piaget, 1962; 1969). These stages are important to consider when thinking about spirituality in children because social workers should be attentive to the spiritual capacity of different age groups. Piaget divided the typical developmental stages of childhood into four distinct categories:

- **Sensorimotor:** This is generally from birth until age 2. During this time children depend on their senses and actions to learn about and experience the world.
- **Preoperational:** This occurs from 2 until 6. Children now are able to represent and understand concepts and things with words and images. It is also a time when the child is egocentric.
- **Concrete Operational:** From 7 until 11. During this stage children have the ability to form logical thoughts about concrete events and analogies.
- **Formal Operational:** This begins at age 12 and lasts through adulthood. During this time individuals are now able to consider hypothetical scenarios and handle abstract thoughts.

Oser's Theory

Oser (1991) developed his own theory of spiritual development. It encompasses five stages and focuses on how children view a God, creator, or ultimate being. These stages are:

1. **The Ultimate Being does it all.** An Ultimate Being is seen as all powerful and children have little direct influence on the Ultimate Being's actions. God is active, people are viewed as reactive. An Ultimate Being is external.
2. **The Ultimate Being does it under certain conditions.** An Ultimate Being is still all powerful, but individuals believe that if they do good or pray they will be rewarded by the Ultimate Being. An Ultimate Being is external.
3. **The Ultimate Being and humankind do it.** Individual actions take precedence here. An Ultimate Being is apart from the world. Individuals no longer believe God is in charge of everything. He has a specific realm instead.
4. **Humankind does it through an Ultimate Being's doing.** This stage does not usually occur until adulthood. God is the base within individuals who choose to become attached to an Ultimate Being because they believe this Being will make their lives more meaningful. They have an indirect union with God.
5. The fifth stage evolves from the fourth but is rare. It is reached through a loving spiritual connection in every action, no matter how insignificant.

As young adults, we begin to create our own identity separate from our parents or parental surrogates. Our ego plays a primary role in this evolution as we come to claim a personal self that reflects who we are. Spiritual writers suggest that this personal self is largely determined by external forces such as our parents, siblings, peers, teachers, coaches, and others with whom we are close. A strong ego has a key role and wants security, comfort, and recognition, as well as some control over what comes next. As we get older, a personal self that is more deeply and authentically within us, sometimes referred to as our true self, begins to emerge. It begins to come out as we face challenges, losses, and struggles in our lives. In many ways we come to terms with the limited control we have over our lives and develop a deeper appreciation of other people and often a Higher Power that answers many of our questions and insecurities. Next, please answer or reflect on the questions in Personal Exercise 7.

Fowler's Theory

Fowler (1995), a developmental theorist and Christian theologian, created a seminal theory on how a person's faith is developed over time. Fowler defined faith as the way a person expresses their religion or spirituality, or what is most meaningful to them whether it is in religious or non-religious form. Faith has also been defined as an ongoing trust in God's faithfulness and assent to God's presence (Steinke, 1993). According to Fowler, while faith is usually meant to be religious, faith struggles are also evident in people who are not actively involved with a religious group. Fowler summarized faith as not being a separate dimension of life but an orientation of the total person, giving purpose and goals to one's hopes and strivings, thoughts and actions. Faith affects the shaping of our initiatives and responses, our relationships and aspirations in everyday life. Faith is a matter most evident in our relationships. As Table 2.1 suggests, Fowler's stages and those

---

Personal Exercise 7: How has your spirituality developed?

1. Describe your understanding of religion and spirituality when you were a child? What were some of your spiritual or religious beliefs and practices? How did you learn about them?

2. Describe your current understanding of religion and spirituality? How is this similar or different from childhood?

3. Describe any past times of spiritual breakthrough or pivotal life events that are relevant to you now.

4. Who/what have been the most influential persons/events in your past? Why are they so important?

5. What have been some of your greatest crises in the past? How have you coped with and moved beyond these crises?

6. From where have you gained strength for living, in past events?

Table 2.1 Fowler's Stages of Faith

FOWLER'S STAGE	ERIKSON'S STAGE	APPROXIMATE AGES	KEY FAITH THEMES
Pre-Stage: Undifferentiated Faith	Stage 1: Trust versus Mistrust	Infancy	Undifferentiated faith
Stage 1: Intuitive-Projective Faith	Stages 2: Autonomy versus Doubt and Stage 3: Initiative versus Guilt	Typically 3 to 7 years	Birth of imagination
Stage 2: Mythic-Literal Faith	Stage 4: Industry versus Inferiority	Typically preadolescent	Automatic acceptance of religious beliefs one is taught
Stage 3: Synthetic-Conventional Faith	Stage 5: Identity versus Role Confusion	Adolescence and sometimes continuing into adulthood	Conformity with and loyalty to family beliefs and practices
Stage 4: Individuative-Reflective Faith	Stage 6: Intimacy versus Isolation	Mid-twenties to forties	Critical reflection and taking responsibility for one's beliefs
Stage 5: Conjunctive Faith	Stage 7: Generativity versus Stagnation	35 years and older	Deepening one's own beliefs and a new openness to others with different beliefs
Stage 6: Universalizing Faith	Stage 8: Ego Integrity versus Despair	Rare for most people	In pursuit of a divinely inspired transformed world for all

of Erikson (1950) evolve together, as our psychosocial and spiritual selves are interdependent.

Fowler (1995) offers six stages of faith preceded by a pre-stage for infants who are not capable of distinguishing their identity, let alone their faith. This stage coincides with Erikson's stage of infancy involving trust versus mistrust as the central psychosocial task to develop.

Faith typically begins to develop in Stage 1: (Intuitive-Projective Faith) around the age of 3 years with the birth of imagination in children. This stage largely coincides with Erikson's Stage 2 (Autonomy versus Doubt) and Stage 3 (Initiative versus Guilt). Fowler refers to imagination in this stage as fantasy-filled with an emphasis on imitating stories and having fluid thought patterns. Imagine how a child in this stage might become completely absorbed in the sacred stories of their religion. The Hebrew Bible, with stories involving deeply mystical and amazing happenings, includes Noah and the ark, Jonah and the whale, the Jericho Wall falling down, and the Exodus story with Moses and his followers escaping across the parting Red Sea. Christian children enjoy these stories too. In addition they imagine with wonder the story of five loaves and two fish becoming enough food for thousands to eat. They also are in awe of the healing miracles of Jesus. Muslim children similarly are filled with excitement and magic imagining the angel Gabriel appearing before Muhammad as he heard Allah literally dictating the Quran to him.

Stage 2, named as Mythic-Literal Faith, involves the evolving faith of pre-adolescent children who are either in elementary or middle school. This stage coincides with Erikson's stage of developing competencies and the struggles between industry versus inferiority. Children automatically accept a literal interpretation of beliefs, moral rules, and attitudes including the religious and spiritual beliefs that they are taught. They accept these stories and beliefs as part of their membership in a church, synagogue or mosque. A person begins to take on the stories, beliefs, and observances that symbolize belonging to a community. However, during this stage children do not usually step back and become reflective and assess the meanings beneath these passages. One 12 year old, for example, cites special Biblical passages periodically on his Facebook page. One passage is from Ephesians 4:29 in the Bible "Do not let any unwholesome talk come out of your mouth, but only what is helpful for building others up according to their needs, that it may benefit those who listen." Another example in the Hebrew Bible is from Psalm 121: "I lift up my eyes to the hills. From where does my help come? My help comes from the Lord, who made heaven and earth." Many children learn these passages from their religious group and find them comforting to recite or share with others. Actually this practice is something that many adults also do when needing comfort. However, the adults are likely to reflect more deeply on the meaning of such a passage when they recite it to themselves.

Stage 3 (Synthetic-Conventional Faith) mostly begins in puberty but could be a permanent place for many adults. A person's experience of the world now extends beyond the family to school or work, peers, the media, and possibly religious institutions. This stage coincides with Erikson's next stage: Identity versus Role Confusion. Erikson points out that the identity crisis (Who am I?), is the single most significant conflict a person must face. By this stage, several disparate ideas or thoughts that did not make sense in a unified way in the past now are coming together and forming an overall understanding of beliefs and other meanings. Abstractions and conceptual understanding are added to a person's capacity to understand during this stage.

This stage is also known as a conformist stage, as a person becomes acutely in tune with expectations and judgments of others who are significant in their lives. Adolescents do not yet have a firm grasp of their own identity so that they can form their own judgment about things and maintain an independent perspective. The beliefs of people are still largely identified as differences in kinds of people (e.g. church attenders and non-attenders) rather than individual differences within and outside one's group. Religious beliefs of one's childhood and family of origin remain most important in maintaining one's spiritual and religious identity. Experimentation outside one's religious group is usually beyond this stage.

Fowler's Stage 4 (Individuative-Reflective Faith) comes next, ideally in the early to mid-twenties, but it can also come in the thirties or forties. Factors precipitating transition to this stage are the experiences of leaving home and going out on one's own emotionally and/or physically. We are expected to take seriously the burden of responsibility for our own commitments, lifestyles, beliefs and attitudes.

Being out on our own forces us to seriously examine what our life is to be about as we truly face the realities of becoming adults. By now, our identity and world-view are differentiated from those of others and become important factors in our actions. We are expected to critically choose our beliefs, values, and commitments by this stage, including religious and spiritual ones. This suggests that we may claim a particular religion on our own or decide to disaffiliate from a church or synagogue of the past. Some who were active in a church or synagogue as children are now withdrawing from all organized religion for a while. Erikson refers to this stage as addressing intimacy versus isolation as many seek to be romantically involved with a partner and settle down with someone with whom they love. Also we are expected to develop a range of meaningful personal relationships with other people during this stage. People in this stage emerge with a developed ego that takes on an inner self which is very important to spirituality.

Stage 5 (Conjunctive Faith) typically does not occur before mid-life, after a person reaches 35 years or older. In this stage, people often relax their belief system, including their religious and spiritual beliefs. We become more open or porous to the beliefs of other groups different from ours. At the same time we are likely to deepen our own belief systems and worldview. Differences and tensions between what we believe and the beliefs of others with whom we have become acquainted become less difficult to accept. We often even appreciate and seek closeness with others with different beliefs and worldviews, a most threatening and objectionable step to have taken in earlier stages.

Supporting social justice causes can become more expansive in this stage as we may become concerned with justice issues affecting people beyond the confines of our social class, religious community, or nationality. If we are Christians, for example, we want Muslims and Jews to have the privileges that we enjoy or at least the opportunities and rights so readily available to us. If we are Muslim, we feel similarly for Christians and Jews. In this stage we are reclaiming and reworking our past as well as becoming open to our inner self and the deeper meaning inside. Our inner life becomes significantly more important to us as we can let go of our strongly held religious beliefs constructed in the past and attempt to explore a larger, often unnamed divine force.

The last stage, (Universalizing Faith), is rare for most people to reach. Those reaching this stage have a deeply felt sense of oneness with all people. They feel a deep concern for the good of all people, a vision of a divinely inspired transformed world, and a selfless passion to pursue it. Such people appear to have a special grace or divinity and seem to stand out to be more fully human than the rest of us. They see reality incredibly clearly without the biases most of us carry. They are also fear-less about dying and prepared to live their lives to the fullest in the here and now.

They kindle our imagination because they embody openness to an almost miraculous world in the future of justice, love, and peace for all. They are appreciated and revered more after death than during their life.

Even though Fowler's stages may still be viewed as the most reliable developmental theory on faith and spiritual development by many communities, especially in the Western world, it has obvious limitations. Being constructed by a Christian theologian, it may not reflect the reality of other religious groups with different worldviews and values. Muslims, for example, may view the theory's emphasis on greater individuality and a diminished collective faith in later stages as contrary to their basic belief system. Also among conservative Christians, these stages at the higher levels may not be viewed in a favorable light. On the other hand, many Hindus who view people of all beliefs as divine and important may find some resonance with Fowler's stages on social justice and concern for all people.

Our spiritual development is not something that grows automatically. It usually develops for most of us as we grow biologically, psychologically and socially. In this regard, a spiritual history may be an important exercise for each of us to explore. It can help us to periodically reflect back on our lives, become more aware of who we were in earlier years, and how we have changed positively and negatively. In addition it can help to reflect on the various people, experiences, and events that have been significant in helping us become the spiritual person we are today. Personal Exercise 8 offers one way to begin this reflective process.

Fowler's Stages of Faith and You

Do Fowler's stages seem real in your life in concrete ways? What stage do you currently see yourself in? How do any of the previous stages of Fowler's theory seem evident in your past life? Overall, which themes from Fowler and Erikson are helpful or resonate with you, if any? Which ones do not?

Personal Exercise 8: What spiritual relationships have you had in the past and present?

1. Write down four or five of the most meaningful relationships, events, or experiences you have had in your life so far.

2. Reflect on each relationship or event, and imagine returning to it and being there for a few minutes.

3. When you are done, give thanks for each of these relationships or experiences and let yourself feel grateful for how each one may have enriched your life.

Experiences with Spiritual Transformation

Some spiritual leaders refer to our spiritual development as a lifelong journey beginning with a "false" self and moving through life to discover a deeper "true" self that awaits us. Our false self is not thought of as being unauthentic but as a self that evolves out of our childhood and is shaped largely by the expectations and pains of growing up and coping with the environment that has been given to us. It also is reflected in the social roles that we take on, such as oldest sibling, mother, or teacher. As we mature, we begin to discover our gifts or talents, which may have been hidden from us in the past. These gifts come in and out of our awareness as we begin to discover and use them and as mentors and teachers help bring them to our attention as well. Discovering a new self that is more authentic and real to who we are grows out of a deeper awareness and appreciation of what life has to offer us and what we can contribute to ourselves and others.

Our ego is our psychological navigating system for getting us through our day. It brings judgment to what we do, distinguishes reality from fiction, discourages behavior that can lead to trouble, makes our decisions, and protects us from potential dangers. While all of these functions are essential to have in surviving, spiritual authors suggest that there are times when we need to suspend these functions and just experience the "here and now" as fully as we can. These "here and now" experiences help bring us into a discovery of our true self. In these instances, we need to let go of all of our controls, remove our protective armor, and set our defenses aside.

Some religious leaders have offered insights about the false and true selves. Rohr (2013), a contemporary Christian author, refers to our false self as a "launching pad"—our body image, our job, our education, what we wear, our money, our car, sexual identity, success, and so on. Rohr refers to these as the trappings of our ego that are very important because they help us grow to maturity and get us through our usual day. But they are limited because they are largely a projection of our self-image and our attachment to it. Our true self, in contrast, is naturally created and given by God as we move beyond our false self (Rohr, 2013). Experiencing it feels like freedom and liberation. Our true self usually evolves and overtakes us if it comes at all.

Jesus taught a familiar principle of living recorded in all four Gospels when he stated "whoever seeks to gain their life will lose it and whoever loses their life will find it" (Luke 17:33). Howes (1984) insightfully interpreted these paradoxical words as meaning that losing one's life is to let down the protective walls around the psyche and giving our life over to something greater. In essence, she is suggesting that Jesus was saying that we have the divine wanting to live within us but needing for us to break the barriers of our egocentricity to allow for it to be born.

The Buddha is well known for his words, "I am awake." He was referring to being "awake" or fully awakened to what is happening in our life right now. To be awake, according to the Buddha, is to be free of attachments or cravings in our inner and outer worlds (Walsh, 1999). Some of the more obvious attachments that people have in our culture are our possessions, such as a fancy home or a sporty car, gaining power, pursuing higher status, or using drugs. These attachments could also be personal characteristics such as being a perfectionist who is never satisfied with what we do, being self-critical to the extent of continually beating ourselves up, or never being satisfied with our partner or our physical surroundings. According to the Buddha, attachments such as these never seem to satisfy our appetites. We always seem to be addicted to wanting more and we never seem to get enough. Our lives, being easily distracted and consumed by our need for attachments or cravings, prevent us from being fully awake to life. Being consumed by such attachments can be viewed as part of our false self that prevents us from discovering who we really are.

Chodron (2012), a Buddhist nun, suggests a way for us to gradually find our true self. She offers a form of meditation that can be helpful to us in monitoring or rehashing our "story line." Our story line is our habitual cognitive patterns that keep us fixed with our current identity. She maintains that there are unlimited possibilities to what we might think, feel, and experience and that for many of us, our sense of who we truly are is possible to find. Meditation helps us to become aware of our story line or fixed identity, as it continually emerges in meditation as internal chatter, and to be curious about it but not to let it control us. The meditation practice is meant to train us not to follow the thoughts (including attachments) but just to observe them and let them go. Over time we can become accustomed to experiencing these emotions and thoughts simply as sensations, free of a story line or fixed ideas of bad and good. At this time explore the questions in Exercise 9.

Personal Exercise 9: Finding your "true self."

Reflect on your life and the opportunities, growth spurts, setbacks, and other changes that have occurred. Spend time identifying what happened during each of these changes.

1. Was there a mentor, teacher, or special friend that played a role in these changes by giving you a new opportunity, access to a new experience, or simply informing you of your talents or pointing out something special about you of which you were not previously aware?

2. Was there something you did differently in your daily life by beginning a new spiritual practice, joining a new spiritual or religious group, or beginning a new job or academic degree program?

Conclusion

The chapter is devoted to exploring our own spirituality. Before we can effectively help our clients with their spirituality and spiritual issues, we need to know something about ourselves. Several questions are identified for the reader to explore and attempt to answer about yourself. Questions revolve around topics such as our religious and spiritual beliefs, moral and ethical positions, our well-being as spiritual people, spiritual group memberships and activities, and how our spirituality has developed over time. Questions are also posed about our experiences with spiritual transformation, our life purposes, possible views and relationships with a Higher Power, and how we may describe an afterlife or reincarnation if we believe in them. These questions are offered to help you explore how you define your spirituality, how developed it is based on some of the developmental theories, and whether or not your spirituality is expressed through any religious lenses.

Discussion Questions and Exercises

1. What have you learned about your spirituality? To what extent are religious beliefs and practices a source for expressing your spirituality? How much is your spirituality based on a non-religious orientation? How developed do you think your spirituality is? Have any of the developmental theories described in the chapter helped you to better understand yourself spiritually?

2. What do you think about the suggestion offered in the chapter about providing students with different opportunities to openly discuss their varied spiritual and religious beliefs with each other? This can be done in small or large groups, within courses and independent of courses. The intent would be to learn more about each other without judging those who have different beliefs. What purposes do you see, if any, in these conversations? What could the benefits be? What are the potential problems? Should the faculty be included or excluded?

3. The concepts of false self and true self are used in this chapter and others. How much sense do these concepts make to you? Have you found yourself discovering, as you have grown older, new aspects of who you are that were previously hidden to you? What are these new discoveries? Were these discoveries the result of something that occurred in your life such as beginning a new spiritual practice, joining a new group, or beginning a new academic degree program?

References

Aria, B, & Gon, R. E. (1992). *The spirit of the Chinese character: Gifts from the heart.* San Francisco: Chronicle Books.

Borg, M. J., & Wright, N. T. (1999). *The meaning of Jesus: Two visions.* New York: HarperOne.

Buechner, F. (1969). *The hungering dark.* New York: HarperCollins.

Canda, E. R., & Furman, L. D. (2010). *Spiritual diversity in social work practice: The heart of healing.* 2nd edition. New York: Free Press.

Chodron, P. (2012). *Living beautifully with uncertainty and change.* Boston: Shambhala.

Cox, K., & Steiner, S. (2013). *Self-care and social work: A guide for practitioners, supervisors, and administrators.* Washington, DC: NASW Press.

Crompton, M. (1998). *Children, spirituality, religion and social work.* Brookfield, VT: Ashgate.

Eastman, C. A. (1997). *Indian heroes and great chieftains.* Dover Publications (www.dover-publications.com).

Ellor, J. W., Netting, F. E., & Thibault, J. M. (1999). *Understanding religious and spiritual aspects of human service practice.* Columbia, SC: University of South Carolina Press.

Erikson, E. H. (1950). *Childhood and society.* New York: W. W. Norton.

Fowler, J. W. (1995). *Stages of faith: The psychology of human development and the quest for meaning.* New York: HarperCollins.

Gardner, F. (2011). *Critical spirituality: A holistic approach to contemporary practice.* Surrey, England: Ashgate.

Harr, C. R., & Yancey, G. I. (2014). Social work collaboration with faith leaders and faith groups serving families in rural areas. *Journal of Religion and Spirituality in Social Work: Social Thought, 33*(2), 148–162.

Hodge, D. R. (2002). Does social work oppress Evangelical Christians? A "new class" analysis of society and social work. *Social Work, 47*(4), 401–414.

Howes, E. B. (1984). *Jesus' answer to God.* San Francisco: The Guild for Psychological Studies, 127–130.

Kelly, T. (2012). *Every good endeavor: Connecting your work with God's work.* New York: Dutton.

McLaren, B. (2010). *A new kind of Christianity: Ten questions that are transforming the faith.* New York: HarperOne.

McLaren, B. (2011). *Naked spirituality: A life with God in 12 simple words.* New York: HarperOne.

Nhat Hanh, T. (2011). Quote in M. Nepo, *The book of awakening: Having the life you want by being present to the life you have.* San Francisco: Conari Press.

Oser, F. (1991). The development of religious judgment. In F. Oser & G. Scarlett (Eds.), *Religious development in childhood and adolescence* (New Directions for Child Development, No. 52). New York: Jossey-Bass, 9–68.

Pew Research Center, Religion and Public Life (2015). America's changing religious landscape. Pew Research Center, Religion and Public Life, Washington, DC, May 12. 2015. Available online at http://www.pewforum.org/2015/05/12/americas-changing-religious-landscape.

Piaget, J. (1962). *Play, dreams, and imitation in childhood.* New York: Norton.

Piaget, J. (1969). The intellectual development of the adolescent. In A. Esman (Ed.), *Adolescent development.* New York: International Universities Press, 104–109.

Reamer, F. G. (2003). Social work, evangelical Christians, and values. *Social Work, 48*(3), 428–431.

Remen, R. N. (1996). *Kitchen table wisdom: Stories that heal.* New York: Riverhead, Berkely Publishing Group.

Rohr, R. (2013). *Immortal diamond: The search for our true self.* San Francisco: Jossey-Bass.

Skovholt, T. M., & Trotter-Mathison, M. (2011). *The resilient practitioner: Burnout prevention and self-care strategies for counselors, therapists, teachers, and health professionals.* New York: Routledge.

Spangler, A., & Tverberg, L. (2009). *Sitting at the feet of rabbi Jesus: How the Jewishness of Jesus can transform your faith.* Grand Rapids, MI: Zondervan.

Steinke, P. L. (1993). *How your church family works: Understanding congregations as emotional systems.* Durham, NC: Alban Institute, 118–120.

Svoboda, M. (2005). *Traits of a healthy spirituality.* New London, CT: Twenty-Third Publications.

Walsh, R. (1999). *Essential spirituality: The 7 central practices to awaken heart and mind.* New York: John Wiley & Sons.

Warren, R. (1978). *The community in America.* 3rd edition. Chicago: Rand McNally.

Willard, D. (1988). *The spirit of the disciplines: Understanding how God changes lives.* San Francisco: HarperCollins.

3

UNDERSTANDING THE SPIRITUALITY AND RELIGION OF OUR CLIENTS

A (religious) path is by no means God himself. One can reach God if one follows any
of the paths with whole-hearted devotion. Everyone should follow their own religion.

(Hindu belief, in Smith, 2001)

In the sky, there is no distinction of east and west, people create distinctions out of
their own minds and then believe them to be true.

(Buddha, in James, 2013)

Smith (2001) discusses three periods of human life: the traditional, modern, and postmodern ages. He suggests that the modern age has given us science while the postmodern age gives us concern for justice, but only the traditional age that preceded both of them has given us a worldview. Unfortunately, the modern and postmodern ages have chosen science as the only means of explanation for what is; they have left religion largely behind as outdated. This is why religion matters, as the title of Houston Smith's widely popular book suggests (2001). Religions, formal and informal, are our sources for understanding beyond physical existence.

Smith (2001) discusses how traditional people divide the world into "this world" and an "other world." He diagrams a small circle within a larger one. The physical universe, or this world, is represented by the smaller circle and the larger circle represents the other world. The other world is understood as a matter of perception, not geography. It contains much of what is invisible to the human eye. It is referred to by some as a spirit world, by others as a world where angels and demons, patron saints, and shamanic allies and others reside.

We know the physical universe, as we can empirically see and measure it through science. Then there is the rest of the world that cannot be informed by science. It includes values, meanings, final causes, invisibles, qualities, and our superiors, according to Smith. This other world is where religions provide meaning, as limited as that is. Smith reminds us that science does a much better job of providing explanations about the physical world than religion can about the invisible one. Yet, this other world is so important to life on this planet in providing us with values and ethics to live by, deeper meaning for what we experience individually and collectively, and so much more that we cannot afford to discount.

Having some understanding of the spirituality and religion of our clients is foundational to the spiritually sensitive approach described in the book (Ellor, Netting,

& Thibault, 1999; Van Hook, Hugen, & Aguilar, 2001). This may seem like an over-whelming task especially when we consider the range of religious groups and especially the needs of clients who are religious. Questions can easily surface when we meet a client who is very different in religious background from us. You may ask, "Am I qualified to help?" Many workers may say, "This case is beyond my expertise or responsibility. I'll refer the client to a clergy person, a church, or a temple." What we often don't consider is that we are not expected to be religious or to know an extensive amount of information about a client's religious group. Some of us may also need to admit to having a subtle underlying bias against working with religious clients.

This chapter introduces a method for becoming more familiar with the client's religion when it is important to the client's spirituality and unfamiliar to us. Imagine this scenario involving a client who is a devout Evangelical Christian and the worker is spiritual but not religious. The client may have what the worker views as "extreme" religious beliefs. The worker may have been raised in a strict Christian family and attended a conservative church that adopts a literal interpretation of the Bible. Yet, the worker has shed her strict Christian upbringing and is no longer attending any church or practicing with any religious group. She is not sure what she believes since leaving home and graduating from college. The worker may be considered a "secular unaffiliated" person based on the language of the Pew Research Center, Religion and Public Life (2015).

Crash Course on How to Learn about Other Religions

How can the social worker prepare to help the client in the above scenario? A set of steps are offered in this section to help prepare social workers generally. These steps can be implemented in their entirety or in part. They are used in a Spirituality and Social Work Course to help students prepare to provide spiritually sensitive social work practice.

Step 1: Learn More about this Religious Group

The first step is a rather basic one. First, it would be good to do some reading about this religious group. Several books are available for this purpose (e.g. Canda & Furman, 2010; Ellor, Netting, & Thibault, 1999; Van Hook, Hugen, & Aguilar, 2001). Also the worker can take a close look at different religious groups' websites. It will likely introduce the group, its important beliefs, and many of its activities. Of the major religions, some are much older than others. Hinduism, the oldest, originated in India. Buddhism evolved from Hinduism in India, as did Sikhism. Of religions with beginnings in the Middle East, Judaism was first, followed by Christianity and later Islam. All three began with the Biblical patriarch Abraham. We focus mainly on Christianity, Islam, Judaism, Buddhism, and Hinduism in the text.

Step 2: Arrange to Visit a Spiritual Event

Next, arrange and visit a worship service or attend a spiritual event in which you can be introduced to the religion's doctrine, beliefs, practices, customs, and maybe most important, its members. It may be wise to call ahead of time and ask the religious group if it would be okay to visit; if so, when would the best time be, how should you dress, and if there is anything else you should know before arriving. Keep in mind that this is like a cultural visit that social workers conduct when they are interested in knowing more about their clients' culture. In this particular instance, the focus would be mostly on the religion of this cultural group, keeping in mind that religion overlaps with many cultural norms and customs.

Step 3: Experience the Client's Religious Service or Spiritual Event

If you know someone from the religious group you visit, it may be easier for you to arrange your visit with them and have them join you or greet you when you arrive. This can greatly facilitate your visit. Once you are at this event, begin to look for some of the elements reflected in most religions, as listed in Figure 3.1. This is not an exhaustive list of important elements, but it can begin to help a social worker obtain some basic knowledge, confidence, and appreciation of this client's spirituality and religion.

When you visit a church, temple, mosque, or other house of worship, you will likely observe a multitude of ways that people worship their God or Higher Power. Christian worship services vary widely across various denominations (e.g. Smith, 1991; Van Hook, Hugen, & Aguilar, 2001; White, 2000). In some instances worship experiences are very formal and follow a rather strict format, sometimes a liturgy. In others it is very relaxed and informal; spontaneous responses like swaying to music

---

Religious Elements

- Beliefs and teachings they have adopted that relate to their daily lives?
- Religious practices important to them (e.g. prayers, meditations, rituals, membership groups, etc.)?
- How these beliefs and practices help them (or do not help them) cope with difficulties when they arise in their lives?
- How they perceive their roles in the family from a religious perspective?
- How these beliefs explain the meaning of life for them—now and in the future when they get older?
- What is sin and evil to them? How are they to forgive and be forgiven for their sins?
- What social supports are available to them from this religious group?
- What are the areas of possible conflict, if any, between their spiritual beliefs and practices and the values and ethics of social work?
- How comfortable are they in talking about these topics?

Figure 3.1 What to Look for at a Spiritual Event: Getting into the Shoes of the Clients of a Spiritual Group

Example of Learning about the Christian Scientists

(Katie McDonnell Hutto)

Before I attended a service at the Church of Christian Scientists, I did some checking about this religion. Not to be confused with Scientology, this church practices a science-based Christianity focused on prayer using the Bible and a textbook called *Science and Health with Key to the Scriptures*. Mary Baker Eddy established The Mother Church in Boston, Massachusetts in 1879 after people began to read, practice, and heal from the ideas in the main texts on Christian Science. I had known that the Christian Scientists believed in healing through prayer, and wondered what going to church there would be like. . . . The service started with a hymn, led by the organ and it was not a typical hymn. The words were different and the melody was an Irish folksong. . . . The Lord's Prayer was then said, and it was odd. After every line, something was added by the two women speakers. At times it would be something scientific in nature, other times it was just a few random words. . . . The booklet we had been given stated that there are no preachers in the Christian Science belief; the textbooks are their preachers. . . . I did notice there was much more material from the Christian Science textbook and Mary Baker Eddy was mentioned more than the Bible throughout the service. . . . The words had no mention of Christ, the tune was Danny Boy and it was only two short verses. . . . Overall, I thought it was a strange experience. I did not get the feeling at all that I had been in a house of God or more specifically a place of Christ. In the literature it noted where you could find nurses and doctors of Christian Science. Being a social worker, it may be good to know what a client who is a Christian Scientist has experienced or believes. If a client does not want to take medication or does not believe they can be helped anymore, finding help in prayer may be a (partial) solution. . . . Though I may not believe like they do, they are all supportive of one another and do have strong faith in what they believe. Addressing this with your client or knowing how to help them in difficult situations can be so important especially in situations where they may feel they have no hope or no one understands.

and saying "amen" to a pastor's message may be welcomed. In Christian churches, worship usually includes prayers, singing hymns, choir music, sacred readings, a homily or sermon, and possibly the Lord's Supper, which re-enacts the Last Supper between Jesus and his disciples. Services tend to have a central focus on the pastor's sermon or the Lord's Supper.

In Islamic services, prayers and a sermon by the imam, or a prayer leader, are always evident (e.g. Ramadan, 2007; Smith, 1991; Umar, 2011). While prayers are required five times a day wherever the person is, Friday prayers are encouraged at the mosque around lunch time or afternoon. Most prayers are ritual prayers and involve kneeling in reverence to Allah. A carpet is provided for kneeling purposes. Everyone leaves their shoes at the door before entering the service, respecting the reverence of kneeling and keeping the carpet clean. Men and women pray in different sections of the mosque for practical reasons of preventing distractions for men when women are in the kneeling position in front of them. The service occurs with everyone facing Mecca, the spiritual center of Islam in Saudi Arabia. Visitors are often allowed to attend services and observe prayers in the back of the mosque. They can also pray silently.

Jews have three major sects: Orthodox, Conservative, and Reform. Their services are conducted in the synagogues on Saturdays and sometimes Friday nights and they are usually in different synagogues based on the particular sect (e.g. Friedman, 2001; Robinson, 2000; Smith, 1991). During synagogue services on Saturday participants are led by a cantor who sings readings and prayers and leads the congregation in prayers. Prayers come from the siddur, or Jewish prayer book. Passages are read from the Torah along with other prayers recited by members. It is a tradition that some members rock their bodies forward and backward during prayers. The Hebrew language is spoken mostly in the Orthodox synagogues and less frequently in Conservative and Reform synagogues. Women are usually required to cover their arms and wear long skirts and a head covering. Men wear a head covering or beanie called a yarmulke.

Some of the religious elements in Figure 3.1 and other questions will begin to get answered by participating in the religious service or activity. Questions can also be answered through discussions with members of the religious group after the activity is over and through reading materials that you may pick up.

Here are examples of what three different Master of Social Work (MSW) students picked up by visiting different religious groups.

- **Visit to a Quaker Meeting:** A student (Sam Rosen) reflected:

    If I were to work with a client who identifies as a Quaker, I would remember the lessons I learned while attending this event. I would encourage the client to consider utilizing their meeting as a source of social support and strength. Whatever concerns, worries or other problems they had, I would ask them if they may want to take the time of silent prayer during services to pray about these issues; (also if they already do this) I would ask if it has potential to help them. Unlike other religious organizations, they would not have a clergy or religious authority to turn to for spiritual guidance. Rather, they would probably consider themselves their own spiritual leaders since Quakers believe in a personal connection to God. I believe that their doctrine can be interpreted as a source of empowerment that encourages them to utilize it as an asset during the course of a practice intervention. It is not likely there would be spiritual barriers to receiving treatment (from a social worker); they have open beliefs to receiving help.

- **Visit to the Hindu Center:** Patrick Swan's comments upon leaving a class visit to the Hindu Center are:

  > I feel like the information I received will be very useful in working with clients that may fit these profiles. I think that I took more personally from this trip, however. I'm very interested in the Hindu religion, now. I think that their underlying spiritual belief in non-materialism and yoga is right in line with my personal beliefs, and what I want to accomplish as a spiritual being. I believe that won't be the last trip I take to the Hindu center. We observed a traditional ritual and enjoyed a home-cooked Indian meal. . . . The Hindu temple was unlike what I was expecting completely. There were multiple deities placed ceremoniously at the front of the temple. These deities seemed to emanate a power, or at least a perceived power. I felt like I could feel the reverence that people placed on them. Thousands of years of worship had gone into these different images, and I felt a great sense of respect for that. I really appreciated the explanations that Mr. T. gave to us for each deity. I was fascinated by the practice of having so many "different" religions and gods that were worshiped under the same roof. Any given night there were different types of services going on offering homage to different deities. I think that's extremely inviting and interesting. A ceremony began (while we were there) that was quaint but still powerful. It involved music and a man visiting each deity and offering prayers with a special set of candles. People sang and played drums and rang bells. I actually found myself enjoying the music, which I wouldn't have guessed. I wanted to know what they were singing, though. I felt a little saddened by the idea I probably never would know what they were singing. Once the ceremony was over, we each were offered a piece of fruit that had been sanctified. I'll finish this journal by listing some of these takeaways. It would be very important for a social worker visiting a Hindu client to have their shoes removed within their living space. It may not be necessary, though, so I believe it would be best to ask first before automatically assuming and removing shoes. Once inside, (seeing) the ohm symbol is something you could use to identify if a client practiced Hinduism. You could also see if there were any specific deities they have displayed either in pictures or tapestries or in statue form. If appropriate and given the right opportunity, a worker could ask about a specific deity and what it meant to them.

- **Visit to a prayer service at a Mosque:** Katie McDonnell Hutto reported that:

  > the service lasted approximately thirty minutes on a Friday afternoon. When I arrived at the mosque, I had to remove my shoes and wear something covering my head. Women sat in the back of the room but were still participating in the same service. There was a prayer leader who did some chanting during the service followed by a message. The emphasis on trusting and serving God alone really came through to me, since I believe it can be hard to truly just let it all go. Many of the prayers were led but there was also time for personal prayer. I did feel different from everyone else, but for the most part I did feel welcome there. This has been

the most "different" spiritual experience I have had yet, but it has not been meditation based. Those that are devout have a regular schedule, and know exactly what will happen when they come to their Friday prayers. I know Islam has a strong focus on keeping your faith in God and trusting in Him. I too believe in this and hearing any messages like this is helpful for me because I feel it is a message that can always be strengthened. God is everywhere, regardless of religion, and hearing that message in different places only affirms that for me. In social work, I believe being able to relate to all your clients is incredibly important. If you have a client that is Muslim, knowing what they believe or that their beliefs somewhat resemble yours can be important. Even if you don't believe in the same thing, the powerful message you can send to your client is that you understand them or you can be there for them and can help on many different levels.

Step 4: Application to Practice

The next step in preparation would be to meet with the clients of your agency and hopefully you will be better prepared to engage them spiritually and religiously (e.g. Ellor, Netting, & Thibault, 1999). I am not suggesting that you are equipped to become well informed about their religion; you will simply have some background and can carry on a brief conversation about their religious issues and it will most likely be noticed and appreciated by the clients. You should see yourself as a social worker tuned in and ready to help if a client introduces her religion in her work with you and your agency. In this case, the client should be viewed as the expert on her religion and you are the student. If a client brings up a religious issue such as the importance of prayer or meditation, an appropriate response could be, "Please explain to me more about the importance of prayer for you if you think this can help me be more supportive of you in our work together."

A Widely Varied Religious Landscape

One of the reasons why many social workers may be reluctant to engage their clients in discussing their religion is because of the widely varying religious landscape of the United States, and possibly in many localities. Our clients represent a wide range of spiritual and religious backgrounds. As described in chapter 1, the Pew Forum's most recent interview study in 2014 found that religious affiliation in the United States is both diverse and changing (Pew Research Center, Religion and Public Life, 2015). According to Pew Forum, Christians make up 70.6 percent of the population. This is a 7.8 percent decline since 2007. While this represents the vast majority of the population, Christians in themselves are an extremely diverse group in denomination, belief, and temperament.

Christians can be categorized into four major groups, which are quite different from each other: Evangelical Protestants, Catholics, Mainline Protestants, and historically Black Churches totaled about two-thirds of the adult population in 2014 (Pew Research Center, Religion and Public Life, 2015). Christians also are affiliated with smaller groups including Mormons, Jehovah's Witnesses, Orthodox Christians, and smaller groups, each being less than one percent of the adult population except for Mormons, who were 1.6 percent in 2014.

In addition, there is considerable variation within these larger categories of Christianity. Mainline Christians, for example, include Methodists, Presbyterians, Lutherans, Episcopalians, Baptists, and other groups. In addition, each of these mainline denominations can be divided up even further. For instance, most of them have a Northern and Southern brand, usually because of schisms of the past that have led the Southern groups to break away and start up new denominations that are more conservative in beliefs and practices. As an example, large numbers of members of the Evangelical Lutheran Church in America (ELCA), mostly in the South, have recently left the ELCA church and transferred to a newly created denomination of Lutherans because the ELCA changed their rules to ordain GLBT pastors in active GLBT relationships and to support GLBT marriages (www.elca.org).

The major non-Christian groups add even more complexity to this diversity. Four major world religions—Judaism, Islam, Buddhism, and Hinduism—make up a total of about six percent of the total U.S. adult population (Pew Research Center, Religion and Public Life, 2015). As with Christians, each of these religious groups has separate sects within them. For example, Jewish groups break down into Reconstructionists, Reform, Conservative, and Orthodox; Muslim groups include Sunni, Shiite, and a smaller mystical sect called Sufis. Beyond these groups a relatively large percentage (22.8 percent in 2014) of U.S. citizens are unaffiliated. This is an increase of 6.7 percent since 2007. Variations in this category have been elaborated on in chapter 1. The largest subcategories are the religious unaffiliated and the secular unaffiliated and smaller numbers include atheists and agnostics. It's important to add that among young adults (ages 18 to 29), about one-third say they are spiritual but not currently affiliated with any religion.

Where can you begin? Let's say that you notice that your caseload now includes three or four new Muslim clients and some of the females are wearing head scarfs and other symbols of importance to them. A visit to a mosque and a quick perusal of the Quran, their holy book, may help you to listen to them with more confidence and sensitivity. Let's say that one of the clients mentions the Quran as a sacred book to them. If you wonder if this is relevant to your helping role, you could say, "The Quran is a very important book to you, isn't it?" This could be followed in a supportive way with something like, "Please share more about your sacred book if you think that will help me understand more about you, your religious supports, and how I can help you."

Religious Holidays

Websites are available for information about the religious holidays of virtually every known religion. One such website is www.interfaithcalendar.org. This website can quickly bring up a calendar of religious events throughout each year and general information on virtually every religion, large and small. Click on the year in which you would like to see the dates of holidays of a religious group. Then click on "Definitions of Calendar Listings" to get to a brief description of all of the religious holidays. Religions are divided into those with one deity (e.g. Christianity, Islam, Judaism), multiple deities, no deity (e.g. Buddhism), and combinations that are less distinct (e.g. Wicca, Native American, Unitarian Universalist). Internet links are available on this website that provide some information about each religion, including suggestions of how people outside the religion can recognize this religion in appropriate ways with their friends from this group. For example, greeting e-cards are available for Ramadan, the most holy Muslim holiday. The website also explains the meaning of the holiday under "definitions," what is practiced and in some instances celebrated during this holiday, and other helpful information such as whether the holiday is a primary or secondary one. As an example, Magha Puja Day is a primary holiday of Buddhists celebrating the presentation of the teachings by Lord Buddha to an assembly of holy men in the month of March.

Other websites on religious holidays are also available and can be found using Google or the websites of specific religious groups. One meaningful way to be introduced to a particular religion of some of your clients is to join other people you know affiliated with this religion in the celebration of one or more of their religious holidays. This could also include recognizing the importance of a religious holiday with clients during conversations and in some instances sending an appropriate greeting card to them. Our clients, like everyone else, have special events or holidays and many have religious holidays of special value to them.

Let's imagine you are working with a Muslim client and you are meeting during their most sacred period of Ramadan. Let's say you decide to find out more about your client's religious holiday and you consult the religious holiday website mentioned above. This website together with another website (www.islam.about.com) will help you find out that Ramadan occurs during the ninth month of the Islamic lunar calendar. It varies each year from the Gregorian calendar that most Americans follow. Each day during the month of Ramadan, Muslims spend the daylight hours in a complete fast. This is a time for Muslims to purify their soul and focus all of their attention on Allah. They are expected to reexamine their lives in relation to the Quran, make peace with those they have wronged, improve their family ties, and rid themselves of bad habits.

Relevant Religious Concepts

Several concepts are commonly addressed in many religious groups that are pertinent to spirituality, including suffering, gratitude, wilderness experiences, mountaintop experiences, sin and repentance, karma, stewardship, social justice, death, afterlife, reincarnation, and faith (Van Hook, Hugen, & Aguilar, 2001). Some, such as wilderness and mountaintop experiences, are metaphors for the spiritual or religious experiences of some people. Wilderness can be a time of struggle, pain, and being lost and confused that people may go through leading eventually to healing and insight at the other end. Mountaintop experiences can be high moments when a person feels inspired, filled with insight, and experiences of unusual breakthroughs in communication with others. Most if not all of these concepts can be important to many clients and therefore have relevance in their work with a social worker. Therefore, social workers should probably know something about these concepts in terms of the meaning they may have for different religious groups. Religious holidays, mentioned earlier, offer explanations and expressions for some of these concepts.

Sin and Repentance

The concepts of sin and repentance are highlighted as one example here (Backus, 2000; Lazarus & Sullivan, 2008; Van Hook, Hugen, & Aguilar, 2001). The concept of sin could possibly have a positive or negative influence on clients depending upon what they believe. For example, committing a sin can be a problem for many clients in that they feel they are sinning and don't know how to stop it; or they may be subconsciously preoccupied or guilt-ridden about what they have done wrong and cannot reverse. Some clients may be acting out problematic behaviors such as mistreating or neglecting their spouse or children, drinking too much alcohol, or perhaps committing petty theft at their work setting. In these instances, their religious group may be a valuable source of support. Or at least their religious friends could be reminding them that their behavior is considered a sin. However, their religious group could have strict conservative beliefs about what sin is and that may be imposing a problem in a client's everyday life. They could be obsessed or torn apart about what they are doing, such as drinking a glass of wine at night or dancing on weekends, knowing that their religious group views these actions as sinful.

Three major religious groups, Christianity, Judaism, and Islam, focus considerable attention on sin and its alleviation (e.g. Lazarus & Sullivan, 2008; Van Hook, Hugen, & Aguilar, 2001). Fasting is required for some, as well as an intensification of prayers, critical self-examination, and sometimes confession. Relevant holidays of the three religious groups are respectively Yom Kippur, Lent, and Ramadan.

Yom Kippur is the holiest day of the Jewish year, when Jewish people observe their holiday with strict fasting, prayers, and ceremonial repentance. It is referred to as the

Spiritual Warfare as an Expression of Sin

(Alexandria Elmore, 2015)

Within the Evangelical Christian Church, the topic of spiritual warfare is a real issue with which some clients may struggle. Spiritual warfare is a war "not with flesh and blood but against spiritual forces of darkness" (Borgman & Ventura, 2014). As social workers, we take a holistic view of our clients by giving consideration to spiritual factors that may influence the client's well-being. Spiritual attacks can become manifested in a variety of ways, ranging from temptations to sin to experiencing a mental illness. When working with clients who believe a personal ailment is the result, at least in part, of a spiritual attack, it is important to recognize the significance of it to them. To determine the best way to help such clients, the social worker can ask them how they view the impact of the spiritual world on why they are seeking help.

One example of a client concern about spiritual warfare was a woman suffering from post-traumatic stress disorder resulting from a sexual assault. This assault caused her to relive it through vivid nightmares and dream anxiety. The woman's nightmares were so frequent and troubling that she would avoid sleeping, and her quality of sleep was very poor. This led to decreased productivity at work, resulting in her subsequent job loss. When working with this client, she expressed the idea that Satan was attacking her with these nightmares. She believed that her sleeping troubles were the direct result of demonic influence and wanted to talk about ways to eradicate this negative force in her life. She strongly believed in the power of prayer, and this spiritual intervention became a critical part of her recovery and healing process.

Because some believe that evil spiritual forces are at work in their life, it may be helpful to explore positive spiritual outlets with them and the spiritual activities in which they can participate to combat these forces (e.g. Eldredge, 2001). For instance, the client may discuss the importance of prayer, reading scripture, or meditating. The social worker can encourage clients to explore their spirituality through the means that they find most comforting and healing. This exploration of spirituality would be in conjunction with other therapeutic interventions relevant to the needs of the client.

Jewish Day of Atonement. Jewish people traditionally observe this entire day with fasting and intensive prayer, and much of this time is spent in synagogue services.

Lent is a period of time in the late winter and early spring for self-examination and often personal sacrifice among Christians. It begins with Ash Wednesday when ashes in the shape of a cross are sketched on the foreheads of members to remind them of their mortality as they come from ashes and return to ashes. Lent is a period of forty days in preparation for Holy Week, when Jesus returns to Jerusalem for the last time, is arrested, crucified, and three days later is resurrected on Easter. Lent is observed by fasting, prayers, more frequent than usual worship, and acts of charity.

Ramadan is a season in which Muslims have their intense focus on their sins and repentance. Ramadan occurs in the ninth month of the Islamic calendar; it varies in time from year to year. Ramadan is devoted to the remembrance of Muhammad's reception of the divine revelation recorded in the Quran. Muslims believe that the Quran was revealed to Muhammad from Allah over a 23-year period through the angel Gabriel. This is the holiest period of the Islamic year and strict fasting occurs from sunrise to sunset. Ramadan may remind many Christians of Lent, which has some similarities, such as giving up things and overcoming bad behaviors.

There is no consensus on a definition of sin among the different religions (e.g. Lazarus & Sullivan, 2008). The various Christian denominations do not even have much agreement on what sin means. So it may be important to explore what a client understands sin to mean if it comes up. In brief, Judaism has the Ten Commandments, also known as the Decalogue. God inscribed the Ten Commandments on stone tablets and gave them to Moses on Mount Sinai. The Hebrew Bible also has numerous laws and instructions about how to live your life. The Ten Commandments are fundamental precepts for Christians as well. These Commandments include recognizing God alone, not worshipping other gods, not using God's name in vain, keeping the Sabbath holy, honoring your father and mother, and prohibitions against murder, adultery, stealing, false witness against your neighbor, and coveting your neighbor's wife or possessions. These commandments and other laws are included in the Hebrew Bible mostly in the books of Exodus, Leviticus, and Deuteronomy.

Along with the Ten Commandments, Christians identify a variety of other sins that are important. While Christians do not have one detailed list of sins agreed upon by all Christians, the two most important commandments proclaimed by Jesus are "Love the Lord your God with all your heart and soul, and love your neighbor as yourself" (Matthew 22:37–39). Any violation of these two most important commandments could be considered sins. Another important passage in the Bible on sin for Christians is Matthew 25:31–46 in which Jesus begins by saying "I was hungry and you gave me food, I was thirsty and you gave me something to drink, I was a stranger and you welcomed me, I was naked and you gave me clothing, I was sick and you took care of me, I was in prison and you visited me." Then when Jesus was asked when these things happened, he responded with "just as you did it to one of the least of these . . . you did it to me." This passage is special for many social workers and has influenced many to choose a career in social work.

There are a range of ways different denominations and sometimes local churches interpret violations of these commandments, varying from a long list of specific attitudes and behaviors explicitly asserted by the elders of many conservative churches, to a more fluid set of principles that can be used by individuals to address their sins in liberal churches (Van Hook, Hugen, & Aguilar, 2001). Conservative Christian teachings about sin may include merely thinking sexual thoughts about another person or prohibiting dancing and alcohol consumption. In these and other instances, the sins are very specific references to unacceptable attitudes or behaviors. In some contrast, many liberal denominations refer to sin in a more humanistic way that often includes a challenge placed on the person committing the sin to reflect on and address it. Some liberal denominations, for example, refer to sin as any instance in which a person is separated from God, others, or oneself in some way. In these instances, sin could include forgetting to pray or denigrating a family member or colleague. In this case, such members are expected to address their sin, sometimes with the help of another person. One female Christian pastor explained her views on sin, in part, based on separations from God and others.

> And yet though I was made by the Creator, I find myself separated from God, from the very source of my being. So again and again God calls me or pulls me back to God's self. This journey doesn't end; it is the spiritual walk. Reconciliation also makes sense regarding my relationships with other human beings, each bearing God's image even as we walk around with 'feet of clay' (an image from the second chapter of Daniel). On an interpersonal level, I go through periods of intimacy and distance with the ones I love the most. The season of Lent invites me to examine these relationships, identify barriers that have gotten in the way, and make amends. But reconciliation is far more than an individualistic notion: it's not only about "me and Jesus" or "me and my relationships." Most hopefully, there is a cosmic dimension: Through Jesus, God draws the world into God's very heart. And there is a social dimension that contributes to this cosmic process. What does it mean as a community to "come-together-again," to be reconciled, across racial and socio-economic lines, right here, right now?

> (The Reverend Joslyn Ogden Schaefer, Associate Rector, St. Peter's Episcopal Church, Charlotte, NC, March 19, 2014)

Muslims have their list of sins as well, including gambling, theft, lying, eating pork, drinking alcohol or taking drugs, being sexually promiscuous and violating other rules included in the Ten Commandments.

It is important to note that not all religious groups find the concept of sin to be important to their belief system or daily life. Followers of Buddhism, for example, are much more inward focused. Rather than focusing so much on their external environment as a source for their moral compass, they seek further clarity and personal development more from within. Kornfield (1993) refers to our demons—for example, grasping and wanting, anger, fear, judgment, restlessness, and doubt. These are some of our emotions and attitudes that prevent us from experiencing wholeness or following a more positive path. He discusses the need for us to recognize and name these demons as they become manifested in meditation or in other introspective exercises. To overcome these demons, we are advised to identify them to ourselves and attempt to accept them as part of who we are, however unwelcomed. Kornfield advises his clients to begin by sitting and being aware of our breath, watching and waiting for their demons, allowing them to come and go, and eventually greeting them as an old friend. Over time, these demons become much less powerful or obstructive in daily living.

Sins at the Macro Level

Addressing sins at the organizational, institutional, and societal levels is also evident for most religious groups. Religious statements on the beliefs about how to treat human beings and other living creatures are often very progressive, especially from the perspective of the Social Work Code of Ethics and CSWE (Council on Social Work Education) accreditation standards. For example, religious groups believe that no one should go hungry. Another macro belief is that world peace should always be preferred over the possibility of war. Violating these religious beliefs and rules, in most cases, would be considered sinful, at least theoretically. In practice however, many of these macro sins may not be taken as seriously as the micro ones because they are thought to be so global and beyond the influence of a particular religious group. Other major reasons why these macro sins are neglected is that they clash with the political persuasions of many religious people, especially those with more political and economic power. Also they can clash with the general norms of the larger community, which tends to emphasize maintaining the status quo.

However, important exceptions need to be added. For example, Quakers not only affirm very impressive ethical principles but they also rigorously stand by and attempt to act upon them (e.g. Gulley, 2013). These principles include promoting world peace, non-violence, and racial, economic, and gender equality. Most African American Churches are also likely to take very strong stands against many macro sins and rigorously oppose them to the extent that they have influence. Racial and economic equality and compassion and social justice for the downtrodden are among their most sacred concerns.

One of the best recent examples is the Civil Rights Movement, most evident in the 1960s and continuing up to the current time in actions such as Moral Mondays in some Southern states. This movement, based primarily in the Christian and Jewish communities, has been a central force leading to the enactment of the national voting rights and employment rights legislation and for the many anti-poverty programs initiated especially in the 1960s. The Civil Rights Movement was empowered by African American Churches advocating for equality, economic justice, and non-violent action. Their beliefs largely originated with the teachings of Jesus and his commitments to justice and non-violence.

Islam also has strong religious positions or ethical principles at the macro level (e.g. Nadir & Dziegielewski, 2001). Racial equality and interracial coexistence are emphasized. The Quran states that income is to be widely distributed and capitalism is approved only if used in a balanced way. Also, the Quran leaves open the possibility of full equality of women with men. While pacifism is not a position taken by Islamic groups, religious tolerance is. The Quran points out that they are to "defend yourself against your enemy but do not attack them first. God hates aggressors."

Many Christian groups take similar positions; they vow never to take an aggressive role against another group unless their own security is violated. The "Just War Doctrine" of the Catholic Church cites four strict conditions for the legitimate defense of a country by military force including 1) the damage inflicted by the aggressor must be lasting, grave, and certain; 2) all other means of putting an end to the aggression must be shown to be impractical or ineffective; 3) there must be serious prospects of success; and 4) the use of arms must not produce evils and disorders graver than the evil to be eliminated (Ramsey, 2002).

Pluralism as a Perspective

Throughout the book, an overall message is that everyone has their own unique spirituality and their own religious or non-religious beliefs. A spiritually sensitive practice approach focuses on our clients' spirituality and religion, not ours. This is about helping our clients and being where they are. Consequently we realize, often over time, that we are exposed to a widely varied set of beliefs and practices of our clients. As we expose ourselves to such a diverse set of expressions, we come to discover that many beliefs and practices of one religious group have similarities to that of other groups. The Golden Rule of "Do unto others what you would want them to do unto you," for example, is adopted by all of the major religions in one form or another. All religions place high value on treating people with dignity and respect, feeding the hungry, caring for the widows and orphans, and seeking peace in the world. Nonetheless, each religion has its own unique beliefs and practices as well; in many instances contradictions and opposing views are also evident. For example, Christianity claims Jesus Christ as the son of God, while Islam proclaims Muhammad as the final and most important prophet, with Jesus being a less important prophet.

Another important view expressed in this book is that pluralism and pluralistic thinking are important concepts to explore and consider adopting as practitioners. Pluralism in the spiritual and religious realms can be described as an appreciation of all religions with the recognition that each has its own contributions to make even though people may have a preference for a particular religion. Each religion shines a little truth on the ultimate truth about God, human existence, and life generally. Some readers may be ready to go even further and take an even stronger view that no group has the ultimate truth but each provides a glimpse of what is true about the ultimate meaning of our existence. This latter view would suggest that it may be in a person's interest to learn about the benefits of several religions. These views are reflected in the most developed stages of faith articulated by Fowler (1995). A student's reflection after his visit to one community church captures some of his

---

A Student's Reflection on Pluralism

(Sam Rosen)

For my spiritual activity, I attended a Universalist Unitarian Church service earlier this morning. I had never been to a Unitarian service before, but had heard about it as a progressive and non-denominational alternative to more traditional religious organizations. . . . What intrigued me most about the service was the lack of specific religious terminology. The hymns and prayers performed during the service . . . referred to "holiness." During one of the pastor's sermons, he explained that "holiness," in its root, is closely related to "wholeness" and it represents how all things and all people are sacred. This church encourages people from all religious backgrounds to take part in their worship. It seems to me that this church attempts to find the common ground behind all spiritual and religious practices.

---

awareness of a religious group's openness to many different beliefs, as summarized in the box above.

Pluralism, by the way, does not mean that you have to sacrifice or give up a strong commitment to your own religious or spiritual group. Actually, those who have enough conviction and comfort with their own religious group often have the easiest time looking beyond it to what can be learned from other religious groups. Conversely, those who rather rigidly hold onto their religious beliefs and affiliations stressing that they are the only course to take may be among those who cannot permit themselves the opportunity to learn from other groups.

McLaren (2012) conceptualizes three different paths that people can take in modern society. Fundamentalism is one path in which you embrace a strong faith identity with your own religious community but have overt or covert hostility toward other religious groups. A second path, relativism, is when you have a weak religious identity but positive feelings toward other religious groups. The third path is similar to a pluralistic view and is likely a later stage of Fowler's stages of faith. In this path, you have a strong faith identity and it is associated with benevolence toward other religious groups. McLaren calls this a theology of interfaith cooperation in which you weave from your own religious resources (e.g. scripture, other doctrine, history, heroes) a coherent theology for being in positive relationship with others.

A pluralistic perspective opens up many important opportunities and benefits to people. As already mentioned, it can introduce other religious beliefs, practices and customs that may be valuable to experience and may enrich a person's spiritual life. For example, a Christian with a strong set of beliefs and practices deriving from their own religious group may not know much about the practice of meditation of Buddhism and Hinduism. Meditation can add another way of praying and also may help such people develop a more grounded, calm, and less stressed lifestyle.

Another benefit of pluralism is that it can create opportunities for a person to meet and converse with other people of different cultures and religions that one may not get to know otherwise. Furthermore, bringing these new people into one's circle of contacts may help overcome stereotypes and biases between groups of people such as Christians and Muslims or Jews and Muslims. Promoting dialogues and mutual understanding among different religious groups, particularly those that experience deeply rooted conflicts and misunderstandings toward each other, is one type of macro spiritual intervention that will be introduced in chapter 10.

The Pluralism Project

The Pluralism Project at Harvard University is an example of an important enterprise that is currently furthering the evolution of pluralism in spirituality and religion. Eck (n.d.) describes pluralism in religion as having salient characteristics. Pluralism is an "energetic engagement" with diversity that involves real encounters and relationships among different religious groups, not mere co-existence. Further, it involves an active attempt and commitment to seek genuine understanding across difference rather than just accepting tolerance. Being tolerant, unfortunately, does not remove ignorance that divides us, but instead accepts a continuation of stereotypes and ignorance about each other. Finally, pluralism requires continual dialogue involving speaking and listening on both sides.

The Pluralism Project: World Religions in America is a 20-year-long research project particularly exploring the communities and religious traditions of Asia and the Middle East that have become more evident in the religious fabric of the United States. Spirituality and Social Work courses are following the lead of this project and others in studying these newer religious communities—temples, mosques, and informal networks as well as the leaders of these groups including shamans, gurus, and others—as they interface with religious and civic traditions and institutions already established in our society. Interfaith groups and networks usually located in most large U.S. cities provide a context for these different groups to meet, get acquainted, and encounter each other. Such groups are important for social workers to find and join in dialogue as well. As will be discussed in chapter 10, these encounters can be viewed as spiritual interventions at the macro level especially when deeply seated conflict is evident between groups like Muslims in their relationships with Christians and Jews.

His Holiness, the Dalai Lama (2010), the head monk of Tibetan Buddhism, believes that the religions of the world can come together rather than remain in conflict in the future. There will always be a plurality of religious traditions in the real world and these differences will become even more apparent in the years ahead, particularly in the United States because of our growing diversity. Therefore, the Dalai Lama stresses that we all need to learn how to coexist in peace and harmony. He claims that when conflicts arise among religious groups because of differences

> **Interfaith Networks in Your Community**
>
> Enquire whether or not there is an interfaith organization in your community that is inclusive in its membership of religious groups and attempts to promote dialogues among groups that are represented in your community. Find out what subjects and issues they emphasize and attend a presentation of interest to you that is sponsored by this organization.

in religious faiths (not political conflicts cloaked in religion), we should understand that the participants of these religions are often sincere in their adherences to their faith, just as we are. The causes of these conflicts happen because of a lack of contact among the followers of the different religions. This lack of contact leads to an ignorance of the genuine value of the beliefs and practices of followers of other religions. Their traditions are genuine just as ours are. The solutions to our conflicts must include the recognition and celebration of our differences. From here the hope is that we can transcend them and move beyond them to a higher level of convergence and a common goal of human betterment and adoption of key ethical teachings. One of the Dalai Lama's specific recommendations is that we share our deep religious experiences with each other with great respect and reverence. We can do this in many sectors of our lives including our human service agencies and community groups.

Conclusion

The chapter emphasizes that we need to have some understanding of the spirituality and religion of our clients if we are to adopt a spiritually sensitive approach as described in the book. Social workers have many ways of responding to this point, including questioning whether they are qualified to help with spiritual issues or even view spiritual issues as relevant to their helping role. The chapter describes a "crash course" for learning about the religion of some of our clients of which we are unfamiliar. First, you can easily learn about this religious group by doing some reading about them and exploring websites of such groups in your community. Next, you are encouraged to attend a worship service or religious event of this group to have some firsthand exposure to them, what they believe, and how they practice their religion. Hopefully, these and other steps described in the chapter provide some beginning background, confidence, and ability to carry on a brief conversation with clients about their religious issues. A basic initial question can often be asked, such as, "Please explain to me more about your religious group if you think this can help me be more supportive of you in our work together." The chapter also covers statistical information on the religious landscape of the United States and its growing diversity. Several spiritual concepts are mentioned as potentially relevant to helping some clients. The concepts of sin and repentance are described in detail as an example of how these concepts can have relevance. Pluralism is a perspective that is described and encouraged to enhance greater mutual understanding among groups and to discover many of the ways that religious groups are similar in belief and practices.

Discussion Questions and Exercises

1. Attend a religious or spiritual event or service that differs from your own background. After your visit, reflect on what you learned. What differences stand out for you the most between this experience and any other religious experiences that you have had? In what ways does this visit increase your comfort level for different expressions of religious beliefs and practices? If it does not increase your comfort level, why do you think this is so?

2. Review the various ways that sin and repentance are viewed by different religious groups. Think about how these two concepts may be relevant to your work with some of your clients. Pick one client and think about how you could explore sin and repentance with them to help them more fully understand their problems. As an alternative exercise, think about how karma can be relevant to your work with Hindu and Buddhist clients.

3. Pluralism in the spiritual and religious realms is described in the chapter as an appreciation of all religions with the recognition that each has its own contributions to make. What are your reactions to this perspective? What do you see as some of the advantages of this perspective? What might be some disadvantages? What do you believe related to pluralism?

References

Backus, W. (2000). *What your counselor never told you: Seven secrets revealed—Conquer the power of sin in your life.* Bloomington, MN: Bethany House.

Borgman, B. & Ventura, R. (2014). *Spiritual warfare: A biblical and balanced perspective.* Grand Rapids, MI: Reformation Heritage Books.

Canda, E. R., & Furman, L. D. (2010). *Spiritual diversity in social work practice: The heart of healing.* 2nd edition. New York: Oxford Press.

Eck, D. (n.d.). The Pluralism Project at Harvard University. Boston: Harvard University. Available online at: http://pluralism.org.

Eldredge, J. (2001). *Wild at heart: Discovering the secret of a man's soul.* Nashville, TN: Thomas Nelson, Inc.

Ellor, J. W., Netting, F. E., & Thibault, J. M. (1999). *Religious and spiritual aspects of human service practice.* Columbia, SC: University of South Carolina Press.

Elmore, A. (2015). Conversation with Alexandria Elmore, MSW, in Charlotte, NC, May 4, 2015.

Fowler, J. W. (1995). *Stages of faith: The psychology of human development and the quest for meaning.* New York: HarperCollins.

Friedman, B. (2001). Judaism. In M. Van Hook, B. Hugen, & M. Aguilar, (Eds.), *Spirituality within religious traditions in social work practice*. Pacific Grove, CA: Brooks/Cole, 96–119.

Gulley, P. (2013). *Living the Quaker way: Discover the hidden happiness in the simple life*. New York: Convergent Books.

His Holiness, the Dalai Lama. (2010). *Toward a true kinship of faiths: How the world's religions come together*. New York: Doubleday.

Interfaith Calendar. Primary Sacred Times for World Religions. Available online at http://www.interfaithcalendar.org.

Kornfield, J. (1993). *A Path with heart: A guide through the perils and promises of spiritual life*. New York: Bantam Books.

Lazarus, W. P. & Sullivan, M. (2008). *Comparative religion for dummies*. Hoboken, NJ: Wiley Publishing.

James, K. (2013). *Enlightenment quotes and passages to awaken the Buddha within*.

McLaren, B. D. (2012). *Why did Jesus, Moses, the Buddha, and Muhammad cross the road?: Christian identity in a multi-faith world*. New York: Jericho Books.

Nadir, A. & Dziegielewski, S. F. (2001). Islam. In M. Van Hook, B. Hugen, & M. Aguilar (Eds.), *Spirituality within religious traditions in social work practice*. Pacific Grove, CA: Brooks/Cole, 146–166.

Pew Research Center, Religion and Public Life (2015). America's changing religious land-scape. Pew Research Center, Religion and Public Life, Washington, DC, May 12. 2015. Available online at http://www.pewforum.org/2015/05/12/americas-changing-religious-landscape.

Ramadan, T. (2007). *In the footsteps of the prophet: Lessons from the life of Muhammad*. New York: Oxford University Press.

Ramsey, P. (2002). *The just war: Force and political responsibility*. New York: Rowman & Littlefield.

Robinson, G. (2000). *Essential Judaism: A complete guide to beliefs, customs, and rituals*. New York: Pocket Books.

Smith, H. (1991) *The world's religions*. New York: HarperCollins.

Smith, H. (2001). *Why religion matters: The fate of the human spirit in an age of disbelief*. New York: HarperCollins.

Umar, M. (2011). *How to pray: A step-by-step guide to prayer in Islam*. Available on Amazon.com.

Van Hook, M., Hugen, B., & Aguilar, M. (eds.) (2001). *Spirituality within religious traditions in social work practice*. Pacific Grove, CA: Brooks/Cole.

White, J. F. (2000). *Introduction to Christian worship*. 3rd edition. Nashville, TN: Abingdon Press.

4

A Closer Look at Specific Religious and Spiritual Groups

> I have discovered that the religious quest is not about discovering "the truth" or "meaning of life" but about living as intensely as possible here and now.
>
> (Karen Armstrong, 2004)

> Regard your neighbor's gain as your gain, and your neighbor's loss as your own loss.
>
> (Taoism in Walsh, 1999)

In this chapter, we take a closer introductory look at some of the major religions. The list of basic elements of a religious group, discussed in the last chapter and used when students visit spiritual and religious group events, is just a starting point for exploration. Nevertheless, it helps a social worker know a little more about a religion in areas that may be relevant to the spirituality of some of their clients. In review, these elements are:

- Their religious beliefs that relate to their daily living.
- Their religious practices that relate to their daily living.
- How these beliefs and practices help members cope with difficulties (or do not).
- How they perceive their roles in the family from a religious perspective.
- How they explain the meaning of life for them.
- What sin and evil are to them.
- What social supports are available to members and others from this group?
- What are the areas of possible conflict, if any, between their spiritual beliefs and practices and the values and ethics of social work?
- How comfortable are they in talking about these topics?

The beliefs of a religious group will vary immensely but most likely they will provide explanations about what is important to believe. Some of these religious beliefs will be more practical to a person's life and these will be the beliefs that will tend to be of most concern to a practitioner. These beliefs will likely derive from the sacred writings of a religious group. The most significant sacred writings of the major world religions are the Torah and the rest of the Hebrew Bible for Jewish people, the Christian Bible for Christians, the Quran for Muslims, the Baghavad Gita and other sacred writings for Hinduism, and the central writings of the Buddha and his disciples for Buddhism.

A special note is important to make about the sacred writings of religious groups (Borg, 2011). They were, in most cases, written thousands of years ago during the times when communication was largely conveyed by oral traditions; also well before the Gutenberg printing press was invented in AD 1440, which printed writings in massive form in the Western world. Therefore, we should keep in mind that what we read today is more of an approximation of what these original religious leaders likely said than it is an exact verbatim account.

Additionally, every religion originated in a particular culture and used the language of that culture (Borg, 2011). Christianity, Islam, and Judaism, for example, had their beginnings in the Middle East, and Buddhism and Hinduism began in the culture of India. The languages of these cultures were used and became a major factor in how their beliefs, doctrine, and teachings were spoken and written. For example, the Jewish Torah was written in Hebrew, the Christian Bible in Hebrew and Greek, and the Quran in Arabic. As Borg points out, religions became, if they survived, a "cultural-linguistic tradition." Their culture's language was their basic vocabulary, and was used to describe their sacred stories and texts, rituals, and practices. These languages were also later used to understand what these early writers were talking about. When some of these religions became world religions their sacred writings needed to be translated into the language of other countries adopting them. Those were naturally times when understanding these religious doctrines began to be confusing and at times misunderstood.

Christian doctrines and texts, for example, were translated into English. In many instances, Hebrew and Greek words were not automatically translatable into English words. Greek language has, for example, four different meanings for love. Thus, the use of these sacred writings by people in the United States should be seen in this light, especially if religious groups take a literal view of them. These sacred writings also need to be understood first as embedded in these original cultures (Borg, 2011). Today, hundreds of existing Christian denominations use many different translations of the original languages used in the Bible. In addition, the more conservative Christian denominations take a literalist view of what is written while the liberal denominations are more likely to go deeper and consider a wide range of interpretations. To further complicate this, all denominations tend to be selective about what religious passages they consider most important, based in part on their primary beliefs as well as on what they feel is most important. Some may say that the conservative and liberal religious denominations in Christianity tend to emphasize different passages to such an extent that outsiders may wonder if they are even referring to the same sacred book. Much of this variability is also evident in the other major religions that were also founded thousands of years ago.

In addition to the religious beliefs, the religious practices of these groups are very important to know about because they can be an even more valuable source of help for our clients in coping with their daily problems and stresses. These religious practices are mostly concrete and many are practical activities that many clients have integrated into their daily routines and lives. One example is Muslims who pray five times each day.

Christianity

Christianity is by far the largest religion represented in the United States in 2014 as 70.6 percent of all Americans claim Christianity as their religion (Pew Forum on Religion and Public Life, 2015). This is the reason why Christianity is covered first and most extensively among the world religions that are introduced. Christianity is challenging to describe because it is composed of over a hundred denominations in the United States alone and it is explained and practiced in so many different ways. Christianity is described here with a brief overview of the beliefs, practices, and traditions of Christianity followed by a description of the four largest groupings of Christianity. They are the Roman Catholic Church and three Protestant groups. The major Protestant groups are Evangelical Christians, Mainline Christians, and Historical Black Churches. In addition, a few other smaller Christian groups are described below that have relatively high numbers of recent immigrants.

The Christian Church has always centered on the figure of Jesus Christ, whose life is described in the New Testament of the Christian Bible (e.g. Harrington, 1999; MacCulloch, 2009). The Four Gospel Books, Matthew, Mark, Luke, and John, were the earliest known recordings of Jesus' life and death; it is widely believed that these early writers were either eyewitnesses or scribes of disciples who were close to Jesus. The relative accuracy of these Gospels, even in Jesus' world of oral tradition, has always been largely assumed by believers. These books of the Bible were written some time within the 1st century, some years after Jesus' ministry and death. As mentioned earlier, the more conservative Christian groups, such as Fundamentalists and Evangelicals, tend to believe that what was written in the Bible is literally God's truth as it is written. Moderate and liberal Christian groups, in some contrast, are likely to view the Bible as generally accurate but open to various interpretations; in part, the more liberal groups make efforts to understand these writings in the context of the Middle Eastern Jewish culture of Jesus' time.

The most significant belief of Christianity is that Jesus is the son of God. His ministry is described over a three-year period while living in Palestine or Israel in the Middle East during the 1st Century (e.g. MacCulloch, 2009). At the end of this time, Jesus was executed on a cross by the Roman occupiers and was resurrected three days later. No other major religion claims that their central figure was resurrected and returned to the world to be with his followers, albeit in a somewhat different form. After Jesus' resurrection, he was reported to have lived among his followers and prepared them to be apostles for forty days before ascending into heaven. This belief in the resurrection offers an enormous source of peace and hope for most Christian believers today. As Christians face the nearness of their own death or are confronted with the death of a loved one, the belief in

Jesus' resurrection and his promise of eternal life can be extremely important to believers.

Jesus' adult life and ministry are described in some detail in the New Testament (Harrington, 1999). They include numerous teachings and healings performed by Jesus. These practices are viewed by many contemporary believers as models of living that can guide their lives as well. Jesus was also known to be devoted to helping people on the fringes of society, such as beggars, the disabled, the blind, lepers, prostitutes, widows, the poor, criminals, and tax collectors. He also often confronted the Pharisees and Sadducees, religious leaders of his time, for being hypocrites in their roles and practices as religious leaders. Jesus was a champion of social justice for these disadvantaged people of his time and offered alternative ways for his society to address their social problems. His ways included speaking out on their behalf, committing non-violent civil-disobedience protests, and preaching love for his enemies. He also argued for elevating the weakest and most powerless to the strongest and most powerful positions while diminishing the strongest to the weakest positions. These approaches have been highlighted down through the ages to help the poor, neglected, and underprivileged.

The Christian Church began as one Church, evolving soon after Jesus' death. Since then the original Church has experienced two major schisms that have splintered Christianity into many more denominations up to the present (MacCulloch, 2009). The *first great schism* occurred in AD 1054 resulting from growing differences and conflicts between Western and Eastern Christians. Out of this schism, two churches emerged, the Roman Catholic Church in the West and the Eastern Orthodox Church in the East. These two traditions have evolved very differently following this schism. The Western Church has been characterized by many for its emphasis on the supremacy of the Pope, the importance of the church hierarchy, and a strict authoritative role emanating from Rome. Other distinguishing characteristics of the Catholic Church have been an emphasis on the Bible as the ultimate truth, mysticism, and the importance of practical religious practices such as recitation of specific prayers and making confessions. The Eastern Church, in some contrast, has given more attention to cultural characteristics of the Eastern world such as meditation and heart-truth over mind-truth, embracing the mystery of miracles more than explanations for them, and using all of the senses in worship, prayers, and other religious practices (Bourgeault, 2008). The Eastern Church, however, is also known for its hierarchy and many traditions, similar to its Western counterpart.

The *second great schism* in Christianity reached its climax in AD 1516 when Martin Luther, a Christian monk, posted his 95 Theses in Wittenberg, Germany as a protest to the Church's claim to the authority of the Pope (MacCulloch, 2009). According to Luther, the Bible was the only source of divinely revealed knowledge from God. This action by Luther ushered in the Protestant Reformation that opened the door for numerous new Protestant denominations of Christianity to spring up over time.

In brief, Christians have several religious practices that are important to them (Van Hook, Hugen, & Aguilar, 2001). They include worship typically on Sunday mornings, prayers in many forms, Bible study and other group activities, a choir and other forms of religious singing, and for some denominations, confession and speaking in tongues. In some denominations, the Communion is the centerpiece of the worship services on Sunday mornings. The Communion is a re-enactment of the Last Supper when Jesus joined his disciples for a last meal and teachings before his crucifixion. Other denominations emphasize a sermon or homily delivered by the priest or pastor as the central focus of the worship service. Many denominations emphasize both the Communion and a sermon. Songs, prayers, and creeds are also important to many Christian worship services. Prayers take many forms, from petitions for help, intercessory prayers to help others, and prayers of thanksgiving, to contemplative prayers involving mostly listening in silence to God. Different prayer forms are described in chapter 9.

Since social workers meet with clients of all different Christian affiliations, it is important to know something about the specific denominations prevalent in the geographic area in which you work. For example, if you work in the Southeastern part of the United States, African American Churches in the Baptist and American Methodist Episcopal (AME) traditions are important. Predominately white churches in the Southeast include Southern Baptists, Catholics, several Evangelical denominations, and many of the Mainline Protestant denominations like the Lutherans, Presbyterians, and Methodists. If you live in a geographic area that draws a large number of recent Latino immigrants, it is important to know that Latino immigrants tend to join and participate in Roman Catholic and Pentecostal churches that have a Latino ministry as part of their identities.

Four Major Christian Groups

According to the Pew Forum on Religion and Public Life (2015), there are four large categories of Christian denominations and numerous smaller groups. Differences exist across every denomination but these larger categories help explain some of the major distinctions. The **Evangelical churches** take a more conservative view of Christianity including a literal interpretation of the Bible, strict rules about moral and immoral behaviors, emphasizing contemporary Christian music in worship, a focus on the word preached by the pastor in worship, and a zeal for missionary work mostly in Third World countries. Evangelical churches are often non-denominational; they may have been part of a larger denomination in the past and later chose to become an independent church. These churches have many different names, such as the Elevation Church and the Venture Church.

The **Mainline Protestants** tend to be more moderate or liberal in their views about Christianity, including a less literal interpretation of the Bible, more historically traditional Christian worship services including singing traditional Christian hymns, and special recognition of several different religious holidays such as Advent leading up to Christmas; Ash Wednesday and 40 days of Lent; the major events during Holy Week; and Easter. Mainline Protestant Christians tend to be involved in a wide range of local community outreach efforts to help the less fortunate in their communities. Less emphasis seems to be on mission work abroad. Mainline churches were among the Protestant denominations that were established and evolved after Martin Luther posted his 95 Theses in protest against the supremacy of the Pope in the Roman Catholic Church. These Mainline denominations today include the Lutherans, United Methodists, Episcopalians, Presbyterian USA, American Baptists, and others. Most Lutherans belong to the Evangelical Lutheran Church of America, which is not evangelical in the same sense as Evangelical churches of today.

Historically Black Churches are another major category of Christians. These are predominately attended by African Americans, whose history can be traced back to the early days of the country. The Black Church has been for its members a unique source of inspiration, belief, and hope (Billingsley, 1999; Martin & Martin, 2002). During slavery in the South these churches served a most important function of protecting, educating, and inspiring black slaves. The pastors of Historically Black Churches today tend to carry important roles beyond just a pastor's role in the traditional sense; they are community leaders, often civil rights leaders and members, and at times spokespersons for the entire Black community. The civil rights movement was founded, conceived, and inspired within the Historical Black Church and provided the major impetus for this movement in the 1950s and 1960s. At that time, the movement was led by a charismatic young pastor, Dr. Rev. Martin Luther King Jr. of the Southern Christian Leadership Conference (SCLC), whose persuasive speeches for equality and economic justice gave direction, inspiration, and substance to the movement. Among others, the movement involved SCLC, the Student Nonviolent Coordinating Committee (SNCC), and Congress of Racial Equality (CORE), The National Association for the Advancement of Colored People (NAACP), and leaders like Rosa Parks, Ralph Abernathy, James Farmer, Andrew Young, Jesse Jackson, John Lewis, and others. Many of these leaders were pastors and lay leaders of churches as well.

Today, many Black Churches are also well known for encouraging a participatory role of the members in worship with jubilant singing, swaying, and open responses of "Amen" in support of the preacher's message. Black spirituals are also notable to these churches. Denominations of the Historic Black Churches have included Black Baptists (Friendship Missionary Baptist Churches and others), AME (African Methodist Episcopal) and AME Zion. More recently, other Black Churches have also emerged that seem to be primarily devoted to ministering to low income people including The House of Prayer for All People and other Black Pentecostal churches.

The Roman Catholic Church has changed over the centuries in some ways and remains committed to historical traditions in other ways. Priesthood is still restricted to celibate males and the worship services consist of a traditional liturgy that is virtually the same in all Catholic Churches. Reforms have occurred in the Catholic Church over the years that have resulted in changes in relatively small ways. The Second Vatican Council established by Pope John XXIII in the early 1960s was a breath of fresh air to the Church in some ways, such as a change in the Mass from Latin to English so members could understand it and opening participation in the Eucharist to Catholic members. Before, only the priests would take the bread and wine while the congregation sat passively and observed it happening. These changes and those anticipated under Pope Francis' tenure are intended to give more control and responsibility to lay members, including new more significant responsibilities for women.

There are numerous smaller Christian groups that do not fit within the four categories mentioned above. Google or the website mentioned earlier (http://www.interfaithcalendar.org/index.htm) can be a resource in identifying many of these religious groups and describing their beliefs and practices. Since the large number precludes mentioning all of them, two groups, Pentecostals and Jehovah's Witnesses, are briefly summarized as examples of groups possibly frequented by many of your clients.

Some Smaller Christian Groups

The **Pentecostal Church** is a smaller religious community that is important in drawing large and growing numbers of recent Latino immigrant participants from Mexico and Central America. This trend is significant as one in four recent Latin American immigrants no longer identify with the Catholic Church (Pew Research Center, 2006; Pew Research Center, 2014). The Pentecostal Churches began in the early 20th century. Pentecostalism gets its name from the Day of Pentecost, described in Chapter 2 of Acts in the New Testament of the Christian Bible, the day when the Holy Spirit was infused into the followers of Jesus after he ascended into heaven. Pentecostal churches are distinguished by their emphasis on spiritual gifts given to people, based on St. Paul's Biblical passage (I Corinthians 12), including the gift of speaking in tongues (O'Connell & Miller, 2006; Tangenberg, 2007). They also believe in miraculous faith healing. Many churches in the Pentecostal movement strongly believe that the second coming of Christ, professed in the New Testament, is imminent in our times. Large numbers of recent, often undocumented, Latino immigrants that join this movement are drawn to it because it stirs in them a sense of hope and empowerment when their lives may be reflecting the opposite.

A MSW Student's Experience as a Pentecostal

Michelle Davis

One MSW student describes her experience growing up in the Pentecostal church:

> Speaking in tongues was considered a great honor, one of the highest forms of worship. It happened to me once at a youth camp revival. Every night after camp activities we attended worship services that were frequently emotionally charged, especially as the final nights of camp drew near. There would be altar calls in which large groups of youths would come to the front to get saved, rededicate their life to Christ, or pray about things bothering them. One night I went down for the altar call and I remember kneeling on the carpeted steps of the stage. My hands were tightly clasped, my eyes were squeezed shut, I was so focused I was almost in a trance. I was distressed because I knew I hadn't been living my life according to the way I thought God wanted me to. As I prayed I began to rock back and forth, overcome with emotion. Suddenly, words and phrases started coming out of my mouth but it didn't feel like I was consciously moving my lips. It felt more like they were moving on their own. I didn't know what I was saying or what I would "say" next. As I continued praying and speaking in tongues, I felt overcome by a presence of God like I had never felt before or since.

(Davis, 2015)

Prayer is an important part of the Pentecostal faith, and two special types of prayer are practiced during Pentecostal services. The first kind of prayer is sometimes referred to as the "Sinner's Prayer." Usually offered by the pastor at the end of the sermon, this prayer is an invitation to any non-Christians in the church to ask God's forgiveness for their sins and to be "born again" (Belcher & Cascio, 2001). The second important prayer involves a practice called the "altar call." This is intertwined with the belief that God can offer divine healing for a variety of physical, spiritual, and mental ailments. In an altar call, a pastor gives an open invitation for any who are suffering in the congregation to come forward to the church altar and to pray and present their troubles to God (Tangenberg, 2007). This practice combines elements of deliverance, spiritual healing, and exorcism, as any evil influence the person may be suffering (including alcoholism or sexual immorality) are viewed as being "driven out" by God (Belcher & Cascio, 2001).

As with many forms of conservative Christianity, Pentecostalism can take an attitude of dismissal or disdain toward what it sees as "worldly influences" (Belcher & Cascio, 2001). This can include things like secular therapy, since this religious group is viewed as preferential to solve difficulties through prayer and submission to God's will as described in the Bible. Therefore, it is critical that a social worker working with a Pentecostal client give particular attention to building trust and rapport. The client may harbor discomfort about seeing a social worker who does not share his or her Pentecostal faith. It is important that the social worker be sensitive to the client's paradigm of divine deliverance and not outright dismiss it or try and convince the client otherwise. Rather, the social worker should approach the client's faith from a spiritually sensitive and strengths-based perspective, acknowledging any success the client has with using spiritual tools such as church attendance or prayer. Instead of trying to supplant these practices, the social worker can recognize the pivotal role these practices play in the client's conceptualization of healing and stress management, and seek to enhance them with interventions that complement the client's established rituals (Belcher & Cascio, 2001).

The **Jehovah's Witness** church is another small but growing church in the United States and the world that attracts many recent immigrants. It was founded in the late 19th century and emphasizes both Bible study and evangelism. Most people may know of the Jehovah's Witnesses (JW) through their personal encounters with JW members during their door-to-door evangelism, in which they attempt to win people over to Christ. This group may be more known for such evangelism than any other church denomination even though many of the Christian denominations, particularly conservative ones, place much emphasis on winning people over to Christ. Jehovah's Witness members are also known for their own unique translation of the Bible and their freely disseminated literature on many religious topics important to them. *Watchtower* and *Awake!* may be their two most familiar handouts given out in public. Unlike the Pentecostals, Jehovah's Witnesses have a centralized body that governs their ministry. While Christian, they do not celebrate Christmas, Easter, or their birthdays because they are viewed as pagan holidays. Further, they believe Armageddon, or the destruction of the world, will come soon. They teach their members to be conscientious objectors with regards to military service, not to salute a country's national flag, and not to receive blood transfusions. Their website, www.jw.org, is a helpful resource for more information on this religious group. In some instances, their strict rules may become an important topic to face when working with JW clients.

In summary, so much has been written about Christianity and its many denominations that you may want to obtain more information. An introductory book titled *Who is Jesus? Why is He Important?* by Harrington (1999) is short, very informative, and introduces Jesus within the context of the New Testament. Longer and widely popular versions about Christianity include *Christianity: The First Three Thousand Years* by MacCulloch (2009) and Christianity as described in *The World's Religions* by Smith (1991).

Judaism

Judaism emerged as a major religion almost 4,000 years ago (Friedman, 2001). The first spiritual fathers of Judaism, known as the patriarchs, include Abraham,

Isaac, and Jacob. Their history is found in the Torah, the sacred Jewish scriptures. Abraham, named Abram at birth, introduced the idea of monotheism to a culture that worshiped numerous idols. God spoke to Abraham, and made a covenant with him, promising to select him as the father of a great nation. Abraham had a son named Isaac, who had twin sons, Esau and Jacob. Jacob received Isaac's blessing and the birthright that he stole from Esau. Jacob fathered 12 sons who became the ancestors of each of the tribes of Israel.

Some 400 years later, the people of Israel became enslaved to the Egyptians. Moses, a key figure in Judaism, led the Jewish people out of Egyptian slavery, originating with a special covenant he made with God as the chosen people. They were commanded to follow the laws of God, and in return, God agreed to make Israel a holy nation. God gave the law to Moses on Mount Sinai, and Moses delivered these laws, the Ten Commandments, to his people. These laws are included in the Torah or the Five Books of Moses.

Modern Judaism is comprised of three main branches, but these branches share several key doctrines (Rich, 2011). Followers of Judaism share an active faith and commitment to the covenant relationship with God established through Abraham and Moses. Within the synagogue, rabbis do not have authority over their congregations. Rather, they are viewed as teachers of the Jewish heritage. The synagogue has three primary functions: it is a place of study, assembly, and prayer. Prayers can have a variety of purposes; for a practicing Jew they are a part of daily life. Prayers can be offered for petition, giving thanks for blessings, praise offered to God, or the confession of sin. With all prayers, introspection and the examination of one's relationship with God is a primary concern. Orthodox Jews view the Torah as the unchanging, literal word of God, and adhere to a dress code, dietary restrictions, and strict observance of the Sabbath. Conservative Judaism holds a more moderate perspective, accepting the original traditions but also being open to interpretation. Those that adhere to this tradition view the law as dynamic and adaptable to a variety of cultural differences. Reform Judaism holds a more liberal interpretation of the law, adapting it to modern ideas of egalitarianism and social justice (Union for Reform Judaism, 2014). In this tradition, the Hebrew Scriptures are not seen as being inspired by God, but rather produced by humans (Rich, 2011).

Jewish services are conducted in the synagogues on Saturdays and sometimes Friday nights and they are usually available in each of the three branches of Judaism. Jews attend synagogue services on Saturdays and they are led by a cantor who sings readings and prayers and leads the congregation in prayers. Prayers come from the siddur or Jewish Prayer Book. Passages are read from the Torah along with other prayers recited by members. It is a tradition that some members sway their bodies back and forth during prayers. The Hebrew language is spoken mostly in the Orthodox synagogues and less frequently in Reform and Conservative synagogues. Women are usually required to cover their arms and wear long skirts and a head covering. Men wear a head covering called a yarmulke or beanie.

When working with a Jewish client, it is important to keep the vast differences among the branches of Judaism in mind. Two clients may both identify as Jewish, but hold very different belief systems. Another important distinction for clinicians is whether the client identifies religiously and/or culturally as Jewish (Institute for Curriculum Services, 2012). As with any population, all Jews do not fit perfectly into predetermined categories. However, some general guidelines about Jewish heritage can be helpful. Generally, Jews do not refer to the Jewish people as a racial group. The Jewish community is made up of people from diverse backgrounds. Also, it is important to be aware that racial categorization is suggestive of the language used historically to classify and discriminate against Jews. Jewish people have been almost continuously persecuted throughout their history with perhaps the most familiar horrific occurrence being led by Hitler of Nazi Germany during World War II. The Holocaust, involving the massacre of six million Jews, was a shocking and dreadful event that still disturbs many Jewish people today. It is very likely that you could be working with a Jewish client who has personally experienced the loss of a family member during the Holocaust. If this is brought up by the client, it is important to be sensitive to the horror of that period and the lasting effect it has had on your client's family including continued preoccupation with discrimination and other anti-Semitic experiences in their present lives.

Many Jews feel connected to their community through their history, culture, and traditions, even if they do not identify religiously (Institute for Curriculum Services, 2012). When working with a client who identifies as Jewish, it can be helpful for the social worker to assume the role of a learner and ask the client to describe the personal significance of their heritage. When visiting a synagogue, one is expected to dress modestly in proper attire. Men typically wear a yarmulke, or skullcap, and the synagogue usually offers them to guests who may need one. In certain synagogues, married women are expected to wear a head covering. A chapel hat is often provided by the synagogue for this purpose. Jewish patrons may be seen wearing a tallit, a type of prayer shawl, or tefellin, a leather pouch containing scrolls with significant portions of scripture. However, non-Jewish visitors should not put on these items because they signify adherence to the law. Depending on which branch of Judaism someone belongs, other customs may also be observed. For instance, in an Orthodox synagogue, men and women are seated in different sections. In any synagogue, attendants stand when the ark, the holding place for the Torah scrolls, is opened. Standing during this time is seen as a sign of respect for God as well as for the Torah.

Islam

Those who adhere to Islam are called Muslims. Muslims are among the fastest growing religious groups of non-Christian people and are also likely to be clients of social workers in some settings. Muslims are a very diverse group made up of recent immigrants, children of immigrants, and Muslims who are U.S. citizens and have been here over many generations (Halim, 2006; Ibrahim & Dykeman, 2011; Memissi, 1996; Ramadan, 2007). Also, Muslims will vary based on their different levels of acculturation to Western society and their culture of origin. There is no particular set of beliefs representative of all Muslims. Their beliefs vary in many ways based on their primary culture and nationality of origin, their worldview, and their degree of spiritual and religious commitment (Hodge, 2005; Memissi, 1996). The impact of the events of 9/11 on Muslims are important to consider as well because of the harassment, rejection, and discrimination experienced by many Muslims in the aftermath of these events.

Islam means "peace" and "surrender;" peace comes when one's life is surrendered to God. Islam's roots are in the Biblical family of Adam, Noah, and Abraham. Abraham took Hagar as his second wife after first marrying Sarah, and Hagar gave birth to Ishmael. Abraham and Sarah also had a son named Isaac. Islam's lineage continues from Ishmael whereas Jewish lineage continues from Isaac.

Muhammad lived from AD 570 to AD 632. He was viewed as a prophet like many before him, including Christ, but he was not viewed as the son of God, as Jesus was. The Quran, the holiest book of Islam, was dictated by Allah to Muhammad over a period of 23 years in a voice later identified as that of the angel Gabriel. The Quran is the central source of Islamic doctrine. It is both a literal message of words and a string of Arabic sounds with a powerful hypnotic effect. The Quran is viewed by Muslims as the culmination of the Word of God. Later in his life, Muhammad became an administrator of the city of Medina, where he melded five conflicting tribes (three of which were Jewish) into an orderly confederation, which became viewed by members of his community as a miracle. After this miracle, people began to flock to him in growing numbers.

In Islamic services, prayers and a sermon by the imam, or prayer leader, are always evident. While prayers are required five times a day wherever the person is, Friday prayers are encouraged in the mosque around lunch time. Most prayers are ritual prayers and involve kneeling in reverence to Allah. A carpet is provided for kneeling purposes. Everyone leaves their shoes at the door before entering the service, respecting the reverence of kneeling and keeping the carpet clean. Men and women pray in different sections of the mosque for practical reasons of preventing distractions for men when women are kneeling in front of them. The service occurs with everyone facing Mecca, the spiritual center of Islam, in Saudi Arabia. Visitors are often allowed to attend services and observe prayers in the back of the mosque. They can also pray silently.

The Five Pillars

Within the Islamic worldview there is the belief that the Quran is the only truth and that it was revealed as a guide for all people (Abdel Haleem, 2004). Allah is at

Social Justice Work of an Islamic Organization

(www.islamic-relief.org)

The Islamic Relief Worldwide is an international relief and development charity based in the United Kingdom. Drawing from Islamic values, it envisions a caring world where people unite to respond to the suffering of others, and it empowers them to fulfill their potential. Toward this end, Islamic Relief promotes sustainable economic and social development by partnering with local communities to eradicate poverty, illiteracy, and disease, as well as respond to disasters and emergencies. Its work focuses on: sustainable livelihood; education, health and nutrition; orphans and child welfare; water and sanitation; and emergency relief and disaster preparedness. For instance, to alleviate poverty and improve the standard of living, Islamic Relief has experimented with the use of microcredit programs to assist poor entrepreneurs who have been unable to receive loans from banks and other financial institutions. Islamic perspectives on social justice issues inspire their work.

the center of the universe and peace is achieved through submission to Allah's will (Abul Fadl, 1991). Commonalities like the five pillars are important to consider (Van Hook, Hugen, & Aguilar, 2001). Each of them may be pertinent when working with a Muslim client. The first pillar is the declaration of faith, which is a prayer or statement that is to be continually affirmed. It is that there is "no god but Allah and Muhammad is the last messenger of God." A second pillar is to pray to Allah five specific times during the day (Umar, 2011). Men are expected to attend religious services on Friday; women are encouraged to attend as well. The times of day to pray and the locations of nearby mosques can be found on websites such as www. Islamicity.com. Alms giving is the third pillar, as Muslims are expected to give a fairly large contribution to their mosque, 2.5 percent of their annual wealth after paying expenses. For the fourth pillar they are expected to fast during Ramadan, their most important sacred holiday. It lasts for 30 days, with no food, water, or impure thoughts permitted during the daytime. The fifth pillar, a pilgrimage to the holy city of Mecca in Saudi Arabia, is required once in a lifetime if a person can.

Gender and Family

Family is central and usually includes extended family from both spouses (Hodge, 2005). Interaction between men and women is traditionally limited beyond immediate family and relatives, and cross-gender social work relationships may be a problem (Springer, Abbott, & Reisbig, 2009). There may be strict adherence to this Islamic arrangement, especially among recent immigrants. For example, Muslim women are perceived by their religion to be held in higher regard in the

Quran than in the Bible. Modesty is an important spiritual and cultural value for many Muslims, especially women; women wear, to varying degrees, Islamic attire, including possibly a veil or hijab, but more likely a head cover and modest clothing. Muslim women are required to wear a covering in public, how much of a covering usually being determined by the woman's cultural group. Men and women are not supposed to shake hands or touch in other ways, such as hugging, outside marriage. Nor are men and women supposed to be together alone except when married. These customs are important to recognize and respect without any judgmental reactions.

Other values largely in common with other religions are reflected in care for others, cooperation between individuals, equality and justice between people, and the importance of social support. Islam especially has similarities with Judaism and Christianity. The Quran includes many references to Jesus and his mother, Mary. Jesus was reported to be born of a virgin, he healed the sick, and ascended into heaven without being killed. Several important theological concepts are similar to those of Jewish and Christian beliefs. For example, Muslims believe in monotheism or one God. God created the heavens and the earth. All three religions had their beginnings with the great patriarch, Abraham. People "sin" by forgetting their divine origin and this mistake needs to be repeatedly corrected. Life is a brief but immensely precious opportunity. Heaven or hell follow and are described in vivid detail.

Differences with Christianity are important to understand. The Quran, not the Bible, is viewed as the culmination of the Word of God, and Muhammad is the final and most important prophet. The prayer requirements for Muslims do not have a counterpart in Christianity. Rules of daily living are very different, as mentioned earlier. Similarities between the Bible and Quran are not as fully recognized or emphasized today as in past centuries. Tensions between Christianity and Islam are significant today in large part because of 9/11. This horrific tragedy has resulted in a new major divide between these religious groups, which calls for continued reconciliation work, often in local communities where Christians and Muslims live side by side. Significant cooperative work is also needed at the institutional level of these two religions, both nationally and internationally.

The implications of all of this for a social worker are many. What might the five pillars say related to an assessment of a Muslim client? The extent to which individual Muslims practice the five pillars may be a good overall indication of their commitment to their faith (Hodge, 2005). Among the issues they bring up are the importance of referring to their higher power as Allah, not God. The declaration of faith and the five prayer times daily suggest that prayer is likely an important spiritual discipline to Muslims if they are committed to regularly practicing it. Also Muhammad is the most important human religious prophet to them. Scheduling visits with the social worker should always take into account the regular times of prayer during the day—at dawn, around noon, afternoon, sunset, and in the evening. If prayer and/or meditation are a relevant topic, they can be explored as a source of hope and strength for such a client.

Fasting is another spiritual discipline that could be meaningful to a Muslim client. When Ramadan occurs, it is important to recognize that the client will likely be fasting during the day. Other things to remember are not to have direct eye contact, as it is a sign of disrespect, and to take off your shoes in a Muslim's home, as the floor and carpet are used for prayer. Do not walk in front of a Muslim praying.

Other instructions include to pray in mosques when you can, wash before prayer, begin in upright posture, climaxing in sinking to one's knees with the forehead touching the floor (signifying human nothingness in the face of the divine). Additional resources about Islam can be found on a website: www.Islamicity.com.

Also, Muslims who are immigrants in particular may be hesitant to be open to the larger American society, other religious groups, and non-Muslim human services. A client's mosque may be their major if not only source of support for a range of spiritual, familial, and educational needs. Thus, social supports offered within their faith community are important to know about and explore.

Sufism, the Mystics of Islam

The two main sects in Islam are the Sunnis and Shiites. These divisions revolve around differing views about who should have succeeded Muhammad. In addition, while these two sects concentrate on the rules for the outer person, Sufism focuses on the inner self, where deeper experiences of God occur (Vaughan-Lee, 2012). Three of the routes to mysticism are poetry of love (e.g. the poetry of Rumi), transcendence or experiencing oneself in a trance-like manner from the outside, and heart knowledge coming from discernment.

Hinduism

Hinduism is a small but growing religion in the United States made up mostly of immigrants from India. According to the Pew Research Center, Religion and Public Life (2015), Hinduism represents only 0.4 percent of all religious affiliations in the United States, but it has so much more to offer to the religious fabric of U.S. society beyond numbers. To many, Hinduism is viewed as more of a way of life or philosophy that provides an ancient foundation from which most religions emerge. Buddhism and Sikhism were founded out of Hinduism in India, and many Hindus claim that anyone can be a Hindu and at the same time, for example, a Christian or a Jew because there is an overall compatibility with many other religions.

Hinduism is the predominant religion of India; Hindu actually means "the belief of the people of India." India is actually known as an ancient melting pot that today is the largest democracy in the world. It has, for example, the largest number of Muslims in the world living within its boundaries coexisting largely peacefully with the majority Hindu population. Many other religions are also represented there, including Buddhists, Jews, and Christians. While Hindus have numerous religious or sacred books, the Bhagavad-Gita is probably the most well-known sacred book. If you can get access to a copy of it, simply peruse it to become more familiar with some of the Hindus' sacred passages.

Many Hindu leaders tend to be very open to dialogue with other religious groups and seem to have little need to challenge the beliefs of others (Smith, 1991). They mostly want to share their very ancient beliefs with pride and confidence and have them considered alongside the beliefs that people have from other religions with whom they are in dialogue. As one Hindu once said, "there are many legitimate spiritual paths."

Hindu beliefs about life are quite profound. Some examples are:

- Apart from God, life has no meaning; it is separation from God that causes human suffering.
- We are prompted by God's will, enacted by God's energy. One expression of this is, "Thou art the doer, I the instrument."
- We carry within us supreme strength, the fullness of wisdom, and unquench-able joy.
- The goal in life is to seek higher levels of being through a variety of yoga philosophies.
- The life span is unending.
- Every moment of our lives is a dying.
- Various religions are but different languages through which God speaks to the human heart.

Hindus have an important concept, karma, central to their beliefs (Hodge, 2004; Satguru Sivaya Subramuniyaswami, n.d.). Karma is the law of cause and effect by which each individual creates his own destiny by his/her thoughts, words, and deeds. Individuals possess free will and have the ability to develop good karma and improve their standing and hope for the future. They also can reap bad karma for wrong attitudes or deeds. Good karma is obviously preferred over bad karma. Hindus also believe in the reincarnations of the soul. The soul evolves through many births until all karmas have been resolved, and liberation from the cycle of rebirth is attained. They believe that no single soul will be deprived of this des-tiny. Knowing this about the soul—that we have to experience life again—has been shown to decrease death anxiety for many Hindus (Parsuram & Sharma, 1992).

While it may sound contradictory, Hindus worship one Supreme Being but they do this in many different forms, usually with deities. Specific deities can be asso-ciated with different denominations of Hindus coming from different geographic and cultural areas. If you visit a Hindu temple, you will sometimes see several dei-ties displayed at the front of the temple. Different people who come in to worship will gravitate toward a particular deity that provides for them the most meaningful connection to the Supreme God. The Hindu religion is known to have several deities, and several denominations and people of a particular denomination tend to worship the same deity. These deities include, for example, Shiva, Goddess Shakti, Lord Ganesha, and Vishnu. Each of these and many other deities are the pathways to God for a Hindu, perhaps somewhat like a holy human figure being a pathway to God for Christianity or Islam.

Hindu beliefs reflect the values of respect, selflessness, and non-violence toward all people, values that are very familiar to social work. The well-known Hindu greeting when meeting people with a bow is, "Namaste," which means "the divine within me honors and greets the divine in you." Meditation practice helps one relate in a clear and open-minded way. Yoga means "union." The practice of yoga means unity of the body, mind, and spirit with the Divine. Yoga practice precedes and prepares Hindus for deeper meditation. Hindus point out that the various versions of yoga widely practiced in the United States are not a preparation for meditation but essentially a good physical workout.

When working with a Hindu client, it can be quite appropriate to keep in mind the common values of Hindus and social workers—that the helping relationship should reflect the values of respect, selflessness, and non-violence as much as possible. When visiting a Hindu in their home, take your shoes off at the door. Be prepared to recognize the special authority and respect given to elders, especially the husband. However, also keep in mind the value of egalitarian family relations between the parents in some families, with the mother usually being the informal household head (Pandey-Eddins, 2012). Spiritual assessments of Hindus should consider identification of particular deities, home or temple-based worship practices, religious teachers, temple priests, and Indian community celebrations; all of these social supports are relevant to the client's sources of strength, resilience, and problem-solving. Meditation practice is very likely to be a popular spiritual practice for Hindu clients, so much so that referrals to complementary healing and stress management yoga practices rooted in Indian culture may be important to consider initially.

Native People and Spirituality

American Indian or Native American spirituality is a topic that covers a variety of belief systems and practices. According to Native Americans, spirituality is an essential part of a person's essence (Robinson, 2008). Native American tribes hold varying beliefs, but there are many common underlying themes that can be found among them. One pervasive idea is the concept of a dual deity. This concept holds that there is a Creator of all things, and this Creator is recognized through rituals. In addition, there is a spiritual world widely accepted in Native American spirituality, with spirits associated with weather and other elements of nature and with these spirits interacting with humans. Some tribal beliefs state that there is a single spiritual force, while others make more of a distinction between spirits. The belief in an afterlife ranges from reincarnation to traveling to another world. We also need to keep in mind that some tribes do not hold any specific beliefs on these topics.

Rituals are a significant part of Native American spirituality and culture. Rituals vary widely among different tribes, but their significance and importance is strong, and widely seen across tribes and throughout Native history. Common ritualistic practices include the use of sweat lodges, hunting ceremonies, medicine wheels, and a variety of other traditions specific to tribes and regions (Robinson, 2008). Sweat lodges, utilized in rituals for purification and healing, involve small buildings, usually comprised of saplings covered with animal hides or blankets. A shallow hole is often dug out in the middle of the floor, where hot rocks are placed. Water can be thrown over the hot rocks to generate steam. This ceremonial practice varies by tribe, but variations in sweat lodges are seen in different regions in North America. Hunting ceremonies, another commonly seen ritual, occur after an animal has been killed. The hunters want to honor and appease the spirit of the animal to ensure that future hunts will be successful.

The Medicine Wheel, or sacred hoop, is a ritual that is used by traditional healers (National Library of Medicine, 2014). It symbolizes each of the four directions (north, south, east, west), but the specific meaning of each direction as related to well-being differs from tribe to tribe. Some examples include representations of the spiritual, emotional, intellectual, and physical aspects of life, and the elements of nature, including fire, water, air, and earth. Medicine Wheels can also be used as a problem-solving tool (Hoover, 2014). The person being counseled uses the wheel by beginning in the east, reflecting on their problem related to their emotions, knowledge, and action taken, followed by any release they experienced and manifestations of the results. Medicine Wheel rituals help individuals understand their problems better, help them become more balanced within themselves and with nature, and help them improve their health and healing capacities.

The powwow is a commonly known Native American ritual, although the significance and history of the ritual is not well understood. The spelling of the term "powwow" is the result of European explorers mispronouncing the word "pauau." The original term, pauau, was used to refer to an official gathering of healers and spiritual leaders (Schultz, 2011). This ritual is often performed for religious purposes, offering healing and wellness. Other purposes of the powwow include a celebration of a victory in battle and recognition of the circle of life. The powwow ritual varies by tribe and has changed throughout history, but typically it involves dance, ceremonial dress, music, and feasting.

The role of spirituality and rituals are important to consider when working with Native American clients. Spirituality is not viewed as a separate part of life for many Native people; rather, spirituality is a core part of one's being. Therefore, it should be given serious consideration by the social worker. The spiritual connection with one's ancestors and the historical trauma associated with the horrific treatment of

Native Americans are both a very real concern for many Native clients (SAMHSA, 2014). The manifestations of historical trauma can be seen in high rates of violent crimes, suicide, and substance abuse, all of which may be a presenting problem for a Native client. Another consideration when working with Native American clients is accounting for how the client has been acculturated as a result of exposure to other cultures. For many Native peoples, cultural history is a significant part of their spirituality. However, their personal spiritual and religious beliefs may be different from the traditional beliefs of their tribe. For example, many Natives are members of Christian churches. Some Natives identify strictly and almost totally with the culture of their tribe, while others identify more strongly with the majority culture. As with any population, the client should be viewed as the expert on his or her own spirituality and culture, and the social worker should be careful not to make incorrect assumptions about the client's belief systems.

When attending a Native American ritual, such as a powwow, certain etiquette should be demonstrated out of respect for the ceremony. It is important to not trivialize any aspect of the ceremony or make any comments that could be perceived as insensitive or disrespectful. For instance, Native American regalia should never be referred to as a costume. These outfits are carefully crafted and often family heirlooms. They should not be touched without asking permission first. Another consideration is photography. A non-Native may want to take pictures of the ceremony, but different tribes hold varying views about photography (Schultz, 2011). Always ask permission before taking pictures at a ceremony or ritual. Overall, respecting the significance of the ritual and what it means to the participants, culturally and spiritually, is the most critical aspect of etiquette when attending a Native American ritual.

Buddhism

Buddhism began with its founder, Buddha. He was born a prince in northern India in 563 bc. The name Buddha means one who is awake. His original name was Siddhartha Gautang. Buddha renounced his royalty when he became a young adult, having already experienced many sorrows in his life. He decided he wanted to devote his life to seeking the truth and overcoming sorrow as a human problem (Kornfield, 1996). The sorrows he wanted to overcome were worldly sorrows that all humans are likely to experience, including losses, aging, sickness, and death and the forces of fear, attachment, greed, hatred, delusions, temptations, and doubts.

Buddha sought freedom and realized that he needed to follow a Middle Path, balancing the inner and outer life. Sitting under a great banyan tree, he meditated until he could see the depths of his consciousness and discover a place of peace at the center of it (Kornfield, 1996). This was his discovery and realization of enlightenment, or Nirvana. Nirvana, for Buddha, was an experience of being free from all kinds of sorrows and entanglements. What he discovered in this enlightened state became the focus of his lifelong teachings that followed. Two overall discoveries were awakened for Buddha—transcendent wisdom and universal compassion.

Buddha came to hold several beliefs. One belief of Buddhism is reincarnation. People are born, die, and are born again as another person. Instead of a personal God, Buddhists are oriented to the meaning of their life in this world and discovery of enlightenment. The Four Noble Truths were formulated after Buddha's experience of enlightenment and serve as a foundation of Buddhism (O'Brien, n.d.). They are:

1. Life is suffering.
2. The cause of suffering is craving that never gets satisfied.
3. The end of suffering and craving is possible.
4. The Eightfold Path frees us from suffering.

This Eightfold Path is Buddha's answer to overcoming suffering. It includes right understanding, right thought, right speech, right action, right livelihood, right effort, right mindfulness, and right concentration. Buddha's teachings explain what each of these paths are and how they can be practiced.

Buddhism is made up of numerous sects based on the individuals who practice it, Buddhist teachers, and the countries they come from. These countries are mostly from the Far East, including Japan, China, Cambodia, Thailand, and others. Buddhism, unlike other major religions, is more likely to be practiced in a person's home than a temple, even though there are Buddhist temples where worship is practiced. Buddhist practice primarily revolves around meditation. Buddha taught a variety of meditation practices to train the mind and open the heart (Kornfield, 1996). They include awareness of the breath and body, mindfulness of thoughts and feelings, use of mantras, visualizations, and practices leading to profound states of consciousness.

When meeting with clients who are Buddhist it is likely you will see a statue of a Buddha in their homes, perhaps on an altar that the family has set up. These statues are helpful reminders of the importance of Buddha and Buddhist teachings. Perhaps, Buddhist clients are likely to be peaceful and have a capacity for inner awareness. They are also likely to have a practice of meditation that may be a regular occurrence. Such a practice is a strength and special source of comfort and peace in times of loss and turmoil. Meditation is discussed extensively in chapter 9 as a spiritual intervention; a basic meditation practice is described along with a more advanced version developed by a Buddhist nun (Chodron, 2008; 2012).

New Age Religions

New Age spirituality can best be conceptualized as an eclectic mix of many spiritual orientations, philosophies, and practices rather than as one cohesive religion (Sutcliffe & Bowman, 2000). Although New Age spirituality reached the peak of its exposure to the public eye in the 1980s and early 1990s, its core concepts and terminology have been around since at least the 1880s (Green, 2000). The term "New Age" arose during this time period and fell in and out of use until the 1930s. According to Green, it was used to refer to a "period of more-than-ordinary life-experiment, spontaneity, and social hope." The milieu of the time was one of questioning toward the arranged social order set forth by established theology. This was compounded by a push toward urbanization and the subsequent desire of some to return to nature. Thus, Christianity was being challenged by the influx of Eastern religions such as Hinduism and Buddhism, and the idea that cities should be centers of life was being challenged by a return to nature through pagan practices. In addition to Eastern religion and paganism, several philosophies arose during this era, which continue to influence modern New Age spirituality. Two of the most influential of these were Theosophy and Jungian Psychology.

Theosophy was developed by H. P. Blavatsky and combines ideas of universal brotherhood, development of higher self, reincarnation, and spiritual evolution into a cohesive orientation (Tingay, 2000). Although Madame Blavatsky did not devise these concepts herself, she and her followers were the first to collect them into the credo of Theosophy, termed "Ancient Wisdom." Jungian psychology became part of the "New Age" milieu by re-conceptualizing religion as a type of ritualized mythology. Jungian archetypes are seen in New Age philosophy as proof of a collective consciousness by virtue of their universality across cultures and epochs. New Age conceptions of religion and who and what God is are based on the inherent divinity of each human life, rather than an external divine force (Segal, 2000).

Because New Age spirituality is broad and includes followers from many spiritual orientations, it lacks a formal doctrine or set of core beliefs (Hedges & Beckford, 2000). Many of the features that give some shape to the New Age orientation are also reflected in other religions, such as:

- **Hope** that the seeds for an enlightened human race have already been sown and are ready for cultivating by those individuals who have worked to find and express their "authentic selves."
- **Criticism** of modern emphasis on productivity and consumerism that stifles natural tendencies for human creativity, compassion, and play. This criticism also extends to religious dogma that uses guilt and fear to spread an agenda.
- **Openness** to new ideas and expression of the higher self, as well as to experiment with new practices and modes of thought that enhance spiritual, mental, and physical well-being.
- **Appreciation** for efforts to minimize exploitation and corruption of the natural world and for recognizing that all beings are interconnected.

There are some considerations to keep in mind when working with clients who subscribe to New Age beliefs. First, in New Age philosophy, the self is considered divine and the highest judge of truth (Bruce, 2000). This may mean that your client, even more than clients of other philosophical orientations, will exercise independence and judgment when listening to your suggestions. Your client may believe, as many New Age spiritualists do, that truth is relative and it is up to the individual to decide whether a particular truth applies to her or him. Not realizing this, a social worker may interpret the client's responses as noncompliant or dismissive. It is important, therefore, to understand that respecting individual determination is critical to your relationship with these clients.

A second practice that a social worker may encounter when working with New Age spiritualists is that of self-healing. When experiencing physical or mental illness, New Age clients may want to pursue holistic or alternative methods of treatment and opt for conventional medicine as a final resort. Some forms of New Age healing are aromatherapy, massage, acupuncture, the use of crystals and other minerals, specialized diets, meditation, pagan healing rituals, aura cleansing, and chakra therapy to name a few (Hedges and Beckford, 2000).

When doing social work with a client who adheres to New Age beliefs, it is essential to keep an open mind (Davis, 2015). Naturally this is important for working with any client with a religious orientation that differs from your own, but it is particularly important given the eclecticism of New Age spirituality. A client with New Age beliefs may incorporate many elements of several religions, such as having a personal altar, wearing a Christian cross, and displaying statues of Buddha in their home simultaneously. It is vital that the social worker understand that for these clients, religious and humanistic philosophies may overlap and strict religious boundaries likely do not apply. When you are unsure about your client's specific beliefs that are relevant to serving him or her, the best policy is always to ask in a genuine and spiritually sensitive way.

An example of a popular contemporary New Age author who also draws ideas from Buddhism and Christianity is Eckhart Tolle. Tolle (2005) refers to the outer self and inner self in a way that is similar to other theorists cited elsewhere in the book. The outer self has a social identity evolving from, among other things, our material possessions, baggage from the past, which he refers to as "pain bodies," and a need to be right and for others to be wrong. All of these and other elements provide a sense of false security. An example is someone who moves up the corporate ladder, works 50 to 60 hours a week, is away from family, and has enormous stress—all to be "successful." Then an inner voice starts breaking through—I'm missing my family, my family is leaving me out, I am not happy in this high stress job, etc.

Tolle (2005) refers to our world as being made up of either form or space. Form refers to areas in which the ego is in charge and involves thinking, feeling, believing, and our attitudes. Space refers to areas in which we are free of ego and can be fully present; this is where consciousness lies. According to Tolle, our inner self is the essence of who we are and is an intensely alive energy field. We need to yield to an acceptance of inner self and as a result, a new dimension of consciousness opens up. Tolle advocates beginning by aligning our outer self to our inner self and its purpose.

Wicca

Wicca is a decentralized, non-monotheistic religion first introduced to the public by Gerald Gardner in the 1950s. Wicca is one form of modern paganism, although not the only type of paganism practiced today (Yardley, 2008). Due to its decentralized nature, Wicca has no established theology or doctrine. However, some common beliefs among practitioners include the belief that nature is sacred, that the divine manifests in both feminine and masculine form, and that nature is composed of spiritual elements. These elements include earth, air, fire, and water and are bound together by the all-encompassing spirit. These four elements together with spirit are symbolized by the five-pointed star, or pentagram, a common Wiccan symbol. Wicca recognizes both a Goddess and God. The Goddess is often characterized as a tri-persona of maiden, mother, and crone, while the God is frequently depicted as a horned god of nature. Because Wicca is not the only form of modern paganism, those that practice may identify with other terms than Wiccan, such as Goddess Worshiper, Druid, or neo-shaman.

A common Wiccan practice is the use of magic to bring about particular outcomes in one's life. Working magic involves focusing one's intention through the use of sacred rituals and can be for practical purposes such as finding a job or overcoming an addiction (Yardley, 2008). Most Wiccans believe that any use of magic to bring about negative outcomes for others will bring harm back to oneself three fold. Wiccans also celebrate some key holidays: the summer and winter solstices, autumn and spring equinoxes, and four Celtic holidays that fall in between. Holiday celebrations and working ritual magic usually involve lighting candles, invocation of the Goddess and/or God, singing or chanting, and occasionally dance.

Followers of Wicca and other pagan religions have long faced stigma and even threats of violence due to their beliefs. Frequently Wiccans are accused of "devil-worshiping," using black magic, or being involved in sacrificial satanic rituals. Therefore, clients who practice this religion may be hesitant to disclose it to a social worker (Davis, 2015). Thus it is important that a spiritually sensitive worker is informed about paganism and is attuned to its subtle cues shared by a client. These cues might include wearing Celtic or pagan jewelry, such as a pentagram or goddess figures. Another clue may be mentioning celebrating the solstices, equinoxes, or other pagan holidays such as Samhain. A client may also refer to their religion as "nature-based" or "earth-based," which may indicate pagan beliefs (Yardley, 2008). As with all religious practices, the worker should remain open to any disclosure but allow the client to take the initiative in sharing it. Due to

Wicca's decentralized nature, it is critical that the worker not make any assumptions about the client's specific beliefs, but rather let the client guide them as the expert.

Conclusion

Religions that are the most frequently represented in the United States are introduced in this chapter along with some of their denominations. The overall purpose is to help social workers know a little more about these religions in areas applicable to spiritually sensitive practice and the spirituality of many clients. Aspects of these religions that are covered include religious beliefs related to daily living, how these beliefs may help members cope with difficulties, the group's influence on members' roles in the family, how they explain the meaning of life, and what social supports are available to members and others from this group. Christianity is by far the largest religion represented in the United States and this explains why Christianity is covered most extensively. Judaism, Islam, Hinduism, and Buddhism are also covered in some depth. The spirituality of Native people and New Age religions are also introduced.

Discussion Questions and Exercises

1. Find your religious group or the group with which you are most familiar among those that are described in the chapter. Was most of the important material about these beliefs and practices similar to what you understand? What was missing or possibly misrepresented? How do you think clients that belong to this religious group may respond to efforts by social workers to engage their spirituality? What might a social worker do to encourage clients from this group to share their spirituality? What should they not do?
2. Select a religious group described in the chapter about which you are unfamiliar and curious. Review the chapter material that describes the group's beliefs and practices. What, if anything, surprises you about this group? How is it similar to other religious groups of which you are personally familiar? How is it dissimilar?
3. Buddhism is a popular religion among many Americans who are not immigrants. What do you think are some of the reasons why the practice of Buddhism has become so popular with so many such people? You may need to do some further reading to come up with an answer. You may want to jump ahead and read about Buddhism in chapter 9, based on the writings of Chodron (2012) and Kornfield (1993), two popular American-born Buddhists.

References

Abdel Haleem, M. A. S. (Trans.) (2004). *The Qur'an.* New York: Oxford University Press.

Abul Fadl, M. (1991). *Introducing Islam from within: Alternative perspectives.* London: Islamic Foundation.

Armstrong, K. (2004). *The spiral staircase: My climb out of darkness.* New York: Alfred A. Knopf, 270–271.

Belcher, J. R., & Cascio, T. (2001). Social work and deliverance practice: The Pentecostal experience. *Families in Society: The Journal of Contemporary Human Services, 82*(1), 61–68.

Billingsley, A. (1999). *Mighty like a river: The Black church and social reform.* New York: Oxford University Press.

Borg, M. J. (2011). *Speaking Christian: Why Christian words have lost their meaning and power—And how they can be restored.* New York: HarperCollins.

Bourgeault, C. (2008). *The wisdom Jesus: Transforming heart and mind—A new perspective on Christ and his message.* Boston: Shambhala.

Bruce, S. (2000). The new age and secularisation. In S. Sutcliffe & M. Bowman (Eds.), *Beyond new age.* Edinburgh, Scotland: Edinburgh University Press, 220–236.

Chodron, P. (2008). *Comfortable with uncertainty: 108 teachings on cultivating fearlessness and compassion.* Boston: Shambhala.

Chodron, P. (2012). *Living beautifully with uncertainity and change.* Boston: Shambhala.

Davis, M. (2015). Wicca and social work. Unpublished paper, School of Social Work. University of North Carolina at Charlotte.

Eddin, Rashmi (2012). Conversation at the Hindu Center, Charlotte, NC, in May, 2012.

Friedman, B. (2001). *Judaism.* In M. Van Hook, B. Hugen, & M. Aguilar (Eds.), *Spirituality within religious traditions in social work practice.* Pacific Grove, CA: Brooks/Cole, 98–119.

Green, M. (2000). New centres of life. In S. Sutcliffe & M. Bowman (Eds.), *Beyond new age.* Edinburgh, Scotland: Edinburgh University Press, 51–64.

Halim, F (2006). Pluralism of American Muslims and the challenge of assimilation. *Journal of Muslim Minority Affairs, 26,* 235–245.

Harrington, D. J. (1999). *Who is Jesus: Why is he important?* Franklin WI: Sheed & Ward.

Hedges, E., & Beckford, J. A. (2000). Holism, healing, and the new age. In S. Sutcliffe & M. Bowman (Eds.), *Beyond new age.* Edinburgh, Scotland: Edinburgh University Press, 169–187.

Hodge, D. (2004). Working with Hindu clients in a spiritually sensitive manner. *Social Work, 49*(1), 27–38.

Hodge, D. (2005). Social work and the House of Islam: Orienting practitioners to the beliefs and values of Muslims in the United States. *Social Work, 50*(2), 162–173.

Hoover, C. (2014). A workshop led by Charlene Hoover, a Native American from Oregon on October 31, 2014 in Charlotte, NC.

Ibrahim, F. A. & Dykeman, C. (2011). Counseling Muslim Americans: Cultural and spiritual assessments. *Journal of Counseling & Development, 89,* 387–396.

Institute for Curriculum Services. (2012). *Are Jews a religious group or an ethnic group?* Available online at http://www.icsresources.org/content/curricula/ReligiousOrEthnic.pdf.

Islamic Relief Worldwide. (2011). Who we are/About us. Available online at http://www.islamic-relief.org.

Kornfield, J. (1993). *A Path with heart: A guide through the perils and promises of spiritual life.* New York: Bantam Books.

Kornfield, J. (Ed.) (1996). *Teachings of the Buddha*. Boston: Shambhala Publications.

MacCulloch, D. (2009). *Christianity: The first three thousand years*. New York: Penguin.

Martin, E. P., & Martin, J. M. (2002). *Spirituality and the Black helping tradition in social work*. Washington, DC: NASW Press.

Memissi, F. (1996). *Women's rebellion and Islamic memory*. New York: Saint Martin's Press.

National Library of Medicine. (2014). *Medicine ways: Traditional healers and healing*. Available online at http://www.nlm.nih.gov/nativevoices/exhibition/healing-ways/medicine-ways/medicine-wheel.html.

O'Brien, B. (n.d.). The four noble truths: Foundation of Buddhism. Available online at http://buddhism.about.com/od/thefournobletruths/a/fournobletruths.htm.

O'Connell, E. & Miller, D. (Interviewee) (2006). *The new face of global Christianity: The emergence of "progressive Pentecostalism"* [Interview transcript]. Available online at http://www.pewforum.org/2006/04/12/the-new-face-of-global-christianity-the-emergence-of-progressive-pentecostalism.

Pandey-Eddins, R. (2012). Conversation at the Hindu Center, Charlotte, NC in May 2012.

Parsuram, A., & Sharma, M. (1992). Functional relevance of belief in life-after-death. *Journal of Personality and Clinical Studies, 8*, 97–100.

Pew Research Center, Religion and Public Life. (2006). *Spirit and power: A 10-country survey of Pentecostals*. Available online at http://www.pewforum.org/files/2006/10/pentecostals-08.pdf.

Pew Research Center, Religion and Public Life. (2014). The shifting religious identity of Latinos in the United States. Washington, DC: Pew Research Center, May 7, 2014. Available online at http://www.pewforum.org/2014/05/07/the-shifting-religious-identity-of-latinos-in-the-united-states.

Pew Research Center, Religion and Public Life. (2015). America's changing religious landscape. Pew Research Center, Religion and Public Life, Washington, DC, May 12. 2015. Available online at http://www.pewforum.org/2015/05/12/americas-changing-religious-landscape.

Ramadan, T. (2007). In the footsteps of the prophet: Lessons from the life of Muhammad. New York: Oxford University Press.

Rich, T. R. (2011). Judaism 101. Available online at http://www.jewfaq.org.

Robinson, B. A. (2008). *Beliefs of Native Americans, from the Arctic to the Southwest*. Available online at https://www.religioustolerance.org.

SAMHSA (Substance Abuse and Mental Health Services Administration) (2014). Tips for disaster responders: Understanding historical trauma when responding to an event in Indian country. HHS Publication No. SMA-14-4866. Washington, DC. Available online at http://store.samhsa.gov/shin/content//SMA14-4866/SMA14-4866.pdf.

Satguru Sivaya Subramuniyaswami (n.d.). Sacred teachings of Satguru Sivaya Subramuniyaswami. Kapaa, HI: Himalayan Academy Publications. Available online at www.gurudeva.org.

Schultz, B. O. (2011). Powwow history. Available online at http://www.powwow-power.com/powwowhistory.html.

Segal, R. A. (2000). Jung's psychologising of religion. In S. Sutcliffe & M. Bowman (Eds.), *Beyond new age*. Edinburgh, Scotland: Edinburgh University Press, 65–79.

Smith, H. (1991). *The world's religions*. New York: HarperCollins.

Springer, P, Abbott, D., & Reisbig, A. M. J. (2009). Therapy with Muslim couples and families: Basic guidelines for effective practice. *The Family Journal, 17*, 229–235.

Sutcliffe, S., & Bowman, M. (Eds.). (2000). *Beyond new age*. Edinburgh, Scotland: Edinburgh University Press.

Tangenberg, K. (2007). Culture, social relationships, and self-perceptions of Pentecostal women. *International Social Work, 50*(2), 229–242.

Tingay, K. (2000). Madame Blavatsky's children: Theosophy and its heirs. In S. Sutcliffe & M. Bowman (Eds.), *Beyond new age*. Edinburgh, Scotland: Edinburgh University Press, 37–50.

Tolle, E. (2005). *A new earth: Awakening to your life's purpose*. New York: Penguin.

Umar, M. (2011). *How to pray: A step-by-step guide to prayer in Islam*. Author. Available online at www.Amazon.com.

Union for Reform Judaism. (2014). *What is Reform Judaism?* Available online at http://www.reformjudaism.org/what-reform-judaism.

Van Hook, M., Hugen, B., & Aguilar, M. (Eds.) (2001). *Spirituality within religious traditions in social work practice*. Pacific Grove, CA: Brooks/Cole.

Vaughan-Lee, L. (2012). *Sufism: The transformation of the heart*. Point Reyes, CA: The Golden Sufi Center.

Walsh, R. (1999). *Essential spirituality: The 7 central practices to awaken heart and mind*. New York: John Wiley & Sons.

Yardley, M. (2008). Social work practice with pagans, witches, and wiccans: Guidelines for practice with children and youths. *Social Work, 53*(4), 329–336.

5

Constructing a Spiritually Sensitive Approach

The more we are concerned for the well-being of others, the closer we will feel to each other.

(Dalai Lama, 5/15/14—Twitter)

Thousands of candles can be lit from a single candle, and the life of the candle will not be shortened. Happiness never decreases by being shared.

A Buddhist Saying (Brainy Quote)

Over the past 25 years, approaches have been proposed, developed, and implemented by several social work educators and practitioners (e.g. Bein, 2008; Bullis, 1996; Canda & Furman, 2010; Cunningham, 2012; Derezotes, 2006; Gardner, 2011; Sheridan, 2013). Support for spiritually sensitive approaches has also been documented in some studies (e.g. Canda & Furman, 2010; Kvarfordt & Sheridan, 2007; Sheridan, 2004). The spiritually sensitive practice approach developed by the author is introduced in this chapter. It has many similarities to the existing approaches as well as some key additional features.

Before introducing this spiritually sensitive approach, prior issues that have been widely discussed and studied are important to consider. They are:

- How should spirituality be initiated in the helping relationship?
- How do social workers view a wide variety of spiritual interventions?
- What is the influence of organizational factors on spiritual interventions?

Views on How the Topic of Spirituality Is Initiated

Some key studies have explored the views of social workers about topics pertinent to a social work approach and spirituality with some key questions repeatedly being asked. A central question pertaining to a spiritually sensitive approach is whether it is appropriate for a social worker to bring up spiritual or religious topics if the client does not. Canda and Furman (1999; 2010) explored this question with their nationally representative samples of NASW members in 1997 and 2008. They found that just over half of the respondents (54 percent) in 2008 took the position that spiritual or religious concerns should only be discussed if the client brought them up. One-third of the respondents believed that it would also be appropriate for the worker to introduce spirituality or religious issues if relevant and appropriate for the client. This still leaves a third smaller group who apparently were not in favor of a social work role at all in discussing spirituality issues with their clients (neither clients nor workers bringing up the topic).

These findings raise some important questions about a spiritually sensitive approach among all three general groups or types of tendencies—those who are comfortable bringing up spirituality as well as responding when their clients do, those who are comfortable addressing the topic only when their clients initiate the topic, and those presumably who are not comfortable discussing it in either instance. Is the first group more likely to have the most robust and effective spiritually sensitive approach than the others? This would seem to be the logical conclusion since they would likely have more opportunities to discuss this topic with their clients than the other two groups. However, on the down side, would this group of social workers also be more likely to bring up spirituality when it was not relevant to the client's situation or when the client was not ready to discuss it? Further, would this group be more likely to inject their own spiritual biases into the work possibly resulting in impeding the work of the client? These are potential dangers.

The second group, those being ready to respond only if the client brings up spiritual issues, would likely be most confident that their clients are genuinely wanting and ready to discuss these issues when it happens. Yet, they may be overlooking important issues that the client wants to discuss but is hesitant to openly initiate. In some of these cases, the client may misperceive that the worker or agency is unwilling or unprepared to discuss these matters.

The third group, those unlikely to view spirituality as an appropriate topic at all, would have different issues. Their most obvious potential problem would be to overlook or to at least be indifferent to pertinent spiritual concerns and resources of clients. Those using this approach may also be less likely to develop their relationship as far with clients who are more spiritual or religious, because these issues are so important to these clients.

The spiritually sensitive approach for social work presented in the book favors the first position—both raising spiritual issues when they are perceived to be helpful to clients and when clients bring up these topics. However, this position can be defended only under particular circumstances. The worker is expected to be comfortable and knowledgeable about spiritual concerns and vigilant in not introducing this topic when clients are unwilling or unready. They must also be relatively free of any tendencies to impose any aspects of their own spirituality or religion. A spiritually sensitive approach to practice is described and elaborated on in this and the remaining chapters.

Practitioners' Views about Spiritual Interventions

This spiritually sensitive approach is based, in large part, on evidence of actual practice that social workers have conducted and supported. Some of the studies that have focused on using a spiritually sensitive practice approach have asked social workers two questions. Which spiritual interventions have they actually used with their clients and which spiritual interventions do they perceive as appropriate for a social worker to use? These studies are important because they provide another form of evidence of the kinds of spiritual interventions social workers are actually using and endorsing. Findings of some of these studies follow.

Canda and Furman (1999, 2010) have categorized spiritual interventions or activities into four types: those used directly with clients, activities suggested to clients for homework, activities made by a social worker privately in preparation for practice, and interventions that connect clients with religious helpers and others in their spiritual support system. While all four of these types of categories are different, they all would potentially be useful in a spiritually sensitive practice approach since all relate one way or another to helping clients.

Canda and Furman investigated how their sample of NASW members would view 21 spiritual activities based on whether they actually used them or whether they viewed them as appropriate regardless of whether they used them. They found that the majority of the respondents (60 percent or more) used the following spiritual interventions or aspects of interventions with some clients. They are listed in no particular order:

- use non-religious spiritual language or concepts;
- use religious language or concepts;
- recommend clients participate in spiritual/religious support systems or activities;
- help clients consider ways their spiritual/religious support systems are helpful;
- help clients consider ways their spiritual/religious support systems are harmful;
- discuss the role of spiritual/religious beliefs in relation to significant others;
- refer clients to a clergy person or other religious/spiritual helper;
- help clients reflect on their beliefs about what happens after death;
- help clients consider the spiritual meaning and purpose of their current life situation;
- meditate to prepare for a client.

In addition, they found strong support (60 percent or more) for the appropriateness of several additional spiritual interventions or aspects that they had not used. In these cases, they may have not had an opportunity to use them because of limitations inherent in their jobs and work settings or possibly they viewed them as appropriate generally but not for themselves because of a lack of readiness or comfort. These interventions are:

- use or recommend religious or spiritual writings with clients;
- help clients develop religious/spiritual rituals as an intervention;

- encourage clients to do regular religious/spiritual reflective journal keeping;
- assist clients to reflect critically on their religious/spiritual beliefs or practices;
- pray privately *for* a client;
- help clients assess the meaning of spiritual experiences that occur in dreams;
- collaborate with a clergy person or other religious/spiritual leaders;
- meditate with a client.

In some contrast, most of the NASW respondents (over 70 percent) in Canda and Furman's 2008 survey indicated that they did not and would not use a few of the 21 spiritual interventions. These interventions were to pray *with* a client, touch clients for healing purposes, and participate in the clients' religious/spiritual rituals as a practice intervention. This is where most of them drew the line between what is acceptable and unacceptable. When comparing their findings of their study of the views and experiences of NASW members in 1997 to 2008, Canda and Furman found similarity in the results but a slight downward trend in approval of some of the spiritual interventions over these 11 years. The respondents who participated in some religious/spiritual courses or training tended to endorse and use more of these spiritual interventions than those who did not. Respondents under 58 years of age were also more likely to approve and use these interventions than those over 58 years.

Another study of social workers' view of spiritual interventions was conducted of licensed clinical social workers in one state by Sheridan (2004), who found similar results. She presented several statements about interventions and asked them two questions—whether they had used these spiritual interventions and whether they considered it an appropriate social work intervention. She found that the vast majority of these social workers supported using the following spiritual interventions or aspects of interventions in both cases:

- the use of religious language, metaphors, and concepts in social work practice;
- gathering information on clients' religious and spiritual background as appropriate;
- help clients clarify their religious or spiritual value;
- recommend participation in religious or spiritual programs;
- recommend regular religious or spiritual reflection;
- help clients consider the spiritual meaning of current life situations;
- help clients reflect on beliefs about what happens after death;
- believe it is important for social workers to have knowledge about different religious faiths and traditions.

Like other studies, Canda & Furman (2010) and Sheridan (2004) usually found more respondents supported the use of these spiritual interventions than actually used them in their own practice. Social workers in Sheridan's study who were more likely to both support and implement these positions tended to participate personally in religious or spiritual practices themselves, participate in current communal religious or spiritual services, and were more favorable to the role of religion and spirituality in social work practice.

Another study explored similar spiritual interventions used by social workers with children and adolescents and found further evidence that the vast majority of the social work respondents have used such spiritual interventions (Kvarfordt & Sheridan, 2007). Over 70 percent of the respondents in this study indicated that they used the following spiritual and sometimes religious interventions:

- help a child or youth reflect on his/her beliefs about loss or other difficult life situations;
- recommend participation in volunteer or altruistic activities;
- gather information on a child's or youth's religious or spiritual background;
- give attention to expressions of spiritual experience or mystical peak experiences reported by children or youth;
- help children consider ways their or their families' religious or spiritual beliefs, practices, or support systems are helpful.

Additional relatively large studies of social workers' views on spirituality and spiritual interventions have also been conducted, report similar findings, and are worth reviewing (Bullis, 1996).

Influence of Organizational Factors on Spiritual Interventions

Studies have also focused on organizational factors of agencies that can both support and impede social workers in using spiritual interventions (e.g. Svare, Hylton, & Albers, 2007). These are important macro concerns for social workers to consider and address as part of their practice role. Numerous organizational factors could influence how and the extent to which spiritually sensitive practice occurs in an agency. Such factors could include an emphasis on spirituality in an agency's mission or vision statement, agency policies supporting spiritual interventions, and any policies or procedures describing how spirituality should be implemented, such as questions in an intake instrument or treatment plan. Most important of all, is the concept of spirituality adequately defined within an agency? We know that this concept is complex and can be defined in many ways, so it is important for an agency to define it so it is understood by everyone in the agency.

Agencies have a responsibility to prepare and train their staff members in how to deliver spiritual services effectively. Staff members will likely need formal and informal training to know how to respond to a range of clients' spiritual issues in a helpful manner (e.g. Rothman, 2009). Also, administrative and supervisory staff should be available to encourage and assist staff members in implementing their spirituality policies and procedures and any other spiritual initiatives of interest to the agency.

An example of a confusing agency spirituality policy and some conflicting communication about it was evident in a psychiatric unit of a community hospital. The assessment form for patients included a standard question about spirituality—"Do you have any spiritual or religious supports?" A student who had a field placement at this hospital asked her supervisor about this assessment question and was told to ignore it. The supervisor said that she could talk to other social workers about it if she wished. Because the student was puzzled and disappointed about this response, she asked other social workers how they dealt with this assessment question. One responded that she "would address (spirituality) if a patient brings it up, but if it isn't important enough for them to bring it up then it probably is not important enough for treatment." Another responded that it was not really something they bring up, and that the question is confusing for the patient; they don't really know what we're asking. A third social worker replied "it's not usually pertinent to their treatment. If they need a chaplain then they'll ask for one or their religious leader will come see them."

Svare, Hylton, and Albers (2007) conducted a study that partially focused on the organizational level of agencies and the elements of organizations that can support or impede spiritually sensitive practice. They gathered data from a focus group of eleven social workers employed in a range of agency settings including medical hospitals, a psychiatric hospital, a faith-based program for pregnant teenagers, a program for seniors with dementia, a child welfare agency, an outpatient mental health clinic, a residential treatment program for incarcerated boys, juvenile probation, and an addiction counseling agency. These researchers were interested in examining the respondents' personal positions on spirituality and religion (e.g. were they religious, spiritual but not religious, or neither), and their personal policies and practice behaviors related to spiritual interventions. In addition, were they influenced by the agency context in which they were employed and did they attempt to influence this agency context?

Svare, Hylton, and Albers offer several helpful examples of the interplay among all of these elements. For example, like other studies, they found that workers who were more religious tended to be more open to the clients' spiritual and religious issues. At the other end of the continuum, social workers who personally viewed religion as restrictive and limiting took the position that these issues were outside the scope of their practice. Sometimes, the workers deliberately worked around agency policies to fulfill their ethical responsibilities; sometimes these efforts were in support of and other times against an agency policy related to religion. For example, the social worker in a faith-based agency for pregnant teens advocated for birth control services even though they were disapproved by the agency; her rationale was that some teenagers needed these services. In a non-sectarian hospital, another social worker partially concealed her effort to assist her client in receiving needed services from a religious organization by only documenting that she provided transportation assistance to an unnamed referral agency.

All of the agencies represented in Svare, Hylton, and Albers' sample used an assessment form that included at least one spiritual or religious question even though the type and depth of spiritual assessments varied widely. All kinds of responses were raised by the presence of these questions, including why these questions were being asked and what their purpose was. One social worker responded that more questions than one or two were needed if these questions were going to help in the exploration of religious supports. Another respondent was concerned that these questions violate the First Amendment to remain neutral to all religions. All of these findings and questions suggest among other things that a good deal of thought needs to go into deciding what kinds of questions to ask to promote a holistic approach to practice. Also, the reasons for these questions are important to identify. Does the agency or an outside organization expect these questions to be asked and why? Is it because of an accrediting agency, the administration of the agency, or interested staff members? Or is it an outgrowth of previous clients' circumstances?

It is suspected that organizational structures related to spirituality services are not evident in most agencies. Or assistance with spirituality issues may be identified as a focus at the abstract level but not adequately operationalized. In these instances some social workers have a tendency to develop their own "personal policies about spirituality" (Svare, Hylton, & Albers, 2007). For example, one social worker who was very religious decided, on her own, to avoid entertaining spiritual or religious concerns of her clients; in her case she worked in a hospice agency that also had a spiritual care worker who could address any religious issues. Other social workers worked out other personal policies in their agency, such as bringing up spiritual issues that were comfortable for them.

Construction of an Approach

Most people agree that spirituality is a key aspect of being human. It is viewed by many as one of the dimensions of being human along with biological, psychological, social, intellectual, and cultural. Others view spirituality as the deeper core of being human that encompasses all other dimensions (Canda & Furman, 2010). With both views, spirituality is present in the makeup of every human being and social workers are encouraged to give greater attention to it in both agency policies and their practice.

A Core of Interacting Factors

What is a spiritually sensitive practice approach and more basically what is spiritually sensitive practice? A **spiritually sensitive approach** *infuses spirituality and* *religion into the helping process whenever it is needed to help our clients.* **Spiritually sensitive practice** *can be defined as the outcome of effectively implementing a spiritually sensitive approach.* The implementation of a spiritually sensitive approach requires a personal commitment to the spiritual and religious needs of your clients. You will also need knowledge about spirituality and religion as they are interwoven into the lives of your clients. Finally, you will need a range of skills to know if, when, and how to help clients with these areas of practice. The spiritually sensitive approach described in the book provides the specific assumptions and beliefs about spirituality and religion (mostly in chapters 1 and 2), specific ethical issues (chapter 6), a knowledge base (most of the book), practice principles and strategies (mostly chapters 7 to 12), spiritual interventions (chapters 9, 10, and 11), and evaluation (chapter 12).

Other Spiritually Sensitive Approaches in Social Work

The approach draws from a core of content evident in many existing spiritually sensitive practice approaches. In recent years, several social work authors have written books describing their construction of a spiritually sensitive social work practice approach (e.g. Bein, 2008; Bullis, 1996; Canda & Furman, 2010; Cunningham, 2012; Derezotes, 2006; Gardner, 2011). The common core of these books have many similarities that are also agreed upon by a broad range of social workers in this field. The core content introduces and defines spirituality and religion, the two key concepts of the approach, and documents the importance of spirituality and religion in clients' lives. Most of these approaches describe a set of practice stages or steps that workers and their clients go through, essentially a problem-solving approach with logical steps; they are engagement, assessment, implementation, evaluation, and termination. These theorists often also describe and illustrate how their approaches are implemented with different groups of clients (e.g. people with addictions, cancer patients) and in different fields of practice (e.g. family, schools, older adults, mental health, and health care).

Canda and Furman (2010) are probably the most well known social work theorists for their introduction of a spiritually sensitive approach. Their very popular textbook has a whole section on "Spiritually Sensitive Social Work in Action," mostly covered in their last five chapters. It is an important culminating section that provides the essentials of a core approach by giving emphasis to both the helping relationship and four phases of work, in their case, understanding, designing, implementing, and evaluating. A valuable set of guidelines are offered to help practitioners determine the extent to which spiritual interventions are warranted based on the clients' initiatives. The harmful effects of a spiritual group on clients are addressed including standards for distinguishing spiritual issues from mental disorders. They refer to their helping process ideally as a transformational one with fundamental changes and growth being hoped for by clients. They describe the stages of such transformation as beginning when disruptions occur in clients' lives, taking advantage of the disruption by moving beyond their status quo, moving through "creative chaos," pulling things together into a new creative order, and finally moving forward hopefully at a higher level of spiritual involvement and a fuller life.

Bein (2008) offers another example of a spiritually sensitive approach that is largely based on a religious philosophy. *The Zen of Helping* is an outgrowth of an American version of Zen Buddhism and also has an infusion of other Buddhist concepts that can be important to the helping process. Bein defines "Zen" as being intimate with what is. Processes of helping are emphasized in Bein's approach rather than an emphasis on defined steps or stages. His approach emphasizes an attitude of openheartedness toward clients and being present with them in the present moment. Bein recommends trusting the present moment with clients with all of its uncertainties rather than depending heavily on practice theories and skills. He suggests letting go of the process of what happens in the helping process with our clients, an unfolding process that presumes we have no control over the outcome. We are to look for client resilience and courage. Bein also points out that we are to care concurrently for our clients and ourselves, as our strength is in our union, not our separateness. We are to focus on the breath to facilitate calmness and mindfulness about what we do. Bein reminds us of the findings of a meta-analysis study that claim that 30 percent of the variance in client outcomes has been found to be attributable to the practitioner-client relationship (Asay & Lambert, 1999). Further, when we add hope, expectancy, social supports, and ecological circumstances to this relationship we find that they all account for as much as 55 percent of client change (Wampold, 2010).

Another approach involves using ethnographic interviewing, which can be a profound way of understanding the client's worldview, including their spirituality (Robert-Lewis, 2011). This anthropological approach has four basic components: the client is considered a cultural guide, global questions are asked, the practitioner listens for cover terms, and asks for descriptors. Viewing the client as a cultural guide means that the client becomes the educator and the worker becomes a student. Questions revolve around asking the client to teach the worker about their religious and spiritual practices with questions like "I want to learn from you so I can understand your point of view." Global questions are very open-ended and ask the client to share and elaborate on their religious practices. Examples of global questions are "Could you help me understand how your religious and spiritual beliefs help you cope with these life challenges that you are reporting?" Cover terms are words used by the client that have particular cultural meanings in their worldview. These cover terms could be reflections of religious traditions such as Holy Communion, yoga, or confession. Once these cover terms are revealed and detected, descriptors could be explored. Descriptors are culturally meaningful information that a client shares related to cover terms; they provide an "inside view" of the client's life and spirituality. If a cover term turns out to be spirituality, descriptors can be explored that offer elaborations, examples, metaphors, and contexts of meaning.

Gardner (2011) offers another approach to a spiritually based practice approach that is similar but also has its own distinct characteristics. She refers to it as "Critical Spirituality." She organizes her approach around four aspects that explain how she defines critical spirituality. First, she recommends that workers recognize the influences of a client's and the community's history and culture on their religious and spiritual experiences. Second, critical spirituality involves celebrating the diversity of spiritual expression with the exception of any form of violence associated with religion or spirituality. Third, workers are required to be reflective and to be acutely aware of our own values, culture, and history that are associated with our religious and spirituality identity and their implications for practice. Fourth, we are to work in a holistic way seeing and appreciating the person as a whole.

Gardner (2011) also has nine practice principles that summarize her approach. First, spirituality is to be viewed as a part of every client's experiences and thus needs to be seen as an integral part of practice. Second, the client's cultural and historical context is to always be considered in exploring spirituality. Third, each person is unique and their experience of spirituality is their own. Fourth, we are to value the differences as well as commonalties in expressions of spirituality. Fifth, practitioners need to be constantly aware of our personal reactions to our clients' spirituality. Sixth, practitioners need to be aware of their own spirituality and the assumptions they may make from their own experience. Seventh, practitioners need to remember that being with clients is as important as doing things for them. Eighth, we need to accept the reality that we do not have all of the answers and uncertainty is evident in much of what we are asked to do. Ninth, we need to recognize our limitations and not offer help beyond our ability; referrals may be needed in these instances.

Key Elements of the Approach

The key features in the spiritually sensitive approach described in the book beyond the above core are introduced and comprise 11 interdependent general principles, some of which distinguish it from the other existing spiritually based social work approaches.

1. It is an approach that works at all levels of client systems—micro, mezzo, and macro.
2. It is designed to meet the core competency requirements of CSWE, the social work accreditation agency.
3. The approach emphasizes being proactive in engaging the spiritual issues of clients.
4. The spirituality of clients and workers must always remain separate.

5. Spirituality is clearly defined and distinguished from religion.
6. Avoid underestimating religion's importance to many clients, especially when religion primarily informs the nature of their spirituality.
7. The engagement component of the practice approach is a critical one for identifying and setting the stage to discuss the clients' spiritual issues.
8. The other three components (assess, intervene, evaluate) also have critical functions in the helping process.
9. Worker preparation is important for each session.
10. Any ethical problems or other negative issues related to the clients' spirituality or religion are addressed.
11. Spiritual work can often be integrated into several widely used general practice approaches. Elaboration of these principles follows.

1. All Levels of Practice—Micro, Mezzo, and Macro

The spiritually sensitive approach described in this book can be implemented with individuals, families, small groups, organizations, and communities. Emphasis is given to describing and illustrating the approach at each of these levels. Micro and mezzo levels of spiritual interventions have been documented extensively in the social work literature, especially work with individuals. Studies have been conducted to find out which spiritual interventions are being implemented by sizeable numbers of practitioners and some of these findings are reported above (Canda & Furman, 2010; Kvarfordt & Sheridan, 2007; Sheridan, 2004).

Macro levels of practice tend to be given less emphasis in the social work literature and many spirituality texts. Yet, many of the important interventions involving spiritual or religious issues are macro in nature. Some can be initiated with clients and others with agencies and other organizations. Macro level spiritual practices involving social workers can be reflected in several forms such as:

- **Agency organizational interventions:** For example, setting up and/or monitoring the implementation of a spiritual component in an agency's mission and vision statement, crafting a definition of spirituality and agency policies supporting the use of spiritual interventions.
- **Community organizing interventions:** These interventions can be efforts to organize and educate people in communities around various collective needs and incorporating a spiritual element in these interventions.
- **Social justice work:** Religious leaders and groups are sometimes at the forefront in promoting community and societal change when major social problems are evident, such as hunger, homelessness, unmet health care needs, war, or illiteracy. A spiritual component is often a motivating factor and an empowering element of these efforts.

- **Faith-based agencies:** Faith-based agencies are becoming increasingly evident in many localities. Traditional sectarian agencies such as Jewish Family Services, Catholic Social Services, and Lutheran Family and Children have been joined by newer religious human service organizations such as teenage pregnancy clinics, family-owned counseling agencies, food banks, and church-sponsored shelters for homeless people. The macro influences of these agencies are important to investigate and learn from.

2. Meets Accreditation Standards of CSWE

Like most existing approaches, this approach revolves around the core competencies of accreditation (CSWE, 2015). All of the core competencies are recognized in one way or another and emphasis is given to the competencies of critical thinking; ethical and professional behavior; diversity and difference; human rights and social, economic, and environmental justice; research-informed practice and practice-informed research; and the components of practice: engage, assess, intervene, and evaluate.

Critical thinking is emphasized in helping social workers develop their own spiritually sensitive approach to practice. Some basic questions have to be addressed critically. For example, when are spiritual issues important to explore with clients? How can spiritual or religious issues be effectively addressed? Are efforts to help based solely on the clients' needs? What spiritual biases of the social worker need to be addressed? Practitioners are exposed to many viewpoints and numerous sources of knowledge to integrate into their practice. Differing and competing views about spirituality and religion are often described, requiring that the readers ultimately think for themselves about what is most important. Critical thinking is evident in all of the components of practice, including engagement, assessment, intervention, and evaluation.

Ethical and professional behavior are stressed throughout the book in different ways. For example, practitioners are encouraged to be personally reflective and understanding of their own spirituality. They are also encouraged to be fully open to self-correction whenever their own spirituality interferes in any way with helping clients with their issues. In addition, the need for training in spiritually sensitive practice is frequently emphasized along with seeking help from supervisors and others. Ethical practice is covered extensively throughout the book. Practitioners are encouraged to manage their personal values so that they do not interfere with their professional values. They are also encouraged to rely on the NASW Code of Ethics and the CSWE accreditation standards to explicitly guide their practice.

Diversity and difference have been conceptualized in the Educational Policy and Accreditation Standards document in 2015 as perhaps the most important reasons to teach spirituality and religion in social work education. These two concepts (spirituality and religion) are included explicitly in Educational Policy 3.0 on

Diversity as two of several dimensions of diversity in clients that are important to understand. In addition, Competency 2 on engaging Diversity and Difference in Practice explicitly identifies "spirituality/religion" along with several other dimensions of diversity to engage because they are believed to shape the human experience and are critical to the formation of identity (CSWE, 2015).

Diversity and difference are partially reflected in the extensive and richly varied descriptions of religious groups, beliefs, and practices in the book. Spirituality is described as having many dimensions and fits well with both religious and non-religious worldviews. The importance of differences in how spirituality shapes the lives of people is evident throughout the book. Practice settings naturally vary widely with regards to how they define and address spirituality and religion. Efforts are made to look at different ways that practice settings can implement a spiritually sensitive approach. Agency organizational factors are also examined to insure that the essentials of agency readiness are present in implementing spiritually sensitive provisions.

Social, economic, and environmental justice and their relationships to spiritual and religious beliefs and practices are highlighted conceptually and by example in several chapters. **Advocacy for human rights** and a perspective of religious pluralism are also described as paramount to a spiritually sensitive practice approach. Chapter 10 on macro spiritual interventions in particular gives extensive coverage to the connections between spirituality and human rights and justice. Macro spiritual interventions are largely described as being important because they draw on the doctrines of religion and spirituality and the beliefs and passions of people in these groups, which emphasize the importance of human rights and justice.

Research-informed practice and **practice-informed research** are also given special coverage. Evidence-based practice is stressed as important at appropriate points in the book and evidence-based programs and practice represent one of the main reasons why research-informed practice is so important. Chapter 12, on evaluation, picks up on several issues that stress the importance of connecting research and practice. Most importantly, agencies are encouraged to conduct more outcome evaluations that provide evidence that their spiritual interventions benefit the recipients.

Based on the 2015 Accreditation Standards, the social work practice approach is now described as four components of a dynamic and interactive process of social work practice (CSWE, 2015). These components are **1) engage, 2) assess, 3) intervene, and 4) evaluate**. While each of these components has a distinctness, they can easily be misunderstood as being implemented in a linear, mutually exclusive way. In actuality the process usually is more like a spiral that moves forward to a new step and then possibly back to a previous step. For example, practice interventions could be explored and possibly implemented while an assessment may still be the primary focus. An illustration of this is a new client wanting to do something immediately to help slow herself down and become more relaxed and centered. In this case, a basic meditation practice could be offered such as proposing a brief period of silence each day, concentrating on breathing during this period, and observing and gently nudging away inner chatter when the client becomes conscious of it. Meditation could be viewed as a homework assignment that could be introduced early on and then discussed extensively in later sessions.

3.   Take Initiatives on Spiritual Issues

The approach encourages practitioners to actively engage clients in the spiritual realm and to do it in a timely manner, as long as it is appropriate to the helping relationship and clients are open to working on these issues. Earlier in the chapter, three possible positions or types of tendencies that a social worker could take were mentioned. The first tendency is for the worker to bring up spirituality when it is appropriate, as well as to respond when clients initiate discussion of this content, the second tendency is to discuss spirituality only when their clients initiate the topic, and the third tendency is to neither bring this material up nor encourage clients to do so. The first tendency is encouraged in the approach when social workers are comfortable with spiritual work and well prepared to implement it. If practitioners are not fully prepared, the second tendency is encouraged to the extent that it is productive for the client. Chapter 7 is devoted to how spirituality can be engaged in the initial phase.

4.   Clients' and Workers' Spirituality Always Kept Separate

The point of view emphasized in the book and in most other existing approaches is that the sole concern is to focus on the clients' spirituality and religion, not on that of the social worker or the social agency for which they work. Exceptions may be possible for sectarian agencies such as Catholic Social Services or Jewish Family Services, even though some of these agencies have taken an ecumenical approach that includes serving clients outside their religious group. The client's spirituality should always be considered in helping the client, whether it is reflected in a religious way or not. When religion plays a role in the client's worldview, specific attention should be given to how their religious connections can help them address their problems. Keeping the worker's and client's spirituality separate is a challenge that is addressed throughout the book and especially in chapter 6, addressing ethical issues and problems.

5.   Distinguish Spirituality from Religion

Social workers should be prepared to engage the spirituality of their clients, especially those who are not known to be religious. The spirituality of a client should be assessed and engaged without having to initiate any religious exploration. Growing numbers of people in the United States are identifying as spiritual but not religious. While their religious background, if it exists, may vary considerably for those with this profile, what is important here is that the social worker is equipped to fully work with clients on spiritual issues without mentioning religious issues. It can also be done in a manner that is relevant and comfortable for the client. Engaging such concepts as meaning, purpose, hopefulness, joy, suffering, forgiveness, and transcendence are relevant to the work of many clients who are spiritual but not religious, as well as religious. Chapter 1 in particular provides a framework for defining spirituality and religion and distinguishing them from each other.

6.   Avoid Underestimating the Importance of Religion to Many Clients

Spirituality and religion, the two central concepts of this approach, are viewed as distinctly different. Spirituality is an inner personal quality that exists in everyone while religion is an external entity that is typically institutional in nature and offers specific doctrine, beliefs, practices, and a community. Social workers tend to be less religious, on average, than their clients, and they may be hesitant to talk about religious issues with their clients though these issues could be appropriate and important to the clients. This hesitation on the part of some workers could be motivated by several things, such as a lack of comfort with this topic or a view that religious topics are outside their expertise (Bullis, 1996; Lips-Wiersma & Mills, 2002; Pargament, 2007; Svare, Jay, Bruce, & Owens-Kane, 2003).

The approach encourages reluctant workers to emotionally stretch some so that they can be more open to allowing the clients' religious issues into their discussions, especially when they can be helpful to the clients. An assumption of the book is that the spiritually of many clients is partially informed by their affiliations with religious groups. The stretching that is encouraged in part involves workers being open to learning about the various religions that are predominant among their clients and within their communities. If several clients of an agency identify as fundamentalist Christians or if the community where a worker is employed has a relatively large segment of people of the Islamic faith, for example, efforts should be made to acquaint oneself with some of the relevant aspects of that religious group. The approach described in chapter 3 introduces practitioners to unfamiliar religious groups important to their clients. Chapters 3 and 4 also provide an introduction to many of the major religions.

7.   Initial Engagement is Critical

This approach involves a set of interactive practice components that workers and their clients follow in a circular manner. These components are engagement, assessment, intervention, and evaluation. The approach gives special emphasis to the first component, engagement. Clients are most likely to share their spirituality and spiritual or religious concerns early in the helping process either directly or in the form of explicit or subtle cues. The explicit cues are often obvious and may appear out of context, such as a comment that a client "could not survive without trusting in the Lord," or a client asking an unexpected question like, "Do you pray?" Many more subtle ways are also likely to be expressed in the engagement phase, such as wearing a head cover or displaying a religious symbol such as a cross. How the social worker responds to these cues in these early exchanges can largely determine whether spirituality becomes a meaningful part of the work that follows. The book stresses that little is likely to happen in terms of spiritual engagement unless the worker offers an authentic and nurturing professional relationship and conveys a welcoming invitation to discuss spiritual issues if they are expressed and seem relevant. Chapter 7 focuses entirely on initial engagement and how it can be used to explore whether spirituality is important to the client.

8.　Other Practice Components Are Also Important

Each of the four components of practice have one or more chapters devoted to it. A special feature of the book during the second component—assessment—is to craft and weave helpful spiritual questions into the overall assessment process in a manner tailored to the client's unique circumstances rather than in the form of typical standardized agency questions that often lack relevance, context, and authenticity. During the third component, the book offers both descriptions of spiritual interventions that stand on their own and a description of how spirituality can be integrated into some of the common approaches used by social workers, such as Cognitive Behavioral Therapy, Person-Centered, and Solution-Focused practice. Assessment is explored in chapters 8, interventions in chapters 9, 10, and 11, and evaluation in chapter 12.

9.　Worker Preparation for Each Session Is Important

Preparation occurs, in specific ways, before each contact with a client. It is important to take time for personal preparation before each session. Shulman (2012) reminds us that the "tuning-in" phase is an important part of practice. It usually occurs a short time before each session with clients. Tuning in means taking time to clear our mind of everything unrelated to the next client contact. It also involves reflecting with our thoughts, feelings, and our spirit to generate empathy for the next client. You could ask yourself several questions. What was discussed during the last session? What do we know or recall about this client or community group that was important to them? What were the client's feelings when you last saw them and how might they be feeling as you anticipate seeing them when you meet now?

Spiritually, tuning in could also mean reflecting on any previous comments, behaviors, or non-verbal expressions about the client's religious affiliation, beliefs, practices, or cues about their spirituality. Spiritual cues are discussed more fully in chapter 7. They can be indirect references to the client's spirituality, mentioned perhaps to see how the social worker might respond. If these cues are ignored by the worker, they may not be mentioned again even though they may be important to a client. Tuning in to spiritual issues might include several questions the worker mulls over. What subtle or obvious spiritual cues have clients mentioned in the prior session? Might the clients be wondering how open you will be to what they want to say? How might you bring up, in a neutral way, the potential importance of their spirituality or spiritual issues when you meet them? The tuning-in period should be a quiet time, hopefully uninterrupted by internal or external distractions. It may even be viewed by some as a meditative or prayerful time. Preparing ourselves with mindfulness can also be an important way to prepare (Gockel, Cain, Malove, & James, 2013). You may ask yourself, for example, "Am I sufficiently centered within myself and free of distractions to be fully present with these clients and open to hearing them at a deeper level?"

Finding the time and developing the capacity to tune in can easily be challenging to implement, particularly as workplaces become increasingly demanding. Especially in situations in which a social worker sees several clients in a day one after another, taking time for tuning in can be difficult. For example, the author has recently become aware of increasing numbers of counseling settings in which social workers are expected to meet with five, six, or seven clients each day in an office setting. Someone else in the agency sets up their appointments that run one after another beginning on the hour and ending 45 or 50 minutes later. Breaks and lunch are usually also built into this schedule. These counseling arrangements are not particularly good for either the client or the worker for obvious reasons, yet they are increasingly springing up in this era of for-profit employers and greater emphasis on brief therapy. These are employment circumstances in which it may be impossible to remain mindful and empathic throughout all of these sessions. It's likely to be exhausting, confusing in terms of keeping the issues of each client separate from one another, and it can result in compassion fatigue very quickly. Yet, in these situations, tuning in may be the only way to remain present to the client personally and to provide a minimally satisfactory provision of help. The 10 to 15 minutes of time provided for tuning in, however short, offer a way to help the worker find a brief moment for rest, bring inner closure to work with a previous client, transition to the next client, and have some success with being mindful.

10. Readiness to Address Harmful Religious Influences

Giving attention to spiritual matters sometimes means becoming concerned and involved in something that can be harmful or negative for a client. A religious doctrine can conflict with professional values or governmental policies, resulting in a problem that needs addressing. For example, domestic violence in a marriage may be less important to a religious group than staying in a marriage. Sometimes these problems are deep seated and derive from religious teachings instilled as early as childhood that need to be dealt with in therapy. A female client, for example, may feel shame or a lack of self-confidence because of early church teachings on humility. Chapter 6 on ethics highlights several ethical challenges that can interfere with implementing a spiritually sensitive practice approach.

11. Integrate Spirituality with Other General Approaches

The approach also offers specific ways to integrate spiritual interventions with other practice approaches that are widely used by social workers, such as Cognitive Behavioral Therapy, the Person-Centered Approach, and Social Justice Interventions. In most cases, integrating a spiritual component into a popular secular approach strengthens both approaches. Chapter 11 addresses several ways to infuse and integrate spirituality into several popular approaches used in social work.

Conclusion

Three key questions were initially examined in the chapter: How should spirituality be initiated in the helping relationship? How do social work practitioners view spirituality and religion? How do organizational factors influence spiritual interventions? Next, the 11 key elements of the spiritually sensitive approach described in the book are introduced and discussed. They are:

- The approach works at all levels of client systems—micro, mezzo, and macro.
- It is designed to meet the core competency requirements of CSWE, the social work accreditation agency.
- It is proactive in engaging the spiritual issues of clients.
- The spirituality of clients and workers must always remain separate.
- Spirituality is clearly defined and distinguished from religion.
- The importance of religion to many clients is not underestimated or ignored.
- Initial engagement is a critical time for identifying the clients' spiritual issues and setting the stage to discuss them.
- The other three practice components (assess, intervene, evaluate) also have critical functions in the helping process.
- Personal preparation for each session is important.
- Any ethical problems or other negative issues related to the clients' spirituality or religion are addressed.
- Spiritual work can often be integrated into several widely used general practice approaches.

Discussion Questions and Exercises

1. How do you think spiritual issues should be initiated in the helping relationship? Roughly three positions have been identified in the chapter. First, there are those who are comfortable bringing up spirituality as well as responding when their clients bring it up. Second, others are comfortable addressing the topic only when their clients initiate the topic, and third, there are still others who presumably are not comfortable discussing it in either instance. Please explain why you took the position that you did and not one of the other positions.

2. Canda and Furman (2010) identified several spiritual interventions that social workers could use in their practice and conducted a study asking a sample of NASW members 1) if they actually used each of them and 2) whether they viewed them as appropriate regardless of whether they used them. What are your responses to these two questions for each of these interventions:

   - Use non-religious spiritual language or concepts.
   - Use religious language or concepts.
   - Recommend clients participate in spiritual/religious support systems or activities.
   - Help clients consider ways their spiritual/religious support systems are helpful.
   - Help clients consider ways their spiritual/religious support systems are harmful.
   - Discuss the role of spiritual/religious beliefs in relation to significant others.
   - Refer clients to a clergy person or other religious/spiritual helper.
   - Help clients reflect on their beliefs about what happens after death.
   - Help clients consider the spiritual meaning and purpose of their current life situation.
   - Meditate to prepare for a client.
   - Use or recommend religious or spiritual writings with clients.
   - Help clients develop religious/spiritual rituals as an intervention.
   - Encourage clients to do regular religious/spiritual reflective journal keeping.
   - Assist clients to reflect critically on their religious/spiritual beliefs or practices.
   - Pray privately for a client.
   - Help clients assess the meaning of spiritual experiences that occur in dreams.
   - Collaborate with a clergy person or other religious/spiritual leaders.
   - Meditate with a client.

- Pray with a client.
- Touch clients for healing purposes.
- Participate in the clients' religious/spiritual rituals as a practice intervention.

3. What are your reactions to each of the 11 features of the spiritually sensitive approach described in the chapter? Which features are easy for you to support? Which ones do you think are controversial? Which ones might you question and why?

References

Asay, T. P. & Lambert, M. J. (1999). The empirical case for the common factors in therapy: Quantitative findings. In M. A. Hubble, B. L. Duncan, & S. D. Miller (Eds.), *The art and soul of change: What works in therapy*. Washington, DC: American Psychological Association, 33–56.

Bein, A. W. (2008). *The Zen of helping: Spiritual principles for mindful and open-hearted practice*. Hoboken, NJ: John Wiley & Sons.

Brainy Quote. Buddha Quotes. Available online at http://www.brainyquote.com/quotes/authors/b/buddha.html.

Bullis, R. S. (1996). *Spirituality in social work practice*. Washington, DC: Taylor & Francis.

Canda, E. R., & Furman, L. D. (1999). *Spiritual diversity in social work practice: The heart of healing*. New York: Free Press.

Canda, E. R., & Furman, L. D. (2010). *Spiritual diversity in social work practice: The heart of healing*. 2nd edition. New York: Free Press.

CSWE (Council on Social Work Education) (2015). *2015 Educational Policy and Accreditation Standards for Baccalaureate and Master's Social Work Programs*. Educational Policy Approved by the CSWE Board of Directors on March 20, 2015; Accreditation Standards approved by the CSWE Commission on Accreditation on June 11, 2015. Alexandria, VA: Author.

Cunningham, M. (2012). *Integrating spirituality in clinical social work practice: Walking the labyrinth*. Boston: Pearson.

Derezotes, D. S. (2006). *Spiritually-oriented social work practice*. Boston: Allyn and Bacon.

Gardner, F. (2011). *Critical spirituality: A holistic approach to contemporary practice*. Burlington, VT: Ashgate.

Gockel, A., Cain, T., Malove, S., & James, S. (2013). Mindfulness as clinical training: Student perspectives on the utility of mindfulness training in fostering clinical intervention skills. *Journal of Religion & Spirituality in Social Work: Social Thought, 32*(1), 36–59.

Kvarfordt, C. L., & Sheridan, M. J. (2007). The role of religion and spirituality in working with children and adolescents: Results of a national survey. *Journal of Religion and Spirituality in Social Work: Social Thought, 26*(3), 1–23.

Lips-Wiersma, M., & Mills, C. (2002). Coming out of the closet: Negotiating spiritual expression in the workplace. *Journal of Managerial Psychology, 17*(3), 183–202.

Pargament, K. I. (2007). Spiritually integrated psychotherapy: Understanding and addressing the sacred. New York: Guilford Press.

Robert-Lewis, A. (2011). Response to Mark Chaves: Practical interventions to assist social work students in addressing religious and spiritual diversity. *Social Work and Christianity, 38*(2), 139–145.

Rothman, J. (2009). Spirituality: What we can teach and how we can teach it. *Journal of Religion and Spirituality in Social Work: Social Thought, 28*(1–2), 161–184.

Sheridan, M. J. (2004). Predicting the use of spiritually-derived interventions in social work practice: A survey of practitioners. *Journal of Religion and Spirituality in Social Work: Social Thought, 23*(4), 5–25.

Sheridan, M. J. (Ed.) (2013). Connecting spirituality and social justice: Conceptualizations and applications in macro social work practice. *Journal of Religion and Spirituality in Social Work: Social Thought,* September issue.

Shulman, L. (2012). *The skills of helping individuals, families, groups, and communities.* 7th edition. Belmont, CA: Cengage Learning.

Svare, G. M., Jay, S., Bruce, E., & Owens-Kane, S. (2003). Going below the tip of the iceberg: Social work, religion, and spirituality. *Social Thought: Journal of Religion in the Social Services, 22*(4), 19–26.

Svare, G. M., Hylton, M., & Albers, E. (2007). On our own: Social workers talk about spiritually sensitive practice within an organizational context. *Journal of Religion and Spirituality in Social Work: Social Thought, 26*(4), 95–113.

Wampold, B. E. (2010). The great psychotherapy debate: Models, methods, and findings. Hillsdale, NJ: Erlbaum.

6

The Ethics of Spiritually Sensitive Practice

A wise person is good to people who are good. She is also good to people who are not good. This is true goodness.

(Lao Tsu, in Walsh, 1999)

Whatever you do, you do to yourself.

(Buddha, in Walsh, 1999)

Ethics and Spirituality

Spirituality is defined in chapter 1 as a very general construct with many subareas that give it specificity and meaning. Unpacking the term "spirituality" can help us illuminate what it means and what it offers to practice. Two specific subareas of spirituality speak to the focus of this chapter. One of these subareas is morality and ethics. Our moral and ethical code, while not often as developed and clear to us as we would like, speaks to who we are spiritually. Most people develop a deeper sense of what they feel is right and wrong, fair and unfair, just and unjust as they mature and grow older. A commitment to social justice for the downtrodden, rejected, poor, sick, disabled, senile, and others who are disadvantaged is a fundamental belief of social workers and the NASW Code of Ethics. The moral and ethical qualities of being human are clearly viewed as elements of our spirituality. Our spirituality often conveys to us a sense of what is right and wrong. When we are faced with a choice, what is fair, peaceful, or egalitarian within an organization, community, or society?

The second subarea of spirituality central to this chapter is similar and involves our personal beliefs, especially our beliefs that form our positions on moral and ethical issues. These beliefs help to define our spirituality and often originate with our religious group, or perhaps a cultural, political, business, or other social group to which we belong. Religious and spiritual groups are major sources for our ethics and morality in today's world. The Golden Rule of Christianity is a good example. According to this rule, "We are to do unto others as we would have them do unto us." All of the major religions of the world have a version of the Golden Rule. Muhammad (Walsh, 1999, p. 143) said, for example, "Wish for others whatever you wish for yourself." The major religions have given focused attention to what they view as the most important ethics to live by (Smith, 1991; 2001; Walsh, 1999).

Confucius, the founder of Confucianism in China, who shaped the ethical code of the Chinese people over 2,500 years ago, proclaimed that a person's moral code determined, more than anything else, what living with wisdom was like (Smith, 1991; Walsh, 1999). Muhammad claimed that all actions are judged by their motives and the most important motives are to help and not harm others. Jesus taught that the last will be first and the first last in his kingdom, so we are to put others before ourselves. Even your enemy is to be loved and treated fairly. Mahatma Gandhi, a leading Hindu religious leader who led the liberation of India from colonization, and Dr. Martin Luther King Jr., a Baptist pastor in the South who led efforts to obtain basic rights to voting, housing, education, and employment for African Americans, succeeded by using an ethical strategy. Both practiced non-violent civil disobedience even when faced with violence from their adversaries. They believed that such an action brought integrity to themselves and respect and dignity for their adversaries, all of which had the greatest chance of bringing about reconciliation of their differences, their ultimate goal.

These are great moral principles to follow, but what are the benefits of doing this? What would motivate someone to follow such a code? It is widely believed that by living unethically and doing things that neglect and hurt others, we are likely to suffer as well. This could also happen in the reverse if others neglect or hurt us. The perpetrator likely ends up with unsettled, defensive, and guilty feelings and a feeling of dejection about themselves (McCullough, Pargament, & Thorensen, 2001; Walsh, 1999). For example, if we talk about someone behind their back in an unfair and negative way, we are likely left with similar feelings for ourselves; we may also be exposing another person to these ill thoughts who can end up thinking, what would he say about me behind my back? In other words, as the Buddha put it, "Whatever we do, we do to ourselves."

What are your ethics? Which ones are most important to you? How difficult is it to live by your ethics? Walsh (1999) identifies several ethical principles to strengthen our resolve as ethical people. These are personal ethics that have implications not only for people but organizations as well. At least three of these ethical principles are directly pertinent to our professional work. They include:

- Do no harm.
- Communicate to heal.
- Right a wrong.

Do No Harm

Do no harm is an important reminder of what we are in business for—helping others. It's important to keep this principle in our consciousness as we take steps on behalf of our clients, the agency that employs us, and all of the other people who may be affected by our actions (NASW, 2008). Doing no harm to our clients is usually straightforward, but not always. For example, we may suggest a resource that we think can help a client, and it turns out that it backfires. So the effects of some of our actions do not become apparent until later, or maybe even after a client is no longer receiving services. That alone would be a good reason to have follow-ups with clients after termination.

Also, thinking about the ethic of helping others, we are sometimes caught between what is best for the agency and what is best for the clients. The agency tells us to do one thing and the client's welfare suggests another action. This can easily happen if the agency with whom we are employed does not always put the client's needs before its own. Some for-profit agencies, for example, that limit the frequency of visits and the particular services the social worker offers are often dictated by financial circumstances—what services will get reimbursed and which ones will not.

Our help also goes beyond the client and agency and affects others affiliated in some way with our client (NASW, 2008). They could be other family members, neighbors, and sometimes adversaries such as a former spouse. When we think about how our actions taken for a client may affect others in the environment we come to realize these actions are not always positive for them either. For example, helping a client may be detrimental to that client's partner or another family member. So it's important to always keep in mind that our actions in helping and not hurting clients may involve other people as well.

Communicate to Heal

What we say to clients, employers, and others each day is often a reflection of our ethics and an expression of our spirituality. Many of the world religions refer to the importance of right speech as well as right action as morals and ethics (Walsh, 1999). No matter who we are talking to, our speech is a reflection of our morals. So one of our ethical challenges as social workers is to be conscious and sensitive about what we say to and about others. We can ask ourselves, from time to time, if we are communicating healing or something else that is counterproductive. Not only what we say but also how we say it is key to communicating healing. Verbal and non-verbal communication are both involved. "I" messages are always better than expressions that begin with "you," so that we openly share our own needs or position for the other person to consider and avoid using "you" statements, which may appear to be attacking or criticizing the other person, or at least putting them on the defensive. We want to express our thoughts and feelings in such a way that our counterpart can freely understand what is going on with us; we do not want to say something that is offensive to them. These behaviors are so much easier to talk about than to practice, as we are often emotional and have a tendency to speak with some impulsivity in our everyday conversations.

Healing words are easier to express to people with whom we are in good standing, especially when things are going well in our relationships. The challenges emerge when we are in conflict or conflict is covertly swarming beneath the surface. We are also challenged when we are communicating with an adversary, someone in a position of authority over us, or a stranger. In these cases, we may have little or no idea of whether our words are healing, partially because we do not know the person very well or at all. In all of these cases, communicating healing becomes our challenge. We need to be thinking about how we can be empathic and in touch with their thoughts and feelings. We need to be as conscious of the other person(s) and how they may be receiving the message as well. We need to work toward what Martin Buber, the Jewish theologian, calls an "I–Thou" relationship, in which we are focusing on what they need, not on ourselves (Buber & Kaufmann, 1970). We are trying to communicate in a loving manner and in a way that will inform the receiver of our message, its intent, and our concern for their well-being.

Right a Wrong

A third ethical expression that also reflects our spirituality is righting our wrongs by facing our mistakes or our part in any difficulties or conflicts, particularly in our work (Walsh, 1999). The wrong could be something like taking office supplies for our own personal use, lying about something when we were too embarrassed to admit fault, or misrepresenting a client when making a referral or doing advocacy. Sometimes it is even more serious, like passing on misinformation to others about a difficult colleague to hurt them, or taking time off from the job and notifying your employer that you were working. Righting a wrong can also be relevant to the wrongs expressed in our society and its institutions. For example, we need to be careful to not be reinforcing racist, sexist or other such disparaging remarks about someone from a minority group by agreeing with these remarks or remaining silent in response to them in our personal lives.

It's difficult but courageous to be open to the thought that we may be wrong, have said something insensitive, or sound self-serving. But we do these things and we usually know we did them when they happen, or later when we look back on our day. Denial that we did anything wrong is one handy defense, as is rationalizing that it was not anything important. Yet, the ethical thing to do is to face up to it, attempt to resolve and undo what we have done, and learn from it. Otherwise, it may just fester within us, nag our consciousness, and interfere with work with others that follows. Perhaps the hardest part of facing it is admitting we were in the wrong. That admission alone is often received unexpectedly and in a healing way by the relevant parties and will likely bring appreciation and disarm others of their own defensiveness. Reconciliation is much more likely to follow with the other parties as well; it brings relief and a resolve to try harder next time.

Controversies about Inclusion of Religion in Social Work

Religion is among the most controversial and challenging topics of discussion in American society. Many people have strong feelings about religion—either in favor of or against it. Further, if they are in favor of it they are usually in favor of their particular religious beliefs and practices, not religious beliefs generally. The United States was founded on the principle of religious freedom because of the denial of that right to those who lived in the European motherland in the 15th and 16th centuries and later. Those European countries demanded allegiance to a national religion, whether it was Catholicism, Anglicanism, Lutheranism, or another group.

Religious freedom and the freedom to choose one's own religious group are still cherished by many Americans today. Yet, in significant contrast, growing numbers are expressing the view that our nation is a Christian nation. This seems to be largely because it is the dominant religion, and perhaps there are perceptions of growing challenges from non-Christian religious groups for rights equal to those given Christians. For example, some religious groups want more recognition given to their religious holidays in the public schools and the workplace. We have a growing number of religious groups in the United States and many of them are increasing (Pew Research Center's Religion and Public Life Project, 2015). Some, such as Hinduism, Islam, and Buddhism, are also viewed as being very different from Christianity. In this regard, Christian privilege is a concept that is receiving greater attention as the number of religions is diversifying in the United States. Christian privilege is similar to white and male privilege and implies that one group has privileges over others, sometimes formal and other times informal (Riswold, 2015). Christian privilege refers to privileges Christians experience in the media, consumerism, schools, workplace, paid religious holidays, favoritism in government, and in many other ways that are in vogue for this group and not others.

Most Christians in this case are largely unaware of this sense of privilege because it is so ingrained in our societal fabric and they are the beneficiaries, while non-Christians may experience it as perceived rejection, neglect, or lower value because of their religious or non-religious affiliations.

The Ethics of Using Spiritual and Religious Interventions

Several studies have been conducted on the views and experiences of three groups in social work in terms of using spiritual and religious interventions—faculty, practitioners, and students in the United States and United Kingdom (U.K.). Sheridan (2009) prepared an extensive summary of such studies. This review also looked for evidence of adherence to specific ethical guidelines in using spiritual interventions. She found ten studies of practitioners revealing that the majority of them reported high or moderate use of most of the interventions. These practitioners represented professional organizations, state licensing boards, and practice-specific registries.

Two student studies found that students used many of these interventions as well but less often. In addition, Sheridan (2009) reviewed 18 studies that included the views of social work faculty, practitioners, and students on inclusion of spirituality in the social work curriculum. However, one limitation was that only three of these studies reported having full-time faculty in their sample. Overall, the findings were mixed, with some favoring inclusion while others reported being more hesitant or opposed. An elective course on spirituality tended to be the most frequently recommended option by faculty of how to include spirituality.

Faculty Views

In several social work programs across the country a significant amount of faculty debate is evident about whether to include spirituality and religion in the social work curriculum (Dudley & Helfgott, 1990; Sheridan, Wilmer, & Atcheson, 1994). Conservative Christian faculty and students, for example, often may want more recognition for their point of view, which may include greater consideration of the

---

Other Examples of Christian Privilege

(Medlin, 2013; Riswold, 2015)

- No need to worry about being accepted or welcomed in most social situations.

- Your beliefs are widely represented on TV and in other pop culture.

- Children engage in Christian activities at school (e.g. Christmas programs).

- Not being told you are going to hell.

- Can easily find counseling services catering to your beliefs.

- Can easily find information about how people of your faith have contributed to society.

- Talking about Islam or Judaism or Buddhism means we are talking about "the other."

- The majority of my classmates have been in a place of worship, and one relatively similar to my own.

- When I talk about God, I can safely assume that others know generally what I am talking about.

- When I say what I think about God's existence, no one will assume I am immoral.

role of faith and religious commitment to social work. They also sometimes feel disrespected and penalized by some faculty and students for their views (Thyer & Myers, 2009). Also, many of this group may want more attention given to a Christian approach to social work under certain circumstances, such as in faith-based agencies with Christian clients. These positions seem to be supported by a growing number of faith-based agencies existing across the country. In terms of the larger picture, this trend is likely to grow as more and more non-Christian religious groups choose social work as a profession. If for example, increasing numbers of Muslims choose to enroll in social work programs, perhaps they will be likely to discuss their religious beliefs and other preferences as practitioners as strongly as conservative Christians. Perhaps, class discussions about the role of religion in practice approaches should be supported in part to help students and faculty realize the ethical problems inherent in some of their wishes.

Another issue is that conservative religious faculty and students tend to assume some religious positions that are controversial in the professional arena of social work. They include such issues as abortion and LGBT rights. In these instances their positions are in conflict with the majority of social work faculty and are also viewed as being in conflict with the NASW Code of Ethics (NASW, 2008). Specific areas of the Code that may be sometimes in conflict with these controversial beliefs are client self-determination, dignity and respect, being non-judgmental, and some areas of social justice.

A counter-position of some social work educators is that the profession must remain neutral with regards to religious issues for a range of important reasons (Dudley & Helfgott, 1990; Sheridan, Wilmer, & Atcheson, 1994). The separation of church and state principle in the First Amendment of the U. S. Constitution is a point of contention for many social work educators, especially those employed in state universities. They believe this constitutional amendment precludes their ability to offer course material of a religious nature. This may be because they sense this material will have a leaning or bias toward one religious group such as Christianity and partake in proselytizing students. Many faculty are also concerned that including spiritual content in the curriculum will conflict with the mission of social work and the Code of Ethics.

The growing number of religions represented by students and faculty at universities and colleges is another reason given for remaining neutral; most social work faculty do not perceive themselves as knowledgeable about the variety of religions that exist; further, they feel they are unprepared to teach religious material. Many educators with these views may also not be religious themselves, which likely influences their desire to remain neutral (Canda & Furman, 2010; Sheridan, 2009). Other educators may be spiritual or religious but choose to be secularists in their work in social work education and practice (Hodge, 2009). The author of this book largely took this position during his first 25 years as a social work educator. Gradually, he came to terms with how important spirituality and religion are to clients and the helping process and he became more convinced that these topics can be taught without imposing particular religious beliefs on anyone.

Other related concerns or reservations about including spirituality in the social work curriculum are many. They include rigidity and dogmatism perceived to be embedded in religion, the blurring of professional boundaries, infringement of client self-determination, the tendency of religion to support the status quo and impede social justice; vague conceptualizations of spirituality; lack of preparation of social workers to address religion and spirituality; and the overcrowded state of the social work curriculum (Sheridan, 2009). When we examine how these ethical responsibilities are to be implemented in spiritually sensitive practice, we discover several ethical challenges.

Practitioners' Views

Practitioners are also at odds with each other on the ethics of introducing these topics in the helping process. Research indicates that social work practitioners are mostly open to a spiritually sensitive approach and may be more favorable to it in general than social work educators (Sheridan, 2009; Sheridan, Bullis, Adcock, Berlin, & Miller, 1992). Studies conducted by Canda and Furman (2010) found that a vast majority of their national sample of NASW members did not believe that integrating religion and spirituality in social work practice conflicts with the Code of Ethics, social work's mission, or the separation of church and state ruling. Other findings of Canda and Furman (1999; 2010) are reported in chapter 5 and many are pertinent to ethics. They found that one subgroup of practitioners in their study apparently was not in favor of a social work role in the clients' spiritual issues and presumably would be unlikely to view spirituality as an appropriate practice topic. Ethical problems are inherent in this subgroup's position, the most obvious one being that these practitioners would be unresponsive to both the spiritual concerns and spiritual resources of their clients. Additionally, they may have more difficulty developing their relationships with the clients who are more spiritual or religious if these issues are important to them.

Finally, Oxhandler, Parrish, Torres, and Achenbaum, (2015) reported on a national study of the views and behaviors of 442 licensed clinical social workers (LCSWs) on how they integrated spirituality and religion into their practice. The vast majority of these practitioners reported having positive views and attitudes about integrating spirituality and religion into their practice but lower levels of actual behavior supporting this integration. As an example, only 57 percent reported actually conducting a holistic assessment that included spiritual issues with each of their clients even though 81 percent reported knowing how to skillfully gather a history from their clients about their religious and spiritual beliefs and practices. Two variables emerged that may offer explanations for these discrepancies: the practitioners' reported degree of intrinsic religiosity (35 percent reported being moderately or very religious) and whether they had prior course work or continuing education on spirituality. Only 53 percent indicated that they had been adequately trained to integrate their clients' religion and spirituality into therapy.

Students' Views

Less is known about the views of social work students on these issues (Sheridan, 2009; Williams & Smolak, 2007). Two studies, one in the U.S. and the other in the U.K., reported on students' use of several spiritual interventions. While they were less likely to use these interventions than practitioners, this seems logical since they likely had less practice experience. The U.K. students tended to have lower favorable responses than the U.S. students on items like "Use religious or spiritual language or concepts," and "Share your own religious or spiritual values." This may be because citizens in the U.K. are thought to be significantly less religious than Americans. Another study conducted in the Southeast region of the country found that most of the students had positive attitudes about religion and spirituality personally but were unsure about how to introduce these topics in their practice (Kaplan & Dziegielewski, 1999). Another study of 208 students at two universities found that the students felt positively about these issues personally and had a tendency to support the use of religious interventions. (Sheridan & Amato-Von Hemert, 1999). Finally, a study by Stewart and Koeske (2006) of students in three universities found that students tended to be favorable to using spiritual and religious interventions in practice. These researchers also examined the predictors of positive views about inclusion of spirituality and religion in practice and found that students who were more religious and spiritual were more likely to be in favor of these interventions in practice. Students who were not affiliated with a religious group tended to be more unfavorable.

Ethical Issues in Using Sacred Readings in Practice

A special section on using sacred materials in social work is inserted here because it raises some important issues related to expressing spirituality and ethics. Sacred material such as passages in the Bible or Quran is often viewed by the respective religious group as the source of ultimate truth about our existence and how we are to live our lives. In other instances, these sacred passages offer important guidance and assistance alongside other non-religious sources.

When members of these religious groups are social workers, they tend to depend upon these sacred books and sometimes draw from them in their practice. The uses vary in purpose and in emphasis. Some examples of the ways that sacred readings can be used are covered next to help the reader reflect on how sacred readings can be both helpful and at times problematic if they are in conflict with the NASW Code of Ethics (NASW, 2008). Three examples are cited. First, sacred readings can be identified as a motivating force, or inspiration, by some social workers. Second, sacred readings can be an important component of some spiritual interventions. Finally, some social workers organize their entire practice approach around sacred readings.

As Inspiration for Some Social Workers

As discussed earlier in the book, many Christians, Jews, and Muslims have been raised in religious homes or have been exposed in other ways to sacred teachings during their childhood. These teachings often become powerful contributors to their worldviews and their choice of a career in social work. Many of the teachings of Jesus found in the New Testament offer examples. For instance, Jesus taught that those who were at the fringes of Palestinian society, such as the blind, lepers, the disabled, orphans, and widows, were to be treated with special care and dignity while those in powerful positions such as the religious leaders were to be confronted and reminded of their hypocrisy and undeserved privileges. "So the last will be first and the first last" (Matthew 20:16) was a frequent message Jesus taught his disciples. This sacred passage still has obvious implications for our times and is often held up as a highly important perspective by some social workers as to how we should respond to the powerless and oppressed in our own day. Muhammad also strongly advocated for helping vulnerable groups among the diverse communities in his life. Many people become social workers because they want to take this responsibility on in their own lives and it seems that using sacred readings in this way can be a very positive influence in one's practice. Possibly an exception to this would be if these sacred passages were used to discriminate against other groups such as the middle and upper classes, who need help as well but do not fit in these categories.

Sacred Readings and Spiritual Interventions

Several spiritual interventions are described in chapter 9. Some of them draw on sacred readings. For example, a client may be asked to select a mantra for meditation that comes from their favorite religious passages. Examples include "Lord have mercy," or "Allahu Akbar" (Arabic for "God is the greatest"), or shorter versions of these popular phrases. Lectio Divina (Latin for "Divine reading") is another example. This intervention, described more fully in chapter 9, can help a client reflect on sacred readings in a heartfelt way by involving the client in reading a short sacred passage over and over; the intention is to help them go more deeply, in a heartfelt way, to hear their Higher Power speak to them. Lectio Divina is a prayer form popular with some groups of Christians in their daily meditation or when they feel a need to face an important decision or circumstance. These efforts to incorporate sacred readings into the help that they are offered by social workers also seems ethically acceptable if the clients are voluntarily seeking this kind of help and if the sacred passages they use are of their own choosing.

Scriptural-Based Counseling

Religious sponsored counseling for individuals and families varies widely and usually is sponsored by faith-based agencies, other religious groups, or private practice settings. Often this type of counseling is designed to be relevant to particular sects of a religious group. Some popular religious counseling approaches are referred to as Christian counseling (for Christians) or Islamic counseling (for Muslims). It is noted that even this type of counseling varies widely among social workers, as illustrated in Scales and Kelly (2012). However, such counseling can be based on a belief in the absolute authority of the respective sacred scriptures.

Christian counseling is widespread in the U.S. and is usually popular with more conservative Christians such as Evangelicals. While most religious counseling approaches rely on sacred scriptures such as the Bible, approaches believing in Biblical authority seem to stand out as somewhat unique. In this case Biblical passages are usually viewed as the main or ultimate source of resolution or the answer to many of the client's problems. While such a counseling approach can be compatible with the Social Work Code of Ethics, there are instances when interpretations of scripture and social work ethics can come in conflict. Examples of such conflicts include LGBT relationships and husband/wife relationships in which wives are to submit to their husbands.

Ethics of Inclusion of Spirituality and Religion

Throughout the book, the concepts of spirituality and religion are presented so that they can be understood as important topics pertinent to the clients and communities that social workers serve. In chapters 2 and 13 emphasis is also given to how these concepts can be important to the professionals serving clients. The viewpoint held by the author is that spirituality and religion are personally important to most people and in many cases they can be empowering to clients. Further, the more social workers view spirituality as important to themselves, the more likely they will be to believe it is important to clients and their communities.

The controversies and challenges of teaching and practicing with these content areas (e.g. separation of church and state, social work mission, Code of Ethics, and others) will likely always be present to some degree and may even become more complicated in the future. Nevertheless, one way to help resolve these controversies and accelerate the incorporation of this material in the curriculum is to take a strong position on a major point emphasized throughout the book: **It's not about us, it's about our clients**. Whatever stake we may have in our own religious affiliation or spiritual perspective, it is not something to present to our clients. We are there for them. We must remember to be where the client is. If our clients are spiritual and/or religious and these topics are perceived by them as relevant to how we can help them, then we have an obligation to invite them into the helping process.

It's not about Us, It's about Our Clients

We should also recognize that our profession is made up of people of all spiritual and religious persuasions—Catholics and Protestants, Evangelical and Mainline Protestants, Christians and Jews, believers and atheists, Muslims, Hindus, Buddhists, and many others. The diverse background of social workers based on religion and spirituality is extensive. Inevitably, it involves a multitude of beliefs pertinent to ethics and spirituality. The self-determination of clients is a basic ethic that we all must support (unless self-determination is harmful to self, others, or society) (NASW, 2008). We should always encourage open and honest discussions among students, between students and faculty, among faculty, between practitioners and faculty, and among practitioners (Reamer, 2003). Such discussions do not seem to happen very often in most programs or localities so we must work harder to insure that they do. That will be a step forward for our profession. While the conflicts among social work groups are real and important, efforts should always be made to keep the dialogue open and respectful for all the different positions that social work faculty, practitioners, and students hold (Hodge, 2003; Reamer, 2003). While there are many differences evident among members of the profession, we must always choose dialogue and mutual understanding over judgment, rejection, withdrawal, silence, and isolation.

Perhaps, because these discussions can be difficult and end up being more unproductive than productive, strategic planning should precede them. Guidelines such as the following can be helpful:

- Initially identify reasonable objectives for a discussion such as to learn more about each other's religious beliefs and practices, to develop an appreciation for the diversity of beliefs and practices among participants, or to find common ground among the various religious beliefs of participants.
- Consider dividing a larger group into smaller subgroups of two to eight so that participants can feel more comfortable sharing their beliefs on a personal level; the smaller number also maximizes everyone's chance of sharing.
- Set up helpful ground rules such as: confidentiality, use "I" messages, respect what each participant shares about their beliefs and practices, and ask questions rather than make statements about what each person shares.
- Encourage participants to give feedback to each other, especially when strengths are evident in what other participants share.
- Avoid using these sessions for participants to promote one religious group over another or for aiming excessive criticism at any group or individual participant.

NASW Code of Ethics as a Resource

The NASW (National Association of Social Workers) Code of Ethics is a founda-tional resource of ethical guidance for all social workers (NASW, 2008). It speaks in general terms, and leaves considerable flexibility for social workers to interpret whether their practice is ethical (Horner & Kelly, 2007). The entire Code is relevant to spirituality services and is organized around responsibilities to different groups including clients, colleagues, practice settings, professionals, and the profession. Several ethical sections of this Code that are considered most important to spiritu-ally sensitive practice are highlighted below.

Ethical Responsibilities to Clients

The major ethical responsibilities especially relevant to *clients* (with emphasis added by the author) are (NASW, 2008):

- **Commitment to clients** (section 1.01) including "to promote the well-being of clients." "In general, clients' interests are primary" except when society or a specific legal obligation supersede them. (A client's well-being includes their spiritual and religious well-being.)
- **Self-determination** (section 1.02) including "to promote the clients' right to self-determination and assist clients in their efforts to identify and clarify their goals" (including any spiritual goals).
- **Informed consent** (section 1.03) about the range of services available and the areas of interest that can be explored (including spirituality).
- **Competence of the social worker** (section 1.04) is important "within the boundaries of their education, training, license, certification, consultation received, supervised experiences or other relevant experiences." "When gen-erally recognized standards do not exist with respect to emerging areas of

---

Ethics Scenario 1

You are assigned to a Muslim family that has been referred to you in a family agency. Their teenage daughter was being harassed at school for wearing a hijab or religious headscarf, an important religious custom to this family. She has also been frequently absent from school during the last several weeks, and it was during the time of Ramadan. You meet the family and find out that the father is the spokesperson for the family. You want to find out how both parents and the teenage daughter view these reported problems and how they can be resolved. What spiritual questions would you ask to help this family?

Ethics Scenario 2

You are the social worker (SW) meeting with Maria, a Caucasian client who lives in a rural area and belongs to a small Southern Baptist church. Maria has AIDS and has two children who are HIV-positive. As the SW, you ask, "How do you do it [keep going as a single mother with these overwhelming circumstances]?" Maria's response is "The good Lord will give me only as much as I can handle." As the SW, what are your thoughts about this comment and how would you explore it as a potential spiritual strength based on Maria's religious background?

---

practice, social workers should exercise careful judgment and take responsible steps, including appropriate education, research, training consultation and supervision, to ensure the competence of their work and to protect clients from harm." This is important in the area of spiritually sensitive practice and can be accomplished by taking spirituality courses in social work programs, participating in staff training and continuing education workshops, consulting others who are knowledgeable about the topic, and taking advantage of other opportunities to learn more about this practice area.

- **Cultural competence and social diversity** (section 1.05) are important in many areas, including spirituality and religion, especially in light of the wide range of ways that spirituality and religion are represented and expressed among different cultural groups. Social workers should have knowledge of the clients' cultures and be able to demonstrate competence in the provision of services that are sensitive to clients' cultures, including the spiritual and religious aspects.
- **Conflicts of interest** (section 1.07) are important to address in many areas (including not allowing a social worker's spiritual biases to interfere in the helping process).

Ethical Responsibilities to Colleagues

Among the major ethical responsibilities to *colleagues* including *peers, supervisees, supervisors, and others,* are other sets of ethical responsibilities (NASW, 2008). While all of them are relevant to spiritually sensitive practice as well, two seem to have the greatest relevance. They are:

- **Respect** (section 2.01) for colleagues and their views on a range of areas (including their spiritual and religious positions).
- **Unethical Conduct of Colleagues** (section 2.11) should be addressed if the social worker is either disrespectful to others (in several areas including

the spiritual area) or the social worker is being disrespected or discrimi-nated against by colleagues (in several areas including the spiritual area).

CSWE Accreditation Standards as a Resource

The accreditation standards of CSWE (the Council on Social Work Education) also support efforts to assist clients with spiritual and religious issues (CSWE, 2015). A summary of many of these issues is provided in chapter 5. Because some of these standards are pertinent to ethical issues, it is important to highlight them. The accreditation standards have a section on competencies that students are expected to demonstrate in practice. Nine competencies are identified in the 2015 report, along with competency-based behaviors that give more specificity to these com-petencies. Some of the competency-based standards and behaviors pertinent to ethics and spiritually sensitive practice are identified next (CSWE, 2015).

Understand Ethical and Professional Behavior (Competency 1)

- Make ethical decisions by applying the standards of the NASW Code of Ethics, relevant laws and regulations, models for ethical decision-making, ethical conduct of research, and additional codes of ethics as appropriate to context (including a code of ethics for spiritual practice).
- Use reflection and self-regulation to manage personal values and maintain professionalism in practice situations.
- Demonstrate professional demeanor in behavior; appearance; and oral, written, and electronic communication.
- Use supervision and consultation to guide professional judgment and behavior (including consulting experts on spiritually sensitive practice).

Engage Diversity and Difference in Practice (Competency 2)

- Apply and communicate understanding of the importance of diversity and difference in shaping life experiences in practice at the micro, mezzo, and macro levels (including spirituality/religion).
- Present oneself as a learner and engage clients and constituencies as experts of their own experiences (including their understanding of their spirituality).
- Apply self-awareness and self-regulation to manage the influence of per-sonal biases and values in working with diverse clients and constituencies.

Advance Human Rights and Social, Economic, and Environmental Justice (Competency 3)

- Engage in practices that advance social, economic, and environmental justice (including practices that are spiritually based).

Engage in Policy Practice (Competency 5)

- Assess how social welfare and economic policies impact the delivery of and access to social services (spiritual policies too).
- Apply critical thinking to analyze, formulate, and advocate for policies that advance human rights and social, economic, and environmental justice (spiritual policies too).

Engage, Assess, Intervene, and Evaluate in Practice with Individuals, Families, Groups, Organizations, and Communities (Competencies 6–9)

- Apply knowledge of human behavior and the social environment, person-in-environment, and other multidisciplinary theoretical frameworks to engage, assess, intervene, and evaluate clients and constituencies. (Infuse these frameworks with spiritually sensitive practices.)
- Use empathy, reflection, and interpersonal skills to effectively engage diverse clients and constituencies.
- Develop mutually agreed-on intervention goals and objectives based on the critical assessment of strengths, needs, and challenges within clients and constituencies (including spiritual interventions).
- Select appropriate intervention strategies based on the assessment, research knowledge, and values and preferences of clients and constituencies (including spiritual interventions).
- Select and use appropriate methods for evaluation of outcomes (including spiritual outcomes).
- Apply evaluation findings to improve practice effectiveness at the micro, mezzo, and macro levels (including spiritual findings).

Specific Ethical Issues in Spiritually Sensitive Practice

When working in these ethical areas, Gardner (2011) recommends that social workers look for common ground between their views and those of their clients as a way of maintaining a creative tension. Also she suggests that practitioners be aware of how their own spirituality could lead them to reflect critically on their clients' spirituality. Introspective questions could be asked, such as, "Why am I struggling to hear and accept that this is this person's experience?" and "How am I making sure that I am not assuming my spirituality is what the person needs?"

While the NASW Code of Ethics and the CSWE Accreditation standards speak to ethical principles related to spiritual interventions in general, there is no widely agreed upon specific code of ethics or guidelines for such interventions (Sheridan, 2009). When we examine more closely ethical problems inherent in

spiritually sensitive practice, we can detect numerous potential challenges needing attention. Canda, Nakashima, and Furman (2004), analyzing qualitative
responses of their national study in 1997, identified several challenges identified by
practitioners:

- not imposing the social worker's perspective;
- the necessity of worker competence;
- fitting spirituality to the timing and goals of clients' developmental
  processes;
- establishing a relationship including mutual understanding about spirituality prior to engagement on this topic;
- focusing only on a client-centered engagement of this topic (not worker-
  centered).

Beginning efforts have been made to develop such guidelines and some of these
efforts are described next.

Canda and Furman Framework

A central question to ask is, when is it ethically acceptable to discuss spiritual and
religious issues with clients? Canda and Furman (2010, p. 292) created a helpful
framework for determining under what circumstances a specific intervention
would be ethical. They begin with a list of four different conditions. They are: A) The
client has *not* expressed interest in the topic; B) The client has expressed interest in
spirituality; C) A spiritually sensitive relationship is well established; D) The worker
has relevant qualifications for particular spiritually based interventions. Obviously,
the first condition is the least likely one to prepare a worker to proceed to discuss
spiritual issues, while a combination of all of the last three conditions are the most
ideal set of conditions for discussing spiritual issues. Of course, if condition A is
where a practitioner is with a client and there seem to be no cues that spiritual or
religious concerns are relevant to this client, the appropriate way to respond would
be to not bring up these issues. However, if condition A is present early in a relationship with a client and spirituality has not yet been explored, the engagement
phase, covered in chapter 7, can be an important place to explore whether spiritual
issues are relevant to helping a particular client.

   Possibly, one way to respond to this spectrum of conditions is to explore how
to move from condition A to conditions B, C, and D although they do not make
up a logical continuum. In this case it would be best to start with condition D. If
the worker is not qualified to practice in a spiritually sensitive way, then the best
response would be to prepare for such practice. Some of the ways that training can
be accomplished are discussed in chapter 5. Next, condition C is something that is
to be developed with clients; training how to practice in a spiritually sensitive way
will help prepare a practitioner to do this. Then, once conditions C and D are met,

a practitioner can respond appropriately with clients who express an interest in discussing spiritual issues.

The Canda and Furman framework also identifies seven fairly typical scenarios that are possible options for offering spiritual activities. One example is direct use of spiritual activities upon the client's request and a second one is direct use of spiritual activities by the worker's invitation. This framework then asks and answers which of the four conditions are needed to implement each of these seven scenarios. For example, a private spiritually based activity by the worker before a session, such as meditation, would be ethically appropriate under any of these conditions, while direct use of spiritual activities by a worker's invitation would require conditions B, C, and D. This framework can be expanded to include several other scenarios, especially those most likely to occur in your agency as a way to further reflect on what is ethically sound practice. It is important to add that the authors always state that caution should be pursued with any of these scenarios.

Expansion of Canda and Furman Framework

By adding additional dimensions to this framework, further opportunities can be offered for reflecting on ethically sound practice. Among other things, other expectations, including issues surrounding the context of a particular agency, can be added to the analysis. The author proposes that five expectations be addressed in a timely fashion, the last three are not included in the Canda and Furman framework. These five expectations are:

Expectation 1: The worker is trained or otherwise prepared to practice in a spiritually sensitive way.

Expectation 2: The clients want to discuss spiritual issues whether they bring them up or not.

Expectation 3: Spirituality or religion are relevant to the problem that the clients are working on.

Expectation 4: The clients' issues are consistent with the agency sponsor's overall purpose and any positions they formally take on spiritual matters.

Expectation 5: There are no obvious biases evident in the worker's practice with a client, whether revealed explicitly or implicitly. If their religious background is similar to their clients', social workers may need to scrutinize their practice even more than normal because practitioner biases can be more easily expressed in these situations.

The first expectation, being prepared to practice in a spiritually sensitive way, necessarily precedes all of the other expectations. This has already been discussed and is a most important starting point. Next, a process of time is likely needed to be able to come to the conclusion that the other expectations are met as well. However, they all should be addressed in a timely fashion and resolved before a contract with a client is worked out. Expectation 2 usually takes time, skillful practice, and some important exchanges between the worker and client. The engagement phase covered in chapter 7 discusses several techniques that can be used to help determine whether or not the client wants to discuss their spiritual issues. While spirituality issues could be raised in later phases of help, they are most likely to be raised in the initial engagement.

While expectation 2 is being addressed, expectation 3, spirituality's relevance to the client's problem at hand, usually needs some time of exploration and assessment as well. The question here is whether spiritual issues are relevant to a case. These issues could be relevant in numerous ways, so all possibilities should be considered. For example, are there spiritual supports—people or organizations that can be enlisted to join to help a client? Are there spiritual or religious issues beneath the surface that have an influence on the problem at hand, positively or negatively? Does the client seem to have strengths that are spiritual in nature that are important to engage?

Expectation 4, consistency of clients' issues with the agency sponsor's policies, is actually an expectation, like the first one, that should be initially addressed in a proactive way. Suggestions for developing policies and procedures to address spiritual issues of clients are introduced in chapter 5 and discussed in more detail in chapter 10. Expectation 5, avoiding spiritual or religious biases of the practitioner, is addressed in several chapters and is a common thread throughout the book. Chapter 7 devotes attention to how workers can aid themselves in avoiding expressions of spiritual biases. As has been said before, biases can emerge either through commission or omission. A worker failing to encourage a client to discuss their spiritual issues when they are relevant can be as detrimental as the introduction of the worker's own beliefs and other biases in an attempt to help. Expectation 5 is the most complex and difficult one to address, is an ongoing challenge to work on, and requires continual vigilance.

Expanding Canda and Furman's framework even further, conditions necessary for ethically appropriate practice could be considered at each of the phases of practice—engagement, assessment, intervention, and evaluation—because circumstances are very different as one moves from emphasis on one phase to another phase. By examining conditions in this way we can help workers consider ethical practice at each phase. Conditions proposed for each phase or component are described in Table 6.1.

Faith-Based Programs and Ethical Challenges

Faith-based agencies are still controversial, particularly around ethical issues like introducing and in some cases imposing the agency's religious position on clients. Expectation 5, described above, may be particularly challenging for faith-based

Table 6.1   Conditions for Ethical Practice by Phases

1. **Engagement**— conditions for bringing up or responding to a spiritual issue with a client:	**Conditions** • Client initiates or brings up a spiritual concern. • Worker indicates that spiritual concerns or issues could be discussed if it helps the client and the client wants to consider it. • Worker picks up on indirect spiritual message of the client, such as carrying a Bible or expressing something like "I would not survive without the Lord." In these cases, the worker's response should be limited to exploring if it has relevance to the type of help the client needs.
2. **Assessment**— conditions for exploring a spiritual concern in more depth:	**Conditions** • Client identifies a spiritual topic relevant to the problem to explore more fully. • A question could possibly be asked about a spiritual topic that has been indirectly mentioned, such as a religious conflict about using birth control. In these instances, the client could be asked if this topic could be explored further because of its possible relevance.
3. **Intervention**— conditions for using a spiritual intervention:	**Conditions** • Client fully understands the intervention and chooses to use it. • Worker recommends a relevant spiritual intervention, explains it fully and how it can help, and suggests it for the client as a possible intervention. Then, the client chooses to use the intervention or not.
4. **Evaluation**— conditions for evaluating a client's spiritual well-being or evaluating the effectiveness of a spiritual intervention:	**Conditions** • If the evaluation is about the client's spiritual well-being, the intent of the evaluation can be explained, including some of the questions to be asked. The client chooses whether or not to participate in the evaluation and is given the option to decline it. • If it is an evaluation of an intervention the client has participated in, the worker explains the importance of the evaluation as a standard of practice and asks the client to participate. The results of the evaluation are shared with the client.

agencies to implement successfully. Expectation 5 refers to having no obvious biases evident in the worker's practice with a client whether revealed explicitly or implicitly. Sherwood (1998), a social worker, shares his struggles with separating his own religious beliefs as an Evangelical Christian from his client's beliefs when employed in both a Christian counseling setting and a secular work setting. In the former setting, for example, he believes he must be careful not to respond too quickly to a client's request for prayer as being genuine on the client's part; he realizes prayer could be used as a defensive position of spiritual denial. In a secular setting he realizes that he has an ethical responsibility to respect the integrity of his own values, his clients' values, and the values of the agency setting. Yet he wants to be bold enough to bring up religious and spiritual issues when they are warranted. He believes that clients often need permission to share spiritual issues they need help with and he feels he has the responsibility to help them tell their story and identify all relevant issues and resources. He concludes that for spiritual and religious assessments and interventions to take place he needs to be open to them, attuned to them, comfortable talking about these issues, and skillful in the way that he does it by being sensitive and appropriate to both the client's values as well as his own.

A closer look at faith-based organizations and how they handle Expectation 5 seems worthy of attention and may be helpful to *all* practitioners using a spiritually sensitive approach. Some studies have focused on the welfare reform legislation passed in the mid-1990s, with shifts in federal policy to Charitable Choice, which allows faith-based agencies to include a religious component in their human service approach (Bielefeld, 2006). This provision among other things eliminated regulatory and contracting obstacles to the participation of faith-based organizations in delivering social services. Some proponents of faith-based agencies suggested that these agencies may be able to offer more than secular agencies because they would be more holistic in their approach and thus have more influence in transforming their clients than secular groups. Proponents also believed that faith-based groups could establish more caring and enduring relationships with clients and they would likely have a more motivated staff with a greater capacity to instill a spirit of hope (Bielefeld, 2006; Netting, O'Connor, & Yancey, 2006).

Some articles have focused on the influence of faith in human service programs related to the Charitable Choice provision, including a study by Hugen and Venema (2009). In addition, Netting (2002) focuses on the use of religiously oriented language in social service programs, and Sherr, Singletary, and Rogers (2009) examined the issue of proselytizing within social work agencies. These articles are relevant to the ethical issues of a spiritually sensitive approach and raise at least two important questions. First, how can the religious orientation of such agencies enrich the services provided to clients? And second, how do these agencies avoid imposing their religious orientation and beliefs on clients with a different religious orientation?

Findings of Hugen and Venema (2009) in their study of 1,110 faith-based programs revealed that over half viewed spirituality as central in their programs. They also looked at how these agencies described the faith-based component. One-third of programs communicated faith implicitly, mostly through acts of caring toward clients, and another one-fourth communicated their faith explicitly and conveyed the view that the role of faith was critical to changes clients could make. Another focus of the study was on how much direct exposure clients had with faith-related elements of the programs. These findings indicated the agencies more frequently communicated faith implicitly rather than explicitly. However, the authors indicated that these agencies differed widely in terms of the intensity of their exposure of faith-related programmatic elements that included processes, values, and relationships.

The survey questions used in the Hugen and Venema (2009) study can serve as helpful guidelines in clarifying when a faith-based program and a spiritually based program in general may be overstepping its ethical boundaries. These different guidelines are important to assess, especially when a program is funded with public money. The programs in this study responded most frequently (33 percent) that "Faith is revealed through acts of caring for participants rather than by any explicit mention of religious or spiritual matters in the program." This seems positive and in keeping with social work ethics. However, another group of programs (26 percent) indicated "Faith is an explicit and critical part of our work with participants, but staff respect the right of participants not to participate in the religious or spiritual aspects of the program." Programs agreeing to this position seemed to be implementing an ethically questionable effort because clients may not have felt comfortable asserting their disagreements with the agency's position because of a power differential and a fear of being rejected from the program or of being relegated to a less valued status. These "explicit efforts" would need to be very cautiously offered to allow clients the complete freedom to say no, which may not be possible in the real world for the reasons noted above. Another smaller group of programs (14 percent) in the Hugen and Venema study indicated that "Faith is an explicit, critical, and mandatory part of our work with participants who choose to participate in the program." In these cases, it would appear to be clearly crossing the ethical line in imposing faith elements, unless these faith elements were based on the clients' faith and not the agency's. Another even smaller number (8 percent) agreed that "Faith is explicitly mentioned to participants, and they are invited to inquire more fully about religious or spiritual matters outside of the program." This position seems to be a reasonable way for these programs to offer their faith-based elements with clients, allowing them to openly choose or reject them.

While many of these 1,110 agencies offered faith-based elements in their programs, the nature of these elements was not shared in detail (Hugen & Venema, 2009). What was partially shared were ethical statements reflecting different points of view. Responses to such statements provide a glimpse of some of the ways faith-based elements were offered. Each statement was followed by a Likert scale for recording responses (0 = never, 1 = rarely, 2 = sometimes, 3 = quite often, 4 = very frequently). The mean or average score for the respondents is described after each statement in the box on p. 145.

Overall, all of the items in the box on p. 145 have scores of 2.05 or less, indicating that respondents were, on average, reporting that these practices were sometimes or rarely used. Because these are average scores, some individual scores are above and some below these averages. Some agencies were likely to implement these practices quite often and some rarely. Also, what is interesting about these statements is that the faith-based elements are always written in such a way that they refer to the agencies' faith and beliefs, not the clients'.

Questions need to be raised about how these agencies and others like them respond to the faith and beliefs of the clients, especially when they are different from those of the agency. Spiritually sensitive practice is based on helping the clients focus on their own beliefs, not those of the agencies. Looking closely at these statements, it's possible that there may be room in some of these practices for clients to express their own spiritual practices when they are distinct from the agency.

Client Exposure to Faith-Related Program Elements

(Hugen & Venema, 2009)

Program participants join in group prayer as an element of our program. (2.05)

Program participants are invited to worship services that are separate from the program. (1.88)

Program participants learn to discuss faith-related beliefs, values, or traditions as an element of our program. (1.80)

Program participants are encouraged to make personal changes in attitudes and behaviors that are based clearly and openly on the faith-related values of our organization. (1.82)

Program participants are encouraged to make personal faith-related commitments. (1.72)

Program participants are encouraged to make personal changes in attitudes and behaviors that are understood but unspoken as being based on faith-related values of our organization. (1.69)

Program participants pray or meditate as an element of our program. (1.60)

Program participants study faith-related texts as an element of our program. (1.50)

Program participants join in worship services as an element of our program. (1.39)

For our program to be successful, program participants must undergo a faith-related transformation. (1.06)

Program participants are required to participate in mandatory faith elements of our program. (0.78)

This is an important overall question to ask faith-based agencies. How much commitment do faith-based agencies have to helping clients work with or engage their own spiritual beliefs and practices when they are different from the agency's?

Sherr, Singletary, and Rogers (2009) investigated whether faith-based agencies cross the ethical line and actually openly proselytize to clients to adopt the agency's religious beliefs and practices against their will. They conducted a case study of a Christian nonprofit agency. They found that this agency was crossing the ethical boundaries and concluded by recommending the following ethical guidelines for practices offered by religious organizations. These guidelines seem very appropriate for other agencies to consider.

- **Clarify worker roles up front**: At the outset of a professional relationship, social workers should negotiate exactly what they are doing and be aware that client self-determination, worker competence, and avoidance of dual relationships are important requirements in providing ethical practice.
- **Avoid opportunities for unethical practice**: Social workers should avoid putting themselves in positions in which clients may feel they are being covertly or overtly pressured to discuss religious beliefs.
- **Acknowledge the potential for unethical practice**: Social workers need to openly acknowledge the potential for unethical practice with each other and with clients. They should also create a milieu of open dialogue about the inherent difficulties of practicing ethically with religious organizations.
- **Create a mechanism for ongoing confidential review with clients**: Social workers should get regular feedback from clients about their experiences, positive and negative, working with social workers at religious organizations.

Sherr, Singletary, and Rogers (2009) offer an important recommendation for practitioners to consider. "Assume that ethical problems can easily emerge and proactively stress the importance of client self-determination, acknowledge the potential for unethical practice on religious issues, especially with faith-based organizations, encourage open dialogue with clients about this possibility, and build in opportunities for regular feedback from the clients on their experiences generally."

Netting (2002) suggests that consumers of faith-based agencies consider asking some questions about faith-based agencies during their first contact. Such questions are likely to bring some balance in the power differential between the agency and client. She identifies several helpful questions for consumers to ask during their first contact or earlier. Some of them follow:

- What does it mean that you are a faith-based provider?
- What faith do you represent?
- What will you do differently than a secular provider of services?
- Will you be careful not to make assumptions about me, to assume that I should share your beliefs, your faith?
- Will you still provide services to me if I do not live up to your moral standards? If I do not profess your faith? If I am skeptical of your faith tradition?
- Will you listen to me even if I do not believe as you believe?
- Will you meet my needs even if they are different than yours?
- Will you be okay if I do not meet your needs?

It may not be easy or realistic for most clients to ask these rather direct and confronting questions even though they are excellent questions to ask. If that is the case, it would be appropriate for faith-based agencies to anticipate that clients may be wondering about some of these questions; in response they could proactively address them in an initial orientation to the agency or during the initial contact, because these discussions can be helpful in clarifying many of these ethical issues.

Religious Beliefs with Ethical Challenges

When people take positions on some social and biological issues, a deep divide can become apparent, sometimes in the extremes. How people view these issues and their solutions can easily bring controversy. They reveal sometimes in uncanny ways what people believe is right or wrong. Strong religious views often can influence these varying and competing positions and they can be based on many things, including beliefs, membership with a religious group, and other forms of peer influence.

At times, social workers differ with each other on these issues and in even more instances we may differ with our clients particularly on the solutions to take. When these issues become pertinent and often central to helping our clients, ethical challenges become critical. In many instances, religion and spirituality are relevant influences. A few examples of clients' ethical challenges and possible religious relevance may help here.

- **Abortion:** Should the decision about an abortion be decided between a pregnant woman and her doctor entirely, should a restricted option be available only under certain circumstances, or should abortion not be an option at all? Existing American law provides the right to an abortion but this right is gradually becoming more restricted by state laws and the courts. Among many people, religious beliefs play a role in their position of favoring the moral right of the embryo to be protected. Among many others, religious beliefs support the mother's right to her own life and well-being as well as her right to choose for herself.
- **Birth Control:** Should birth control be banned for everyone but marital couples, or is it a right of all women and their partners to choose a birth control method? Again, religious views can inform these questions from both sides in a way that may be similar to the abortion issue.
- **Medical Interventions versus Religious Interventions:** Should a medical intervention recommended by licensed medical personnel always be the preferred or even mandated option for treating a person, or can it be replaced by prayer, a special diet, or another non-medical, religious intervention if that is what a client chooses? A patient's religious affiliation and beliefs often influence how they proceed in accepting or rejecting a medical intervention. This ethical issue particularly becomes important when the medical intervention may be necessary to save someone's life.

- **Euthanasia:** Euthanasia refers to a practice of ending one's life to relieve pain and suffering. Should life be continued against the will of a person who chooses to die because of unbearable chronic pain or severe brain damage? Or should the affected person have the right to choose to live or die? Some religious groups believe that life is sacred and to be preserved above all else. Others believe that a person has a moral right to choose what is best for them, including terminating their life.
- **LGBT Issues:** Should LGBT people be allowed to marry each other if they wish or should this be denied them because sacred scriptures, interpreted by some, view marriage only being between a woman and man? Some conservative religious groups interpret their sacred texts to condemn homosexual behaviors while other religious groups believe that every person is a child of God and must be respected and valued for who they are. The latter group also believes that the Bible and other sacred texts do not take a clear and convincing position on this issue.
- **Death Penalty:** Should a person who willfully kills someone be eligible for execution under some circumstances or should their lives always be spared? Religion can play a role in this decision on either side of the issue. Some religious groups believe that every life is sacred and thus should be spared in all cases, while another religious view follows the Biblical passage, Leviticus 24:20, known as the "an eye for an eye" passage in the Old Testament, in which "The one who has inflicted the injury must suffer the same injury."
- **Religious Practices in Public Places:** At a macro level, should students' religious practices such as saying prayers or wearing a head covering for religious reasons be permitted in the public schools? Or should prayers, head coverings, and other religious practices be disallowed because of the doctrine of separation of church and state?
- **Relations between Marital Partners:** Should the relationship between marital partners be egalitarian in that neither person has a power advantage over the other? Or, based on the religious traditions of some conservative Christians, Hindus, Jews, and Muslims, is the male considered the head of the household and the person through whom a social worker may be expected to speak directly, with the woman deferring to her husband's words in such conversations?
- **Women as Leaders in Religious Organizations:** Should women be denied a leadership role, especially a cleric position, because this is part of the culture of some religious organizations? Or should they be encouraged to find a religious organization that welcomes them to explore such a leadership role, where their talents can be fully expressed?

These and other ethical questions can be complex and bring incredibly different responses from different people and groups. For example, even the terminology

One Person's Viewpoint

The truth is that male religious leaders have had—and still have—an option to interpret holy teachings either to exalt or subjugate women. They have, for their own selfish ends, overwhelmingly chosen the latter. Their continuing choice provides the foundation or justification for much of the pervasive persecution and abuse of women throughout the world.

(President Jimmy Carter, 2009)

used to simply identify these issues alone can reveal some of the differences. Hodge (2003), for example, presented some of the ethical issues separating Evangelical Christians from other social workers. Here is how he identified some of the value conflicts that some social workers are likely to face:

- social workers who believe in egalitarian marriages interacting with couples who affirm complementary marriages;
- social workers who believe in a biological origin of homosexuality interacting with people who believe that homosexuality is socially constructed;
- social workers who are morally opposed to spankings interacting with clients who affirm the importance of spankings as a disciplinary method;
- social workers who believe that morality and law are socially constructed working with clients who believe in divine revelation.

How We Can Help with Ethical Challenges

Let's consider how a social worker can be effective when they are assigned to help clients with such ethical challenges. One basic and critical question for social workers to consider is, when does client self-determination end and either societal law or the Code of Ethics preempt it? In most cases, it is not up to the social worker to decide. We are expected to help the clients make their own decisions and help them realize when their positions are in conflict with social work values and societal laws. We are to assist clients in coming to terms with a range of issues before them, some being their basic morals and ethics and how they may be in conflict with others'

What Language Would You Use?

What are your reactions to Hodge's wording of these ethical differences? How would you identify them using your own words and understanding? In what ways do the words that you may use, in themselves, create problems in overcoming these ethical conflicts?

morals and ethics. Our role involves carefully hearing and clearly understanding the client's side, their moral code, and how it affects their decisions. We also have a responsibility to help them explore the other side(s) that conflicts with their position, whether it is a societal law or professional ethics. When we are assisting two clients, such as an estranged couple or a parent and child, we are also helping them understand each other's positions and instances in which their positions may be different.

A process of assistance to a client when a religious or spiritual issue is relevant could begin with encouraging them to openly and freely tell their story (Bein, 2008). What do they perceive the problem or their situation to be, and what are the various ways that they and their significant others view it from a spiritual and religious perspective? How specifically do their religious and spiritual beliefs play a part? How important are these beliefs to them and their significant others? How do these beliefs influence their perspective? Are there alternative spiritual or religious beliefs that could also be considered in this regard? A report in the box below of a social work student on a visit to a Seventh Day Adventist Church illustrates some of these issues if the client belonged to this church.

Two ethical areas, abortion and LGBT rights, are perhaps among the most controversial in social work education, and religion and spirituality usually play a role in both controversies. These ethical issues are among the most controversial among social worker faculty and students and they often become evident in classroom and hallway discussions in social work programs. The political positions of more liberal

---

Visit to a Seventh Day Adventist Church

(Patrick Swan)

After visiting a Seventh Day Adventist Church, a student journaled:

A belief that is apparently commonly held within this denomination is that people's lives and destinations are predetermined. "God has a plan for me" was a line in one of the songs, for instance. As I mentioned, the pastor spoke about how it was asinine to try to shorten or prolong life. I feel like this could create an issue with a social worker working with a client with these beliefs. If a person held this ideology, they may think taking action to better their situations or preventing avoidable hardship may be futile. Nevertheless, I think this could be an opportunity to reframe a situation with a client. A possible scenario may be a client who has been diagnosed with diabetes believing that changing his eating habits is pointless. A way of reframing this in reference to the client's relationship to their Higher Power could be to ask if they believe God would want them to suffer needlessly. This denomination seems to also prescribe to free will, so that strategy may be effective.

professionals, the vast majority, seem often to be at odds with those who are more religiously conservative, particularly Evangelical Christians (Hodge, 2002; Reamer, 2003).

While Reamer (2003) recognizes this reality among social workers, he makes an important distinction that is also made by the author earlier in the chapter. We must distinguish acknowledging differences among social workers about their ethical positions on abortion, LGBT issues, and other matters from how we help clients. We must always be prepared and willing to help clients decide for themselves where they stand on these issues as they address their problems and what their options for solutions are. For example, if a social worker is uncomfortable with the rights of LGBT people to marry, this position must not interfere with helping a LGBT couple decide for themselves whether they wish to get married. Similarly, a social worker could be in favor of LGBT rights and be working with parents of an LGBT individual who are unwilling to accept their adult child's sexual orientation; this worker also has an obligation to help these parents decide for themselves how they will view their adult child, including examining all of their options. As Reamer (2003, p. 429) points out, "social workers should be as willing to serve and assist people whose values and lifestyles are different from their own—whether the clients are more or less liberal or conservative politically, or more or less religious in their beliefs and practices—as they are people whose values and lifestyles are similar." Reamer also reminds us, "In our professional capacity we do not have the right to interfere with clients whose views and actions differ from ours so long as the clients' views and actions do not violate social work's mission and ethics" (p. 430).

Conclusion

This chapter focuses on moral and ethical issues that can come into play in spiritually sensitive practice. Our moral and ethical code usually has a strong association with our spirituality and this code has been introduced in chapter 1 as one of the manifestations of spirituality. Our beliefs are also an important topic of the chapter, particularly our beliefs that form our positions on moral and ethical issues. Religious and spiritual groups are major sources for the ethics and morality of many people. Inclusion of religion and spirituality in social work education and professional practice brings controversies for some people and often such inclusion raises ethical issues, such as: Is this a violation of separation of church and state? And can religious beliefs interfere with our social work mission? Ethical concerns are also raised when social workers do not engage and respond to the spiritual issues of their clients. The NASW Code of Ethics and Accreditation standards are described as a helpful source of information and support for including spiritual issues in our practice. A helpful framework is included in the chapter that offers guidelines for determining if and when to engage spiritual and religious issues with individual clients. Faith-based agencies face some unique ethical challenges and some of the ways to consider addressing them are also covered. Finally, several ethical challenges can be raised when working with some religious clients. Issues like abortion, birth control, euthanasia, and relationships between married couples are examples and need to be thoughtfully worked out.

Discussion Questions and Exercises

1. Three ethical principles that have relevance to the professional life of social workers are mentioned early in the chapter. They are: do no harm, communicate to heal, and right a wrong. Pick one of these principles and apply it to an ethical issue with which you are grappling. Describe this issue and how you have resolved or wish to resolve it using this ethical principle.

2. Many ethical challenges are evident in our work with clients. They often have a spiritual or religious element in them. Several of these issues are discussed in the chapter, including abortion, birth control, the death penalty, euthanasia, medical interventions and religious opposition, religious practices in public places, LGBT issues, relations between marital partners, and women in leadership roles in religious organizations. Select one of these ethically challenging issues and attempt to answer the specific question it raises in the chapter. Then imagine that you have a client with this issue. What would you consider doing to help them face this issue?

3. In the chapter, Hodge (2003) presented some of the value conflicts that he believes separate some social workers from their more conservative religious clients. Here is how he identified some of the value conflicts that social workers are likely to face with each other or with some clients:

   - social workers who believe in egalitarian marriages interacting with couples who affirm complementary marriages;
   - social workers who believe in a biological origin of homosexuality interacting with people who believe that homosexuality is socially constructed;
   - social workers who are morally opposed to spankings interacting with clients who affirm the importance of spanking as a disciplinary method;
   - social workers who believe that morality and law are socially constructed working with clients who believe in divine revelation.

   What are your reactions to Hodge's wording of these ethical differences? How would you identify them using your own words and understanding? In what ways do the words that we use, in themselves, create problems in overcoming these ethical conflicts?

References

Bein, A. W. (2008). *The Zen of helping: Spiritual principles for mindful and open-hearted practice.* Hoboken, NJ: John Wiley & Sons.

Bielefeld, W. (2006). Investigating the implementation of charitable choice, *Journal of Religion & Spirituality in Social Work: Social Thought, 25*(3–4), 151–173.

Buber, M. & Kaufmann, W. (1970). *I and thou.* New York: Touchstone.

Canda, E. R., & Furman, L. D. (1999). *Spiritual diversity in social work practice: The heart of healing.* New York: Free Press.

Canda, E. R., & Furman, L. D. (2010). *Spiritual diversity in social work practice: The heart of helping.* 2nd edition. New York: Oxford University Press.

Canda, E. R., Nakashima, M., and Furman, L. D. (2004). Ethical considerations about spirituality in social work: Insights from a national qualitative survey. *Families in Society, 85*(1), 1–9.

Carter, J. (2009). Losing my religion for equality. Speech reported as an opinion piece by President Jimmy Carter in *The Age*, July 15, 2009. Available online at http://www.theage.com.au/federal-politics/losing-my-religion-for-equality-20090714-dk0v.html?page=-1.

CSWE (Council on Social Work Education) (2015). *2015 Educational Policy and Accreditation Standards for Baccalaureate and Master's Social Work Programs.* Educational Policy Approved by the CSWE Board of Directors on March 20, 2015; Accreditation Standards approved by the CSWE Commission on Accreditation on June 11, 2015. Alexandria, VA: Author.

Dudley, J. & Helfgott, C. (1990). Exploring a place for spirituality in the social work curriculum. *Journal of Social Work Education, 26*(3), 287–294.

Gardner, F. (2011). *Critical spirituality: A holistic approach to contemporary practice.* Burlington, VT: Ashgate.

Hodge, D. R. (2002). Does social work oppress Evangelical Christians? A "new class" analysis of society and social work. *Social Work, 47*(4), 401–414.

Hodge, D. R. (2003). Hodge responds. *Social Work, 48*(3), 431–432.

Hodge, D. R. (2009). Secular privilege: Deconstructing the invisible rose-tinted sunglasses. *Journal of Religion & Spirituality in Social Work: Social Thought, 28*(1–2), 8–34.

Horner, R., & Kelly, T. B. (2007). Ethical decision-making in the helping profession. *Religion & Spirituality in Social Work: Social Thought, 26*(1), 71–88.

Hugen, B., & Venema, R. (2009). The difference of faith: The influence of faith in human service programs. *Journal of Religion & Spirituality in Social Work: Social Thought, 28*(4), 405–429.

Kaplan, A., & Dziegielewski, S. (1999). Graduate social work students' attitudes and behaviors toward spirituality and religion: Issues for education and practice. *Social Work and Christianity, 26*(1), 25–39.

McCullough, M. E., Pargament, K. I., & Thoresen, C. E. (Eds.) (2001). *Forgiveness: Theory, research, and practice.* New York: Guilford Press.

Medlin, A. (2013). Atheism. An unpublished manuscript presented to the School of Social Work, University of North Carolina at Charlotte.

NASW (National Association of Social Workers) (2008). Code of Ethics of the National Association of Social Workers. Washington, DC: National Association of Social Workers. Approved by the 1996 NASW Delegate Assembly and revised by the 2008 NASW Delegate Assembly. Available online at http://www.socialworkers.org/pubs/code/default.asp.

Netting, F. E. (2002). Reflections on the meaning of sectarian, religiously affiliated, and faith-based language: Implications for human service consumers. *Social Work & Christianity, 29*(1), 13–30.

Netting, F. E., O'Connor, M. K., & Yancy, G. (2006). Belief systems in faith-based human service programs. *Journal of Religion and Spirituality in Social Work: Social Thought, 25*(3–4), 261–286.

Oxhandler, H. K., Parrish, D. E., Torres, L. R., & Achenbaum, W. A. (2015). The integration of clients' religion and spirituality in social work practice: A national survey. *Social Work, 60*(3), 228–237.

Pew Research Center, Religion and Public Life. (2015). America's Changing Religious Landscape. Pew Research Center, Religion and Public Life, Washington, DC, May 12, 2015. Available online at http://www.pewforum.org/2015/05/12/americas-changing-religious-landscape.

Reamer, F. G. (2003). Social work, Evangelical Christians, and values. *Social Work, 48*(3), 428–431.

Riswold, C. D. (2015). Teaching the college "nones": Christian privilege and the religion professor. *Teaching Theology and Religion, 18*(2), 133–148.

Scales, T. L., & Kelly, M. S. (Eds.) (2012). *Christianity and social work: Readings on the integration of Christian faith and social work practice*. 4th edition. Botsford, CT: North American Association of Christians in Social Work.

Sheridan, M. J. (2009). Ethical issues in the use of spiritually based interventions in social work practice: What are we doing and why? *Journal of Religion & Spirituality in Social Work: Social Thought, 28*(1–2), 99–126.

Sheridan, M., & Amato-Von Hemert, K. (1999). The role of religion and spirituality in social work education and practice: A survey of student views and experiences. *Journal of Social Work Education, 35*(1), 125–143.

Sheridan, M. J., Bullis, R. K., Adcock C. R., Berlin, S. D. & Miller, P. C. (1992). Practitioners' personal and professional attitudes and behaviors toward religion and spirituality: Issues for education and practice. *Journal of Social Work Education, 28*(2):190–203.

Sheridan, M. J., Wilmer, C. M., & Atcheson, L. (1994). Inclusion of content on religion and spirituality in the social work curriculum: A study of faculty views. *Journal of Social Work Education, 30*(3), 363–376.

Sherr, M. E., Singletary, J. E., & Rogers, R. K. (2009). Innovative service or proselytizing: Exploring when services delivery becomes a platform for unwanted religious persuasion. *Social Work, 54*(2), 157–165.

Sherwood, D. A. (1998). Spiritual assessment as a normal part of social work practice: Power to help and power to harm. *Social Work and Christianity: National Association of Christians in Social Work, 25*(2), 80–90.

Smith, H. (1991). *The world's religions*. New York: HarperCollins.

Smith, H. (2001). *Why religion matters: The fate of the human spirit in an age of disbelief*. New York: HarperCollins.

Stewart, C., & Koeske, G. (2006). Social work students' attitudes concerning the use of religious and spiritual interventions in social work practice. *Journal of Teaching in Social Work, 26*(1–2), 31–49.

Thyer, B. A., and Myers, L. L. (2009). Religious discrimination in social work academic programs: Whither social justice? *Journal of Religion & Spirituality in Social Work: Social Thought, 28*(1–2), 144–160.

Walsh, R. (1999). *Essential spirituality: The 7 central practices to awaken heart and mind*. New York: John Wiley & Sons.

Williams, M., & Smolak, A. (2007). Integrating faith matters in social work education. *Journal of Religion & Spirituality in Social Work: Social Thought, 26*(3), 25–44.

7

INITIAL ENGAGEMENT OF SPIRITUAL ISSUES

Much as we wish, not one of us can bring back yesterday or shape tomorrow. Only today is ours, and it will not be ours for long, and once it is gone it will never in all time be ours again.

(Buechner, 1969)

[W]e cannot escape our own beliefs and value systems. To truly hear someone, it is necessary to take the stance of "not knowing," without losing sight of the goals of the work. This means jointly creating a view of the problem with the client, whose own understanding of it is key to its resolution.

(Gotterer, 2001)

Based on the core competencies required by the social work accreditation agency, social work programs are required to prepare students to use a practice approach that has four components of a dynamic and interactive process beginning with engagement (CSWE, 2015). The other components are assessment, intervention, and evaluation. The next six chapters look closely at how a spiritually sensitive social work approach implements these four components. This chapter explores the first phase, engaging clients.

A client's spirituality is sometimes evident especially in the initial contact with a social worker. This is particularly the case when it is a religious expression. It can take a verbal form such as mentioning a church or synagogue affiliation or a non-verbal form such as wearing a religious head covering. It can be revealed by clients explicitly, as in a casual comment such as "I meditate" or implicitly by the client informing you they are not available on Wednesday nights because of an important commitment.

Possible scenario—an elder female client

Client: "Prayers are so important to me in getting through my day. Are you allowed to pray with me in this session?"
Question for reader: How would you feel about this question? What could you say that would be engaging the client to share the meaning and importance of prayer to her?

Bringing Spirituality into Initial Discussions

The initial component is referred to as engagement or engaging the client. This is a time of exploration, negotiation and relationship building (Canda & Furman, 2010; Cunningham, 2012). We are exploring what the client needs and negotiating how we can help. From these explorations, we can begin to determine if and how the agency can help. Often this involves the worker not only asking the clients questions about what they need but also communicating, in a variety of important ways, how the agency can help them. One of the things that a spiritually sensitive social worker could do during engagement is communicate, in a neutral way, that the worker is open to discussing spiritual or religious concerns if they are pertinent to what is needed. This communication can most easily be mentioned in response to spiritual cues offered by the client.

Clients may share spiritual cues in the initial interview to communicate that they have a spiritual or religious background or a spiritual issue to bring up. If such a cue is ignored, it may not be brought up again in later sessions. Therefore, a worker

---

Some Examples of Spiritual Cues to Consider from Clients

1. Verbal expressions—e.g. "I don't know what I would do without the Lord."

2. Religious symbols—e.g. wearing a cross around her neck or a head covering.

3. Seeking help with changes in her life.

4. Wanting to experience inner peace after the loss of a special friend.

5. Mentioning social supports—e.g. "I attend a support group in my neighborhood."

6. Having difficulty facing a recent diagnosis of a terminal disease.

7. Client's schedule—e.g. "I cannot meet on Fridays." (He attends prayer service at his mosque.)

8. Indirect non-verbal expressions: When asked about spirituality, she smiles as if she is very familiar with this concept.

9. Questions about the agency or service provisions: "Do I have to share my situation in the group? What kinds of things am I expected to share?"

10. Awareness that the client is struggling with guilt about something they recently did.

needs to recognize when a spiritual cue is expressed or indirectly manifested by recognizing the value of this spiritual cue to a client and possibly expressing an explicit openness to bringing it into the conversation. In addition, the worker may want to explore further what this cue may mean to the client. A welcoming ear to hear more rather than silence or indifference may be important. An example of such an encounter with a homeless person carrying a Bible illustrates this in the box below.

Spiritual cues often may be difficult to understand in the form that they are presented and could be viewed as more negative than positive. An example of this came up in a Spirituality and Social Work course when the concept of spiritual cues was first introduced. Several of the students mentioned spiritual cues of their clients that they viewed as "crutches"; they also viewed them as excuses by clients for not doing anything about their situations. An example involved a client saying "Jesus, take the wheel." This comment seemed potentially troubling, possibly because the student did not know how to respond. "Jesus, take the wheel" may be a client's way of saying they are feeling overwhelmed by their circumstances and have to depend upon Jesus to help them. As a response, one way to keep the conversation going could be to say, "You seem to depend upon Jesus to help you in difficult times. Do you want to share more about how Jesus helps you?"

As an exercise, consider next how you might respond to another comment brought up by this student group. How would you respond to the comment of the client with ALS disease on p. 158?

If the client does not share any spiritual cues in this initial contact, it may or may not be appropriate for the worker to initiate a brief comment inviting the client to share any spiritual issues if they are helpful. A possible comment by a worker at the appropriate time could be something like, "Spirituality is something that is important to some people coming to our agency. If it is important to you, I want to encourage you to share your spiritual background or any spiritual concerns that may be relevant to the help that you are seeking (e.g. housing, job, a relationship issue). If

---

Initial contact of a client seeking help from a faith-based homeless clearing house

A homeless man openly carries his Bible into the interview with the intake worker. He refers to his Bible as his only important possession.

Worker: I see that the Bible seems to be really important to you.
Client: Yes I use it all the time.
Worker: Would you like to share how it helps you? I am interested in hearing about it.
Client: I read special verses in it when I am having problems.
Worker: Feel free to bring your Bible into our discussions whenever you think it can help us in our efforts to find you housing.

spirituality is not important for you in our discussion, just ignore my comment as it will not be relevant to you." This statement might lead the client to share something spiritual or religious; it may also open up a discussion about what spirituality means to the client. Or it may be something that the client remembers and brings up later. If a client asks what spirituality means to the worker, it would be important to point out that every human being has a spiritual aspect or dimension; it can be religious or it may not be. A simple definition of spirituality could be added by the worker since the term takes on different meanings to different people.

Forging a Spiritually Sensitive Relationship

Little is likely to happen when clients share their spiritual issues unless they are expressed in the context of a nurturing professional relationship being developed during the engagement. Relationship building is important to all social work relationships and it has a special role to play for a spiritually sensitive worker. When we meet with a client, we are expected to view them in a holistic way as a biological, psychological, social, mental, cultural, and spiritual being. As a spiritually sensitive worker, in particular, we honor our client as a spiritual being. Honoring a person spiritually can be like honoring the still small voice within them that can guide them and inform them about what is right for them to do. So what is involved in a nurturing professional relationship? It involves attending to empathy, being open to intuition, identifying spiritual strengths of clients, and fostering self-determination, among other things.

> **Exercise**
>
> A student was assigned a client who has ALS disease (also referred to as Lou Gehrig's Disease, a progressive neurodegenerative disease). At one point in the interview, this client said, "God brought me to this [problematic] physical condition."
>
>   In response, explore how you might supportively respond to this client. As part of your response you may want to consider helping the client explore more positive ways that his God might view him and his disease.

> **Exercise**
>
> If the client does not share any spiritual cues in the initial contact, what might be the down side of the worker making an introductory comment as suggested above? How might this comment be detrimental to the worker/ client relationship?

Empathy

Empathy is about getting into the shoes of a client and trying to feel what they are feeling. Empathy is important during the entire helping process but it is especially important in the beginning phase of engagement (Rogers, 1951; Shulman, 2011). We recognize that every human being is very complex and often initially hesitant to share very much of who they are; thus they often openly reveal only a very small part of themselves and it could be a superficial side. Their strengths, for example, may be initially difficult to find or easily overlooked. Or they may be overshadowed by current problems that are looming before them.

Transcendence, a concept described earlier in the book, is important to consider here. Spiritually sensitive social workers are expected to transcend their own being to be where the client is (Rogers, 1977). We make every effort to be totally present with this person, undistracted by our own internal chatter or personal insecurities. Indeed, we strive to be in the present. "I am only here with my client who needs my help" is a mantra that we can recite to ourselves. We are trying to listen and understand with what a Hindu person might refer to as the third eye, holding back on talking, and mostly listening at a deeper level.

Hodge (2004) offers a few principles that expand upon the importance of empathy for the spirituality of a client. First, it is important to respect a client's spiritual autonomy. This includes refraining from discussing spirituality if the client chooses not to discuss it. Another is to use language drawn from the client's worldview, for example, shifting to Allah rather than God, or synagogue instead of church when these terms are relevant to clients. Another principle is to demonstrate interest and curiosity in a client's spirituality along with encouraging the client to elaborate on their experiences with it when appropriate (Patterson, Hayworth, Turner, & Raskin, 2000). Also it is important to be sensitive to the biases and misunderstandings that clients from some religious groups may experience from social agencies and other groups. Some examples of such groups are the Jehovah's Witnesses, Evangelical Christians, Mormons, and Muslims. Finally, Hodge points out that some social workers who may have rejected their childhood religious affiliation may be inclined to share this experience with clients if they feel similarly; Hodge (2003) cautions that we need to be careful not to work through our own unresolved issues with a client who may be in a similar place.

Intuition

As we build empathy in our relationship with a client, we are also anticipating our intuitive side to emerge. Luoma (1998) defines intuition as an act or process of coming to direct knowledge without reasoning. It involves an inner voice, or knowing without logical thought and without actually knowing how we know. Instead of "thinking" about the person we engage, we are feeling something with or about them. Luoma also points out that intuition is manifested not as something that can be turned on or off; it just happens without explanation. Intuition often is evident before thought processes even become evident, or it could emerge as conversations with clients are evolving. Intuition is something that some people have an easier time experiencing than others. Yet, it is something that most people can experience if they are comfortable enough to give attention to it. Many people may admit that they sometimes experience a deeper sense of something or an insight that they cannot explain in terms of its source; and this message could be very profound or useful in helping a client (Luoma, 1998). Muller (2010) adds to the meaning of intuition suggesting that humans have an intimate capacity to discern what is true. It is an inner compass, a visceral knowing, that indicates what is right to do or to become. Besides intuition, he suggests it could have other names such as our spirit, our spark of divinity, a still small voice inside, or our inner light.

We emphasize that intuition is one of several tools at our disposal in the helping relationship. We intuit what is going on with our client beyond what might be expressed. While our intuitive thoughts are but one source of evidence that often needs confirmation from other sources, they can be important as we explore what the client needs and may be expressing. These intuitive thoughts are also, by virtue of their nature, tentative and important to explore in the form of questioning rather than accepting them as absolute truths. For example, a worker may sense that a client, in silence, is hesitating to share something very important but private. A worker's possible response could be, "Are you possibly wanting to share something difficult to express, or something that you may not yet trust me enough to share?"

Facilitating an Openness to Being Intuitive—An Exercise

- Find another person to work with on this exercise.

- Close your eyes for a few moments and get quiet and centered inside.

- Next, face the other person. Close your eyes for a moment. Quiet yourself inside. If there are distracting thoughts, just become aware of them and gently nudge them away. Use your mantra (a special word that calms you) if distractions come.

- For a few minutes, just simply look at the other person. Just look into their eyes in gratitude for who they are. Try to imagine that you are communicating with their soul—soul to soul.

- Afterward, share what happened with your partner for a few minutes.

- Finally share any ideas or reactions about what you experienced with the class. Were any thoughts or feelings related to intuition evident? If so, was it confirmed as accurate by the other person?

While this question is viewed as just one of many possibilities, the important point is that it is shared as a question that can be passed over if the client finds that it is not pertinent.

Spiritual Strengths

Client strengths are important to consider as we engage new clients in a relationship. To engage these aspects of a client, we need to become aware of them and their importance and use the exploratory process to identify them. Spiritual-related strengths could be an almost unlimited number of things and vary from one person to the next.

Social workers should become keenly aware of their clients' strengths and how to bring these strengths into the discussion with this client (Saleebey, 2013). Yet, we have a tendency to easily overlook or minimize the importance of our clients' strengths related to spirituality or religion (Banerjee & Canda, 2009). What are your spiritual strengths? Are they easy for you to identify? Compare your strengths with a colleague's and determine how they are similar and different.

Examples of Possible Spiritual Strengths

- an affiliation with a spiritual or religious organization;

- active participation in such an organization;

- having a spiritual discipline such as prayer, meditation, chanting;

- awareness of one's own spirituality;

- can identify a personal spiritual characteristic, such as being intuitive;

- desire to know more about one's spirituality;

- actively seeking to develop oneself spiritually;

- having spiritual or religious friends;

- a capacity to be intuitive;

- comfort in talking about one's spiritual needs;

- feeling empowered by one's spirituality;

- having access to spiritual resources;

- using spiritual resources available within a group;

- comfort with the spirituality of other people of different religious backgrounds.

> **Exercise**
>
> When you think about spiritual strengths, what things come to mind for you?

Self-Determination

Client self-determination is a basic ethical standard that guides what happens in every relationship between a social worker and client (NASW, 2008). Clients tend to know what is best for themselves in most cases. While some may lack judgment about what they need, they always have an inherent right to decide what is in their best interests unless there is a danger to themselves, others, or to society. Self-determination includes a client's right to their own spiritual and religious beliefs. This is an especially critical assumption to make when we enter into a discussion of spiritual or religious matters with a client. One of the most important reasons why some social workers are hesitant or even opposed to helping clients with spiritual issues is the fear that they will bring their own religious positions into these discussions and attempt to proselytize or convert their clients. Some religions, including Christianity and Islam, include among their central tenets the importance of evangelism; people are to be recruited to become followers of Christ or Muhammad. So this temptation is very real for social workers affiliated with such religious groups (see Dialogue box on p. 163).

In chapter 2, the emphasis was on social workers knowing themselves as spiritual and religious or non-religious people. This is important so that they will have a heightened awareness of who they are spiritually and what their worldview is related to religion, spirituality, and related topics. The importance of knowing their spirituality is not for purposes of using these beliefs to influence clients. To the contrary, the point is to consciously avoid doing this. The purpose of knowing themselves is to appreciate their own spirituality so they can appreciate the potential importance of spirituality to their clients. Then we need to listen objectively to what our clients share about their spiritual beliefs and yearnings. We also need to intervene, verbally and non-verbally, in ways that support the healthy maturation of our clients' spiritual beliefs and practices.

Self-determination is an ethical principle that is central to a spiritually sensitive social worker. In this regard, mindfulness is a philosophical orientation that workers can adopt to help them remain focused on the client in the present, and not on their own personal issues. A mindful worker learns to be as fully present to who the client is and what the client brings and shares.

In most instances, social workers will not be working with clients of similar spiritual and religious backgrounds. In our increasingly diverse religious society, we must prepare ourselves for differences to exist as the rule, not the exception. The importance of spiritual sensitivity may be most challenging when working with

---

Dialogue between a social work field instructor and a new student

Student: When do I tell the client that I am a Christian?
Field Instructor: You don't. It's not about you; it's about your client!

---

client populations underrepresented among social workers and social work educators who teach them. Examples include Evangelical Christians (Furman, Perry, & Goldade, 1996; Sheridan, Wilmer, & Atcheson, 1994) and Muslims (Canda & Furman, 2010; Ibrahim & Dykeman, 2011). Ibrahim and Dykeman (2011) recommend, for example, that engaging Muslim clients not involve asking too many questions because it may be perceived more as interrogation than a helpful exploration. Instead, these authors suggest giving more emphasis to active listening, positive asset search, paraphrasing, clarifying, and moving slowly in efforts to take into account the central importance of their religion.

Any number of combinations of spiritual and religious affiliations are possible between a social worker and their clients, as the examples in Table 7.1 suggest. The list of possible combinations is almost limitless, as the below examples suggest. Further, one can see from any of these combinations that the workers will truly be challenged to maintain an objective ear and an open heart in listening to a client share their problems within their own spiritual and cultural contexts. What are some of the reasons why some of these combinations may be difficult for you? How easily can you transcend your own spiritual background to be comfortably present with the background of your clients? What do you or can you sometimes do to succeed in keeping your spiritual beliefs and biases in check while working with a client of a different spiritual background?

Personal Obstacles to Deeper Exploration

Several obstacles are likely to interfere with our readiness to explore a client's deeper spiritual issues. These obstacles are important to consider during initial engagement when a relationship with a client is beginning to take form and the

Table 7.1 Examples of Spiritual and Religious Combinations between Social Workers and Clients

WORKER	CLIENT
• Mainline Protestant Christian	• Orthodox Jew
• agnostic	• Evangelical Christian
• New Age enthusiast	• practicing Catholic
• cultural (but not religious) Jew	• Christian Fundamentalist
• Evangelical Christian	• Hindu
• European-American Buddhist	• Muslim
• non-practicing Catholic	• atheist

client is sizing up the worker with questions such as, "Can I work with this person?" and "How well can they understand me?"

Taboos as Obstacles

Some researchers (Rice & Dudley, 1997; Shulman, 2011) suggest that some of these obstacles can be thought of as taboos. One such taboo is that social workers have a tendency to consider the realm of their social work exploration and assistance to be essentially limited to psychosocial, cultural, and biological sciences. Concerns outside these areas, the reasoning goes, are assumed to be beyond social work's expertise. Religion, for example, is thought of as a topic that social workers know little if anything about and we automatically think of it as something for another professional to address, such as a clergy person.

Social workers primarily focus on the psychosocial functioning of a client's life, but that could mean addressing psychological issues at a deeper level that may touch on their spirituality as well as cultural issues entwined with it. We also stress the importance of being holistic—considering all factors that may be relevant to a case, including religious and spiritual ones (CSWE, 2015). For example, if clients are searching for more meaning in their lives and want to talk about joining a religious community such as a church, synagogue, or mosque, that could be a potential social support worth exploring with them.

A Latina teenage female client in the public schools offers another example. An MSW student presented a case involving this teenager in her MSW practice class. The teenager recently began seeking advice from the MSW student, her school social worker, because of difficulties she has been having with her parents. She was involved in heated arguments with her parents because she wanted to be taking birth control; she perceived this decision as being that of a responsible young adult. She had a boyfriend but stated she was not having sexual intercourse with him. However, because of her parents' strong Catholic religious beliefs, among other issues, they were strongly opposed to this student's decision and threatened to kick her out of the house or severely punish her for this decision. As the MSW class explored what this student's next steps might be, a suggestion was made to explore the teenager's religious beliefs as a Catholic and how they may play a role in her birth control decision and in her differences with her parents. For example the worker could ask several questions such as, "As a Catholic, how do you feel about birth control? Do you have different views than your parents based on your beliefs?"

Exercise

What do you think? If you were assigned this case, would this be a potential topic of relevance to you? Explain why or why not.

In the class discussion, some MSW students rather emphatically argued that social workers should not be discussing her Catholic beliefs in the public schools. The topic seemed to them to be a taboo in a public school.

Another taboo identified by Bein (2008) is similar to the first. Many social workers do not perceive themselves as experts in any area of spirituality or religion. They especially know little about someone's religion if it is different from their own. If a client brings up a religious issue such as personal prayer as a discipline or recites religious passages from the Torah or Quran, many social workers are likely to feel inadequate in responding, particularly if the client's religious practices are unfamiliar to them. They rationalize that they cannot comfortably carry on a meaningful conversation about what is essentially a religious practice of the client. Instead, the tendency is to explain that they know little or nothing about this topic, or they may simply listen and move to another subject as soon as respectfully possible because of their hesitancies to continue it.

In these and other taboo areas, many social workers seem to forget that we do not have to be an expert on a topic to discuss it (Bein, 2008). You only need to be attentive to what the client is saying and interested in learning more about it to determine if it is relevant to why they are seeking help. Once a client shares a spiritual topic or concern of some sort, a discussion of that concern can naturally follow in which a worker can find out how and why this topic is important to the client.

Nevertheless, even if social workers want to engage the client's spirituality, they usually do not know what to do next. While many think that they have nothing to offer in this area and revert to silence or changing the subject, a worker using a spiritually sensitive approach would want to support the client's right to self-determination and respond as they would to any other pertinent topic. They could ask the client to elaborate on it.

A referral to a clergy person is often one possible way to help. A further discussion about this may lead the worker to believe that clergy are the experts and a referral is actually needed. Yet, if we do not initially assess what the religious issue is or whether it possibly relates to the other problems that the client is meeting with us about, how can we make a responsible referral? What would be the specific reasons we would be referring a client to a clergy person? We probably would not have enough pertinent information to know.

We are also not experts in several other areas. Take housing as an example. We are, in most cases, not experts in housing unless we are employed in a housing agency; yet, we initially explore these issues with clients to find out what kinds of help they may need and what agencies to consider for a referral. In addition, it may turn out that their housing concern is related to why they are seeing us. Help may be needed by a couple, for example, if they are in disagreement about which housing option to select and need help with making a decision.

So how far into a conversation on spirituality should we go if we are not sure the discussion is going to be directly relevant to our agency's function? This is often an underlying question that needs careful consideration and professional judgment. Workers could make the mistake of delving too far into a topic that is not relevant to a particular client's problem or in contrast they could stop the discussion abruptly and overlook the importance of the topic to them. One fear that some social workers may have is that they will get so far into discussing spirituality that they will find themselves well beyond their capacity and expertise to help.

Barriers of Overly Zealous Workers and Clients

Instances are always possible of an overly zealous social worker pursuing spiritual issues with clients or overly zealous clients doing so with their social workers (Bein, 2008; Canda & Furman, 2010; Gardner, 2011). In either case, obstacles can easily emerge that can interfere with engaging a spiritual concern at a deeper level. Let's take the instance of overly zealous clients. Let's imagine an encounter between a social worker not affiliated with any religious group and a client who has newly joined a Pentecostal church and wants to enthusiastically share it with anyone who will listen. Possibly such a client may subconsciously wish to win the worker over to her beliefs as well.

The workers in these instances could be facing a personal barrier if they are not aware of their own biases against the client's religion or a bias against the client continually making reference to it. A worker may react by holding back and not engaging the client's religious comments because of their perceived intensity and passion. Or the worker may just listen and look for an opportunity to change the subject. Such a worker should be in touch with their biases and/or any internal resistance they may feel toward the client. In addition, they should prepare themselves to do what a spiritually sensitive worker may do. This could be a time to recognize and affirm the client's religious affiliation, share what seems to be a perceived spiritual strength of the client based on their religious comments, and begin to explore how these strong passions can be channeled into the helping process to effectively address the client's problem at hand.

The other possibility would be workers who are overly zealous about their religion meeting with clients who do not openly share any particular spiritual cues. For example, if a client does not mention any spiritual affiliations, the worker may comment that joining a spiritual group could be very important to one's life. Or the worker could keep probing with questions in search of the possibility that the client feels something similar to what the worker feels. In these cases the worker should become aware of the possibility and potential danger of sharing their religious beliefs or orientation in one way or another (Gardner, 2011). It is important for the worker to become aware of such religious biases and be prepared to do what a spiritually sensitive worker would do. If the client does not seem to mention any spiritual issues, the overly zealous worker should probably move on to explore other pertinent areas.

The Influence of the Agency

Another potential obstacle to discussing spiritual concerns with a client is the agency in which a social worker is employed (Bein, 2008; Svare, Hylton, & Albers, 2007). An important question to consider is what the agency's policy is about discussing spiritual and religious matters with clients. This is a good question to explore and get clarification on if there are any ambiguities. Often there is no explicit agency policy on discussing religious issues, and discussing spirituality may even be less evident in a policy because of the multitude of ways in which spirituality is defined. Further, when there is no policy, the views of different administrative and supervisory staff may be different from each other and often merely reflect their own personal views.

An example of ambiguous agency policy and procedures was evident in a community mental health facility that was used as a field practicum by MSW programs in a large populated area. An assessment instrument used by the social services department included the question, "Do you have any spiritual or religious supports?" To the surprise of a student who was placed there, she was explicitly instructed by an administrative person not to ask this question or any other questions about religion. No explanation was given for this contradictory message. This student had been prepared to conduct a spiritual assessment based on what she had learned in a Spirituality and Social Work class but she ended up remaining silent about it because of these instructions.

A related obstacle to an ambiguous agency position is a perception by employees that an employer does not want them to discuss spiritual issues with clients (Svare et al., 2007). This is not a position that has been confirmed explicitly by the agency or any administrative staff but it is simply something that is suspected. In this case these workers may have a tendency to be new and sufficiently hesitant about working with clients on these topics. This is more likely to occur in public or quasi-public agencies and large bureaucratic agencies in which policies and procedures of how to proceed are quite extensive, technical, and difficult to comprehend. Thus, the topic of spirituality is avoided and ambiguity remains about whether it can be discussed with clients.

This perceived obstacle is one that can be assertively explored and overcome by a social worker using a spiritually sensitive practice approach. Such a social worker can bring this concern to the administration of an agency for clarity about a policy. A highly desirable response could be that a spiritually supportive policy is not only discussed, but also developed and implemented if there was no prior policy. Such a policy should include a clear working definition of both spirituality and religion. In addition, an explanation can be given of how these two concepts can be relevant during assessment and intervention work with clients. An explanation is also needed about when these topics should not be brought up or discussed with clients. In the absence of a policy, a formal understanding could be provided indicating why

> **Exercise: Agency Clarity about Discussing Spirituality and Religion**
>
> Recognizing that discussing spirituality could be perceived as a taboo topic in some agencies, consider how you would obtain clarity about this issue in your agency. Ask colleagues and administrators if there is a policy or formal position about discussing spirituality or religion with clients. If so, how are these two concepts defined? Under what circumstances is spirituality allowed or encouraged? Are there safeguards that preclude a worker from bringing up their own spirituality and imposing it on clients? If there are safeguards, how are they explained? If none of these issues are clarified, ask whether it would be appropriate to set up such a policy or formal position.

and how spirituality may be an appropriate topic to discuss in client-worker conversations. This could be done in a staff meeting or during a training session.

Deeper Exploration in Engagement

How deeply or extensively should a practitioner delve into a spiritual concern with a client when it is explored? The answer to this question will vary based on the client, agency setting, and other factors. We may only need to explore a spiritual concern for a few minutes and then realize that it is not relevant to a case. Or we may find out in a brief conversation with a client that we need to make a referral to another agency to obtain help with this issue. In this case we will want to know the relevant spiritual and religious resources that are available and the eligibility requirements and admission procedures. Or another possibility is that we could open up a deeper conversation that is appropriate for the worker and client to continue. Of course there can be other possible options as well. Let's look at some of the ways that a spiritually sensitive worker can respond to a relevant spiritual concern at a deeper level of engagement.

First, we would acknowledge that this appears to be an important topic of the client and encourage them to continue to share. Expressing an interest in the client's concern and an openness to what the client wants to share is not to be underestimated; it expresses deeper empathy and conveys an openness to hear more about this topic. This is a good time for the worker to concentrate on an internal mindfulness exercise such as concentrating on the breath and gently nudging away internal chatter. Safe space needs to be created for clients to begin sharing their beliefs, views, and experiences without any sense of being rushed, interrupted, or judged. We follow the client's lead, helping them share, in a free-floating manner, what is in their minds and hearts. They need to listen to what they are sharing as well. This is important because what they share may seem new even to them as this may be a rare opportunity for them to share these personal spiritual concerns with someone else. This sharing could be viewed as storytelling, which can be very therapeutic (Bein, 2008). The worker can draw on the techniques of the Person-Centered Approach involving active listening, probing for elaboration, and conveying a deep respect for the values that are apparent in what is being said; all to hear the deeper messages that are person-centered (Corey, 2011; Rogers, 1951).

Many different questions could be asked at this point in the discussion in order to move it forward. Some examples are:

- This seems to be important to you. Please tell me more if you wish.
- Can you give me an example of what you are saying?
- Can you share with me how this topic (e.g. meditation, religious passages, etc.) may help you with your problem?
- How can I help you? Does it help if we discuss this topic further?
- Is there anyone else who is available to help, possibly within your support network?

Engagement leads to assessment. Many of the topics and particular supports mentioned during initial engagement are naturally pursued further. What begins to unfold in engagement can be given more complete attention when the emphasis is on assessment. Thus a well-rounded, comprehensive, and holistic assessment brings together the exploration of different sets of concerns, those of the client and those related to the agency's overall purpose. It is suspected that in most cases, spiritual concerns and supports are likely to come up early in engagement when introductions are being made and a relationship between the worker and client is being explored around how they can work together.

A Sacred Way to Greet Our Clients

The Hindus greet each other with "Namaste," which means in Sanskrit, "The divinity in me greets the divinity in you." It is based on the Vedic principle (from the ancient Hindu scriptures called the Vedas) that the divine energy is everywhere and in all beings. This sacred Hindu custom suggests that we leave our ego at the door. Our ego is our psychological navigating system for getting us through our day. It brings judgment to what we do, distinguishes reality from fiction, discourages us from behaving in ways that lead to trouble, makes our decisions, and helps protect us from potential dangers. While all of these functions are essential to have to survive, spiritual authors suggest that there are times when we need to suspend these functions and just experience the present time as fully as we can. So "leaving our ego at the door" means letting go of all of our controls, removing our protective armor, and setting our defenses aside.

When we greet the divine in the other person, what do we mean? Martin Buber, the prominent Jewish theologian, proposed an "I–Thou" relationship that helps us to be fully with another person without pretenses, masks, or hidden motives

(Buber & Kaufmann, 1971). We enter this relationship to enhance the other person in some way and to truly share ourselves. In contrast, Buber refers to an "I–It" relationship as one in which we hold back and share with another in a guarded way and with personal advantages in mind. Buber points out that we tend to move in and out of these "I–Thou" moments.

Let's consider more closely how the greeting "Namaste" and the concept of I-Thou can be relevant to the helping relationships. For example, we may be helping a homeless person, a troubled teenager, or a homebound elderly person. In any of these helping relationships, our ego can easily become an obstacle for us if we do not leave it at the door. When we assist others who may need our help, we can easily have distracting or even conflicting motives for helping them, such as wanting to feel good or to get some credit or recognition. Or we may feel a sense of our importance as the giver and inadvertently look down on the recipient. Our ego can also be an obstacle if we jump in too quickly; we may be offering answers to clients' problems before we fully learn what they need or whether they even want our help.

According to Bein (2008), an American Buddhist social worker, Zen Buddhism offers a similar approach and helps clarify the meaning of this sacred Hindu custom of Namaste. Zen is a sect of Buddhism that teaches the helper to be "awake and intimate" with their clients and the helping process; we are to be authentic; have an open, compassionate heart; and accept our clients' pain and fear, their successes and failures. We trust in the present moment and we focus on our breath to facilitate our calmness and mindfulness. Bein proposes that we maintain a "strong back" or a stable posture capable of holding the clients' suffering and pain so that the clients can feel comfortable exploring their thoughts, feelings, circumstances, hardships, and stories. We also are to maintain a "soft front" or an open-hearted disposition toward our client.

Leaving our ego at the door and greeting our client with whom we meet with "Namaste," is no easy task to take on. It takes lots of practice and lots of trial and error in attempting to behave differently than the usual ways we interact with others. But if it's true that this divine energy is everywhere including in us and other people with whom we interact, what could be more fulfilling? In fact, this most profound way of greeting each other could become something that catches on and mutates out of control.

Conclusion

An important feature of the spiritually sensitive approach described in the book is that the initial engagement component of social work practice is likely a critical one. It is important for at least two reasons. First, it is often the first and possibly the last time that clients are likely to communicate cues that spiritual issues are important to them. Second, if this is so, it is a time to welcome clients to discuss these issues if they are pertinent to the helping process. Forging a spiritually sensitive relationship is important during initial engagement and depends upon the social worker communicating empathy, being intuitive, recognizing and affirming spiritual strengths of clients, and encouraging client self-determination. These are all important aspects of setting the stage for helping a client. Obstacles to exploring spiritual issues are also discussed in the chapter. One obstacle is to view the spiritual or religious issues of the client as a taboo not to be discussed. A second obstacle could be either a social worker who is overly zealous in approaching this topic or an overly zealous client. Another obstacle could be the agency sponsor that has no explicit agency policy or position on discussing the clients' spiritual or religious issues; in this circumstance workers are left without clarity on how they are supposed to respond to these issues.

Discussion Questions and Exercises

1. Over time, many lively discussions have occurred among social work faculty, students, and practitioners across the country revolving around how to respond when clients bring up prayer. If a client asked you to pray with them, for example, what would you likely say? How can your response be supportive of the client's needs and at the same time authentic to your views on prayer in the helping process?

2. Review the table on religious combinations between the worker and client presented earlier in the chapter. Which religions of clients do you think you will find most challenging in your practice? Which ones do you think will be the easiest for you? What are some of the reasons why some combinations are difficult for you? How easily can you transcend your own background to be comfortably present with the spirituality of these clients? What do you think you will need to work on to be able to effectively do this?

3. The agency that you work for can be a valuable ally or an obstacle for you in discussing pertinent spiritual and/or religious issues with your clients. Explore whether your agency (or field placement agency) has a policy or any other guidelines on the relevance and importance of spirituality in its programs. If so, ask how they define spirituality and whether they differentiate it from religion. Under what circumstances is spirituality allowed or encouraged as a topic of discussion with clients? Also ask if there are any safeguards to prevent a worker from bringing up their own spirituality and imposing it on their clients? If there are safeguards, how are they explained? If none of these issues have been clarified, ask whether it would be appropriate to work on such a policy or at least arrive at a formal position on these issues.

References

Banerjee, M. M., & Canda, E. (2009). Spirituality as a strength of African-American women affected by welfare reform. *Journal of Religion and Spirituality in Social Work, 28*(3), 239–262.

Bein, A. W. (2008). *The Zen of helping: Spiritual principles for mindful and open-hearted practice.* Hoboken, NJ: John Wiley & Sons.

Buber, M., & Kaufmann, W. (1971). *I and Thou.* New York: Touchstone.

Buechner, F. (1969). *The hungering heart.* New York: HarperCollins.

Canda, E. R., & Furman, L. D. (2010). *Spiritual diversity in social work practice: The heart of healing.* 2nd edition. New York: Free Press.

Corey, G. (2011). *Theory and practice of group counseling.* 8th edition. Belmont, CA: Thomson.

CSWE (Council on Social Work Education) (2015). *2015 Educational Policy and Accreditation Standards for Baccalaureate and Master's Social Work Programs.* Educational Policy Approved by the CSWE Board of Directors on March 20, 2015; Accreditation Standards approved by the CSWE Commission on Accreditation on June 11, 2015. Alexandria, VA: Author.

Cunningham, M. (2012). *Integrating spirituality in clinical social work practice: Walking the labyrinth.* Boston: Pearson.

Furman, L. D., Perry, D., & Goldade, T. (1996). Interaction of evangelical Christians and social workers in the rural environment. *Human Services in the Rural Environment, 19*(2/3), 5–8.

Gardner, F. (2011). *Critical spirituality: A holistic approach to contemporary practice.* Burlington, VT: Ashgate.

Gotterer, R. (2001). The spiritual dimension in clinical social work practice: A client perspective. *Families in Society: The Journal of Contemporary Human Services, 82*(2), 187–193.

Hodge, D. R. (2003). The challenge of spiritual diversity: Can social work facilitate an inclusive environment? *Families in Society, 84,* 348–358.

Hodge, D. R. (2004). Spirituality and people with mental illness: Developing spiritual competency in assessment and intervention. *Families in Society, 85*(1), 36–44.

Ibrahim, F. A., & Dykeman, C. (2011). Counseling Muslim Americans: Cultural and spiritual assessments. *Journal of Counseling & Development, 89,* 387–394.

Luoma, B. B. (1998). An exploration of intuition for social work practice education. In Canda, E. R. (Ed.) (1998). *Spirituality in Social Work: New Directions.* Philadelphia: Routledge, 31–45.

Muller. (2010). *A life of being, having, and doing enough.* New York: Three Rivers Press.

National Association of Social Workers. (2008). Code of Ethics of the National Association of Social Workers (approved by the 1996 NASW Delegate Assembly and revised by the 2008 NASW Delegate Assembly). Washington, DC: Author.

Patterson, J., Hayworth, M., Turner, C., & Raskin, M. (2000). Spiritual issues in family therapy: A graduate level course. *Journal of Marital and Family Therapy, 26*(2), 199–210.

Rice, D., & Dudley, J. (1997). Preparing students for the spiritual issues of their clients through a self-awareness exercise. *Journal of Baccalaureate Social Work, 3*(1), 85–95.

Rogers, C. (1951). *Client-centered therapy.* Boston: Houghton Mifflin.

Rogers, C. (1977). *Carl Rogers on personal power: Inner strength and its revolutionary impact.* New York: Delacorte Press.

Saleebey, D. (2013). *The strengths perspective in social work practice.* 6th edition. Boston: Pearson.

Sheridan, M. J., Wilmer, C. M., & Atcheson, L. (1994). Inclusion of content on religion and spirituality in the social work curriculum: A study of faculty views. *Journal of Social Work Education, 30*(3), 363–376.

Shulman, L. (2011). *The skills of helping individuals, families, groups, and communities.* 5th edition. Itasca, IL: F. E. Peacock.

Svare, G. M., Hylton, M., & Albers, E. (2007). On our own: Social workers talk about spiritually sensitive practice within an organizational context. *Journal of Religion and Spirituality in Social Work: Social Thought, 26*(4), 95–113.

8

Spiritual Assessments

The deeper we go, the more we find that all things possess the potentiality for meaning.

(Harris, 2002, p. 148)

The familiar charge to "meet the clients where they are" includes their spirituality in whatever form it appears . . . spirituality is a complicated topic that eludes clear-cut guidelines.

(Gotterer, 2001)

Assessing what clients need is an important practice component throughout the helping process. It is given focused attention early in the helping process and promulgated as a core competency by the social work accreditation agency (CSWE, 2015). In-depth spiritual assessments usually occur after a relationship has been established with the client and it is evident that the social worker and agency are a good fit for what the client needs. With a spiritually sensitive social work approach, a spiritual assessment is an important part of this process.

Assessing the clients' issues related to spirituality will vary depending on the role that spirituality plays in an agency's service provisions and how the agency views spirituality. As indicated in previous chapters, spirituality can be viewed in a number of ways. It can be viewed as a reflection of the whole person, the central core of a person, or in a more limited way as one aspect of the person (Canda & Furman, 2010). However, spirituality may also not be considered at all if an agency does not view it as important to its mission, vision, and programs. So the agency's view of spirituality, how it defines it and takes it into account, will likely determine how it is assessed. If the agency views spirituality as a reflection of the whole person or as the central core, it will likely be a major part of the assessment process. If viewed as one aspect, it will likely involve a more narrowly focused set of questions. Faith-based and sectarian agencies may also be likely to use a more extensive spiritual assessment than secular agencies.

Spiritual assessments are a complex topic and include many different features. This chapter will cover these features as follows:

- What spiritual assessment questions to ask.
- Looking at a client's spirituality from different angles.
- Implicit and explicit assessments.

- Spiritual assessments for specific client populations.
- Different methods of conducting spiritual assessments.

What Spiritual Assessment Questions to Ask

Moore (2003) reflected on what the focus of an assessment should be. His exploration raised several questions that are still relevant today. Should a spiritual assessment focus primarily on spiritual strengths? In this case, what about the potential negative aspects of spirituality? Or should it primarily focus on new developments in a person's spirituality or other areas?

As mentioned earlier, spiritual assessments will vary widely depending on the interest of the agency in the spirituality and religion of their clients. Further, the focus varies with the background of a specific social worker and the needs of a client. For example, does the degree of competence of the social worker assigned to the client need to be taken into account since an assessment may be exploring something well beyond what a worker can address? Also, what about limiting questions to what is relevant to a client's case plan? There may not be an adequate rationale for going beyond that focus. Finally, among other things, social workers almost always help clients connect with necessary resources. In this regard, it would make sense that a spiritual assessment focus on the resources that clients will need. Moore (2003) concludes by offering a schematic diagram for how to determine what spiritual questions to ask. It begins by asking whether spirituality is relevant to a client case. Proceeding to further questions would depend upon a response of at least a "maybe." More in-depth questions could be asked if the client identifies spirituality as either a strength or a problem respectively.

Spiritual assessments can take a variety of forms in agency settings depending upon the purpose of the agency and the needs of the clients. Implicit (non-religious) and explicit (religious) assessments are possibilities. Brief and detailed assessments are another way to distinguish them. They are typically implemented at the beginning of a helping relationship, after initial connections with a client are made and a good fit is established. They can also be asked throughout the helping process.

Spiritual assessments can be conceptualized as a two-stage process (Canda & Furman, 2010; Pargament, 2007). A brief preliminary assessment comes first, followed by a more comprehensive assessment if it is warranted. The brief assessment would occur during the initial engagement when the client and the agency are exploring whether the agency is the best fit for what the client needs. If this initial exploration indicates that the agency can help them, a more comprehensive assessment of spiritual issues is warranted and follows.

It is important to add that a spiritual assessment is always an ongoing process that begins at the first contact with the agency and continues until the end of this relationship. This is particularly important to remember as spiritual concerns may not be comfortably shared by a client until much later in the helping relationship, possibly when the client more fully discovers the connections of their problems with their spirituality or when the client becomes more fully comfortable and trusting of the worker. Griffith and Griffith (2002) point out that social workers should have their "spiritual radar" on throughout the helping relationship.

How Spiritual and Religious are Clients?

What are some of the ways to focus a spiritual assessment? At a basic level, it may be helpful to initially find out how spiritual and religious a client is. As Canda and Furman (2010) suggest, there can be many different configurations such as 1) someone who is spiritual but not religious, 2) religious but not spiritual, 3) religious and spiritual with spirituality being only one part of the client's religion, 4) spiritual and religious coinciding, and 5) neither spiritual nor religious. We also need to be open to the possibility that none of these configurations provide a helpful fit for some of our clients. Finding out how spiritual and how religious someone is and the sources for their spirituality involve asking questions of each person about each of these issues.

An example is offered in Figure 8.1 of a set of loosely connected spiritual questions that focuses on determining how spiritual and religious a person is. These questions are drawn from other studies (e.g. Canda & Furman, 2010; Millison & Dudley, 1990; Sheridan, 2004). Other questions could be added such as directly asking someone how spiritual and religious they are. Note that these questions include both closed and open-ended ones.

One challenge in crafting a questionnaire on the spirituality and religiosity of someone is to sort out questions that are spiritual and non-religious from those that are spiritual and religious. For example, questions about mindfulness could be considered spiritual and non-religious while questions about attending religious services are explicitly religious.

- How often do you attend spiritual or religious services? (Response options: weekly or more often, two to three times a month, monthly or less often, once or twice a year, almost never.)
- Do you have spiritual or religious supports when you need help? (Response options: yes, no.) What are they? (Response options: a blank space for the answer.)
- How often do you pray each week? (Response options: a blank space for the answer.)
- How often do you meditate each week? (Response options: a blank space for the answer.)
- Are you familiar with mindfulness? (Response options: yes, no.) How would you define mindfulness? (Response options: a blank space for the answer.) How often do you use mindfulness exercises each week? (Response options: a blank space for the answer.)
- Do you believe in a Higher Power? (Response options: yes, no.) How would you describe your Higher Power? (Response options: a blank space for the answer.) How is this Higher Power important to you? (Response options: a blank space for the answer.)
- Have you ever had a transformative experience? (Response options: yes, no.) Please describe what this (these) experience was like? (Response options: a blank space for the answer.) How, if at all, did this experience change you? (Response options: a blank space for the answer.)

Figure 8.1 How Spiritual and/or Religious Are You?

In chapter 2, the focus was on describing the spirituality of social workers. Several very general questions were identified and are listed in Figure 8.2. These questions were selected because they are among the most relevant and helpful ones that the author and others have used with students and they also seem helpful for professional people wanting to explore their understanding of their own spirituality.

As you review these questions in Figure 8.2, which ones seem appropriate for you to bring up with clients if they are relevant to a particular case? As you can see, some are religious and some are not religious. Some may appear religious to some people and not others. Religious questions are obviously among the ones to

---

1. What are your most important spiritual and religious beliefs? Please describe at least two or three of each one.
2. Do you believe in God, a spiritual Higher Power, or some other sacred force? Please describe. If not, please describe what you do believe.
3. What beliefs do you question or find upsetting?
4. What is most meaningful to you and your life? Please explain how your spirituality or religion may relate to this.
5. How often do you feel like life is joyful and worthwhile? Please explain how your spirituality or religion may relate to this.
6. How strongly do you feel a connection with something inspiring that is greater than yourself, such as God, nature, or sacredness? Please explain.
7. What are the main moral principles and values that guide your life?
8. Where do these principles come from?
9. How do these principles influence your life? What moral principles do you struggle with accepting?
10. When you have been at a time of crisis or serious need, what spiritual or religious supports have been useful to you? Please explain what they are and why they were chosen.
11. Do you belong to and participate in any spiritual or religious groups? If so, please describe them. How often do you meet with them?
12. What kinds of spiritual or religious practices do you participate in? Please describe them and indicate how often you do them (e.g. prayer, meditation, reading a sacred text, music, support group, etc.)
13. Describe your understanding of religion and spirituality when you were a child. What were some of your spiritual or religious beliefs and practices? How did you learn about them?
14. Describe your current understanding of religion and spirituality? How is this similar or different from childhood?
15. Describe any past times of spiritual breakthrough or pivotal life events that are relevant to you now.
16. Do you believe in an afterlife (life after someone dies)?
17. How would you describe this afterlife? Do you view it in terms of a heaven and hell?
18. How important is an afterlife to you in comparison to your life on earth?
19. How do you think it will be determined where you will go after you die? What types and severities of sin, if any, may determine where you will likely go?
20. Do you believe in reincarnation (returning after death as another person or animal)? How would you describe what reincarnation is to you? How would you like to return if you had a choice?

Figure 8.2   General Questions That Could Be Explored

consider with clients who are religious, while the non-religious questions may be more suitable to clients who are spiritual but not religious. These questions are likely to be inappropriate for clients who reveal neither spiritual nor religious connections. Note that some of the questions, such as the questions about an afterlife and reincarnation (questions 16–20) may only be suitable to ask clients in a hospice or palliative care program; yet many religious people who are not involved with hospice view the afterlife as a central part of their general religious beliefs. Finally, it needs to be noted that this is not intended to be an exhaustive list of general assessment questions that could be asked. Many other general questions are also possible. Maybe you can identify one or two of them that you feel have been overlooked.

Looking at a Client's Spirituality from Different Angles

It seems that there are numerous ways to focus on a client's spirituality when an agency setting has a relatively open format for exploring it. Often, such an open format is not available. However, let's consider that it is open for now. Let's look more closely at the topics of the client's spiritual practices, spiritual coping sources, spiritual identifiers during an initial contact, spiritual distresses, spiritual integrity, and others.

Spiritual Practices and Spiritual Coping Sources

A client's spiritual practices could be explored by directly asking what practices a client uses when they are struggling or possibly as a regular daily practice (Canda & Furman, 2010). Examples could be given such as praying, meditating, reading a sacred book such as the Bible or Quran, worship or other types of liturgies, singing, and chanting. Spiritual coping sources could also be a focus especially when a client is struggling with a problem that is not becoming readily resolved. Some spiritual coping sources for clients could be seeking hope, attempting to find meaning and purpose in one's life, finding ways to experience internal comfort and peace, etc.

Spiritual Identifiers

Questions that help reveal spiritual identifiers of the clients are another appropriate focus if there is an interest initially in finding out if and how the spirituality of the client is relevant to explore. Holloway and Moss (2010), for example, identified six general topics that researchers have explored to find out if a client has a spiritual background that is relevant to explore in the helping process. These topics are described in the form of closed-ended questions that could be rephrased as open-ended questions to more effectively elicit helpful responses.

Six Spiritual Identifiers

                                                    (Holloway and Moss, 2010)

- Is there purpose to the client's life?

- Are the clients able to transcend their suffering?

- Are they at peace?

- Are they hopeful or do they despair?

- What nourishes their sense of self-worth?

- Do their beliefs help them cope?

Spiritual Distresses and Pain

Spiritual distresses and pain are another topic that could be initially explored in an assessment. Burton (2004) refers to such pain as operating at a deeper level of consciousness and manifested, for example, as actual chronic and constant pain, withdrawal from spiritual supports, conflict with loved ones, general anxiety and fears, and in other forms. Spiritual pain and distress may be easy to identify as symptoms through observations and the client's comments, but the challenge may be to determine how much it is viewed as a deeper spiritual phenomenon or primarily a psychological one. Holloway and Moss (2010) suggest three sources if it stems from spiritual roots. It could involve a deep conflict within the inner self; a dark night of the soul when a person has difficulty finding God, as described by St. John of the Cross; or it could result from a loss of faith (St. John of the Cross, 2003).

Spiritual and Religious Supports

Knowing about the client's social supports is an important part of virtually every social worker's job in assisting clients; we often make referrals to these supports when they are needed. Spiritual and religious supports are an important but often overlooked component of these social supports and are important to assess. Questions 10, 11, and 12 in Figure 8.2 address questions about supports such as identifying spiritual supports that have been useful in times of crisis, the client's group membership in any spiritual or religious groups, and their spiritual practices that may or may not be connected to membership in a religious group. These questions seem to be a good way to begin assessing the client's spiritual and religious supports.

Religious groups are or could be a central part of the social supports of some of our clients. In some cases, religious groups can offer worship experiences weekly or more frequently. Child and adult education could also be important on a variety of spiritual topics. Religious groups sponsor social events to help people get acquainted and have fun. Other social supports could include Bible or Quran study groups, women's and men's support groups, choir and other singing groups, prayer groups, meditation groups, senior social groups, retreats for study and worship, charity and social justice outreach efforts to help disadvantaged people, consumer or self-help groups such as wellness clubs, yoga and reiki classes, book clubs, and other activities. Most important, many of these religious groups provide regular churchgoers with larger social networks, more types of social supports, and more positive relationships than their counterparts who are not churchgoers (Ellison & George, 1994).

Canda and Furman (2010) mention several other types of supports of a spiritual but not necessarily religious nature. Family and friends who contribute spiritual encouragement are a source. Spiritual support groups and book discussion groups that meet regularly in a library or someone's home are others. 12-Step programs are a possible support for people struggling with addictions. Yoga and meditation classes are available in various settings including Buddhist and Hindu temples, YMCAs or unaffiliated meditation centers. Retreat centers in the mountains, near rivers, by lakes, and in wooded areas are also available for rest, inspiration, healing, and counseling.

Implicit and Explicit Assessments

Explicit assessments involve asking assessment questions that directly ask about the clients' religious issues (Canda & Furman, 2010). In many cases, agencies are openly interested in addressing spiritual and religious concerns because this is important to their mission and vision. Many hospice and addiction settings are examples. Established sectarian agencies such as Jewish Family Services and Catholic Charities and smaller faith-based agencies are other examples. Agencies that are accredited with national accrediting agencies such as the Joint Commission on Accreditation of Healthcare Organizations are required to assess the spiritual issues of clients and address them if requested by the client. The questions in Figure 8.2 are primarily examples of explicit assessment questions. Most of them make reference either directly or indirectly to religious factors. As noted earlier, these are examples, but readers need to be selective about which questions are appropriate to their agency purpose and their clients' needs.

Assessments of spirituality can also be implicit assessments without mentioning religious terms and experiences (Canda & Furman, 2010; Hodge, 2013). These assessments are especially useful with clients who do not identify themselves as religious. These assessment questions can often get to the underlying spiritual issues of such clients without possibly antagonizing some who may not wish to discuss religious issues. These assessments can also be useful to clients who are not ready to share their religious beliefs or affiliations, perhaps in the early stages of the helping relationship. Many clients use terms and phrases that may implicitly signal the existence of spiritual issues. They often describe thoughts, experiences, and feelings that parallel the spiritual (Hodge, 2013). These descriptions can signify the existence of relevant practice topics that call for further exploration. The word "sacred," for example, may be viewed as a non-religious spiritual word used by some clients. They may use it to describe an activity such as gardening, walking in the woods, climbing a mountain, painting, writing poetry, sewing, feeding people who are hungry, and other activities (Crisp, 2010; Griffith & Griffith, 2002; Pargament, 2007). According to Hodge (2013), these activities can provide a transcendent sense of connection, meaning, and purpose. While these activities and the thoughts associated with them might be considered by many people to be purely secular, they are accorded a spiritual role in some clients' lives. Other examples of words that could be used by clients who are spiritual but not religious include amazing, holy, earth-shattering, joyous, fortunate, grateful, exhilarating, blessed, providential, astounding, incredible, wonder, mind-blowing, miraculous, awesome, reverence, and the list goes on and on.

Hodge (2013) provides a helpful list of questions that could be used in an implicit spiritual assessment. Some examples of these questions are included under the subtitles of past spirituality, present spirituality, and future spirituality in Figure 8.3.

Throughout the book, the topics of spirituality and religion are discussed in ways that often overlap for some people and not others. Non-religious spirituality is an important area of assessment for clients who are not religious but could be deeply

---

Past Spirituality

- When you think back, what gave you a sense of meaning (or purpose or hope for the future)?
- When were you the happiest (or most joyful)?
- How did you cope with challenging scenarios in the past?

Present Spirituality

- When do you most fully feel alive?
- What causes you the greatest despair/suffering?
- What things are you most passionate about in life?
- Who or what do you put your hope in?
- For what are you most grateful?
- What are your deepest regrets?
- What sources of strength do you draw on to keep pressing forward?
- Where do you find a source of peace (inspiration)?

Future Spirituality

- What are you striving for in life?
- Why is it important that you are in this world?
- How would you like people to remember you after you are gone?

Figure 8.3   Questions That Could Be Asked in an Implicit Spiritual Assessment (Hodge, 2013)

Non-Religious Aspects of Spirituality

- seeking meaning for our lives

- finding purpose

- pursuing hope

- embracing love

- seeking an inner source of peace

- experiencing wonder and joy

- mystery

- a personal relationship with a Higher Power

- morality and ethics

- personal beliefs

- a capacity for connectedness, transcendence, and oneness with others.

spiritual. The challenge is in how we can engage these clients without bringing up religious terms or content. Implicit assessments are an important way to do this. As pointed out in chapter 1, non-religious spiritual concerns can be described in many ways as indicated in the above box.

Hoyt (2008), a self-identified non-spiritual social worker, raises questions that practitioners may need to take into account when conducting a spiritual assessment with clients who are both non-spiritual and non-religious. If we claim that everyone has some form of spirituality but find that some clients deny this, how do we conduct a spiritual assessment that is meaningful to them? Hoyt suggests assessment questions that can be initially raised that do not assume the client to be either spiritual or religious. They are:

- How do you make sense of the situation that brings you to therapy?
- Is there anything in your worldview or belief system that helps you with this situation, or that has an influence on the situation?
- What gives your life meaning?
- What are your sources of comfort, encouragement, support, and guidance?

Hoyt would say that these questions can be peceived as either spiritual or not. If the client is spiritual, these questions offer opportunities for this to be revealed and elaborated on in their responses. However, we also need to be aware that there are others who may view some of these assessment questions as neither religious nor spiritual.

Spiritual Assessments for Specific Client Populations

Spiritual and religious questions are also likely to be asked in specific agency settings or for specific reasons that apply to some client groups and agencies and not others. For example, questions could go into more depth in a general spiritual history that is used by agencies that view spirituality as encompassing the whole or core person. Spiritual assessments can also be partially distinct among different ethnic groups such as American Indians, Muslims, Hindus, Buddhists, and others who are affiliated with religions other than Christianity. Chapter 4 focuses on many of these religious groups and identifies specific assessment questions that could be important to ask clients affiliated with such a group. According to Ibrahim and Dykeman (2011), for example, assessments of Muslim clients, if they are immigrants, should begin with exploring several cultural issues. They include an assessment of the importance of the clients' culture of origin and worldview, their commitment to the Quran and the regular practice of the five pillars, and their level of acculturation and socialization into American society.

Assessments can be conducted, for example, with children, adolescents, couples, older adults, people who are LGBT, people with mental health problems, health care patients, and those with addictions or terminal illnesses. Let's look next at some of the specific topics and assessment questions that could be asked of such groups. Coverage of spiritual assessment questions is limited to those that have been reported in the professional literature. These reports largely fall into three different categories. Some are practice reports describing assessment questions that have been used successfully with specific client groups. Others come from research articles that identify assessment questions as findings of their study. Finally, some are spiritual assessment regulations and requirements of accreditation organizations. All three categories have as their purpose attempting to define or assess spiritual needs. Thus, the assessment questions for particular client groups reported in this section are not exhaustive of all of the client groups needing them. Instead, they offer a sample, albeit rich, of specific spiritual domains and assessment questions recommended for a variety of groups. It is hoped that the reader can use them as they develop their own assessment questions for their client groups.

LGBT (Lesbian, Gay, Bisexual, Transsexual) Clients

Assessment questions often need to be added to a spiritual assessment for people who are LGBT in either topic or specific question form. Spiritual assessment questions already mentioned for people generally are, of course, appropriate for people who are LGBT. They have the same spiritual and religious needs and issues that anyone has. In addition, people who are LGBT may also have spiritual and religious issues that are somewhat unique to them and these may need to be added to a spiritual assessment for them. Negative social attitudes about homosexuality cause a variety of harmful and painful consequences for people who are LGBT including fears resulting from being told they are going to hell, depression, low self-esteem, feelings of worthlessness, and suicide (Barton, 2010; Van Metter & Kelly, 2010).

Adolescents reporting to have strong fundamental religious beliefs are likely to have greater conflicts if they are lesbian, gay, bisexual, or transsexual because homosexuality is taught in fundamentalist groups to be an unacceptable and ungodly sin (Cates, 2007; Plugge-Foust & Strickland, 2000). This is not only true with fundamentalist Christians but also some Catholics, Mormons, and Jewish (Lynch, 1996) and Muslim groups (Davidson, 2000). Many other conservative to moderate religious organizations—for example, many Mainline Protestant groups—are also likely to maintain, in more subtle ways, a position that homosexuality is morally wrong. In recent years these religious groups are beginning to change and be more accepting. Yet, people who are LGBT must decide painfully which of their two identities must be rejected or at least concealed—their religious affiliation or their sexual orientation (Wagner, Serafini, Rabkin, Remien, & Williams, 1994). The coming-out process for some people who are LGBT is also important to consider in an assessment. Bowland, Foster, and Vosler (2013) stress the importance of asking questions about these issues, especially when the clients are conservative Christians or live in a conservative culture.

On the positive side, many churches and synagogues are increasingly welcoming LGBT groups into their communities with a progressive, healthy spiritual view of homosexuality. These groups in the Christian community include some Episcopalians, Evangelical Lutherans of America, Presbyterian-USA, United Church of Christ, United Methodists, Quakers and others. A Christian denomination called the Metropolitan Community Church is also springing up that primarily serves the needs of Gay Christians within the Christian Church. All of these groups and others are obviously important social supports to tell LGBT groups about (Bowland, Foster, & Vosler, 2013). These new and very different experiences with the Christian Church can be very healing and renewing to the identity of people who are LGBT.

Buchanan, Dzelme, Harris, and Hecker (2001) offer questions that can be asked of LGBTs that help them deconstruct how they may have thought of their identities in the past and to help them explore preferred ways of being for the future. These questions can be used as assessment questions that fall under the headings of intrinsic and extrinsic spirituality. Intrinsic spirituality is more associated with one's inner world and spirituality while extrinsic is associated more with the external world especially one's religious affiliations. Some of these questions are shared next.

Extrinsic/Religious Beliefs:

- In what ways do your religious practices impact your life in regard to your sexual identity? In what ways do they guide your life?

- In what ways does your family's religious background impact your life regarding your sexual identity?
- What support have you found within your church, doctrine, and canon for your sexual identity? What have been the limitations you have found within these?
- What can you do to inform yourself of the positive influences of these religious beliefs or practices?
- In what ways do your practices facilitate the experiencing of your sexual identity?

Intrinsic/Spiritual Beliefs:

- Where did you gain your spiritual beliefs? What has influenced your spiritual beliefs?
- How have these beliefs directed your life? In what ways are you gaining guidance from these beliefs?
- What are the effects of these spiritual beliefs and behaviors on your life and on your relationships?
- How do these spiritual beliefs encourage you in developing relationships with others of your same gender? How have these beliefs discouraged you from forming new relationships?
- In what ways do these spiritual beliefs contribute to your quality of life as a person? In what ways have these beliefs subtracted from your quality of life?

Several other questions are also suggested by Buchanan et al. (2001) that help LGBT people externalize problematic beliefs and thinking, open up space for new ways of thinking about their spiritual and sexual identity, and explore deeper meaning for them and their lives.

Health Care Clients

Health care clients typically utilize agencies and hospitals that are accredited. Many of the larger accreditation agencies at the national level require their member agencies to conduct spiritual assessments (Hodge, 2006). A notable one is the Joint Commission (formerly Joint Commission on Healthcare Organizations and previous to that the Joint Commission on Accreditation of Hospitals). The Joint Commission accredits more than 20,000 health care providers including hospitals and home care agencies. While the Joint Commission leaves it up to their agencies to determine the content and scope of a spiritual assessment, they suggest several possible in-depth questions as follows:

- Who or what provides the patient with strength and hope?
- Does the patient use prayer in their life?

- How does the patient express their spirituality?
- How would the patient describe their philosophy of life?
- What type of spiritual/religious support does the patient desire?
- What is the name of the patient's clergy, minister, chaplain, pastor, or rabbi?
- What does suffering mean to the patient?
- What does dying mean to the patient?
- What are the patient's spiritual goals?
- Is there a role of a church/synagogue in the patient's life?
- How does the patient's faith help them cope with illness?
- How does the patient keep going day after day?
- What helps the patient get through this health care experience?
- How has illness affected the patient and the patient's family?

(Joint Commission, 2015)

As you can see as you review these questions, all of them are very general and could fit with almost any agency setting. Only a few seem exclusively applicable to health care. Questions using the words "suffering," "dying," "illness," and "health care experience" could be viewed as directly referring to the patient's current illness and health care.

Other accreditation agencies like Community Health Accreditation Program (CHAP) and the Commission on Accreditation of Rehabilitation Facilities (CARF) also require spiritual assessments without requiring coverage of specific topics or questions. In these instances when specific requirements are not made beyond requiring a spiritual assessment, agencies accredited by these organizations have an excellent opportunity to devise their own questions based on their first-hand knowledge of what their clients need. However, such vague requirements can also be problematic if some member agencies do not take them seriously and possibly pass over them.

A team of nurses (Galek, Flannelly, Vane, & Galek, 2005) conducted a literature search of articles on spiritual assessments in the health field published in nursing and medical journals and found seven major constructs. They included 1) love/belonging/respect; 2) the Divine; 3) positivity/gratitude/hope/peace; 4) meaning and purpose; 5) morality and ethics; 6) appreciation of beauty; and 7) resolution/death. From there they constructed a very useful 29-item quantitative spiritual assessment questionnaire that identified spiritual needs falling under these constructs. Examples of items under each construct are as follows:

1) love/belonging/respect

- to be accepted as a person
- to feel a sense of connection with the world
- for compassion and kindness
- for respectful care of your bodily needs

2) Divine

- to participate in religious or spiritual services
- to have someone pray with or for you
- to read spiritual or religious material
- for guidance from a Higher Power

3) positivity/gratitude/hope/peace

- to feel hopeful
- to feel a sense of peace and contentment
- to have a quiet space to meditate or reflect
- to be thankful or grateful

4) meaning and purpose

- to find meaning in suffering
- to find meaning and purpose in life
- to understand why you have a medical problem

5) morality and ethics

- to live an ethical and moral life

6) appreciation of beauty

- to experience or appreciate music
- to experience or appreciate nature

7) resolution/death

- to address unmet issues before death
- to address concerns about life after death
- to have a deeper understanding of death and dying
- to forgive yourself and others
- to review your life.

For each spiritual need, the patients were to identify if it was evident to them while they were in the hospital, using the choices of yes or no. A scale was also used to indicate how important each need was; patients were to choose: slightly, moderately, very, or extremely.

Hodge and Horvath (2011) examined eleven studies focusing on health care needs from the clients' perspectives. Their meta-analysis resulted in the identification of six primary themes. These themes were 1) meaning, purpose, and hope; 2) their relationship with God; 3) spiritual practices; 4) religious obligations; 5) interpersonal connection; and 6) professional staff interactions. Some of these themes overlap with themes in studies already reported above. Other themes offer additional information about patients' spiritual needs. The theme "their relationship with God" included questions of God such as pleading for healing and worrying about who was to blame for their condition. Also they mentioned a desire to want to get right with God, trust God's will, and ask for help in accepting what has happened to them. They also wanted to be reassured of God's presence and care of them. The theme "religious obligations" included Jewish and Muslim respondents requesting special types of religious food such as kosher or halal food, respect for modesty, particularly in gender roles, and specific practices surrounding death and burial. Jehovah's Witnesses requested avoidance of blood transfusions. The "interpersonal connections" theme included a need for visiting with family members and others who share their spiritual values, receiving prayers from others, seeking forgiveness from people they may have wronged in the past, and bereavement activities.

Mental Health Clients

Studies of mental health clients indicate that many of them view spirituality as an important positive aspect of their lives and in some cases a means of getting better (Gotterer, 2001; Sullivan, 2009). In contrast, past religious experiences of other mental health clients have been problematic to their well-being, with trauma and abuse being part of them. A study by Fitchett, Burton, and Sivan (1997) of the religious needs of 51 psychiatric patients that were hospitalized found that 58 percent responded affirmatively that they had religious needs. In addition, in some cases higher percentages responded affirmatively that specific concepts relevant to religion were important. Eighty-four percent indicated affirmatively that they knew of God's presence, 80 percent indicated prayer was important to them, 75 percent responded favorably about their purpose and meaning in life, 65 percent wished to have a chaplain visit and pray with them, 51 percent indicated they wanted relief from fear of death, and 39 percent wanted the sacraments of their religion. This study and others remind us that general questions about spirituality often need to be followed up by specific questions that go in more depth related to issues of importance to clients. In this case, the term "religion" by itself does not help them identify all that religion may be to them.

When mental health clients have psychotic episodes, care must be taken to distinguish content of a spiritual nature from a psychotic episode. For example, clients who say that they hear voices from God or Jesus calling them may be truly aware of an inner sense of a call or it could be a psychotic episode (Gotterer, 2001). Hodge (2004) suggests that an effort be made to discern whether such a comment is an isolated one or one in a collection of many. Also he suggests exploring it in terms of the client's worldview. For example, a Pentecostal church and possibly other religious groups could be teaching and encouraging such metaphysical experiences as normal. Such a statement as hearing the voice of God should also be assessed in light of the clients' overall functioning and other comments of a similar nature that they make (Fallot, 2001b; Fallot, 2001a). Practitioners who wish to engage these issues with mental health clients will need to have highly specialized skills in the areas of clinical work on religious issues and mental health and likely a long-term relationship with the clients as well (Sullivan, 2009). Clergy affiliated with the client's religious denomination as well as psychiatric professionals should be consulted to help with these distinctions and how they can be determined.

Gotterer (2001) recommends keeping in mind that spirituality and religion can be both a source of strength and confusion to mental health clients. Their strength can be manifested in emotional solace, inspiration, community, structure, security, and guidance. They can also be a source of confusion, pain and conflict. The challenge becomes detecting the difference and helping clients distinguish between what is helpful and what is harmful. Hodge (2004) also suggests several spiritual assessment questions be asked of people with mental illness. Five of them are mentioned here as general starting points for exploring more specifically how the clients' spirituality may help them with a specific disorder.

1. I was wondering if you consider spirituality or religion to be a personal strength.
2. In what ways does your spirituality help you cope with the difficulties you encounter?
3. Are there certain spiritual beliefs that you find particularly helpful in dealing with problems?
4. Are there certain spiritual practices that you find particularly helpful in dealing with problems?
5. Do resources exist in your church (or religious) community that might be helpful to you?

Most of these questions are similar to questions that have already been identified in this chapter but these questions seem to be exploring more directly a possible link between the clients' spirituality and their specific mental condition. Further questions could be asked in which a client could think about how their particular problems may be helped by specific spiritual interventions. For example, a client with an anxiety disorder may be asked if she has ever found meditation or prayer help her lower her anxiety.

Older Adult Clients

Spirituality and religion are viewed to be important to many older adults as they move into the later stages of life. Research has found connections between older adults' ability to cope with chronic illness and religion (Lee & Sharpe, 2007; Mackenzie, Rajagopal, Meibohm, & Lavizzo-Mourey, 2000), grief (MacKinlay, 2002), and facing their own mortality (Hermann, 2001). Nelson-Becker, Nakashima, and Canda (2006) suggest that other factors facing older adults may also suggest a need to explore connections to their spirituality. On the positive side, spirituality and religion could be explored when it is important to an older adult, influences their views of dying and death in a positive way, and provides important social support. On the negative side, they suggest exploring spiritual and religious issues when clients experience depression, chronic and terminal illness, anxiety about death, the need for bereavement, a need for caregiving, substance abuse, physical or emotional abuse or neglect; trauma, or a crisis of faith.

Nelson-Becker, Nakashima, and Canda (2006) recommend finding out about an older adult's interest in discussing their spirituality before attempting any in-depth exploration because many older adults view this topic as very personal and possibly private. Asking about it initially can also encourage clients to share topics that they might not otherwise share. They recommend initial questions such as, "1) Are spirituality, religion, or faith important in your life? 2) What terms do you prefer? Please explain." Nelson-Becker and colleagues have identified eleven domains of spirituality that could be relevant to assess for older adults. They suggest that combining questions from each of these domains offers an important framework for assessing the spirituality of older adults. Their spiritual assessment domains include: 1) spiritual affiliation; 2) spiritual belief; 3) spiritual behavior; 4) emotional qualities of spirituality; 5) values; 6) spiritual experiences; 7) spiritual history; 8) therapeutic change factors; 9) social support; 10) spiritual well-being; and 11) extrinsic/intrinsic spiritual focus (Nelson-Becker et al., 2006). Since most of these domains have been covered in this and earlier chapters, only the assessment questions that have not been identified will be mentioned. They are included under emotional qualities of spirituality and therapeutic change factors.

Emotions are possibly a major source for describing and experiencing spirituality (Nelson-Becker et al., 2006). People's spirituality can cause them to feel joy, awe, mystery, and hope; anxiety, shame, guilt, and many other feelings. Some believe emotions are the essence of one's spirituality or religion. Some assessment questions that could be asked related to emotions are:

- Have you recently experienced an emotion such as anger, sadness, guilt, or joy in the context of religious or spiritual experience?
- What significance, if any, did this have for you?
- (Or if a client is describing an experience, one can ask) what feelings did you have in response?

Nelson-Becker et al. (2006) refer to therapeutic change factors as the clients' strengths and resources harnessed for healing, growth, and overall well-being, assisted by spiritual support groups and rituals. They give the example of a client who promotes healing from a severe illness through a rite of anointment or laying on of hands (Dossey, 1993). A set of assessment questions that may be able to capture therapeutic change of a spiritual nature for a client are:

- What might be an object or image that symbolizes/represents your spiritual strengths?
- Could you tell me a story of how spirituality helped you cope with difficulties in the recent past?
- How do you see this particular spiritual strength as being able to help you in your current problems?
- What spiritually based strategies, rituals, or actions have helped you to cope with times of difficulty or to experience healing or growth?

Clients with Terminal Illnesses

A few field settings naturally include spirituality as a central focus in their assessments and interventions. One of them is hospice and palliative care for clients who are dying. In these settings, it is important to be prepared to explore a wide range of topics and questions on spirituality. Doka (2011) suggests that spirituality and religion may be critical resources for clients trying to find meaning in their illnesses, especially life-threatening ones. Making sense of their suffering, anticipated death, and their life become so important to many such clients. Therefore, he urges agencies with clients with terminal illnesses to go beyond asking about the clients' religious affiliation in their spiritual assessments. Asking clients when and where they feel most spiritually connected could begin this deeper exploration. Also they could be asked about spiritual practices that help them. They may want to share stories, prayers, or songs they utilize. Further, an exploration of meaning and hope could be very useful as clients decline and anticipate their death and a possible afterlife.

Hospice clients often utilize hospice settings that are accredited by the National Hospice and Palliative Care Organization (NHPCO). This national agency recommends a spiritual assessment for patients and to use a Social Work Assessment Tool (SWAT). It is an instrument that patients can fill out as a questionnaire or answer via an interview schedule with assistance from a social worker. Among 11 items that are assessed, six directly explore spiritual or religious issues and are as follows:

1. Do the patients' medical treatments match up with their religious and cultural beliefs?
2. Are the patients handling their feelings of grief pretty well?
3. Do patients have good support from friends, family, and places of worship?
4. Do patients feel a higher purpose in life and a sense of connection with all?
5. Are patients extremely upset to the point of thinking about suicide or wanting to hasten their death?

6. Are patients fearful about dying?

This assessment instrument is quantitative in nature and includes a 5-point Likert scale measuring from extremely likely to extremely unlikely. If the answers to these questions indicate a problem, follow-up questions of an in-depth nature would likely be asked such as, "Can you tell me more?" Or, another follow-up question could be, "What can we do to more fully help you?"

Dudley, Smith, and Millison (1995) conducted a study of the spiritual assessments used by 53 hospice workers in three states. They reported using assessment questions that included some questions that were religious in nature and others that were spiritual but not religious in nature. Religious questions that they asked included some that were basic about the clients' religious affiliation and others that were open-ended and pertinent to various religious issues. Almost all of their assessment forms asked the basic questions about religious affiliation mostly with the intention of finding out if they should be referred to an outside religious organization. These affiliation questions essentially are:

- What is your religion/denomination?
- Do you belong to a particular church or synagogue or mosque?
- Who is your clergy person?
- Do you want for him/her to contact you?
- Have you grown up in a religious tradition? (Asked particularly if client answered "no" to the previous questions.)

Other more in-depth religious questions were also asked. Some attempted to find out if the clients' religious beliefs were a source of support. For example, some asked: What is the role of your religious beliefs in your daily life? What role does religion play in dealing with your illness? Have your beliefs or practices changed since your illness? In addition, some hospice programs also asked whether or not the clients needed or wanted to share religious rituals or traditions with someone and if these particular rituals were helpful in controlling their pain or comforting them. Specific rituals mentioned on many of these forms were prayer, scripture readings, other religious readings, receiving the sacraments, meditation, worship service, expressing feelings toward God, sacrament of the sick, anointing, confession, and penance.

Still other questions explored whether clients experienced possible religious problems or barriers in coping with their illness (Dudley, Smith, & Millison, 1995). Examples of these questions were:

- Are you estranged from (angry with) your church/synagogue (or God)?
- Do you have religious conflicts with palliative care?
- Do you have confusion or doubts about your religious beliefs (or do you have unanswered prayers)?
- Are you having difficulty carrying out your religious duties?

- Do you have a wish for more faith (or stronger religious beliefs, or greater belief in an afterlife) to help you with your illness?
- Do you have a need for dealing with guilt and/or a need for forgiveness?

Other questions were spiritual in nature and not explicitly religious. Both a non-religious and religious person may find them relevant. Several spiritual topics were identified in these assessment instruments that could be explored with clients. These topics fell under "problems" and "other" topics. The problem-centered topics included: fear of death, abandonment, hopelessness, spiritual emptiness, unresolved grief, loss of meaning in life, unresolved past conflicts or experiences, confusions or doubts regarding beliefs, why me?, need for reconciliation with or forgiveness from other people, need for comfort and peace, need to receive love from others. Other spiritual topics not problem-centered included: philosophy of life, expressions of spirituality, important past or current events, feelings about God and self, belief in life after death, existential meaningfulness, things uncompleted, faith and hope, and support systems.

Still other spiritual questions were used that were open-ended. They included:

- How do you express your spirituality? How do you feel about your current spiritual practices?
- How would you describe your philosophy of life? How are you feeling about your philosophy of life at this time?
- Do you have a philosophy about illness (or your illness)?
- How do you understand hope? For what do you hope?
- What helps you the most when you feel afraid or need special help?
- What is especially meaningful or frightening to you now?
- How has being sick made any difference in how or what you believe?
- What do you think is going to happen to you?
- What does death mean to you? Do you have a belief in an afterlife?
- Do you have feelings of bitterness or resentment towards anyone? How do you handle feelings of bitterness, resentment, guilt, or anger? Do you desire spiritual support to deal with such feelings?
- Do you have any unresolved guilt or anger surrounding your illness or about the illness itself?
- What are the most important relationships in your life? Why are they important? Would the loss of any relationship change the purpose of your life?
- Do you feel a source of love from God or any spiritual being?
- Has spiritual support been helpful to you in the past? What is your source of strength during your current illness?

It should be noted that some of these spiritual topics, such as fears, bitterness, unresolved conflicts, and hope, could also be interpreted as psychological in nature.

However, the nature of the assessment process would be quite different based on whether it is a spiritual or psychological assessment.

Different Methods of Conducting Spiritual Assessments

Let's briefly highlight some of the methods of data collection that are relevant to conducting assessments. Assessments involve asking questions and there are three essential ways of asking questions—asking clients in an interview format, asking clients to fill out a questionnaire, and assessing by observing them (Dudley, 2011; Hodge, 2005a).

Assessments Using Interviews

Assessments are usually most effectively conducted in face-to-face interviews with the clients. Questions can be clarified if misunderstood and clients' non-verbal expressions can be observed. Interviews can have questions that are structured, semi-structured, or unstructured. Unstructured interviews, also referred to as in-depth interviews, use a very flexible format and mostly use open-ended questions that are well suited to spiritual assessments (Hodge, 2001; Dudley, 2011). An interview guide is used composed of a purpose, a list of all of the topics to be explored, and possibly some specific questions to be asked related to some of the topics. Usually, the interviewer formulates many of the specific questions and asks them in an order suited to the individual client's needs in each interview. An unstructured interview format would be a good choice when an agency views spirituality as reflected as the whole person or the core person. The interview feels a lot like a conversation because it has a somewhat spontaneous flow to it. It is only different from a conversation in that the flow of information is mostly coming from the client to the worker; also these interviews are private, confidential, and have a purpose.

An unstructured assessment interview is also similar to the ethnographic interviewing approach, which can be a profound way of understanding the client's spirituality (Robert-Lewis, 2011). This anthropological approach views the client as a cultural guide, which means that the client becomes the educator and the worker becomes the student. Questions revolve around asking the client to teach the worker about their religious and spiritual practices with questions such as, "I want to learn from you so I can understand your point of view." "Global questions" are typically asked; global questions are very open-ended and ask the client to share and elaborate on their religious practices. A global question could be "Could you help me understand how your religious and spiritual beliefs help you cope with these life challenges that you are reporting?" "Cover terms" are another characteristic of ethnographic interviewing. These cover terms are words used by the client that have particular cultural meanings in their worldview. These cover terms could be reflections of religious traditions such as Holy Communion, yoga, chanting, or confession. Once these cover terms are revealed and detected, descriptors could be explored. Descriptors are culturally meaningful information that a client shares related to cover terms that provide an "inside view" of the client's life and spirituality typically not known by an outsider. If a cover term turns out to be spirituality, for example, descriptors can be explored through elaborations, examples, metaphors, and contexts of what spirituality means to the client.

Motivational interviewing techniques are also relevant to this exploration. While open-ended questions are very helpful for clients in exploring their spirituality and spiritual issues, reflections may be just as important (Matulich, 2013). Reflection can be in many forms. For example, you could simply repeat an element of what a client says. Or you can infer the meaning of what is said and reflect it back in new words. Or you can also emphasize the emotional dimension through a feeling statement. Matulich suggests stems to begin reflection statements such as "It sounds like . . .", "You're wondering . . ." and "If I understand you correctly . . . ." He believes that many people feel listened to, understood, and cared about with reflections, even maybe more than questions. So, for example, if clients are disappointed because they are not finding answers from God to a tragedy, a helpful reflection could be "You're wondering how and when God will help you make meaning out of this tragedy."

Assessment interviews that are structured, semi-structured, or unstructured can easily be adapted to group interviews. A group interview could be used to assess a family, a support group, treatment group, or a community group. A group interview has advantages, such as the group dynamics, that can be used to facilitate discussion among all of the participants (Corey, 2004; Toseland & Rivas, 2011). This is particularly important with a topic like spirituality that may not be easily discussed. Group members are often a helpful catalyst for each other in stimulating discussion on a topic of common interest. One interviewee, for example, might express a spiritual belief that encourages another interviewee to express a similar or differing belief. Yet, if participants in group interviews are reluctant to express their views on a sensitive subject like spirituality, a false homogeneity of views may result. For example, a teenager may be hesitant to discuss her views on the religious belief of her parents about birth control for fear it may bring disapproval from her parents.

Assessments Using Questionnaires

Questionnaires, like interviews, can be constructed at different levels of structure—structured, semi-structured, or unstructured (Dudley, 2011). Mailed questionnaires can be used, for example, for prospective clients to explore their thoughts about their spirituality before they attend an assessment interview. The questionnaire could be composed of a set of closed and open-ended questions. However, if you use a questionnaire, keep in mind that the worker is not readily available to offer assistance in clarifying the questions on a questionnaire, in contrast to an interview.

Questionnaires need to be devised so that they are as self-explanatory as possible. Using mailed questionnaires do have an advantage of giving you easy access to numerous people who may live a long distance away (Dudley, 2011). Administering a mailed questionnaire simply requires a mailing address, an envelope, and postage. Also, electronic or computerized questionnaires are the latest development in questionnaire studies. A computerized self-administered questionnaire can be sent via an e-mail attachment, or it can be accessed on a website or an electronic bulletin board. The responses can be saved and maintained on an electronic file that is automatically prepared for data analysis. However, keep in mind that a major disadvantage of electronic questionnaires is that they exclude anyone without access to a computer.

Unstructured questionnaires can be helpful in many instances. A spiritual assessment used by an agency that views spirituality as a key aspect or the central core of clients may find questionnaires to be a creative way to learn more about their clients and their spirituality. Several open-ended questions could be asked about clients' spiritual development or pressing spiritual issues. For example, clients at the point of entry to a program in a hospice setting can share the ramifications of what they believe and what is important for them at this point in time (Doka, 2011).

Assessments through Observations

A third way to gather data for assessments is to observe clients when meeting with them in an office interview, and when visiting them in their own home (Dudley, 2011). The importance of observational methods in conducting assessments is often overlooked. Observations offer numerous opportunities to further understand people on a spiritual and religious level. We can learn something about people through the religious and spiritual symbols that they wear, such as a Christian cross or a shirt with the affiliation to a religious or spiritual group. A peace sign, for example, on someone's paraphernalia could tell a lot about their spiritual positions, or possibly nothing. Head covers for Islamic women, yarmulkes for Jewish men, and colorful robes worn by Hindu women from India are also potential indicators that could open up opportunities for discussions about religious and spiritual meanings. Facial expressions are also sometimes relevant to assessments, such as a big smile by a client when religion or spirituality is mentioned or being silent in a group session because of particular religious customs that discourage self-disclosure to strangers or people outside someone's religious group.

Spiritual Histories

Spiritual histories may imply a rather lengthy assessment that is comprehensive and includes several different questions. The focus would necessarily be determined based on the mission of an agency. For example, if it is a family counseling agency like Jewish Family Services, the history would concern issues in the past and present related to family relationships. Questions could explore religious and spiritual teachings from the past and their importance to the children and adults in the family; also questions about marriage, the fathers' and mothers' roles, single parenting, divorce, and cohabitation. Their views about raising children could also be explored with the emphasis being placed on their religious and spiritual training received in the past.

Several lengthy spiritual histories are available in the literature. Two of them are noted here as examples. Boyd (1998) offers a comprehensive religious/spiritual assessment tool that has questions about several topics of the past. They could include the person's spiritual upbringing, life-shaping experiences, any conversion/ peak/mystical experiences, spiritual crises and emergencies, their current social environment, religious identity, commitment level, and religious affiliations and involvements. They could also include codification of beliefs, rituals/image symbols/behavioral enactments/observances/practices, God images, concepts of evil and the demonic, a person's spiritual developmental stages, effects of their spiritual identity on life style, meaning of life issues, and their moral frame of reference.

Hodge (2001) introduces a spiritual history assessment that emphasizes qualitative methods. His assessment instrument asks questions about the clients' religious and spiritual traditions growing up, highlights of their spiritual experiences that stood out in retrospect, their current spiritual/religious orientation and strengths, and an exploration of questions about spirituality. These questions could also focus on clients' affective life (e.g. coping with life's pain), behavioral life (e.g. spiritual rituals and practice that help the client cope), cognition (e.g. their current spiritual and religious beliefs), communication with a Higher Power, conscience (e.g. how they determine right and wrong), and intuition (e.g. experiencing intuitive hunches).

Other Spiritual Tools

Spiritual tools provide another way of assessing spiritual issues of clients. Canda and Furman (2010) describe a **spiritual development timeline** exercise representing a client's life that is plotted on a graph. It can be diagramed with the assistance of a practitioner or by clients alone. Its intent is to describe a special form of spiritual history, a visual image of a client's spiritual development. Such an assessment is useful to clients who want or need to have an in-depth examination of their spirituality. Such an exercise can begin wherever the client wants to start—as a young child attending Sunday school, an exhilarating episode during adolescence while at a church retreat, or around an episode of a painful betrayal by a church pastor. Some of the advantages of using a spiritual development timeline are that it shifts communication away from direct verbal sharing by a client to a more neutral object, the graph (Hodge, 2005b). Children and youth as well as those who are highly sensitive about discussing their spirituality in particular may find a timeline more comfortable to use. Also, creativity can be encouraged in drawing the timeline using a wide range of art materials, magazine pictures, and various colors.

Spiritual genograms are another assessment tool. Most social workers are familiar with family genograms that help clients understand their family dynamics going back two or three or more generations. Spiritual genograms add another layer to family affairs, the spiritual and religious influences (Hodge, 2005b). The spiritual genogram can help a client visualize and gain insights about these various influences. Standard genogram conventions recommend using circles and squares along with lines to describe close, distant, and uncomfortable relationships. Colors, shades of colors, and possibly spiritual symbols can be used to reflect different orientations to religion (e.g. Jewish or Southern Baptist). Dates can be added to reflect when someone began participating in a particular religious group and how and when they made changes in their affiliations. Degrees of involvement in these religious and spiritual groups should also be indicated, possibly by using shades of colors and other artistic tools. The relationships among family members, past and current, are most important to describe (Collins, Jordan, & Coleman, 2007). As in other family genograms, lines with arrows indicate the flow of energy and influence both ways or one way. Lines are used to reflect the nature of these relationships with thicker lines signifying stronger relationships, dashed lines representing more tenuous relationships, and jagged lines symbolizing conflicted ones. Spiritual genograms are especially useful when family systems play a role in the client's issues. For example, immigrant families with strong religious traditions, extended families with intergenerational religious influences, interfaith marriages, blended families, and other types of families can particularly benefit from genograms (Poole, 1998).

Spiritual ecomaps are another assessment tool that is useful in social work assessments (Collins, Jordan, & Coleman, 2007). Spiritual ecomaps help clients visualize what is going on around them in spiritual terms in the context of their social environments. These assessment tools are mostly for the current happenings in the clients' lives while family genograms focus more on the past. An individual or family client system is included in the inner circle of the ecomap. Outside this circle is an open area in which spiritual supports and problems are identified. Generally, the closer these entities are to the inner circle of the client system, the more influence and regular involvement they are likely to have.

These entities may include memberships in religious groups, spiritual support groups like Alcoholics Anonymous, youth groups, or a church Bible study group that meets regularly. In addition, key people who are spiritual supports are included, such as a mother who has a close relationship with a client and her family. Spiritual problems are also added, such as a connection to a problematic religious group and people that bring spiritual tension or unhelpful critical encounters. Hodge (2005b) suggests that these ecomaps can be used to explore the nature of the spiritual aspects of the clients' relationships with others with whom they are close;

they can focus on such things as their beliefs in a Higher Power and transcendence experiences. For example, a Muslim client who practices prayer five times each day could include the locations where her prayers are usually practiced, any people that join her, employers and others with whom she has to negotiate time away, and the mosques that she attends.

Spiritual ecograms combine the information and visual advantages of ecomaps and genograms into a more comprehensive assessment that takes into account the benefits of past generations in a spiritual genogram and the current spiritual environment of an ecomap. Canda and Furman (2010) and Hodge (2005b) among others describe helpful illustrations of spiritual ecograms and lifemaps. According to Hodge, the client system is placed in the center of the ecogram. The top half of the page describes the client's intergenerational spiritual history using a genogram diagram. The bottom charts the client's current relationships, positive and negative, using the structures of a genogram. The genogram provides a visual description of how people and events in the past may influence present relationships with people and organizations. A Hindu immigrant family from India, for example, is likely to be significantly influenced by previous generations in the family who provide a strong religious and cultural bond that keeps these families together.

Conclusion

The chapter covers the assessment component or phase of the practice approach described in the book. Numerous articles have been written on spiritual assessment in social work. The chapter covers five different aspects of this topic: what spiritual assessment questions to ask, looking at a client's spirituality from different angles, implicit versus explicit assessments, specific assessment questions recommended for different client groups, and some suggestions on different methods to use in conducting spiritual assessments. The assessment issues focusing on specific client groups covered in the chapter include people who are LGBT, clients in health care settings and mental health settings, older adults, and clients with terminal illnesses.

Discussion Questions and Exercises

1. How spiritual are you? How religious are you? Answer the set of questions asked in Figure 8.1 to help you answer these two questions for yourself. Which questions are particularly helpful? What questions are missing that are important to you?

2. Several questions about spirituality and religion are listed in Figure 8.2. If you were to select a set of five key questions to ask your clients in a spiritual assessment, which of these questions do you think are most important to ask? What other questions may be left off of this list that you would also want to ask a client?

3. The chapter includes an in-depth look at the spiritual assessments of five different client groups. Select one of these client groups or another client group of which you have interest. Then develop five assessment questions that you would like to ask that address the special spiritual needs of this particular client group.

References

Barton, B. (2010). "Abomination"—Life as a Bible belt gay. *Journal of Homosexuality*, 57(4), 465–484.

Bowland, S., Foster, K., & Vosler, N. R. (2013). Culturally competent and spiritually sensitive therapy with lesbian and gay Christians. *Social Work*, 58(4), 321–332.

Boyd, T. (1998). Spiritually sensitive tools for social work practice. In B. Hugen, *Christianity and social work: Readings on the integration of Christian faith and social work practice*. Botsford, CT: NACSW, 239–255.

Buchanan, M., Dzelme, K., Harris, D., & Hecker, L. (2001). Challenges of being simultaneously gay or lesbian and spiritual and/or religious: A narrative perspective. *American Journal of Family Therapy*, 29, 435–449.

Burton, R. (2004). Spiritual pains: Origins, nature and management. *Contact*, 143, 3–13.

Canda, E. R., & Furman, L. D. (2010). *Spiritual diversity in social work practice: The heart of healing*. 2nd edition. New York: Free Press.

Cates, J. A. (2007). Identity in crisis: Spirituality and homosexuality in adolescence. *Child & Adolescent Social Work Journal*, 24(4), 369–383.

Collins, D., Jordan, C., & Coleman, H. (2007). *An introduction to family social work*. 2nd edition. Belmont, CA: Thomson Learning.

Corey, G. (2004). *Theory and practice of group counseling*. 6th edition. Belmont CA: Thomson Learning.

Crisp, B. R. (2010). *Spirituality and social work*. Surrey, England: Ashgate.

CSWE (Council on Social Work Education) (2015). *2015 Educational Policy and Accreditation Standards for Baccalaureate and Master's Social Work Programs*. Educational Policy Approved by the CSWE Board of Directors on March 20, 2015; Accreditation Standards approved by the CSWE Commission on Accreditation on June 11, 2015. Alexandria, VA: Author.

Davidson, M. G. (2000). Religion and spirituality. In R. M. Perez, K. A. DeBord, & K. J. Bieschke (Eds.), *Handbook of counseling and psychotherapy with lesbian, gay, and bisexual clients*. Washington, DC: American Psychological Association, 409–433.

Doka, K. J. (2011). Religion and spirituality: Assessment and intervention. *Journal of Social Work in End-of-Life & Palliative Care*, 7, 99–109.

Dossey, L. (1993). *Healing words: The power of prayer and the practice of medicine*. San Francisco: Harper.

Dudley, J. (2011). *Research methods for social work: Being producers and consumers of research*. 2nd edition (updated edition), Boston: Allyn & Bacon.

Dudley, J., Smith, C., & Millison, M. (1995). Unfinished business: Assessing the spiritual needs of hospice clients, *American Journal of Hospice and Palliative Care*, March/April, 30–37.

Ellison, C. G., & George, L. K. (1994). Religious involvement, social ties, and social support in a southeastern community. *Journal for the Scientific Study of Religion*, 33(1), 46–61.

Fallot, R. D. (2001a). The place of spirituality and religion in mental health services. In R. H. Lamb (Ed.), *New directions for mental health services*. San Francisco: Jossey-Bass, 79–88.

Fallot, R. D. (2001b). Spirituality and religion in psychiatric rehabilitation and recovery from mental illness. *International Review of Psychiatry, 13*, 110–116.

Fitchett, G., Burton, L. A., & Sivan, A. B. (1997). The religious needs and resources of psychiatric inpatients. *The Journal of Nervous and Mental Disease, 185*, 320–326.

Galek, K., Flannelly, K. J., Vane, A., & Galek, R. M. (2005). Assessing a patient's spiritual needs: A comprehensive instrument. *Holistic Nursing Practice, 19*(2), 62–69.

Gotterer, R. (2001). The spiritual dimension in clinical social work practice: A client perspective. *Families in Society, 82*(2), 187–193.

Griffith, J. L., & Griffith, M. E. (2002). *Encountering the sacred in psychotherapy.* New York: Guilford Press.

Harris, B. (2002). *The father quest: Rediscovering an elemental psychic force.* Cheyenne, WY: Fisher King Press, 148.

Hermann, C. P. (2001). Spiritual needs of dying patients: A qualitative study. *Oncology Nursing Forum, 28*, 67–72.

Hodge, D. R. (2001). Spiritual assessment: A review of major qualitative methods and a new framework for assessing spirituality. *Social Work, 46*(3), 197–201.

Hodge, D. R. (2004). Spirituality and people with mental Illness: Developing spiritual competency in assessment and intervention. *Families in Society, 85*(1), 36–44.

Hodge, D. R. (2005a). Developing a spiritual assessment toolbox: A discussion of the strengths and limitations of five different assessment methods. *Health & Social Work, 30*(4), 314–323.

Hodge, D. R. (2005b). Spiritual assessment in marital and family therapy: A methodological framework for selecting from among six qualitative assessment tools. *A Journal of Marital and Family Therapy, 31*(40), 341–356.

Hodge, D. R. (2006). A template for spiritual assessment: A review of the JCAHO requirements and guidelines for implementation. *Social Work, 51*(4), 317–326.

Hodge, D. R. (2013). Implicit spiritual assessment: An alternative approach for assessing client spirituality. *Social Work, 58*(3), 223–230.

Hodge, D. R. & Horvath, V. E. (2011). Spiritual needs in health care settings: A qualitative meta-synthesis of clients' perspectives. *Social Work, 56*(4), 306–316.

Holloway, M., & Moss, B. (2010). *Spirituality and social work.* New York: Palgrave Macmillan.

Hoyt, C. A. (2008). What if the spirit does not move me? A personal reconnaissance and reconciliation. *Social Work, 53*(3), 223–231.

Ibrahim, F. A. & Dykeman, C. (2011). Counseling Muslim Americans: Cultural and spiritual assessments. *Journal of Counseling & Development, 89*, 387–396.

Joint Commission. (2014). Standards FAQ details: Spiritual assessment. Revised November 24, 2008. Available online at http://www.jointcommission.org/standards_information/jcfaqdetails.aspx?StandardsFaqId=290&ProgramId=47 (accessed February 14, 2014).

Lee, K. O., & Sharpe, T. (2007). Understanding religious/spiritual coping and support resources among African American older adults: A mixed-method approach. *Journal of Religion, Spirituality & Aging, 19*(3), 55–75.

Lynch B. (1996). Religious and spirituality conflicts. In D. Davies & C. Neal (Eds.), *Pink therapy: A guide for counselors and therapists working with lesbian, gay and bisexual clients.* Buckingham, England: Open University Press, 199–207.

Mackenzie, E. R., Rajagopal, D. E., Meibohm, M., & Lavizzo-Mourey, R. (2000). Spiritual support and psychological well-being: Older adults' perceptions of the religion and health connection. *Alternative Therapies, 6*(6), 37–45.

MacKinlay, E. (2002). Health, healing and wholeness in frail elderly people. *Journal of Religious Gerontology, 13*, 25–34.

Matulich, B. (2013). How to do motivational interviewing: A guidebook. 2nd edition. www. motivationalinterviewingonline.com.

Millison, M., & Dudley, J. (1990). The importance of spirituality in hospice work. *The Hospice Journal*, 6, 63–78.

Moore, R. J. (2003). Spiritual assessment. *Social Work*, 48(4), 558–561.

Nelson-Becker, H., Nakashima, M., & Canda, E. R. (2006). Spiritual assessment in aging. *Journal of Gerontological Social Work*, 48(3–4), 331–347.

Pargament, K. I. (2007). *Spiritually integrated psychotherapy: Understanding and addressing the sacred.* New York: Guilford Press.

Plugge-Foust, C., & Strickland, G. (2000). Homophobia, irrationality, and Christian ideology: Does a relationship exist? *Journal of Sex Education and Therapy*, 25, 240–244.

Poole, D. L. (1998). Politically correct or culturally competent? *Health & Social Work*, 23, 163–166.

Robert-Lewis, A. (2011). Response to Mark Chaves: Practical interventions to assist social work students in addressing religious and spiritual diversity. *Social Work and Christianity*, 38(2), 139–145.

St. John of the Cross. (2003). *Dark night of the soul.* Mineola, NY: Dover Publications.

Sheridan, M. J. (2004). Predicting the use of spiritually-derived interventions in social work practice: A survey of practitioners. *Journal of Religion and Spirituality in Social Work: Social Thought*, 23(4), 5–25.

Sullivan, W. P. (2009). Spirituality: A road to mental health or mental illness. *Journal of Religion & Spirituality in Social Work: Social Thought*, 28(1–2), 84–98.

Toseland, R. W., & Rivas, R. F. (2011). *An introduction to group work practice.* 7th edition. Boston: Pearson.

Van Metter, K., & Kelly, J. (2010). Religious and spiritual impact in LGBT populations. Unpublished report, School of Social Work, University of North Carolina at Charlotte.

Wagner, G., Serafini, J., Rabkin, J., Remien, R., & Williams, J. (1994). Integration of one's religion and homosexuality: A weapon against internalized homophobia. *Journal of Homosexuality*, 26(4), 91–110.

9

Spiritual Interventions

Each time a (person) stands up for an ideal, or acts to improve the lot of others, or strikes out against injustice, he sends forth a tiny ripple of hope, and crossing each other from a million different centers of energy and daring, those ripples build a current which can sweep down the mightiest walls of oppression and resistance.

(Bobby Kennedy, Cape Town, South Africa, 1966)

If you cannot find truth where you are, where do you expect to find it?

(Zen Dirt, 2011)

Interventions that are spiritual in nature are the focus of this and the next two chapters. Introducing spiritual interventions is the third component of the dynamic and inter-active process of social work practice promulgated by the accrediting agency (CSWE, 2015). Spiritual interventions primarily at the micro and mezzo levels are described in this chapter. Chapter 10 focuses on macro spiritual interventions and chapter 11 explores ways to infuse spiritual concepts into several general practice approaches.

Once an initial spiritual assessment has been completed, spiritual interventions are usually introduced. Unfortunately, however, spiritual interventions may not naturally derive or result from spiritual assessments. In reality some social agencies are organized so that intake workers in one unit conduct assessments and prac-titioners in another unit implement interventions. Continuity in this case can be challenging. Even when the same worker carries out assessments and interventions as a continuous process, one step may not easily follow the other unless the assess-ment includes explicit recommendations about possible interventions to introduce.

Dudley, Smith, and Millison (1995) reviewed the spiritual assessments instru-ments of 53 hospice workers in three states to determine if any of their questions focused at all on possible interventions beyond simply a referral to a clergy person. They found about half of the forms made reference to an intervention plan with questions such as, "What type of spiritual/religious support does the client desire?" Yet in most of these instances, there were no guidelines for recommending any particular spiritual interventions beyond referrals. These researchers concluded that the omissions of references to interventions likely indicated that the spiritual assessments were probably not used in planning an intervention. So we need to keep in mind that conducting an assessment and implementing a spiritual inter-vention may not be directly linked in the helping process. Because of this omis-sion, it is recommended that spiritual assessments focusing on particular problems include a set of questions that explore how various interventions could address the problem (CSWE, 2015, Competency 7).

Introduction to Spiritual Interventions

Canda and Furman (2010) have categorized spiritual interventions or activities into four types: those used directly with clients, activities suggested to clients for homework, activities made by a social worker privately in preparation for practice, and interventions that connect clients with religious helpers and others in their spiritual support system. While all of these types of categories are different, they could all potentially be supportive of a spiritually sensitive practice approach since all relate one way or another to helping clients. All of these activities are covered in this chapter except activities made by a social worker in preparation for practice; these activities are explored in chapter 13. Several spiritual interventions are described in this chapter. In actuality, there are what may seem like an unlimited number of spiritual interventions that could be used in a spiritually sensitive approach to practice. Canda and Furman (2010, pp. 360–361) describe an extensive list of 73 "spiritually-oriented helping activities."

Spiritual interventions are in some cases religious and in other cases non-religious. Often interventions can be used in either circumstance with minor changes in wording. As has been discussed in prior chapters, some religious and non-religious activities can be difficult to differentiate as practitioners may disagree over which they are. Practitioners should choose how they will view these interventions and they can define them in a way that is acceptable to their clients and agency. Mindfulness provides a good example of this. In most cases mindfulness can be implemented as non-religious, but it can also be used in a religious context as a means of becoming attentive to God or a Higher Power. So it's important to be as flexible as possible in implementing these interventions. Governmental agencies, for example, typically do not introduce religious activities and only focus on non-religious ones. If a spiritual intervention can be used as a religious one with some clients and a non-religious one with others, this expands its utility in practice.

A spiritual intervention is defined in the book as *an action with a spiritual focus introduced in the helping process.* The collection of spiritual interventions described in the chapter are varied and suitable for clients with a diverse set of backgrounds, spiritual orientations, and religious and non-religious affiliations. However, this is not intended as an exhaustive list. Social workers are likely to introduce clients to many of these interventions and hopefully they will naturally emerge out of conversations and decisions involving clients. Ideally, all of these spiritual interventions are developed by practitioners and clients working together, tailored to the client's specific needs. For example, a labyrinth may be an appropriate spiritual intervention for a restless and hyperactive teenager living in a residential facility but it would have to be relevant to the teenager's specific needs and space would be needed for the labyrinth. The labyrinth is an ancient spiritual tool that is a form of walking meditation described later in the chapter (Cunningham, 2012).

Some spiritual interventions could originate as spiritual practices of the clients. They can be viewed as spiritual interventions under some circumstances. A key circumstance would be that the client's spiritual practices are viewed by both the worker and client as relevant to resolving the client's problems. An example would be clients who depend significantly upon prayer for support or inner peace. In these cases, a worker could encourage a client to openly discuss their spiritual practice, learn how it helps the client, support its continuance when it is relevant to resolving the client's problems, and possibly work to strengthen the spiritual practice.

Spiritual interventions can be introduced at different levels of practice—micro, mezzo, and macro. Some interventions are designed especially for individual clients. Others for small groups. Still others are useful with families. Other interventions focus on helping communities and organizations at the macro level and will be covered in the next chapter. Some of these interventions can be used at several levels of practice. The interventions described in this chapter are limited to only some of the pertinent ones that could be used with clients. There are too many to cover in a few chapters of a book. Forgiveness therapy, art therapy, and music therapy are a few examples of intervention that are popular but not covered (Land, 2015; McCullough, Pargament, & Thorensen, 2001). Please keep this in mind as you proceed. The spiritual interventions described in the chapter include mindfulness, meditation, prayer, metaphors and guided imagery, and altars.

Mindfulness

In recent years, mindfulness has become a very popular concept and a spiritual practice in social work circles and in the larger society. It is a philosophy or way of life that derives from Buddhism. The key principle of mindfulness is to be present in the moment and experience life more fully now. The reasoning goes like this—we cannot return to the past and the future is beyond reach. "Now" is all that we have. The focus of mindful people is totally on themselves and the people and social circumstances they are with now. Mindful social workers attempt to be totally present with their clients in mind, body, and spirit.

Mindfulness is a difficult concept for most Westerners to fully understand and practice because our culture emphasizes busyness, focusing on the future, sometimes dwelling in the past, getting ahead, and taking on as much or more than we can handle in the present. Our external environment is often filled with demands, interruptions, and noises. We check our cell phones to keep up with others, spend an inordinate amount of time in front of television, and become absorbed in our computers and iPads. When we are driving or walking somewhere, we are listening to our iPod or radio or talking on our cell phone. Silence is not a comfortable part of the lives of most of us.

Mindfulness Exercise

For about ten minutes, find a quiet location to complete this exercise. Put everything that you are doing aside and just spend this time doing nothing. Sit in a comfortable position upright in a comfortable chair with your feet on the floor and your hands resting on your lap. Close your eyes so that you won't be distracted. Concentrate only on your breath. Just observe the breath going in and out in a normal pattern. If chatter comes up in your consciousness become aware of it but don't hold onto it. Just observe it as a sensation that comes and goes. If the chatter continues, as it usually will, select a word or mantra that is special to you (e.g. love, hope) and silently say your sacred word to gently nudge the chatter away when it comes. Then return to the breath and concentrate on breathing in and out. Journal about this experience afterwards including sharing what the silence was like, what chatter emerged, how easy or difficult it was to nudge it away, and how you felt after the exercise.

Most Americans also have a substantial amount of chatter going on inside. Our minds seem to be continually thinking of one thing or another. Often this inner chatter is unproductive and moves from one thought to another in the past or future, not the present. Chatter is negative in various ways and tends to interfere with our daily functioning. Negative chatter can be messages or tapes from the past that tell us over and over that we are not worthwhile or important, or we are not up to the tasks before us.

A desire for mindful living encourages us to search for regular times and places that encourage inner quietness and contemplative listening. Such places could be a church or synagogue, the woods or beach, the library, or any other quiet oasis that we can find or develop. We need to find times and quiet places where we can turn off our sound and electronic devices (e.g. cell phone, computers). We need to rewire our minds to welcome the sheer silence in our midst and to develop an appreciation and comfort with it. Initially we need to learn how to stop everything and do nothing. We focus on our breath and a mantra can be introduced when we experience internal chatter.

Mindfulness is a basic spiritual practice that has huge implications for our work with our clients. Every social worker is encouraged to develop a regular mindfulness practice (Hick, 2009). Just keep in mind that it is always a work in progress and the goal is to simply make it a comfortable part of your routine each day. Mindfulness, some will say, can change your life over time. Its benefits are many including helping you to slow down, to manage your internal chatter, bring about greater inner peace, and be more relaxed and present in the here and now wherever you are. Mindfulness can fairly easily be taught to clients, particularly those who are open to learning about it and especially those who need to be relieved of the stresses in their lives.

Mindfulness has many benefits. Another benefit to mention is that the here-and-now experience of mindfulness can actually be viewed as an organism forming what the person's next step will be in their particular situation (Norton Professional Books, 2014). This can be especially beneficial, for example, to people with anxiety about what will happen in their future. People who are often filled with such fears can practice mindfulness that overtime can replace some of their fears with a deeper wisdom within themselves resulting from being fully present.

Mindfulness can easily be taught in groups. A combination of providing useful mindful exercises and processing what happened afterwards is one format to follow. Group members can often gain more insight and encouragement about the benefits of mindfulness from the feedback of their peers in the group than the leader. Clients of all different backgrounds including clients with acute and chronic mental health problems have benefitted from mindfulness group experiences. Many books are available on mindfulness and how it can be used in social work practice (e.g. Nhat Hanh, 1976; Hick, 2009). In addition, Altman (2011) offers a practical book of 50 one-minute mindfulness exercises that can be both practiced by practitioners and taught to clients. Mindfulness is a non-religious spiritual intervention that can be used in any agency, school, or hospital setting. Mindfulness as practiced by Buddhists and others has many dimensions to it. Often there are mindfulness groups available for those who want to pursue this practice in more depth. An example of this is Thich Nhat Hanh's (2012) mindfulness training topics which include non-attachment to views, freedom of thought, awareness of suffering, taking care of anger, true community and communication, truthful and loving speech, reverence for life, and generosity.

Mindful Eating

Mindfulness can influence many aspects of our lives. One of them is how we eat. Many people are so much on the go that they eat without even realizing what they are consuming. It is sometimes referred to as "wolfing down" our meal. A key concept of mindful eating is that one is aware of what he or she is eating with each bite of food and enjoying the taste (Nhat Hanh, 2014). While eating mindfully, we can replace concentration on the breath with concentration on each bite of food. We appreciate the taste and the aroma, chew a normal amount that can be easily digested, and take another bite only after the previous bite is fully digested into the stomach. Mindful eating offers us awareness of why and what we are eating including the many dimensions of eating. Bays (2009) describes several dimensions of hunger for food, the point where eating begins. They are eye hunger that is satisfied by the attractiveness of what we eat, nose hunger satisfied by the fragrance of the food, mouth hunger satisfied by the sensation of the food when tasting it, stomach hunger satisfied by digesting the right amount of food, and mind hunger that is difficult to satisfy if our thoughts are always changing.

Albers (2008) suggests that people have many problems with eating. Among them are eating until you are too full and then feeling guilty; eating when you are bored, stressed or anxious rather than hungry; grazing on food without really tasting it; mindlessly munching on snacks while zoned out in front of the TV; eating a meal at the same time each day whether you are hungry or not; skipping meals; and not paying attention to your hunger signals. Mindful eating has been found to be helpful with clients having gastrointestinal problems, obesity, eating disorders, and other eating problems.

Meditation

Meditation is a central spiritual practice of Hindus, Buddhists, and other groups in the United States, while Christians, Muslims, and Jews are more likely to depend upon prayer as a spiritual practice. Nevertheless, some Christians, Muslims, Jews, and those who are non-affiliated are increasingly using meditation as a spiritual practice as well. Meditation is a practice used to communicate with one's Higher Power, whether it be a divinity within, God or Allah, or something else. It is also a popular practice for finding balance in one's life and becoming more centered. Some forms of prayer also have similarities to meditation. Centering prayer, a contemplative Christian spiritual form of prayer, involves sitting in a disciplined form of silence and discerning what God wants. In contrast, most prayer forms primarily involve talking to God, not listening.

Meditation is a spiritual intervention that is practiced by growing numbers of people (Nhat Hanh, 1976). Actually, it is an increasingly popular intervention that practitioners are offering to their clients. Many clients in mental health, family services, criminal justice, substance abuse, and other settings are usually faced with increasing stress in their lives. Their problems sometimes seem only to worsen by increasing distractions, challenging relationships, and a diminishing sense of well-being and self-confidence. While other interventions are offered to counter these problems, meditation can be added as well to address these stresses and related problems.

Carlson and Larkin (2009) make a case for using a group meditation approach for clients with addiction problems. They point out that stress both contributes to substance abuse and is one of the consequences of using substances. Stress can be either psychological (e.g. anxious, unfocused, scattered thinking, immobilized) or physiological (e.g. rapid breathing, increased blood pressure, tense muscles, gastrointestinal and urinary reactions). Meditation in groups can become a coping intervention for such problems. Carlson and Larkin describe their approach of mindfulness meditation to help clients be fully present in the moment, focusing on the breath, and quieting the mind. They point out that detached meditative awareness in recovery of an addiction allows for difficult thoughts, feelings and cravings to be observed and seen as transitory rather than controlling and immobilizing. Meditation involves letting go of these transitory urges and cravings and returning to a meditative stance in the present moment. Helpful outcomes for clients include witnessing the constantly shifting stream of inner and outer experiences without getting caught up in them, and mindfully responding to stressful events instead of reacting impulsively without much thought. Carlson and Larkin (2009) discuss several specific topics with their clients as part of their approach of mindfulness meditation. These topics include cultivating awareness of the moment, encouraging clients to find times of silence and doing nothing, and focusing on the breath and breathing patterns. Other topics that are discussed address how to quiet the mind and deal with internal chatter. Clients are helped to distinguish unproductive from productive thoughts, respond mindfully rather than impulsively to stressful events, and to use empowering mantras in managing chatter. Clients are also helped to develop a regular routine of mindfulness techniques.

Meditation is practiced by many religious groups. Most meditation practices introduced in recent decades in the United States have originated in the practices of the Eastern World, especially India and other Far Eastern countries like Nepal. They are often led by gurus who come to reside in the United States. Generally, meditation appears, at least on the surface, to be practiced in similar ways by different religious groups. However, the practice of meditation can vary in its emphasis for different religious groups. As an example, yoga originated as a Hindu practice that prepares a person for deeper meditation. In some contrast, many American groups that practice yoga view it as a practice that has many benefits revolving around exercise, such as stretching, developing balance, building strength, improving circulation, and focusing (Kirk, Boon, & DiTuro, 2006).

According to writers of meditation, there is one most important time—now (Chodron, 2012; Nhat Hanh, 2009; Tolle, 2005). The present moment is the only time over which we have dominion and we need to embrace and cherish it. Along with the present moment, the most important people to us are those with whom we are *now* and the happenings of the moment are where we should focus our full attention. When asked who he was, the Buddha replied, "I am awake." Being fully awake to the moment is most important as we are reminded that most of us are only partially awake much of the time. Nhat Hanh suggests, for example, that our most important pursuit is lessening the suffering of the person standing next to us and making them happy, for that alone is the pursuit of life in this moment. The Dalai Lama professes that his religion is simply about kindness and our most important purpose is to be kind to whomever we are with.

The purpose of meditation varies depending upon who is describing it. Meditation among Hindus is a practice of going deeply within oneself to experience Nirvana or union with the Divine. Similarly, the Buddhists seek in meditation an egoless state of stillness and peace. Nothing is more important in life than being in this state.

A Visit to a Buddhist Center

(Michelle Davis)

The room was filled with about fifteen people, and then she appeared. A woman of average build wearing a brightly colored red robe with yellow cloth draped from her shoulder . . . came out and lit a candle. Her head was not quite shaved but had very closely cropped gray hair. Everyone stood in reverence and clasped our hands in prayer position. She turned to greet us, introduced herself and stated that the class was on Meditation for Beginners.

Sitting in lotus position, she asked us some questions: What is the mind? What can meditation do for us? Answering her own questions she explained how meditation can reduce stress and help us achieve a state of happiness no matter what else is going on around us. . . . We ended with a meditation of loving kindness. We were instructed to visualize someone we cared for deeply. I visualized my husband. Then we were instructed to think about their lives when they weren't with us. Their daily activities, their joys, their sorrows, and their suffering. We were supposed to envision their suffering in the past, present, and even in the future, even to the moment of their death. And then we were told to breathe in their suffering like a black cloud of smoke. She told us to take it into our bodies and to purify it there into white light that represented joy. With this joy, we would breathe it out into our loved one with every exhalation. And so it went, breathing in their black smoke of suffering and breathing out the light of joy. This meditation made me feel very centered and it made me happy to practice it. I can see how expanding it slowly beyond someone you love and eventually even to strangers could help you practice "virtuous action," as the monk discussed.

Michelle Davis, graduate student, School of Social Work, University of North Carolina at Charlotte, Charlotte, NC.

Contemplative Christians also seek this deeper spiritual experience of emptying themselves of worries, concerns, and other thoughts. They describe meditation as a process of becoming liberated from our ego and all of our personal baggage to which our ego attaches. Centering prayer, Lectio Divina, and other Christian contemplative meditative practices are important as they free followers to explore themselves more deeply and to discover a Higher Power. Some call this seeking to find the true self as opposed to an existing largely false, outer self.

Many other groups, religious and non-religious, see meditation primarily as a means of stress reduction and self-care (Zanzig, 1990). Many people, including practitioners and their clients, are becoming increasingly busy, going many directions at once, trying to cram more in the day, and in the process experiencing less happiness!

As a result, meditation has become an important practice. Buddhist centers, Hindu Temples, and other meditation centers like Insight Meditation, Transcendental Meditation, and mindfulness meditation groups are springing up all over the United States. Their common purpose seems to be to help people slow down, be more in the present, and become more mindful and grateful for their lives in the present.

Basic Meditation

Basic meditation has a set of simple steps that can be taught, but the implementation of these meditative steps can be challenging if attempted on a regular daily basis. This seems to be the case because so many people have difficulty slowing down, finding a quiet time and place, and being in silence for any length of time. The steps, in brief, are to begin by finding a quiet comfortable place to meditate, and sitting in a comfortable posture. A largely silent practice, as meditation begins we are to find our breath and stay attentive to it. The breath is the anchor to meditation. The breath and its rhythm are basic to our well-being and often forgotten. When we tune in to them, breathing in and out in a normal rhythm, we can become largely free of our distractions around and within us. After we breathe in we can simply let go as we exhale; notice our muscles around the chest and shoulders relax and then notice how they can deepen and spread throughout your body (Walsh, 1999). This may be a good time to do a body scan of each part of your body to see if tension or pain is evident anywhere (Leung, Chan, Ng, & Lee, 2009). Also as you breathe, be in touch with the feeling of restfulness and contentment that you may feel inside by just breathing and just enjoy it.

When inner chatter emerges in our silence, which almost always occurs, we are helped to simply observe it and view it as a transitory sensation. We let it pass by rather than dwell on it and let it control us. The overall purpose of meditation is to remain silent, calm, centered, and free of distracting thoughts and feelings. A mantra or sacred word or phrase (e.g. hope, love, all is well) is often added to this practice when a sensation appears in our consciousness. We observe a thought and gently nudge it away by saying our sacred word to ourselves and returning to an inner openness and silence. We say the mantra until the thought disappears and then return to silence.

> Meditation allows you to carve out a relationship with the inner presence that is the deepest part of yourself. Eventually you find that you can rest in that presence through the storms of life and so that everything you do comes from the awareness that that's who you are.
>
> Sally Kempton—Swami Durgananda, in Gates, 2006

The benefits of meditation are usually not easily realized and appreciated without continuing the practice for a long time on a regular basis. Some of the benefits, however, can be immediate. During meditation, we can do a body scan, focusing on each part of our body for a moment until we have taken a full inventory. In this way, we become more aware of our bodies and how we may be in pain in various places or carrying localized tension and tightened muscles. In the past, we may have been unaware of the tension and pain that we often carry. However, most benefits become evident not so much during meditation as afterwards. Over time our lives become calmer, more grounded, and less burdened by our day-to-day stressors. We can become more aware of what is happening around us in the present and more grateful for all that we have and focus less on what we may not have.

Buddhist Meditation

Buddhist meditation offers a more complicated version of basic meditation. Chodron (2008), an American Buddhist nun, describes Buddhist meditation as a practice. She describes three parts—posture, the object of meditation, and the way we relate to thoughts. First, she describes in some detail the importance of posture during mediation, a posture that is noble, upright and relaxed. Our seat should be flat and balanced in a chair, legs comfortably extending in front of us, our torso upright, our hands on our thighs with palms down, eyes open and gazing softly downward or closed, and our mouth slightly open and relaxed. The object of meditation, part two, is the breath. Staying in touch with the breath keeps us present. When the mind wanders, the breath brings us back to the present over and over again. Chodron suggests that typically we focus on the breath one-fourth of the time and three-fourths of the time on space around the breath. The breath goes out and dissolves in space.

Part three of Chodron's practice is the way we relate to thoughts in meditation. When thoughts emerge, one option is that we can label them (e.g. harsh, passion). Meditation gives us a way of working with our thoughts, emotions, fears, doubts, and temptations triggered by outer circumstances. We can learn that these thoughts are short-lived, dissolving, elusive, never predictable, and empty of any danger. Over time we can become more open and receptive to our outer circumstances and the people we encounter; in difficult times we can function in a healthier way when we cannot find a job, face a difficult boss, or have strong cravings. Our energy changes as we let go of these difficult circumstances and become more refreshed, liberated, and inspired.

Kornfield (1993), another American Buddhist monk, who is also a teacher and therapist, relates meditation more directly to the helping process. He explains that before many people can develop a capacity for concentration and quiet, they may need help in healing their mind, body, and spirit from deep-seated past wounds. Meditation is where our deep-seated problems often surface. He refers to them as "demons." Demons could be such things as self-doubts deriving from

---

Value of Meditation to You?

1. Have you ever meditated?

2. If so, what has your experience been like? How has meditation been a useful spiritual tool for you?

3. If you have never meditated, have you ever spent time alone in silence for any length of time? What was that like for you?

---

childhood, deep anger over past events, fears from the past, or addictions. When these demons surface, Kornfield suggests that we name them and allow ourselves to feel them until they pass, rather than avoid or suppress them. Then we are to return to concentrating on our breathing until these demons reappear. Over a long period of work on demons they will hopefully lose their power over us and maybe dissolve.

Meditations with Repeating Mantras

Another type of meditation involves silently repeating a mantra over and over. In traditional forms of meditation, mantras are only used when internal chatter appears; once the chatter disappears, the mantra is discontinued. Mantras are only used to nudge away distractions. Repetition of a mantra is a more unusual form of meditation. An anonymous wandering pilgrim (Anonymous, n.d.) known to be a serf in 19th-century Russia was solely in search of finding God. He wanted to know how he could pray without ceasing, a phrase recorded in one of the letters of St. Paul in the Christian Bible. This pilgrim wandered all over Russia looking for the answer to his question, but he was without success for years. Finally he came upon a staret, a wise old religious sage, who gave him a satisfactory answer. The old sage informed him that he was to reject all thoughts and only repeat what has since become the Jesus Prayer ("Lord Jesus Christ, son of God, have mercy on me a sinner.") at all times, in all places, even during sleep. At the end of the first day, the pilgrim recited this prayer 12,000 times; he continued to devote his life to doing this for months and then years until the prayer finally became a part of him and recited itself within him without any effort on the pilgrim's part.

The Buddha taught his followers "the loving kindness meditation" that is another example of a mantra prayer (Walsh, 1999). It is a slow and gentle repetition to yourself of the words "May I be happy, kind, loving, and peaceful." As the prayer is repeated over and over, and begins to settle into your deeper being, you can change it to "May you be happy, kind, loving, and peaceful." The final step is to extend your prayer to embrace all creatures with "May all *beings* be happy, kind, loving, and peaceful." This prayer can be continually repeated or if not, you could return to it whenever internal distractions occur. Other words besides happy, kind, loving, and peaceful can be incorporated into your meditation. Choose words that are most meaningful to you. One purpose of contemporary mantra prayers is to find a personal God. Another related purpose is to rid yourself of all thoughts that are not of God.

Walking Meditation

Walking meditation is an alternative to meditation sitting down. Often movement of the body during a prayer helps in staying awake and being attentive to the moment. Nhat Hanh (1985), a popular Vietnamese Buddhist monk, describes a walking meditation as an example. He refers to walking meditation as going without a destination, taking peaceful and anxiety-free steps, being aware of your breathing to preserve peace and mindfulness, and walking in rhythm with your breathing pattern. He claims that the practice of walking meditation opens our eyes to wonders in the universe and helps us become aware of pain, suffering, and anguish in the world. Stations of the Cross is another walking meditation based on the last hours of Jesus' life (Brown, 2003). Each of the fourteen stations represents a location along the way from when Jesus was praying at the garden of Gethsemane to the tomb where he was buried. In Jerusalem, where this journey actually occurred, stops are made at Gethsemane, the ruins of the temple, the fortress where Pilate condemned Jesus, the Pond of Siloam, the place where he was prepared for burial, and the tomb. This walking meditation can occur anywhere with signs or locations symbolizing each station. A social justice dimension of the Stations of the Cross can be added if the locations are contemporary sites in a city or town such as city government, the jail, the courts, a convent of nuns, a home for orphans, and a memorial to the six million Jews executed by the Nazis during World War II.

Walking the Labyrinth

The labyrinth is an ancient spiritual tool that is another form of walking meditation. While the labyrinth is an archetype, a divine imprint, found in all religious traditions in various forms around the world, it is typically used as a non-religious spiritual intervention (Cunningham, 2012; Mansfield, n.d.; Semmens, 2014). The labyrinth path leads to a center, where one pauses before they return to where they began. Everyone moves through it at their own pace. Like life, the labyrinth with its twists and turns can be used for exploring goals or meaning in a difficult situation. Labyrinths can be found located throughout most communities at hospitals, hospice centers, YMCAs and YWCAs, low income residences, community centers, churches, and synagogues. It is an individual experience but often groups of people join together to participate in it. In this way, the group can be introduced to the

Figure 9.1   An Example of a Labyrinth

labyrinth together and they can process the experience together afterwards. One example of a labyrinth is shown in Figure 9.1.

Creating Mandalas

Mandala means "sacred circle" in Sanskrit. Mandalas are an art form traditionally used by Tibetan Buddhists, American Indians, some Christian, and others. In some spiritual traditions, mandalas are used to facilitate meditation and as a transformative tool to assist with healing (Brown, 2003). The symbolic form that is created results from a very careful introduction of a variety of colors of sand into the outline of the spiritual symbol.

The Tibetan Buddhist mandalas are an act of meticulously painting with many colors of sand. See an example of a mandala in Figure 9.2. Painting a mandala focuses the participants' attention and assists in meditation as a visual form of mantra.

Figure 9.2   Buddhist Monks Working on a Mandala

After the completed mandala is displayed and admired, often for weeks, the sand is brushed together into a pile and poured into running water to symbolically spread the mandala's blessings to others. Destroying this beautiful art form that took such a long and arduous time to create is meant to symbolize our impermanence as humans. It conveys a central Buddhist teaching that all creatures beautiful and otherwise are never permanent. Mandalas are now used as a form of meditation among health professionals and their clients. Instructions and examples of how one university has introduced mandalas as a spiritual practice with students, staff, and faculty is available online (University of New Hampshire Health Services, n.d.).

Prayers

Prayer is a practice that is well known in most religions in the United States and is a key spiritual practice of Christians, Muslims, and Jews. Prayer and meditation are similar in some ways. Both are efforts or attempts to communicate with a Higher Power, such as God or Allah. However, they are different in some ways. Prayers tend to involve active participation by the person praying while meditation emphasizes silence and listening. Yet, some people may even use the two terms interchangeably. In these instances, it may be important to ask them to clarify how they are different or to explore how clients define both prayer and meditation.

Prayers are typically spiritual practices of clients, which can also become spiritual interventions if they are viewed as an important element in the helping process. During the initial phase of work together, for example, a client may share some of the spiritual practices that are important to them. Prayer may be one of them. Prayers of clients are a source of numerous discussions and sometimes debates among social work students and practitioners, especially concerning how to respond to clients' questions about prayer. Many clients sometimes ask their worker questions about prayer such as:

- Do you pray?
- Would you pray for me?
- Would you pray with me?

These specific questions have highlighted discussions by numerous social work groups over the years because they illustrate some of the controversy between those who favor and oppose discussing spiritual topics with clients. Some students and practitioners believe prayer is not appropriate to discuss under any circumstances in the helping process. Others feel that clients should be able to bring up the topic but the workers should remain neutral and largely silent in their responses. Still others are open to engaging this topic and including prayer in their discussions. An even smaller number believe that praying with clients is an acceptable practice under certain circumstances. Ethical issues have been investigated when deciding on whether and when prayer with clients is acceptable (Sheridan, 2010).

Prayer is a practice that is well known in most religions in the United States. According to a 2012 Pew Research survey, about three-quarters (76 percent) of Americans said that prayer is an important part of their daily life (Pew Research Center for the People and the Press, 2013). Even among those who are religiously unaffiliated, 44 percent said they pray daily (Pew Research Center on Religion and Public Life, 2012). People pray for numerous reasons. Bade and Cook (2008) identify many of the reasons why Christians pray—for comfort, guidance, understanding, changes desired, to stay focused, to decrease fear, as a ritual, for acceptance, for strength, to seek advice, to seek God's will, and for healing.

Prayers are not usually a spiritual intervention introduced by a social worker. Sectarian agencies such as a Christian counseling agency or Jewish Family Services may be exceptions if prayers are a normal spiritual practice of their clients. Usually it is the clients who either directly or indirectly bring up prayer as a spiritual practice that is important for them. Yet, the way in which a social worker responds to this client initiative on prayer is what is important for us to consider. If prayer is something brought up by a client as a significant source of support and comfort, it is important for a practitioner to explore what these prayers mean to the client and how praying may be something that a client should be encouraged to continue as part of an overall plan of action. For example, praying may give the client renewed strength or greater hope. In these discussions, the workers' views and practices are inappropriate to share unless the clients inquire about them. In other words, all workers ideally approach this topic essentially the same way, including both workers who pray regularly and those who do not pray at all. For these and other reasons, it would be helpful for practitioners to know something about prayers and their potential importance to these clients. Knowing the different forms that prayers can take and understanding what can happen in prayer experiences are something that a practitioner should know and support if it is a healthy practice for clients especially when these prayers are relevant to helping them.

Common Prayers

Countless authors of the major religions have written extensively about prayer and the different forms it can take. Even more authors have written actual prayers that have been recited repeatedly down through the ages until the present. While prayers are a most important way that most people communicate with their Higher Power, the amount of time, attention, and energy that is put into these practices is likely to determine how much people get out of them. Guenther (1998) states that while the quality of people's prayer can vary, the most effective prayers may be those that involve us in loving attentiveness to our Higher Power to whom our prayers are directed. Numerous authors (e.g. Bloom, 1970; Brown, 2003; Guenther, 1998; Rupp, 2007; Webster, 2009) describe several different types of prayers common especially in Christianity, Judaism, and Islam. Adoration, thanksgiving, confession, intercession, and petition are five of the most familiar and commonly used prayers.

Prayers of adoration—awestruck by the beauty of the world: Prayers of adoration are evident when we view a beautiful sunrise or sunset, a budding flower, millions of glistening stars on a clear night, or an unexplained profound happening of which people are awestruck (Brown, 2003; Guenther, 1998). These prayers can also be in adoration of other things, such as a poem that speaks a truth in a new inspiring way, a sacred reading or music that lifts you out of your seat, a painting or sculpture that communicates volumes of meaning. The list goes on and on. These prayers usually come spontaneously as a response to one of these encounters.

A Prayer of Seeking God

(Meister Eckhart, a 12th-century Christian mystic)

If you will seek God, you will find God together with every good thing.
What you sought before, now seeks you.
What you once pursued, now pursues you.
What you once fled, now flees you.
Everything comes to the person who really approaches God, bringing all that is God with it, and causing all that is alien to God to fly away. . . .

Chilsom (1996)

Adoration prayers can be religious or non-religious, be expressed formally as a prayer or just an unexpected testimonial to another person or a whisper to one's self. Such prayers can be useful to many clients—someone who is depressed, suffers from an anxiety disorder, or is simply in a bad mood, has low energy, or a feeling of self-pity.

Prayers of thanksgiving and gratitude—thank you for . . .: Prayers of thanksgiving are expressions of gratitude to God, our Higher Power, the Universe, or another person, whomever we consider the source (Guenther 1998; Webster, 2009). The object of gratitude could be a brief encounter with someone or the gift of a new possession or it could be much bigger, such as having a healthy family, a special friend who understands and loves you, or successful surgery. These prayers could be either religious or not. Who the thankfulness is directed to may help us know but often our expressions of gratitude give emphasis to the gift, not the giver. These prayers can be spontaneous or planned. A client may pray herself to sleep every night thanking her God for each special thing that happened to her that day. Similar to adoration, many of our clients can easily become disappointed, anxious, feel helpless and hopeless, or feel sorry for themselves and their circumstances. These gratitude prayers can replace such compelling thoughts with awareness of what we *do* have and the realization that our lives always have both positives and negatives. Exercises on gratitude can sometimes be inserted in a practice session with clients, whom we ask to identify three or four things that they are thankful for. This is in no way intended to negate or play down a difficult situation that a client may be facing. In retrospect, thanksgiving prayers can help us realize that we have more than we previously realized. This insight can help clients adapt to their situations a little easier, at least in the present moment.

Prayers of confession—forgive me for my wrongdoing: Prayers of confession are also popular among Christians, Jews, Muslims, Hindus, Buddhists, as well as other groups. Confessions mean that we are acknowledging our sins to our Higher Power or superiors (Brown, 2003). We are admitting we have hurt someone or committed an unfair or insensitive act. According to Guenther (1998), the more specific

---

We can be grateful even when things are not going so well

(Norton Professional Books, 2014)

- We can be grateful when we are sick for the times we are well.

- We can be grateful in difficult situations by finding positives even when they are not readily apparent, such as a car accident that we survived with our lives.

- We can be grateful in the presence of loss for the prior time we had together and for our healthy lives as long as they occurred.

Forgiveness Prayer

(Unitarian Universalists)

If I have harmed anyone in any way either knowingly or unknowingly through my own confusions I ask their forgiveness.

If anyone has harmed me in any way either knowingly or unknowingly through their own confusions I forgive them.

And if there is a situation I am not yet ready to forgive I forgive myself for that.

For all the ways that I harm myself, negate, doubt, belittle myself, judge or be unkind to myself through my own confusions I forgive myself.

---

these confessions are, the more helpful they can be. For example, "Forgive me for that hurtful remark that I made to my friend today" or ". . .the way I yelled at my son when he talked back at me." These confessions should attempt to identify patterns in our behavior to confess if possible rather than just one behavior by itself. Also we should be letting go of our sin or wrongful act once we have confessed it so that we can move beyond it.

Prayers of confession and forgiveness can be shared in a religious context such as a formal confession to a priest, rabbi, or imam, an informal admission to a spiritual director, or as a sorrowful comment to another confessor (Brown, 2003; Webster, 2009). Various worship services are designed for confessions and to seek forgiveness, such as a Lenten service or a Eucharist ritual in a Christian church, or a fasting and atonement ritual during Ramadan or Yom Kippur. Many sacred readings are also helpful guides in confessions and exercises to seek forgiveness. Parables in the Bible, such as the story of the prodigal son (Luke 15:11–32) can help us look deeply within for how God or a parent might lovingly respond to our sins. Confessions to another family member or colleague can also be a non-religious form of confession that can set the record straight that a confessor has wronged another and is sorry. It should be noted that prayers of confession are different than prayers of reconciliation between two people (Guenther, 1998). Confession is one-sided and focuses only on us whereas reconciliation focuses on two sides or parties coming together.

Prayers of intercession—please help another person: Prayers of intercession are very frequently used when family members, friends, and others are in need of support or help from our God or a Higher Power. We are placing ourselves before God, Yahweh, or Allah on behalf of another. We pray for people who are troubled or suffering in our midst and are either near or afar and have experienced a tragedy or loss. Intercessory prayer can be more powerful in a community than alone as the other participants add conviction and hope to the effort. Guenther (1998) suggests that intercessory prayers are more effective when they exclude our own desires

Suggestions for Intercessory Prayers

(Guenther, 1998)

- View yourself as a channel of love through which God can reach a person.

- Do it anytime that the thought pops up.

- This prayer can be powerful when done together in a community.

- Find a way to make it happen—agreeing to do it is easier than actually doing it.

- Empty ourselves of our own desires and preoccupations.

- Pray for the whole person, not just their special need.

- An answer to such a prayer may be for us to help them.

- We are likely to see this person in a whole new light different than the person we thought we knew.

- We may grow in our awareness of people suffering and have greater awareness of injustices.

and preoccupations and only focus on the person being prayed for. Also, it may be better to pray for the whole person, not just their special needs.

While one should not expect answers to our prayers or in some cases what could be considered miracles, some scientific studies have found that prayers can be effective in overcoming or ameliorating someone's disease and illness (Dossey, 1993; Hagerty, 2009). Debate continues on whether findings of these clinical studies and others are convincing evidence of prayer's effect, but what may be more important is that efforts are being made to find out using the scientific method. The efficacy of prayers is discussed more fully in chapter 12 in discussions about evaluation. An NPR (National Public Radio) series on science and spirituality also explores this important question (http://www.npr.org/templates/story/story.php?storyId=104466652). An advantage of intercessory prayers, whether or not they change the person who is the focus, is that the one who prays may see this person in a new light and may grow in their concern about their suffering and any injustices. Further, this awareness in itself may lead them to reach out and actually help this person.

Prayers of petition—please help me: Prayers of petition are a fifth type of common prayer. These may be the most common of the five types of prayers, according to Guenther (1998). Petitions are prayers to God or our Higher Power for something on our own behalf or something we need. People commonly pray for all kinds of things—food, relief from stress or suffering, avoidance of temptations or evil actions, a job opportunity or a new marital partner, resolutions of conflicts, and numerous other requests. Sacred readings, such as the Torah, Bible, and Quran, often encourage prayers of petition but also are likely to caution the person to look for what God wants out of this petition beyond what the person is requesting. In other words, God knows what we need well beyond what we think we need. A most familiar Bible passage that encourages believers to pray is: Ask and it will be given to you, search and you will find, knock and the door will be opened to you (Luke 11:5–13). In other words, the passage suggests that we not be afraid to ask and keep at it; answers will come.

Numerous other prayer forms are also frequently used. These are prayers that may be familiar to some and not others. They include prayers using sacred readings; centering prayers; recitation prayers; body prayers; and praying with beads, icons, and mandalas.

Prayers Using Sacred Readings

Prayers using sacred readings are another form of prayer. Religious people often read the sacred books and other writings of their religious group. They may also sing these readings as a hymn of praise or chant. At times people may also pray these readings. These prayers are more of the heart than the head. Jews and Christians often use the Psalms in the Bible in this way. Many of the Psalms may have originally been sung as hymns in Jewish synagogues as well as used as prayers. They are poetic, sometimes repetitive, and lend themselves to a more affective prayer than readings that focus on understanding with the mind.

Lectio Divina is a good example of an affective prayer involving sacred or special readings. Lectio Divina, which translates from Latin to English as "divine reading" originated in Christianity in the 4th and 5th centuries. It involves four steps and can

---

Exploring Your Prayer Practices

Five common types of prayers in the United States have been described above: adoration, thanksgiving, confession, intercession, and petition.

1. Which of these prayer forms, if any, have you used in recent months? Which prayer forms have you used the most?

2. How important are they to your personal daily life? In what ways are they helpful? Not helpful?

3. How often if at all do your clients mention using any of these prayer forms? How have you responded?

be used with either religious or non-religious spiritual material (Brown, 2003). It begins with selecting a passage. A passage can come from a sacred book, poetry, or other religious or non-religious material that has spiritual meaning. It should not be too long, possibly a page of writing at most. The four steps begin with *reading* the passage, possibly two or three times slowly and with a pause between readings. The second step is to *meditate* and linger on the reading, especially the words, phrases, and ideas that speak to you the most at a deeper level. This step occurs especially during the second and third readings. The third step is to *contemplate and pray* on the material that moves you the most in terms of what message your Higher Power or an inner voice is sending to you. Finally, the last step is to be *resting and living* in what you have received or how you have been moved.

The Buddha also has many profound sayings that could be viewed as prayers (Vishupadi, 2013). They are usually asking us to think more deeply about who we are and what we are going through right now. Some examples of Buddha's sayings that could be read and meditated on are:

- "Peace comes from within. Do not seek it without."
- "Do not dwell in the past, do not dream of the future, concentrate the mind on the present moment."
- "Wonder of wonders! Intrinsically all living beings are Buddhas, endowed with wisdom and virtue, but because (people's) minds have become inverted through delusive thinking they fail to perceive this."

Meditating on the last parable can help a person first think about how they have deluded their potential and then reflect on the potential wisdom and virtue in them that may want to be more manifested and distinct in their lives.

Centering Prayer

Centering prayer, while labeled as a type of prayer, seems to be more like meditation. Centering prayer is a Christian version of Eastern meditation. Centering prayer (CP) is a receptive, deep method of silent prayer. It is a contemplative prayer form that does not usually use any external guides, such as icons, ritual prayers, music, or sacred readings (Brown, 2003; Keating, 2006). This prayer form exposes a person to the sheer silence that is always available but so seldom apparent within and around us. It helps to address the active chatter within us that often increases when we sit quietly alone. The person selects a sacred word (e.g. love, peace) that they say to themselves whenever their chatter emerges into consciousness. Over time most people gradually become more comfortable with centering prayer and can sit through it for longer periods of time. The goal is to experience CP regularly, preferably daily, and increase the time of the prayer as a person feels comfortable. They may begin with only ten minutes at each sitting and expand it to 20 minutes or more. The benefits of CP are not as evident during the prayer time except in being comfortably in silence longer and perhaps in managing internal and external chatter more. The benefits of doing centering prayer on a regular basis, as with other types of meditation, are to become more centered and present, slowing a person's pace, and listening more and hearing God's call.

Ritual Prayers

Ritual prayers are prayers promulgated by a religious group that are immediately familiar to them and often recited as part of worship or as an individual prayer. These prayers usually come from a sacred book and are memorized and ingrained in the person's mind. The obligatory prayers of Muslims recited five times a day, for example, are one of their five pillars. The first chapter of the Quran is recited early in a Muslim service. An abbreviated description of the Muslim prayers typically recited five times daily usually in Arabic are (Instructions for Performing Muslim Prayers, n.d.):

Muslim Prayers (One Version)

Step 1: Have a sincere intention to perform the prayers purely for the sake of God. Raise both hands up to the ears (palms facing the direction of Mecca) and say: Allahu Akbar "God is the greatest."

Step 2: Next, place the right hand on top of the left hand on one's chest and say: a) "I seek God's shelter from Satan, the condemned" b) "In the name of God, the most Gracious, most Merciful. All praise is due to God, Lord of the Worlds, The most Gracious, the most Merciful, Master of the Day of Judgment, You alone we worship and You alone we ask for assistance. Guide us along the straight path. The path of those upon whom You have bestowed Your blessings, not the path of those with whom You are angry nor the path of those who have gone astray." c) Select verses from the Holy Qur'an to read.

Step 3: Bowing with the back and leg perpendicular to each other, the following prayer is recited three times "Glory be to my Lord, the Almighty."

Step 4: While going back to standing position this prayer is said: "God hears those who praise Him." "Our Lord, praise be to You."

Step 5: Say "Allahu Akbar" ("God is the greatest") and then prostrate. While prostrating, say the following prayer three times. "Glory be to my Lord, the Most High."

Step 6: Say "Allahu Akbar" then sit for a moment, repeat "Allahu Akbar," prostrate once again and repeat the prayer in step 5.

Step 7: Then say "Allahu Akbar," stand up straight and then repeat steps 2 through 6.

Step 8: Recite these prayers: "Salutations, all good things, and all prayers are for God. The peace and mercy of God be upon you, O Muhammad. Peace be upon all of us, and upon His righteous servants. I bear witness that there is no God except God and I bear witness that Muhammad is the Messenger of God." "O God bestow honor upon Muhammad and upon his family just as You have bestowed honor upon Abraham and his family. And O God, bestow Your blessings upon Muhammad and his family just as You have bestowed Your blessings upon Abraham and his family. In all of the worlds, You are the most praised and the most glorious."

Step 9: Having said the above mentioned prayers, turn to face the right and recite the following prayer: "May the Peace and mercy of God be upon you." Note: This Salam (Prayer for Peace) is directed to the angels and the worshippers to the right and to the left.

Step 10: Then turning the face to the left, the prayer above is said again: "May the Peace and mercy of God be on you."

(Source: Instructions for Performing Muslim Prayers, n.d.)

The "Lord's Prayer" or "Our Father" is another example of a ritual prayer in the Christian tradition and is usually included in their weekly Sunday services. "Hail Mary" prayers are ritual prayers of the Catholic faith. The Serenity Prayer by Reinhold Niebuhr ("God, grant me the serenity to accept the things I cannot change, the courage to change the things I can, and the wisdom to know the difference.") is recited regularly in 12-step programs such as Alcoholics Anonymous and Narcotics Anonymous as a self-help group prayer without an affiliation to any particular religious group.

Body Prayers

Body prayers refer to different types of prayers using our bodies. While we always use our body in some way in every prayer, such as concentrating on the breath, body prayers involve more focal attention given to the body (Brown, 2003). Body prayers often use music as an aid in facilitating body movement. The types of music can vary widely from meditative to upbeat hip-hop. **Yoga** is an example of a body prayer. Yoga has been discussed previously as an initial step of Hindu meditation; yoga has also been mentioned as a popular set of exercises practiced by many Americans. In addition however, some of the poses of yoga can be used in body prayers, such as sitting cross-legged on the floor, slowly extending your arms out in front of you as you inhale, and returning to a prayer position as you exhale. Or a person can use their imagination as they experience yoga while standing, sitting, or lying down. As a person stands or sits, for example, they can be guided to imagine their Higher Power's gentle presence flowing through the back of their neck, down their spine to their buttocks, then through their thighs and calves, and through their heels into their toes. Gentle music in the background is also a preference of many doing body prayers.

Dance is a special body prayer form that is popular with several religions. God is the audience of dance prayers. Dance can be spontaneous, fun, and playful. It involves the whole person using all of the body senses and expressing our deepest passions and delights. The **powwow for Native Americans** is another example. This is a type of activity or event in which Native American people meet, dance, and preserve their heritage as American Indians. The website, www.powwows.com, is a helpful source of information about powwows and includes a calendar of powwow events held across the country. Powwows vary in length from one day to a week.

The Sufi sect of Islam is also known for praying to their God through dance. **Sufi dancing** is both a meditation and mystical journey of Sufis to their God (http://www.artof4elements.com/entry/60/sufi). Sufi spins are a beautiful form of Sufi dance in which the dancer spins around and around and symbolically lets go, abandons ego, and surrenders to God. The spinning appears like a hypnotic experience taking the form of a cosmic rhythm. Rumi, Persian Sufi poet and philosopher of the 13th century, wrote thousands of verses of poetry about divine love and spiritual bondage and was the likely founder of using music, poetry and dance as a path to reach God. Hindus and Jews, among other religious groups, are also known to use dance as a form of prayer.

Praying with Beads

Praying with beads adds further variety to prayers and meditation experience. Praying with beads is popular with most religious groups even though the specifics vary (Brown, 2003). The beads are laced flexibly together so that they have some movement. As aspects of a ritual prayer are recited silently, a new bead is held in the fingers. The beads serve as a kind of mantra that helps a person focus on the breath and the message in the ritual prayer in a tactile form. Catholics are well known to use prayer beads to say the "Hail Mary," a ritual prayer, and other prayers. They usually have 54 beads that are held one at a time from the beginning to the end of a prayer. As soon as the last bead is held, the prayer comes to an end. Episcopalians, a Protestant denomination, typically uses 33 beads divided into four sections. One example of a prayer done with beads is an Episcopal prayer, "I *give you* (God) my mind that I may better understand, I give you my eyes that

I may see more clearly, . . . my ears that I may hear with greater compassion, . . . my mouth that I may speak your truth with greater gentleness, . . . my heart that I may love others more fully, . . . my hands that I may do your service, and . . . my feet that I may go joyfully wherever you call." Then the cycle begins again with "*Bless* my mind, and repeats the other parts of the body . . ." Then "*strengthen* my mind, etc." And finally "*Use* my mind," etc. Prayer beads are also popular with Hindus, Muslims, and people of the Baha'i faith. In addition, prayer beads and prayer wheels are very popular with various sects of Buddhists including Tibetan Buddhists.

Praying with Icons

Praying with icons is another popular form of prayer and meditation among some religious groups. Orthodox Christians are an example (Nes, 2004). When visiting an Orthodox church that is Russian, Greek, Bulgarian, or of another Eastern European ethnic group, one quickly understands the importance of icons. They are colorful paintings of Christian religious figures on a board. Some have a singular focus—Jesus, Mary and the baby Jesus, a disciple, or a saint. Other icons have a Biblical scene or story, as icons have been an important way to teach children about the Bible. Usually Orthodox churches have a patron saint, a historical figure in Christianity such as St. Paul, and have an icon of that figure noticeably displayed in the front of the church sanctuary. The Orthodox churches have an iconostasis that divides the sanctuary up into the larger area where the participants gather and worship, and the smaller area behind the iconostasis where only the priests meet and prepare the elements for the service. Participants in the Orthodox Church use all of the senses to experience their God. The icons surround them in a visual sense, the liturgy is sung in early Slavonic Russian emphasizing the hearing sense, incense permeates the sanctuary and brings out a sharp sense of smell, and the service is experienced standing often for two or more hours, drawing on the limits of our physical capacity. Among others, Hindus and Muslims also display icons of

---

Exercise in Exploring Unfamiliar Prayer and Meditation Forms

It is likely that some of the more unusual prayer and meditation forms presented above are familiar to you and others are not. They include prayers using sacred readings, centering prayer, ritual prayers, body prayers, praying with beads, praying with icons, and praying to deities. Which prayer forms are familiar to you? Which ones are unfamiliar? If any of these prayer forms seem ambiguous or strange to you, select one of them and do some research to find out more about it.

Figure 9.3   Orthodox Christian Icon of Our Lady of Vladimir

meaning to their religions in their temples. A famous Russian Orthodox icon displayed in Figure 9.3 is titled Our Lady of Vladimir.

Praying to Deities

Worshipping deities is also evident in some religions. Hindus have gods and goddesses that are sometimes part human and part animal (Achuthananada, 2013). A popular one is Ganesh, an elephant-headed Hindu deity. Ganesh is the son of Shiva and Parvati. He has the face of an elephant with a trunk and big ears, along with a huge pot-bellied body of a human being. Ganesh is one of five primary deities. Ganesh is viewed as the lord of success and the destroyer of evils, and as the god of education, knowledge, wisdom and wealth. He is displayed in Figure 9.4.

Figure 9.4 The Hindu Deity Ganesh

Upon visiting a Hindu Temple, you are likely to see one or perhaps several deities set up on a stage slightly above the level of the worshipers. Various sects of Hinduism tend to gravitate to different deities as their primary but not exclusive worship focus. Hindu sects are likely to come from different regions of India.

Metaphors and Guided Imagery

Metaphors

A metaphor is a figure of speech in which we describe something difficult to grasp, such as love or God, as being like something else more concrete and comprehensible (Walsh, 1999). Metaphors can be a helpful way for clients to address some of their cognitive issues. Like so many other spiritual interventions, this one gives more emphasis to heart-felt efforts and less to the mind and thinking processes. All or some of the five senses are often drawn on when working with metaphors. Spiritual metaphors in particular can be useful to use with clients who are more religious or tend to depend upon sacred readings such as the Bible or Quran. The internal cognitive messages of many clients, such as negative self-image messages, can easily interfere with or obstruct their capacity to function in healthy ways. Assisting such clients by introducing spiritual metaphors can help them reframe their thinking in more healthy ways. For example, people with little confidence in themselves may benefit from the mustard seed parable, in which a tiny seed can become a mighty, huge tree once it grows.

Metaphors also help clients delve more deeply into their issues and alternative ways of examining their problems. In this regard, an example of a metaphor is a glass partially filled with water. Is it half full or half empty? This is a wonderful metaphor to ponder with a client only looking at the negative side of their situation. After taking a half-empty view, they can be helped to see what the half-full metaphor may suggest about what is working. Jesus offers numerous metaphors in the New Testament implanted in his stories and parables. He explained that finding the way is like being the mustard seed, being the shepherd's sheep, the Good Samaritan, or the Prodigal Son. Walsh (1999) offers several metaphors on what spiritual transformation can be like. These metaphors can be helpful to clients from different religions as well as non-religious clients. A spiritual transformation is like:

- **Awakening:** We are thought to be only semiconscious or in a slumber and our spiritual practices awaken us.
- **Enlightenment:** Spiritual disciplines bring us out of inner darkness to understanding, light, and vision.
- **Metamorphosis:** Spiritual practices can transform us from a caterpillar into a beautiful butterfly.
- **A journey:** We are viewed as traveling to find ourselves and we are forever here and now awaiting our recognition of this.
- **A mountaintop experience:** An unusual set of moments of insight about life and its meaning.

Enlightenment quotes and passages in Buddhism and Eastern thought generally provide another rich source of ideas to ponder. Many such authors of Eastern thought offer brief sayings that are thought-provoking and expand their understanding of a problem in a more introspective manner (James, 2013). Examples are:

- "To the mind that is still, the whole universe surrenders" (Lao Tzu).
- "All that we are arises with our thoughts" (Buddha).

- "We assume we will awaken to something else, something bigger and more grand. But really it is awakening to yourself, to what is here, has always been here. That is the startling, refreshing, wonderful good news" (Gangaji).
- "Fear is a natural reaction to moving closer to the truth" (Chodron, 2012).
- "Before you embark on a journey of revenge, dig two graves" (Confucius).

Guided Imagery

Guided imagery is another spiritual intervention that can help a client in a heartfelt way (Naparstek, 1994). Among other things, it can have a spiritual component to it. A guided imagery is a fantasy that a practitioner can describe step by step to help a client imagine being in it. Guided imagery exercises choose themes capturing qualities or situations that a client is having difficulty facing. Clients who are stressed or seem to rigidly hold onto certain routines and images of who they are and what they can do are helped in a guided imagery exercise to explore alternative ways to live their lives. A guide imagery can help the client imagine being in a more pleasant situation as an alternative—on the beach, in the mountains, or planting flowers in the garden. The scene is described and developed so the client can, step by step, gradually get into the situation using their senses and imagination. For example, imagine standing on the ocean beach, . . . sinking your bare feet into the soft and comforting sand, . . . smelling the salty water, . . . being mesmerized by the waves coming in and out, etc. Such an intervention focuses on the client's senses rather than their thinking and helps them develop an awareness of how they can change their circumstances.

Another example is the theme of helping a client self-disclose or share their deepest feelings about their struggles. The story can be imagined that you are walking along and you look over and see in the distance someone sitting under a large mulberry tree. You continue walking along and observe that this person is getting up, waving to you, and walking toward you. You stop and see who he is and it looks like Jesus (or another religious or admired figure of importance to the client). As this person comes closer, you realize that it actually is Jesus. You become very excited. As this person comes closer you see that he is overjoyed to see you. He comes up and puts his arms around you. After greeting you, he asks you to sit down next to him, possibly under the mulberry tree. Then he asks you to share all of the struggles that you have been holding inside and wishing you could share with someone. He seems to have all of the time in the world. Now, share what you would like to say to him.

Altars

The altars and other objects in the front of a church sanctuary or Jewish temple often hold considerable sacred meaning. In the Christian churches the cross is

Figure 9.5   Altar of a Jewish Synagogue

usually displayed at the center. Also the Bible and possibly the Communion elements are present. In the Jewish synagogue, the symbols of the Jewish six-point star and the nine candles of Hanukkah are displayed and the Torah is present as well. Important symbols in the front of a mosque are usually simpler and include the symbol of Islam and carpets for kneeling prayer. Hindu temples also have sacred altars; they are often the deities that Hindus worship and each has special meaning for a particular sect of Hindus.

Altars and shrines in homes are also important. When you visit a client in their home, you may be fortunate enough to see a family altar. Altars are often set aside as a place for prayers and devotions that occur regularly or sporadically when needed. It is a sacred place in most homes. A Hindu altar may include a statue of a deity, an Islamic altar a Quran, and a Christian altar a cross. As religious altars, they usually have religious symbols on them like a sacred book, photo of the founder of their religious group, or icons. Examples include possibly the Star of David for Jews, the star and crescent for Muslims, a statue of Buddha for Buddhists, or the crucifixion or resurrection cross for Christians.

Altars can also be non-religious but spiritual (Taylor, 2009; Linn, 1999). As non-religious altars, they might include flowers or plants, photos of family members, or sacred quotes of a revered person. These altars can sit on a table or chest of drawers, a window sill, or anywhere they can be easily observed and appreciated. They can provide a focal point for family members to connect with their spiritual realm. And they can be used to assist in a journey of healing, grieving of

---

An Altar to Help Students Grieve their Losses

An exercise used in a spirituality and social work class involves asking students to bring a memento reminding them of a family member or close friend who has died. Mementos can be photos, or a hobby of the person who was lost, a memorable event, or any number of other reminders. Each student is to bring the memento to the altar, describe the person who was lost, and leave the memento at the altar. The author uses this exercise to help students get in touch with their losses and draws attention to helping them partake in the grieving process.

---

a lost family member, recovering lost religious roots, or celebrating the beauty of nature.

Nhat Hanh (2014) suggests that an altar can be set up in your kitchen. This altar could remind you to practice mindfulness while cooking and later eating. The altar could be big or small and could have whatever is meaningful to you on it. It could have a photo of someone special to you, a flower in a vase, incense, a religious symbol, or maybe your favorite recipe book. The current altar of the author stretches across his desk and includes photos of him and his wife and another of his parents, an icon of Jesus, and a vibrant red shawl given to him by a Hindu friend as a blessing while he writes. He also has a framed note from his father-in-law that reads, "You can do it with my help . . . God."

Asking clients what they would include on their private altars can be a helpful exploratory exercise in identifying important symbols that have deeply-felt meaning for them and can bring comfort when there is suffering or a feeling of hopelessness (Taylor, 2009). Clients could also be encouraged to set up their altar in their home and develop some spiritual exercises to use with it. Altars can be created by clients perhaps with assistance from a social worker if it helps them address a concern for which they are being seen. For example, if a client is grieving a loss of a loved one, an altar can be a way to honor and say goodbye to that person (Linn, 1999). An altar could also be created to help a parent let go of a child who is growing up and leaving home; in this case, photos can be shown of a child at a graduation ceremony and possibly during earlier stages of life. An altar could also be helpful in recognizing the conclusion of a special relationship that had to be ended such as a divorce; in this case, separate photos of the two people could be displayed on the altar.

According to Linn (1999), the power of altars lies in their visible appearance. Each item can hold a special meaning for the family. While they are physical objects, they can also represent more abstractly an ideal, belief, or idea, or a relationship with a Higher Power or some other person. With the growing pace of life today, altars become more important to connect people to the sacred elements of their lives.

These objects can also infuse the most ordinary aspects of life with the divine. They can also honor the hallowed places within people's lives and selves. An altar could also be developed to celebrate a new job or the purchase of the first home after several years of apartment living.

The Medicine Wheel

The Medicine Wheel is a sacred circle of many Native American tribes, and in some ways an altar. The circle can be used in many ways as it can represent the great cycles of life including birth, death, and rebirth; the cycle of all of the seasons; the four basic elements of life (air, water, earth, and fire); and the four directions (north, east, south, west) (Linn, 1999). At the center of the wheel is the most sacred point of the altar because it symbolizes the Creator and the connecting point between visible and invisible realms. The east, for example, is symbolically the beginning of the wheel and is the home of new beginnings, spring, the dawning of the day, among other things. It contains within it excitement of new life and new birth. From there, one can explore the south, west, and north.

Conclusion

Several spiritual interventions are described in the chapter that can be helpful to many clients. This is not an exhaustive list of interventions but does represent many of the most popular ones. Many of these spiritual interventions can be implemented on one or more levels of practice. All three levels of micro and mezzo practice (individual, family, and small group) are potentially relevant. Of course this will vary with each client's religious or non-religious beliefs and affiliations as well as their openness to wanting this intervention.

Table 9.1 is offered as a beginning point for discussion of how far social workers can go in implementing these spiritual interventions. For example, meditation has been reported to be offered to clients individually and in groups with some success (Carlson & Larkin, 2009; Waechter & Wekerle, 2015). Also, mindfulness seems to be a widespread practice at all levels of practice even though this is not yet well

Table 9.1   Spiritual Interventions at Different Levels of Practice

SPIRITUAL INTERVENTION	INDIVIDUAL	FAMILY	SMALL GROUPS
Mindfulness			
Meditation			
Prayers			
Metaphors/Guided Imagery			
Altars			

C = considerable use now

P = possible use but not too often now

documented in the literature (Hick, 2009). Other times a spiritual intervention may seem possible but is not common practice. Prayer, for example, may be an intervention that is beginning to be considered if the client and worker both find it to be a helpful part of the client's treatment plan (Dossey, 1993). Prayers can take numerous forms, as is evident in the above section on prayer.

As an exercise, reflect on if and when the spiritual interventions covered in the chapter have been used in your agency or by others that you know. Fill out Table 9.1 as you view current practices that use these spiritual interventions. Place a "C" in any cells in which you think an intervention is used considerably and a "P" in cells in which an intervention is possibly being used or tried but not too often. Maybe you will want to take the initiative and explore implementing some of these spiritual interventions with interested clients. The next chapter takes a close look at spiritual interventions that can be introduced at the macro level.

Discussion Questions and Exercises

1. Have you ever meditated? If so, what has your experience been like? Has meditation been a useful spiritual tool for you? If you have meditated, how comfortable have you been with the silence? How have you dealt with internal chatter when meditating? What difficulties have you had? Set aside 10 to 15 minutes and attempt to implement one of the above methods of meditation ("Basic Meditation" or the approach described by Chodron).

2. Some prayer forms are described in the chapter that are unfamiliar to many people. They include prayers using sacred readings, centering prayer, ritual prayers, body prayers using yoga poses or dance, and praying with beads, icons, and mandalas. Which of these prayer forms are familiar to you? Which ones are unfamiliar to you? How could you respond in a supportive way to a client who mentions depending upon one of these prayer forms?

3. As an exercise, review Table 9.1 and think about how realistic it may be to implement each of these spiritual interventions with interested clients in your agency at each of the three levels of practice. When would it possibly be inappropriate to use them with clients in your agency? When do you think it would be appropriate to consider them even though obstacles are likely to be evident? In these instances, what would you consider doing, if anything, to encourage your agency to support such offerings when you believe they can help clients?

References

Achuthananada, S. (2013). *Many many many gods of Hinduism: Turning believers into non-believers and non-believers into believers.* North Charleston, SC: CreateSpace Independent Publishing.

Albers, S. (2008). *Eat, drink, and be mindful.* Oakland, CA: New Harbinger Publications.

Altman, D. (2011). *One-minute mindfulness: 50 simple ways to find peace, clarity, and new possibilities in a stressed-out world.* Novato, CA: New World Library.

Anonymous. (n.d.). *The way of a pilgrim and the pilgrim continues his way.* Translated by R. M. French. San Francisco: Harper & Row.

Bade, M. K. & Cook, S. W. (2008). Functions of Christian prayer in the coping process. *Journal for the Scientific Study of Religion, 47*(1), 123–133.

Bays, J. C. (2009). *Mindful eating: A guide to rediscovering a healthy and joyful relationship with food.* Boston, MA: Shambhala Publications.

Bloom, A. (1970). *Beginning to pray.* Ramsey, NY: Paulist Press.

Brown, P. D. (2003). *Paths to prayers: Finding your own way to the presence of God.* San Francisco: Jossey-Bass.

Canda, E. R., & Furman, L. D. (2010). *Spiritual diversity in social work practice: The heart of healing.* 2nd edition. New York: Free Press.

Carlson, B. E. & Larkin, H. (2009). Meditation as a coping intervention for treatment of addiction. *Journal of Religion and Spirituality in Social Work: Social Thought, 28,* 379–392.

Chilsom, R. (1996). *God awaits you: Based on the classic spirituality of Meister Eckhart.* Notre Dame, IN: Ave Maria Press.

Chodron, P. (2008). *Comfortable with uncertainty: 108 teachings on cultivating fearlessness and compassion.* Boston: Shambhala.

Chodron, P. (2012). *Living beautifully with uncertainity and change.* Boston: Shambhala.

CSWE (Council on Social Work Education) (2015). *2015 Educational Policy and Accreditation Standards for Baccalaureate and Master's Social Work Programs.* Educational Policy Approved by the CSWE Board of Directors on March 20, 2015; Accreditation Standards approved by the CSWE Commission on Accreditation on June 11, 2015. Alexandria, VA: Author.

Cunningham, M. (2012). *Integrating spirituality in clinical social work practice: Walking the labyrinth.* Boston: Pearson.

Dossey, L. (1993). *Healing words: The power of prayer and the practice of medicine.* New York: HarperCollins.

Dudley, J., Smith, C., & Millison, M. (1995). Unfinished business: Assessing the spiritual needs of hospice clients, *American Journal of Hospice and Palliative Care,* March/April, 1995, 30–37.

Gates, J. (2006). *Yogini: The power of women in yoga.* San Rafael, CA: Mandala Publishing.

Guenther, M. (1998). *The practice of prayer.* Boston: Cowley Publications.

Hagerty, B. B. (2009). *Fingerprints from God: The search for the science of spirituality.* New York: Riverhead Books.

Hick, S. F. (2009). *Mindfulness and social work.* Chicago: Lyceum Books.

Instructions for Performing Muslim Prayers. (n.d.). In Arabic with diagrams of positions for each step. Islamic Center of Southern California. Available online at http://www.icsconline.org/docs/MuslimPrayerbyJihadTurkandJoshHerman.pdf.

James, K. (2013). *Enlightenment quotes and passages to awaken the Buddha within.*

Keating, T. (2006). *Open mind, open heart.* New York: Continuum International Publishing Group.

Kirk, M., Boon, B., & DiTuro, D. (2006). *Hatha yoga illustrated*. Champaign, IL: Human Kinetics.

Kornfield, J. (1993). *A Path with heart: A guide through the perils and promises of spiritual life*. New York: Bantam Books.

Land, H. (2015). *Spirituality, religion, and faith in psychotherapy: Evidence-based expressive methods for mind, brain, and body*. Chicago: Lyceum Books.

Leung, P. P., Chan, C. L., Ng, S., & Lee, M. (2009). Towards body-mind-spirit integration: East meets West. *Clinical Social Work Journal, 37*, 303–311.

Linn, D. (1999). *Altars: Bringing sacred shrines into your everyday life*. New York: Ballantine Wellspring.

Mansfield, K. (n.d.). Charlotte labyrinths. Available online at http://www.charlottelabyrinth group.com/labyrinths.

McCullough, M. E., Pargament, K. I., & Thorensen, C. E. (Eds.) (2001). *Forgiveness: Theory, research, and practice*. New York: Guilford Press.

Naparstek, B. (1994). *Staying well with guided imagery*. New York: Warner.

Nes, S. (2004). *The mystical language of icons*. Cambridge, UK: Wm. B. Eerdmans Publishing.

Nhat Hanh, T. (1976). *The miracle of mindfulness: A manual on meditation*. Boston: Beacon Press.

Nhat Hanh, T. (1985). *A guide to walking meditation*. Norwich, CT: Thames Printing Company.

Nhat Hanh, T. (2009). *You are here: Discovering the magic of the present moment*. Boston: Shambhala.

Nhat Hanh, T. (2012). The fourteen mindfulness trainings for engaged Buddhists. *Mindfulness and meditation in the tradition of Zen master*. Available online at http://www.peacefulc-ity.org/2012/04/revised-14-mindfulness-trainings-now-available-april-2012.

Nhat Hanh, T. (2014). *How to eat*. Berkeley: Parallax Press.

Norton Professional Books. (2014). *Morning meditations: Daily reflections to awaken your power to change*. New York: W.W. Norton.

Pew Research Center, Religion and Public Life. (2012). Religion and the Unaffiliated. Washington, DC: Pew Research Center. Available online at http://www.pewforum. org/2012/10/09/nones-on-the-rise-religion.

Pew Research Center, Religion and Public Life. (2013). Section 6: Religion and Social Values. Washington, DC: Pew Research Center. Available online at http://www.people-press. org/2012/06/04/section-6-religion-and-social-values.

Rupp, J. (2007). *Prayer*. Maryknoll, NY: Orbis Books.

Semmens, H. R. (2014). *The labyrinth as a spiritual tool*. Unpublished paper. Charlotte, NC: School of Social Work. University of North Carolina at Charlotte.

Sheridan, M. J. (2010). Ethical issues in the use of prayer in social work: Implications for professional practice and education. *Families in Society, 91*(2), 112–120.

Taylor, B. B. (2009). *An altar in the world: A geography of faith*. New York: HarperCollins.

Tolle, E. (2005). *A new earth: Awakening to your life's purpose*. New York: Penguin Group.

University of New Hampshire Health Services. (n.d.). *Mandalas as spiritual practice*. Available online at http://unh.edu/health-services/ohep/spiritual-wellness/mandalas-spiritual-practice.

Vishupadi, R. (2013). *Quotes of wisdom: 99 Buddha's quotes*. Available online at www.Amazon. com.

Waechter, R. L. & Wekerle, C. (2015). Promoting resilience among maltreated youth using meditation, yoga, tai chi and qigong: A scoping review of the literature. *Child and Adolescent Social Work Journal, 32*(1), 17–31.

Walsh, R. (1999). *Essential spirituality: The 7 central practices to awaken heart and mind*. New York: John Wiley & Sons.

Webster, R. (2009). *Prayer for beginners: Discovering the language of your soul.* Woodbury, MN: Llewellyn Publications.

Zanzig, T. (1990). *Learning to meditate: Thirty-day introduction to the practice of meditation.* Winona, MN: Saint Mary's Press.

Zen Dirt. (2011). *Fill your mind with emptiness.* April 22, 2011. Available online at http://www.zendirt.com/if-you-cannot-find-the-truth/502.

10

Macro Spiritual Interventions

Our world is one of terrible contradictions. Plenty of food but one billion people go hungry. Lavish lifestyles for a few but poverty for too many others. Huge advances in medicine while mothers die every day in childbirth and children die every day from drinking dirty water. Billions spent on weapons to kill people instead of keeping them safe.

(Ban Ki-Moon, U.N. Secretary General)

I ask everyone with political responsibility to remember two things: human dignity and the common good.

(Pope Francis, 5/1/14, Twitter)

Spiritual interventions are usually most familiar to people at the micro and mezzo levels of practice. Macro interventions, the topic of this chapter, are just as important. Macro levels of practice tend to be overlooked in the larger realm of spiritually sensitive practice (Hill & Donaldson, 2012; Sheridan, 2012a). The chapter covers several different aspects of spirituality related to macro practice. They are:

- developing spiritually sensitive human service organizations;
- a closer look at faith-based organizations and their macro issues;
- spirituality and religion infused in social movements;
- spirituality's role in community practice.

A spiritual intervention has been defined as an activity, type of treatment, or action with a spiritual focus introduced in the helping process. A macro spiritual intervention has a few additional distinctions. Macro spiritual interventions typically involve activities that are introduced at the organizational, policy, or community levels of practice. These interventions are likely to serve large numbers of people and bring about change that can impact social structures, such as laws, agency policies and programs, as well as people. Macro spiritual interventions often focus on larger social issues and problems such as hunger and food insecurities; homelessness and inadequate housing; unemployment and low wages for the employed; intergroup conflicts among different religious and cultural groups; access to quality health care; women's and children's rights; voters' rights; immigration reform; and environmental efforts such as supporting the use of alternative energy sources and joining causes that seek to protect the health of the Earth.

The collection of spiritual interventions described in the chapter are varied and suitable for implementation in both human service organizations and communities of different sizes and compositions. Macro spiritual interventions are not as numerous in number or as well documented as micro ones (Hill & Donaldson, 2012). Yet, the chapter offers an introduction to several different spiritual models, formats, and strategies that could be used. The organizational interventions that are included address issues of human service organizations such as how spirituality or faith elements can be effectively introduced in clinical programs and how these elements can be used to inspire and effect positive changes in clients. Community interventions with a spiritual component, described later in the chapter, aim to improve the quality of the lives of people in several different social and economic areas. These interventions are usually driven, at least in part, by the religious and spiritual beliefs of the organizations that are involved.

Practitioners who are likely to introduce these interventions can be generalist social workers, community organizers, administrators, or planners, among others. The clients, community participants, and other recipients of these interventions are likely to have a diverse set of backgrounds, spiritual orientations, and religious affiliations. In all instances, the choice of a macro intervention, like micro and mezzo ones, is likely to be implemented most successfully if it emerges out of a close working partnership between macro practitioners and community participants.

Develop Spiritually Sensitive Human Service Organizations

It is important for social workers to address organizational factors in their agencies that can support the help provided to clients with spiritual issues. These are important macro concerns for social workers to know about and address as part of their practice role. One concern is that social workers and other helping professionals cannot be fully prepared to offer spiritually sensitive interventions to their clients until their employer is prepared as well (Doe, 2004). This point was emphasized earlier in chapter 5. Ideally, the agency sponsor (or school or hospital sponsor) of a spiritually sensitive practice approach needs to take the first step in conceptualizing what spirituality and religion mean to the agency in terms of helping their clients (Doe, 2004; Svare, Hylton, & Albers, 2007). Agencies are also responsible for preparing practitioners to become equipped to help clients with their spiritual issues. Several other areas of agency preparation are also important, including defining spirituality and religion, developing procedures for spiritual assessments, implementing spiritual interventions when they are helpful to clients, and evaluating how well these interventions work. A social worker's part in all of this may be to assume some responsibility for facilitating efforts to implement these organizational tasks or at least to bring these issues up with the appropriate agency administrators or their supervisors. This involves a set of macro interventions that focus on organizational development and change.

Conceptualize the Clients' Needs for Spirituality and Religion

Several questions should be initially considered by agencies about spirituality and religion and the needs of their clients. Is the concept of spirituality in the agency's mission or vision statement (Doe, 2004)? Are there agency policies supporting the introduction of spiritual interventions? And are there any policies or procedures describing how spirituality can be implemented, such as in an intake instrument or treatment plan? Some studies (e.g. Svare, Hylton, & Albers, 2007) suggest that an absence of clear and complete policies and procedures on spirituality can lead practitioners to develop their own positions and practice on spiritual issues often based on their own religious beliefs. Moreover, it is likely that several different versions of practice will emerge to the detriment of the clients involved.

An agency should have, at the very least, a policy about spirituality and spiritual services if they intend to offer any services of a spiritual or religious nature (Doe, 2004). As part of this policy, they should define what spirituality means in the context of services provided to their clients, and also how religion may be relevant as a topic of discussion for some clients receiving these services. Each agency will be different in this regard and should focus on the specific spiritual needs of clients in their setting. For example, if the setting is a hospital, spirituality can be important to patients in coping with various diseases and other medical conditions. Prayer and meditation, for example, may be important to address. Chaplain services may be beneficial and a diversity of available clergy may be needed for patients affiliated with the Catholic and Protestant churches, Islam, and other religious groups. These services can provide comfort, meaning, and reassurance for patients and their families, and also provide them with religious rituals, grief counseling, and burial services (Harr & Yancey, 2014).

Prepare the Agency and Practitioners

Once these policies are in place, agency administrators and supervisors can be actively involved in informing direct service personnel about these policies. Do staff members understand these policies and how to implement them? A related question is whether or not staff training, formal or informal, is offered or made available outside the agency. Staff members will need to be prepared to respond to spiritual issues in ways that are helpful to clients. Some form of staff training will be needed as part of this preparation, as well as supervisory assistance in implementing these policies over time with clients. Training sessions to prepare staff members are crucial to success. Portions of this text can be used as training material.

The content of the book provides a helpful framework for topics to be covered in such training. This framework, in an abbreviated form, can be as follows:

- Understanding the concepts of spirituality and religion (chapter 1).
- Understanding how these concepts can be relevant to the needs and problems of clients served by the agency (chapter 1).

- Discuss and address the general needs and questions of staff members that can help prepare them to effectively work with clients (chapters 2 and 13).
- Identify and learn about the religious groups represented by the client population of the agency, especially religious groups that are unfamiliar (chapters 3 and 4).
- Develop a spiritually sensitive approach to practice that can be modeled after the approach described in the book (an introduction in chapter 5).
- Explore and understand the ethical issues and dilemmas that are important to address in using this approach (chapter 6).
- As part of the approach that is chosen, gain understanding about how to work with clients during each of the four major components or phases: engagement, assessment, intervention, and evaluation (chapters 7, 8, 9, 10, 11, and 12).

Many other problems at the organizational level have spiritual implications that could be addressed. For example, mindfulness is an approach that can be practiced in an organization's life and can address many organizational problems (Birnbaum & Birnbaum, 2008; Hick, 2009). Staff members can meet in support groups that help them develop mindful sensitivities, such as being fully in the moment, responding to exhaustion with rest, being attentive to their own inner needs related to body pain, and setting priorities instead of trying to do it all. Mindfulness can be taught to staff members and encouraged as a way of interacting with each other. Mindfulness can also be practiced in staff meetings by taking a few minutes in the beginning to help attendees be in touch with their breathing and the importance of deliberating in the present moment. These mindful techniques can be mentioned in a subtle and humorous manner, such as by asking people if they are breathing and if their breathing is slowing them down enough to partake in what is going on. A few moments can follow for doing this. These comments can be cues that a mindful discussion can help the group communicate directly and openly, be respectful of each other and readily hear what each person says, and cooperate on the tasks before the group.

Many social agencies and hospitals provide spiritually sensitive interventions to their clients and patients (Canda & Furman, 2010). Their stance is usually to provide assistance to clients in all aspects or dimensions—psychological, social, mental, biological, cultural, and spiritual. Yet often, organizational policies and procedures for implementing these interventions are not fully developed or are missing. Some of the critical areas that could be considered are the following:

- Craft a widely agreed upon concept or definition of spirituality and religion in the context of the agency's services.
- Develop procedures to assess the spiritual needs of clients in the assessment phase.
- Identify any spiritual interventions that are routinely used or should be considered for some clients.

- Evaluate the effectiveness of spiritual interventions and spiritually sensitive practice.

Craft a Working Definition of Spirituality

If human service organizations are wanting to optimize their spiritually sensitive practices, then it is important to have some explicit guidelines or even policies that apply to the entire agency (Doe, 2004). Otherwise, what could happen is that practitioners who are comfortable and favorable to engaging their clients on spiritual issues will apply their own approach, with some approaches being acceptable to the agency and others not (Svare, Hylton, & Albers, 2007). Others in the agency who are not inclined to be open to helping clients with spiritual issues will likely be avoiding or only superficially addressing these concerns. If the agency does not have such a definition or at least a clear perception of what spirituality and religion mean in the realm of their services, the problems mentioned above will inevitably occur. Most of the staff members of agencies that the author has talked with about these issues indicate that their agencies do not have clear, consistent messages on this topic.

An agency using a spiritually sensitive practice approach takes the first step in defining and clarifying what spirituality means to them, what religion means and how it can be related to client needs and problems, and how practitioners can help clients in these areas of spirituality and religion. As mentioned earlier, the social worker's part may be to assume some responsibility for facilitating these efforts or at least bringing these issues to the attention of the appropriate agency administrator or their supervisor.

A definition of how each agency views the concept of spirituality for helping their clients is a way to encourage implementation of an entire range of services that are spiritually sensitive. How can this happen? First, it would be important to select a committee to propose a definition to agency administrators. This committee of six to ten should have representation from all levels—administration, supervisors, evaluators, and direct service staff from different programs and disciplines. Possibly a board member, volunteer, and client could also be considered. Upon beginning its task, the committee should review the literature on how social work and other professions define these two concepts. Reviewing chapter 1 illuminates the idea of the many dimensions of both spirituality and religion. In constructing definitions, it will be very important to differentiate spirituality and religion, as there is often confusion about how they are different. Some even think that spirituality is religion. Formulating a non-religious and religious definition of spirituality could help with this issue. Also helpful would be to create a set of guidelines for when staff members' responses to a spiritual issue are unacceptable. In large part, this is important in order to discourage practitioners from introducing their own personal point of view in the helping process. Chapter 6, on ethics, offers some helpful guidelines for avoiding introduction of such biases. An alternative to using a committee could be to have a few staff members formulate the definitions and then seek feedback from a wide range of agency personnel and volunteers. Either way, the more that all stakeholders participate, the more likely the outcomes will be supported and utilized.

After these two concepts are defined in a general way, it will also be important to develop explanations for how these concepts have meaning for clients. For example:

- If the clients are children, it may be important to emphasize such spiritual concepts as wonder, openness to mystery, and freedom to explore (Fuller, 2006). If the children are being served by a faith-based agency, storytelling of favorite religious stories from sacred writings may be another option.
- Older adult clients may respond to spiritual interventions that help them explore and reminisce about their lives in the past, claim their legacies to be passed on to others, help them resolve past conflicts with family and close associates, and find meaningful ways to live fully in the time ahead (Seeber, 1990).

Develop Agency Procedures for Spiritual Assessments

The author's experiences in talking with agencies is that many of them have a spirituality question or two that they ask clients initially as part of a larger assessment process. Typical questions are often, "Do you have any spiritual or religious supports?" Or "Are you affiliated with a particular spiritual or religious group like a church or synagogue?" In both circumstances, if the response is yes, a follow-up question is usually needed to find out what they are. Unfortunately, such questions are not often viewed as important because they are not usually explored in more depth and they do not lead to follow-up questions about possible interventions.

Chapter 8 is devoted to spiritual and religious assessment questions and is a good resource for an agency to review in preparing more comprehensive spiritual assessments. One approach could be to begin with a few general questions that open up discussions about spiritual topics pertinent to the agency's purpose, followed by specific questions that are linked as closely as possible to interventions that an agency can offer. The general questions should be tailored to the client population's needs. Examples are:

- An agency serving LGBT teenagers could ask some general questions such as, "What are your spiritual and religious beliefs?" (Tan, 2005). These questions could be followed by specific questions that help them explore their beliefs. For example, how have their beliefs encouraged and discouraged them from forming new intimate relationships? How have their religious beliefs contributed to and detracted from their quality of life as people?

- A hospice agency would likely want to explore how their clients find meaning in their lives now (Doka, 2011). What concerns and unresolved issues do they have? How do they view life after death and what meaning may it have to them?
- A mental health inpatient facility may want to assess what spirituality and religion mean to their clients by asking them specifically about their religious and spiritual beliefs and practices, how important they are to them, and how these practices can help them function more effectively in their daily lives (Hodge, 2004). For example, "Do you have spiritual or religious practices that you have used in the past or would like to use now?" If these practices are relevant to their treatment goals, how can the staff members help them implement these practices?

Implement and Evaluate Spiritual Interventions

Sometimes agencies may believe that a spiritual intervention is an important part of their service delivery provisions. Spiritual interventions described in chapter 9 provide many examples. Substance abuse agencies, for example, have found meditation to be a helpful approach in assisting clients in letting go of addictive impulses when they arise (Carlson & Larkin, 2009). Mindfulness is a general practice that can be used in many agencies to help clients learn how to become more comfortable in the present, where they can be most in touch with their needs and be able to change their circumstances. Prayer can be a useful practice for clients suffering from a loss through death or divorce, surgery, a chronic medical condition, an anxiety disorder, a family member's challenging circumstances, peace in their family, or a volatile neighborhood.

Evaluations are also essential especially at a time when faith-based agencies and other agencies offering spiritual practices are being criticized for not having enough accountability for what they do. Evaluations address many questions, including basic things like defining what spirituality means in the agency's practice context as well as determining the extent to which the agency's practitioners are adequately prepared to provide spiritually sensitive practice. Ethical concerns should also be carefully examined, such as avoiding the introduction of spiritual biases unwanted by the clients. Most important, evaluations provide a means of objectively determining the extent to which clients are being helped with their problems; ultimately, evaluations are needed to provide evidence that spiritually sensitive interventions and practices work or are effective.

Faith-Based Organizations and Macro Issues

Faith-based organizations, in contrast to many other agencies, often consider spirituality and religion when defining their overall purpose, mission and vision statements, and many of their interventions. These organizations are currently providing a diverse range of services in our society (Ammerman, 2001). They provide services to people in food pantries and soup kitchens, housing shelters, clothes closets, and child care. They are also involved in health screening, financial aid, and transportation assistance. Also, educational and cultural activities such as substance abuse prevention, tutoring, youth camps, and job counseling are examples of services they provide. In addition, senior centers, neighborhood and community outreach efforts, support groups, and self-help groups are sometimes faith-based. Evangelistic outreach activities and humanitarian efforts in Third World countries are also provided by some of these agencies. Finally, public advocacy organizations that provide civil rights work and coalitions on environmental or health and social service issues can be faith-based and macro in nature.

Faith-based agencies and programs have not always been available with such diverse purposes as they are now. A few decades ago, there were far fewer such agencies in number and they were mostly referred to as sectarian or denominational agencies. Denominational agencies are established religious-sponsored agencies that have become largely integrated into the human service system. Examples include Jewish Family Services, Catholic Social Services and Catholic Charities, the Salvation Army, and Lutheran Family and Children. These agencies are discussed later in the chapter. More recently, these agencies have been joined by a diverse set of new and expanding religious enterprises. Many of these newer agencies have come about because of the Charitable Choice provision of the Welfare Reform legislation passed in the mid-1990s (Bielefeld, 2006; Sheridan, 2012a). Among other things, this provision eliminated some regulatory and contracting obstacles to the participation of faith-based organizations in delivering social services. This was done because proponents of faith-based agencies believed these agencies, with their added faith component, could be more effective than secular groups (Bielefeld, 2006: Netting, O'Connor, & Yancey, 2006).

Some studies have focused on the shifts in federal policy to Charitable Choice that allows faith-based agencies to include a religious component in their human service approach (Bielefeld, 2006). As discussed in chapter 6, some proponents of faith-based agencies suggested that these agencies may be able to offer more than secular agencies because they would be more holistic in their approach and thus have more influence in transforming their clients than secular groups. Proponents also believed that faith-based groups could establish more caring and enduring relationships with clients and they would have a more motivated staff with a greater capacity to instill a spirit of hope (Bielefeld, 2006; Netting, O'Connor, & Yancey, 2006). Other proponents claimed that faith-based organizations can also be more effective in changing the behavior of individuals than traditional nonprofit agencies, perhaps because of their experiences with moral teachings (Kennedy & Bielefeld, 2002).

Among other things, these studies focus on describing key components and processes of faith-based programs, descriptions of faith-based services for particular client populations, and the influence of faith in human service programs. The findings of Hugen and Venema (2009) in their study of 1,110 faith-based programs revealed that over half of them viewed spirituality as central in their program. They also looked at how these agencies described the faith-based component. One-third of programs communicated faith implicitly, mostly through acts of caring toward clients, and another one-fourth communicated their faith explicitly and conveyed the view that the role of faith was critical to changes clients could make. Another focus was on how much direct exposure they provided to clients with faith-related elements. Findings indicated the agencies differed widely in terms of the intensity of their exposure to faith-related programmatic elements that included processes, values, and relationships.

While many of these agencies offered faith-based elements in their programs, the nature of these elements was not shared in the study in detail (Hugen & Venema, 2009). What was shared was evident in responses to a set of Likert scale statements in Figure 10.1. Responses to some of the statements provide a glimpse of some of the general ways faith-based services were evident at the organizational level. A five-point Likert scale (0 = never, 1 = rarely, 2 = sometimes, 3 = quite often, 4 = very frequently) was used and the average scores appear after each statement in Figure 10.1.

Each of these statements reflects, in different ways, the specific messaging communicated by each agency about its faith. However, these statements are worded in such general terms that it is difficult to know what they actually do. To find out more, each of these items could be used in a follow-up study by any agency, faith-based or not, to inquire specifically about how faith is communicated at the organizational level. They are:

- In what specific ways are the faith elements of your program reflected in your services and care of your staff?
- In what specific ways do the program participants perceive or think about your program as faith-based?
- Are the faith elements clearly communicated in your program? If so, what are they? If not, how are they unclear?
- What is communicated in the faith-related literature available to clients in your program?

Another part of the study by Hugen and Venema (2009) included Likert scale statements representing several different ways that faith-based elements could be

---

- The faith element of our program is primarily reflected in the service and care of our staff. (3.00)
- Program participants perceive or think about our program as faith-based. (2.54)
- The faith elements incorporated into our program are clear and open. (2.49)
- Program participants see faith-related literature on display in our program. (2.22)

Figure 10.1 Client Exposure to Faith-Related Program Elements (Hugen & Venema, 2009)

introduced within service provisions. Because many of these statements focused on important ethical issues, they are discussed in chapter 6. Other issues surrounding the nature of faith-based interventions, their outcomes, and evaluations are discussed and examined more closely in chapter 12.

On another note, the importance of collaboration between faith-based organizations and secular agencies within the larger human service system is important to maximize benefits to clients and stress efficiency in the use of dwindling human service resources. In this regard, little seems to be known about the nature and extent of such collaboration between faith-based and secular agencies working in the same fields or with the same client populations. Thomas (2009) conducted a national study of 15 faith-based agencies to learn more about these inter-agency relationships. One concern raised in her qualitative study is that such collaboration may be limited and that barriers may exist to forging greater cooperation. More research is encouraged in this regard.

Denominational Agencies

Traditional denominational agencies are one type of faith-based agency that have existed for several decades. Examples include the Salvation Army and Catholic Charities. Most of these faith-based agencies are different from the more recently developed faith-based agencies because they are well established and probably have learned from experience how to communicate their faith in ways that are acceptable to the larger network of human service agencies. They may have needed to "soften" the faith elements of their services to clients to qualify for funding outside their denomination. They may also offer their services to people outside their religion. Further, they may have removed barriers to working closely with other religious and non-religious agencies. The list in Figure 10.2 represents some of these denominational agencies at the national level. Select one and explore its website. When was it founded? What does the website reveal about faith elements that are part of its service provisions?

Christian denominations include Mainline Protestant sects such as Presbyterian, Methodist, Lutheran, Baptist, and Episcopalian, and many of these and other denominations are typically divided further into more conservative and liberal sects of their denomination. For example, a Baptist church could be affiliated at the national

---

- The Association of Jewish Family & Children's Agencies (AJFCA) (http://www.ajfca.org/home/)
- ICNA (Islamic Circle of North America) Relief USA (http://icnarelief.org/site2/index.php)
- Catholic Charities USA (http://catholiccharitiesusa.org/)
- Salvation Army (http://www.salvationarmyusa.org/)
- Lutheran Services in America (http://www.lutheranservices.org/)

Figure 10.2   List of Some Denominational Agencies

level with the American Baptist Association, the Southern Baptist Convention, the National Baptist Association, USA (predominately African American), or possibly with none of them. A local Lutheran church could be affiliated with the Evangelical Lutheran Church in America, the Lutheran Church-Missouri Synod, or another less known regional synod. Other Christian denominations include Roman Catholic, Orthodox, Mormon, Jehovah's Witnesses, Pentecostal, and others. Further, there are Associations of Muslims, Hindus, and Jews among others as well that could be sponsoring a denominational human service agency. To become more acquainted with a denominational human service agency of particular interest to you, complete the exercise in Figure 10.3.

Example of Jewish Family and Children's Services

The Association of Jewish Family & Children's Agencies (AJFCA) is a national membership organization for Jewish human service agencies in the United States and Canada (http://www.ajfca.org/). AJFCA has approximately 125 member agencies, representing most of the eligible Jewish family and children's agencies in North America. They state that their local agencies provide services to clients of all ages, faiths, and economic backgrounds. Their services, in general, include counseling families, feeding the hungry, assisting the elderly and protecting the vulnerable. They stress that they are united by the values of their Jewish tradition and work together toward their common goal of Tikkun Olam, or repairing the world. Their website provides a map and links to the locations of all of their AJFCA agencies throughout the United States and Canada. The website provides links to websites for each local Jewish Family and Children Services in your locale once you select your location of interest.

Among the Association's fundamental Jewish values are:

- **Tzedakah:** the obligation of the Jewish community to create justice in the world;

---

1. Google a denominational human service agency of interest to you in your community.
2. Visit the website of the agency.
3. Review the mission and vision statements of the agency and any other religious and cultural information that is provided.
4. What are their preferences, if any, about who is qualified to receive services, especially based on a client's religion? (E.g. do they give preference to people of their religious group for any services? What are their policies abut clients from other religious backgrounds?)
5. What faith elements do they mention, if any, that they introduce in the helping process and how do they introduce these elements? (E.g. do they promote their religious beliefs in any way? Do they expect clients to follow their religious practices? Do they expect clients to attend their worship services or join their groups?)
6. Contact the agency and ask to interview a social worker to find out more about how faith is introduced in their agency.

Figure 10.3 Denominational Human Services: Questions to Ask before Making a Referral

AJFCA and its member agencies proudly represent the current chapter of a long and distinguished Jewish history. The Jewish story is an amazing chronicle of survival through the ages. From our suffering as slaves in Egypt, through years of exile and wandering, surviving pogroms in Russia, the horrors of the Holocaust and centuries of attack, the Jewish people have overcome and reached freedom and prosperity. Today, our network of Jewish family service agencies provides a platform for us to stand up and be counted as Jews who survive and achieve. Without our sense of AMCHA* and Jewish peoplehood, this survival would not have been possible. We were all slaves in Egypt, we were all present to receive the Ten Commandments at Sinai and we are linked together generation to generation, each taking our place in this long and distinguished history.

* AMCHA is the Hebrew word meaning "Your People" and refers to grassroots and ordinary people. AMCHA Initiative is a national organization committed to addressing anti-Semitism at institutions of higher education in the United States.

Figure 10.4   A Chronicle of Survival through the Ages (www.ajfca.org)

- **Tikkun Olam:** the collective obligation to work toward making the world right and whole;
- **B'zelem Elohim:** treating others with the inherent dignity that arises from the belief that all human beings were created in the image of God.

The AJFCA agencies are strongly rooted in Jewish tradition and values, as their website states. Some of their cultural values are described further on the website under "Jewish connection," which includes a Jewish holiday calendar. One of their values statements relates their unique history especially as a community of survivors.

The history of Jewish people as survivors is well documented and important to remember when working with Jewish people or others of different religious groups that have been persecuted in the past and possibly in the present. While it is most appropriate to wait for a Jewish client to bring up any past history of actual persecution or memories about the Holocaust, it is likely that older Jewish people in particular will remember the Holocaust during World War II and lives of family members and friends that have been lost and persecuted during that historical period. Most importantly, practitioners should pause and just listen to what Jewish clients share about the Holocaust and try to imagine the extreme horror that still is likely to be residing deep within them. Then it would be important to listen for how the horrors of that time may be a part of their current insecurities and fears. Explore these insecurities gently if they are shared and relate to the helping process.

The Jewish Family Service Agency (JFSA) in Las Vegas is an example of a local JFSA agency. They state that "While our focus is on the Jewish community, Jewish Family Service Agency serves all individuals without regard to religion, race, age, disability, sexual orientation, national origin" (http://www.jfsalv.org/). Their stated purpose is to serve the entire community, but their priority would be Jewish clients. JFSA—Las Vegas states that they provide a variety of services for the community's changing and emerging challenges (http://www.jfsalv.org/). Their website indicates that they provide counseling and psychotherapy to all ages individually

Catholic Charities (CC) is another well-known denominational agency (www.catholiccharitie-susa.org). Catholic Charities, in brief, is among the largest private providers of social welfare among sectarian social welfare organizations in the U.S. Degeneffe (2003) reviews the history of CC and describes the many important programs and services offered by it at both the local and national levels. He also discusses controversies about Catholic Charities receiving public funding while having a direct and formal allegiance to the Catholic Church. Among other issues, Degeneffe discusses whether CC can and does provide nonbiased and fair services, especially related to some of the Church's controversial policies such as abortion. Consider reviewing his article to become more informed about the many contributions of Catholic Charities as well as how they have addressed some of the common ethical challenges facing faith-based agencies. Then possibly compare this agency with other denominational agencies such as the Salvation Army and Lutheran Family and Children.

Figure 10.5   Catholic Charities USA

and in groups. They provide services to seniors in three areas: Holocaust survivors, seniors living at home, and senior case management. They also offer adoption services and emergency services. They provide professional services free of charge, on a sliding scale, or using third party insurance. Temporary financial aid is provided in emergency situations only to Jewish clients.

Faith-Based and Macro Interventions

Spiritual interventions are evident in faith-based agencies at many levels of practice. In this section, faith-based interventions are highlighted at the macro level. Here is where we find the expressions of some of the most deeply rooted religious values, such as social and economic justice, compassion, dignity for all, peace and non-violence over war, and fairness. The scriptures and teachings of most religious groups reveal strong commitments to these and other values that are similar to social work values.

There is a relative absence of professional literature on how spirituality plays a role in macro practice in faith-based agencies. To find out about such practice, we need to expand our search beyond professional literature to include literature provided by religious groups. The work of Councils of Churches in many states is one source. These Councils have websites that can be found using Google. Many of them are directly involved in advocating for public policy and legislative changes in their states. In addition, the National Council of Churches (http://www.nationalcouncilofchurches.us/), their parent group, is involved at the national and international level in a range of peace and justice issues. One of their priorities involves reversing the trend of mass incarceration of people on drug charges, the bulk of them being people of color. Another priority is developing closer ties among different religious groups including Christians, Jews, and Muslims in the U.S. One aspect of this work area is to help reduce anti-Muslim and anti-Semitic sentiment in a post-9/11 world and another is to develop more understanding of other religious groups such as Buddhism and Hinduism. Other examples of national religious organizations include the U.S. Conference of Catholic Bishops (http://www.usccb.org/) and the Jewish Social Justice Roundtable (http://jewishsocialjustice.org/about-us).

Local spiritual or religious groups are also possible resources for learning more about faith-based social justice activities. Ethical Societies, or Ethical Humanistic Societies, are one source. They are in several cities and regions including Philadelphia, St. Louis, Baltimore, New York, and northern Virginia. An example of a local faith-based social justice group focusing on reconciliation is Mecklenburg Ministries (http://www.meckmin.org/) in Charlotte. This group is an interfaith, interracial, and multi-ethnic organization with over 100 member congregations representing more than a dozen faith traditions that builds bridges across many differences. Much of their work focuses on racial justice and fostering dialogue among different racial groups in Charlotte.

Numerous other religious organizations are actively involved in peace, social justice, and non-violence at the national, state and local levels. Some religious groups also have magazines that describe various types of faith-based social justice activities including describing the spiritual strategies and tactics that they use. A popular Evangelical Christian social justice magazine, *Sojourners: Faith in Action for Social Justice* (http://sojo.net/), provides an example. An article in a recent issue of their magazine describes the activities of the Cincinnati Union Bethel (CUB), a faith-based organization that runs a low income single women's housing complex. This housing group was being intimidated by a large financial group wanting to buy it as an investment to build high income housing as part of gentrification of that community (Araujo, 2013). CUB organized an ad hoc faith coalition to protest this financial group's actions and led prayer vigils and letter writing efforts in pro-test. CUB also set up a nativity scene (symbolizing the stable where Jesus was born because there was no room in the inn) near the financial group's nativity scene to highlight the irony of the financial group's nativity scene and its opposition to a place for these women to live.

A Model Faith-Based Agency

Some articles in the literature describe how faith-based agencies operate. A model faith-based agency that is comprehensive and ecumenical is one example. Kaseman & Austin (2005) describe a macro faith-based agency committed to both service and advocacy that they view as a possible prototype for comprehensive faith-based human service organizations in the future. They view it as distinctly different from traditional church programs and sectarian organizations like Catholic Social Services. They identify several components of importance to their agency that may be useful to other faith-based agencies. Some of these components are noted here. First, they stress the importance of holding onto and sustaining the spiritual calling that undergirds their effort. As they explain, if the staff and volunteers of an agency are called to serve in a social ministry, they should trust their instincts and moral compass, especially a call that identifies with the poor and vulnerable and believes in divine justice and love. Second they are committed to their own personal spiritual renewal. For example, they incorporate such things as personal sharing, prayer, and guided meditation into their activities with each other, such as during staff meetings. Third, they pursue ecumenical and interfaith missions with all of their partners despite the challenges this may bring rather than having an enterprise that is controlled by one denomination or faith group. This component is related to the view expressed in chapter 3 about pluralism and persistently looking for the commonality in the beliefs evident in all religions. Fourth, they enlist the involvement of a diverse set of leaders that reflects the ethnic, racial, religious, sexual orientation, and socioeconomic structure of the greater community. Most essential, they stress that the focus be on clients and that they continually remind themselves that their ministry exists for that reason. While these faith-based components were reported from only one agency, they may provide guidelines for other agencies.

Example of Church of the Saviour

Another faith-based group, the Church of the Saviour, has been perhaps one of the most effective in obtaining social and economic justice for large numbers of lower income people residing in the District of Columbia (http://inwardoutward.org/the-church-of-the-saviour/churches/). This non-denominational church over the past 70 years has created an amazing collection of human service provisions including a medical respite facility for homeless people, transitional housing for women and children, a medical clinic, a hospice for people with AIDS and others, extensive affordable housing for low income people, a child development center, a nurturing integrated home for people with developmental disabilities and those without disabilities, a senior center and apartments, financial education and support, and foster care, to name only some of their ministries.

The spiritual approach of Church of the Saviour may be the most instructive aspect of this church for other faith-based groups. The church is made up of seven smaller churches and each member belongs to one of these churches. Members commit to several spiritual disciplines including attending weekly worship, regular reading of the Bible, tithing, work with one and only one mission group, participating in weekly mission group meetings of prayer, and participating in project activities. The overall theme of this group is an "inward journey and outward journey" suggesting that members must go inward or inside themselves to find God's call for them and then develop a lasting commitment to that call or mission; the call is then carried out in the outward or outside world as a ministry of social justice guided and sustained by their ongoing inward journey (O'Connor, 1975). The human service provisions mentioned above are just some examples of these mission projects. Anyone can initiate a new mission focus by "sounding the call" to the larger community and waiting for enough members with a similar call to join them. A new mission may take a year or more to get started because of the kind of commitment that it requires. They want these missions to be grounded deeply in scriptures and committed to survive for a long period of time.

Spirituality and Religion Infused in Social Movements

Prophets of Judeo-Christian History

The prophets of Jewish history are extensively documented in the Hebrew Bible (also the Old Testament of the Christian Bible) and were well known for their extraordinary influence in furthering social justice. They focused much of their attention on opposition to the kings and their abuse of authority especially when the kings put their own personal greed and gains before the needs of the people (Heschel, 1962: Williams, 2003). These prophets included Jeremiah, Isaiah, Hosea, Amos, Micah, and others. A large segment of the Hebrew Bible is devoted to the lives and actions of these prophets. They were known for their prophetic voices as messengers of Yahweh; they were also well known for their clever and often unorthodox ways of protesting to get the public's attention. Much could be learned from them today about how to pursue social justice.

The prophets were not popular or accommodating to what made sense to public order (Heschel, 1962). Their words and actions were often designed to confront the status quo and get the attention of the public in any way that they could. Often they were viewed as disturbers of the peace, strange crackpots, and troublemakers. Jeremiah provides a good example. In a gathering of the king's consultants who were debating whether to resist Babylon's attack on their Jewish state, Jeremiah let his views be known by walking around wearing a wooden yoke (used on oxen) around his neck to symbolize that his country should surrender to Babylon instead of fight. His warning was ignored and Jerusalem, the capital, was destroyed and most of the population with it.

Jesus was also well known for his key role in advocacy for social justice (Williams, 2003). He was often confronting the religious leaders of his time with their hypocrisy in teaching Jewish law but overlooking how it affected the downtrodden. His focus was unswervingly on assisting and liberating the least advantaged in Palestinian society—the blind, deaf, epileptics, lepers, disabled, mentally ill, prostitutes, widows, orphans, foreigners, and others who were the most disadvantaged. In his introduction to his ministry in his hometown synagogue, Jesus unveiled his profound hope for the disadvantaged when he proclaimed that he was sent from God "to bring the good news to the poor, proclaim liberty to the captives, sight to the blind, and freedom for the downtrodden . . ." (Luke 4:18–19). These scripture passages and similar ones from other religious groups throughout history have inspired and empowered countless people to work to change the social orders of their nations on behalf of the downtrodden.

The Black Church and Civil Rights of the 1960s

The Civil Rights Movement of the 1960s is probably the best example of an effective social movement driven by religious groups and beliefs. The movement was led by African American Christian Churches in the South with support from Jewish and Christian groups in the North (Williams & Bond, 1987). Dr. Martin Luther King and other Southern religious leaders like Jesse Jackson, Andrew Young, and Ralph Abernathy began to stage unrelenting acts of opposition against Jim Crow laws and other injustices in the 1950s and 60s. These actions ultimately resulted in a massive civil rights movement engaging the entire Southern region of the country. Dr. King was a young charismatic pastor of an African American Baptist Church in Atlanta whose gifted eloquence as a speaker and deeply rooted commitment to social justice inspired the nation to face its moral responsibilities to African Americans (e.g. King, 1990; King, 1986). He and others in this movement persistently educated and inspired people through sermons, speeches, and protests. They exposed the disenfranchisement of African Americans in many areas including obstruction of voting rights; employment discrimination; segregated housing; "separate but equal" public facilities such as schools, hospitals and public transportation; forbidding African Americans from using private facilities such as restaurants and recreation centers; and an absence of equal justice under state and local laws. This movement later became a national movement expanded to include all poor people in the Poor People's Campaign and protests against the Vietnam War. Among other things, they exposed and confronted many of the horrific crimes and brutalities of the Jim Crow era such as murdering and abusing civil rights workers, lynching, and indiscriminate jailing of African Americans who challenged the status quo.

Most importantly, what motivated Dr. King and other Black leaders was their strong Christian beliefs and convictions, which became the main impetus for Dr. King's eventual successes. Dr. King's famous speeches were well known to be based in Christian teachings and practices. For example, in his letter to white Southern pastors from the Birmingham Jail in 1963 he emphasized the interconnection of all people, the importance of non-violence in all actions that expose injustices to some people, doing what is right, demanding freedom for the oppressed, and claiming that change comes from tireless and persistent efforts of people in partnerships with their God (King, 1990). A specific example of Christian teachings in this Birmingham letter was:

> Was not Jesus an extremist in love? "Love your enemies, bless them that curse you, pray for them that despitefully use you." Was not Amos an extremist for justice—"Let justice roll down like waters and righteousness like a mighty stream." Was not Paul an extremist for the gospel of Jesus Christ—"I bear in my body the marks of the Lord Jesus." Was not Martin Luther an extremist—"Here I stand; I can do none other so help me God." Was not John Bunyan an extremist—"I will stay in jail to the end of my days before I make a butchery of my conscience." Was not Abraham Lincoln an extremist—"This nation

cannot survive half slave and half free." Was not Thomas Jefferson an extremist—"We hold these truths to be self-evident, that all men are created equal."

Examples of Recent Social Movements

The community work of religious groups, sometimes affiliated with social workers, has been the catalyst for beginning many social movements. Recent large scale social movements like the Living Wage Movement in Baltimore (Hutchison, 2012) and the Moral Monday Movement for voters' rights and other protections for citizens in North Carolina are examples. Both have been led by religious groups or religious leaders and have been inspired by religious doctrine. Of the models of community work mentioned above, building coalitions around common goals like fair wages and voters' rights are often emphasized. Also these community efforts become engaged in political action even though this sometimes becomes controversial for some religious groups, such as conservative and moderate church members. As was mentioned earlier, some of the most deeply rooted values of religious groups concentrate on social justice, dignity for all people, and fairness. The scriptures and teachings of the major religious groups clearly enunciate commitments to these values.

The initial impetus for the living-wage law in Baltimore came from a largely church-based organization known as BUILD—Baltimoreans United in Leadership Development (Niedt, Ruiters, Wise, & Schoenberger, 1999). Many of the pastors in the poorer sections of Baltimore noticed that a growing number of employed people were frequenting the soup kitchens and other charitable services offered by their churches. It became increasingly apparent to them that a large population of working poor in the city could not live on their employment income. Therefore, BUILD joined with the Industrial Areas Foundation organizers and unions, such as the American Federation of State, County, and Municipal Employees (AFSCME), and launched a campaign focusing on city contracts, contending that tax dollars should not be used to support private firms if they were paying their workers poverty wages. This religious-initiated effort eventually led to passage of an ordinance demanding living wages for their employees.

The Moral Mondays Movement came about in a similar way, with the emphasis being on "moral grounds" for opposing a series of extreme measures taken by a recently elected conservative state government in North Carolina (Barber & Zelter, 2014). Moral Monday leaders, mostly from churches, claim that their religious doctrine teaches them that the poor in spirit and income should be considered first not last in the state budget. The leaders of Moral Mondays continually pointed out that Christian teachings emphasize that the last will be first and the first last as a centerpiece of Jesus' teachings. This theological underpinning of the movement has given an inspiring and convincing justification to many folks to go out and join the protest against these extreme state measures. Many of the protesters had not joined protests in the past.

Moral Mondays is a protest movement in North Carolina, led by Rev. William Barber, a pastor and president of the NAACP in North Carolina. A large percentage of the protesters are citizens who belong to local churches and synagogues and several religious progressive social movements. This movement has sparked similar protests in other states like South Carolina and Georgia. The protests are usually on Mondays, when the legislature begins its week. They emphasize they are protesting issues of morality evident in the recently passed legislation of a conservative Republican-controlled state government. These issues include voting rights being suppressed by the requirement of a new photo ID and a reduction in days for early voting, environmental issues such as allowing fracking without regulations, severe cuts to social programs and public education, tax changes that favor the wealthy, and restrictions on abortion centers, among other issues. Medicaid expansion and the National Affordable Care Act were also voted down, which would have brought new health insurance to approximately 500,000 lower income citizens. The protests of some of the people involve civil disobedience by entering the state legislature building and being arrested peacefully.

Figure 10.6   Moral Mondays Movement

From Charity to Social Justice

Dudley (2014) developed and implemented a model for churches and other religious groups wanting to place more emphasis on social justice in their largely charity-oriented outreach efforts. Religious organizations tend to focus on charitable acts that meet the immediate and temporary needs of people struggling to survive rather than pursuing social justice efforts that may seem more nebulous, challenging, and controversial. As Figure 10.7 indicates, charity involves providing help to some people having a dire need such as hunger or homelessness. Charity

CHARITY	> Pathway to Social Justice >		SOCIAL JUSTICE
Solely help a small group of people with dire needs	Help this group but also *explore* developing new permanent structures to address the causes of their problems	Emphasis is on *developing* new structures addressing the causes that help some people with particular dire needs	Create or renew structures that help all people with particular dire needs
• Temporary	• Begin to explore underlying causes	• Address underlying causes for some people	• Permanent solutions
• Doesn't address causes			• Addresses all causes
• Dependency remains			• Self-sufficiency

Figure 10.7   Continuum of Social Justice

is short-term and does not usually address the underlying causes of the problems people are having, such as finding well-paid jobs or adequate housing. Social justice, in contrast, addresses the causes of people's problems by establishing and supporting structures that help people become more in control of their lives.

Often charity and social justice are viewed by religious communities and other groups as two separate efforts that have different tracks. The Continuum of Social Justice model, in contrast, suggests that a charity intervention can move in small steps toward greater social justice. As Figure 10.7 indicates, a first step could be to respond to the immediate needs of people who live nearby. An example could be a food pantry for people who are hungry or food insecure. First, this charitable effort could become involved in handing out food for a while and group members could become more intimately acquainted with the recipients and their circumstances. If the group found that their efforts were not improving the long term food security of these people and maybe were even drawing more people to them who needed food, the group could decide to search for longer term and more permanent solutions for these recipients.

Next, the group could explore some of the reasons why people are hungry and seeking food relief by conducting a needs assessment (Dudley, 2014). They could ask the recipients questions about their circumstances when they come in for food. They could also consult community groups that have effectively addressed this problem in other areas. In their search for causes, maybe they would find out the people need help with learning how to cook nutritious meals or shopping in a more frugal way for groceries. They may also find out that some of them qualify for food stamps but haven't applied. They may also find that they have trouble paying their bills and managing their money, as some may be unemployed or have low paying jobs and no relevant job skills.

From these discoveries, new steps would become apparent (Dudley, 2014). The food pantry could join a network of food pantries and shift its resources somewhat to add, for example, cooking classes and grocery shopping classes, counseling from the local credit union on financial matters, and referrals to governmental food programs. Some of these religious groups may also set up small scale job training programs and offer GED (General Education Development) programs. They could also attempt to involve the local newspaper in developing stories about this problem and become advocates for a more active role from the local government in eliminating food insecurity across the city.

Spiritual Roles in Community Practice

Community-level practice in general, whether faith-based or non-faith-based, involves engaging and organizing people for a collective purpose. Gamble and Weil (2010) define community practice as an empowerment process strengthening the participation of people in democratic processes, advocating for social and economic justice, and improving the effectiveness and responsiveness of public and private systems. They identify several overlapping models of community practice including:

- neighborhood organizing;
- organizing functional communities (e.g. an advocacy group for a client population such as people with mental illness);
- social, economic, and environmental development;
- designing inclusiveness in program development;
- social planning;
- building coalitions around common goals, political action, and movements for progressive change.

All of these models are involved, to varying degrees, in the practice of bringing positive social change to a community and at times the society at large. All of them also have the potential for having a spiritual component.

Macro levels of practice tend to be underplayed in most of the spirituality literature of social work (Sheridan, 2012a; Sheridan, 2012b). There are several exceptions to this pattern, such as a special issue on macro practice and spirituality in the *Journal of Religion & Spirituality in Social Work: Social Thought* in 2012. An extensive review of the literature on community practice and spirituality by Hill and Donaldson (2012) concluded that spirituality is often important to the work of many community organizers but there is surprisingly little evidence of *how* spirituality plays a role or is infused in actual community practice. Community organizers have shared how spiritual rejuvenation is a key resource for them in developing energy and direction for their work on social justice; also spirituality deepens their grounding in compassion for their client communities (Canda & Furman, 2010). But studies could not be found in social work that described an actual community practice intervention with an explicit role for spirituality.

While many interventions involving spiritual or religious components can be macro in nature, it seems to be easier to describe how spirituality is infused in the micro and mezzo aspects of community work. As an example of this, one practitioner shared that their interfaith small groups begin each meeting with different religious rituals to highlight the religious diversity of the group (Hill & Donaldson, 2012). Other groups inject a moment of silence for prayer or mediation at the beginning and conclusion of their meetings.

12-Step Programs and Addictions

The 12-step programs are important to mention at this point. These programs are an example of a self-help group with a spiritual element that is central to it (Alcoholics Anonymous World Services, 2004). While 12-step programs may be viewed by many as mezzo in nature because they are clinically oriented, they could also be viewed as a community movement because they usually draw large numbers of participants to their meetings and they meet regularly in thousands of places across the country. Alcoholics Anonymous and other self-help groups such as Narcotics Anonymous, Overeaters Anonymous, Gamblers Anonymous, Sex Addicts Anonymous, and Co-Dependents Anonymous are stand-alone self-help programs that are based on the 12-step program. According to principles embedded in the 12-steps, a person with an addiction is helped to believe in a Higher Power, recognize their dependence on this Higher Power, and examine in an in-depth way their own shortcomings and the need to change. The 12-steps for alcoholics are described in Figure 10.8.

Alcoholics Anonymous (AA) and other 12-step groups have been found to be among the most successful programs in helping people overcome their addiction problems (Bliss, 2007; Brown et al., 2007; Tonigan, Rynes, & McCrady, 2013). Decreased drinking intensity and increased abstinence were found to be strongly correlated with spiritual change occurring in these self-help groups. Belief in a Higher Power or God, committing to prayer and meditation, and compiling critical personal moral inventories have all played a role in bringing about these changes (Mullins, 2010). Success is also attributed to the program's use of common mantras, having sponsors, and the self-help and accountability aspects of the programs.

Nonetheless, this relative absence of professional literature on how spirituality plays a role in macro practice suggests that we need to expand our search to include timely literature on spirituality and macro practice in other areas. Several suggestions of religious sources are described in the previous section on faith-based organizations. The literature of other professional disciplines similar to social work is another possible source. The disciplines of community psychology, ecological psychology,

---

1. We admit we are powerless over alcohol—that our lives had become unmanageable.
2. We come to believe that a power greater than ourselves could restore us to sanity.
3. We make a decision to turn our will and our lives over to the care of God as we understood Him.
4. We make a searching and fearless moral inventory of ourselves.
5. We admit to God, to ourselves, and to another human being the exact nature of our wrongs.
6. We are entirely ready to have God remove all these defects of character.
7. We humbly ask Him to remove our shortcomings.
8. We make a list of all persons we have harmed, and become willing to make amends to them all.
9. We make direct amends to such people wherever possible, except when to do so would injure them or others.
10. We continue to take personal inventory, and when we are wrong, promptly admit it.
11. We seek through prayer and meditation to improve our conscious contact with God as we understand Him, praying only for knowledge of His will for us and the power to carry that out.
12. We have had a spiritual awakening as the result of these steps, and try to carry this message to alcoholics, and to practice these principles in all our affairs.

Figure 10.8   12-Step Program of Alcoholics Anonymous

cross-cultural psychology, social psychology, political science, nursing, public health, sociology, and community development are all possible resources for such literature.

Spiritual Activism as an Approach of Macro Practitioners

The macro literature offers other helpful ideas about how spirituality can be connected to macro practice. "Spiritual activism" is an example, as it describes an approach of macro practitioners that can guide and shape many different types of spiritual interventions. Sheridan (2012b) suggests that this relatively new or possibly reemerging perspective is becoming evident among some social work activists at the macro level of intervention. Sheridan states that spiritual activism is offered as an alternative to traditional approaches to social activism that are not spiritual in nature and tend to lead macro practitioners to burnout and polarization. She cites seven themes describing spiritual activism in the writings of several macro practitioners.

1. **Having spiritual motivation for doing justice work:** This means that the spiritual qualities with which macro practitioners identify (e.g. peace, compassion, love) are central to why they are doing this work (Lee & Barrett, 2007).
2. **Recognizing and cultivating an awareness of the interdependence of everyone and everything:** This means perceiving this awareness as a transformative force that helps us see "life as an interdependent web of which all are a part . . ." (Dylan & Coates, 2012).
3. **The means we choose in setting activism goals are important, as are the outcomes:** Our interventions, strategies and other processes are as important as our goals. For example, if peace and equality are part of who we are as spiritual beings, then we should foster peacefulness and equality as we participate in our action.
4. **Assuming a perspective of not knowing what the outcome will be or what lies ahead:** While practitioners have positive intention, they let go of any notion of a particular outcome and recognize that their outcome may be different and beyond that anticipated by any group.
5. **Openness to suffering and grieving:** This means practitioners, being fully present with their hearts, open them as they experience the suffering in those whom they help; in this way they can also experience their joy.
6. **Outer change requires inner work:** The work of practitioners on justice issues reflects qualities they are developing in themselves.
7. **Commitment to a personal spiritual practice:** These practitioners choose to develop their own spiritual practices in keeping with their personal faith journey, which provides grounding, inspiration, and motivation for their involvement.

A Discernment Process and Decision-Making

Community practice, like mezzo and other macro interventions, often involves making group or community decisions (Farnham, Gill, McLean, & Ward, 2011). Group decision-making can be very important to what happens next in groups. Decisions can be major or minor ones, and can be related to anticipating outcomes, selecting new members, or deciding when to meet next. The processes that are instituted to initiate decision-making are too often given little attention and can possibly create irreparable problems for groups of all types if decisions are not made well. Examples of problems could be participants feeling they or their positions on issues have not been taken into account. Or possibly participants view the process as too political and their political persuasion was overlooked or trampled on by other more dominant political sentiments. Some may also think that decisions may be unequal based on racial and ethnic differences in participants in a group. Decisions in groups are often a power issue that can easily interfere with what is in the best interest of all participants. Spiritual discernment is one effective way of addressing such concerns. Spiritual discernment promotes spiritual concepts like inclusiveness, appreciation of diversity, no losers, empowerment, and self-determination.

Spiritual discernment is a process of helping someone listen more deeply to how to live their life and what they should do (Farnham et al., 2011). This is viewed in the Christian community as listening for what God wants them to do, but it could also be a helpful non-religious concept for others. Discernment is a spiritual concept of importance at many different levels of practice. Spiritual direction, for example, usually involves a relationship between a spiritual guide (sometimes called a spiritual director) and a directee. This approach is used in Christian communities but could also be used within other religious or non-religious contexts. It is especially evident in Quaker communities. The spiritual guide's role is to help the directee discern what God or their Higher Power wants them to do generally or in response to specific circumstances, such as selecting a new vocation, getting married, or possibly moving to a new region of the country or abroad. Discernment is furthered when the guide helps the directee listen to the Spirit in a variety of ways, such as prayers, meditation, and encounters with others. The spiritual guide's role is not to give advice or recommend what the guide thinks needs to be done.

In a community context, a spiritual discernment process can also be important in helping the group make collective decisions (Farnham et al., 2011). Discernment usually involves arriving at a consensus on a decision rather than forcing a vote with winners and losers. A consensus promotes inclusivity in a group or community because everyone feels that their input and contributions were heard and taken into account. All views are considered and no one view is likely to prevail. Group members are expected to have less investment in the final decision and more in the process of getting there. While their own thoughts are important to the process, so are all of the other participants' views and the synergy that can emerge as all of their viewpoints are considered together. Usually, the group members feel that the final decision reflects, at least in part, their views but they are also likely to see the views of others who may disagree with them in the final outcome. A compromise can be evidence that everyone is satisfied with the outcome and moving ahead with positive feelings about the collective and its future impact. Also everyone is likely to want to continue to give the group or community their all rather than dropping out or cutting back.

One group, Listening Hearts (www.listeninghearts.org), has a long history of helping religious groups use their version of a spiritual discernment process in their activities. This group emphasizes engaging a Higher Power's guidance, being alert to signs of the Spirit, and praying in ways that involve deep listening. Deep listening is reflected in some of the spiritual interventions described in chapter 9, like centering prayer and meditation. Listening Hearts offers a set of guidelines that can be used in community groups to implement spiritual discernment. A slightly modified version of their guidelines is (Farnham et al., 2011):

1. Begin by taking time to be settled in God's (your Higher Power's) presence.
2. Prepare yourself to listen to others with all of your senses, feelings, intuition, imagination, and thinking.
3. Each person speaks once and not again until everyone has had a turn.
4. Pause between speakers to fully absorb what has been said.
5. Do not interrupt.
6. Do not challenge what others say.
7. Do not formulate what you want to say while someone else is speaking.
8. When you speak, speak for yourself only, expressing both your feelings and thoughts, and refer only to your own experiences. Avoid broad generalizations and hypotheticals.
9. Listen to the group as a whole—to those who have not yet spoken as well as those who have.
10. Hold your desires, opinions, and convictions lightly.

Conclusion

This chapter examines several developments in the realm of spirituality and macro practice. The chapter begins by pointing out that more research and case examples are needed in social work that recognize the role of spirituality in macro practice. In addition, the chapter discusses the need for more organizational work in social agencies that explicitly addresses how and why the spiritual issues of clients are to be addressed proactively. Faith-based agencies are described to have their own unique organizational issues related to spirituality, and the chapter identifies some of their advantages and challenges. Social movements are highlighted, as many of them are influenced if not driven by spirituality and religion in one way or another. Key examples of these social movements are offered. Finally, spirituality plays a role in community practice in different ways. Spirituality is evident in the personal lives of many macro practitioners, in decision-making processes of communities, and in some large-scale program areas such as the 12-step programs.

Discussion Questions and Exercises

1. Muslim Family Service agencies exist in several cities that have relatively large numbers of Muslim residents. Google "Muslim Family Services" and select one of these local agencies. Assume that you are wanting to refer one of your Muslim clients to this local family agency. Visit the website. Review their mission statement and any other religious and cultural information that is provided about them. What faith elements do they mention, if any, that are part of their services? What additional information would you want to know, if any, before making this referral?

2. A model faith-based agency is described in the chapter (Kaseman & Austin, 2005). Some of the faith-based components of this agency are reported and can provide guidelines for other agencies to follow. Imagine you are creating a faith-based agency and attempt to answer the following questions.
   - What do you think about each of the components of the faith-based agency described above by Kaseman and Austin (2005)?
   - What are the advantages of each component?
   - What are the disadvantages?
   - What other components would you consider if you were an administrator in a faith-based agency?

3. If you work in a social agency, investigate how your agency addresses spirituality as a client issue. Are there policies in place that clarify what spirituality is and how the clients' spiritual issues are to be addressed in your agency? If not, how would you go about informing the agency of the need to add some explicit policies and other guidelines? What definitions of spirituality and religion would you propose to the agency?

References

Ammerman, N. T. (2001). *Doing good in American communities: Congregations and service organizations working together.* Hartford, CT: Hartford Institute for Religious Research, Hartford Seminary.

Araujo, D. C. (2013). No room at the inn. *Sojourners: Faith in Action for Social Justice*, June, 2013, 36–39.

Barber, W. J. & Zelter, B. (2014). *Forward together: A moral message for the nation.* Atlanta: Chalice Press.

Bielefeld, W. (2006). Investigating the implementation of charitable choice, *Journal of Religion & Spirituality in Social Work: Social Thought*, 25(3–4), 151–173.

Birnbaum, L., & Birnbaum, A. (2008). Mindful social work: From theory to practice. *Journal of Religion & Spirituality in Social Work: Social Thought*, 27(1–2), 87–104.

Bliss, D. L. (2007). Empirical research on spirituality and alcoholism: A review of the literature. *Journal of Social Work Practice in the Addictions*, 7(4), 5–25.

Brown, A. E., Pavlik, V. N., Shegog, R., Whitney, S. N., Friedman, L. C., Romero, C., & Volk, R. J. (2007). Association of spirituality and sobriety during a behavioral spirituality intervention for twelve step (TS) recovery. *American Journal of Drug & Alcohol Abuse*, 33(4), 611–617.

Canda, E. R., & Furman, L. D. (2010). *Spiritual diversity in social work practice: The heart of healing*. 2nd edition. New York: Free Press.

Carlson, B. E. & Larkin, H. (2009). Meditation as a coping intervention for treatment of addiction. *Journal of Religion and Spirituality in Social Work: Social Thought*, 28, 379–392.

Degeneffe, C. E. (2003). What is Catholic about Catholic Charities? *Social Work*, 48(3), 374–383.

Doe, S. S. (2004). Spirituality-based social work values for empowering human service organizations. *Journal of Religion & Spirituality in Social Work: Social Thought*, 23(3), 45–65.

Doka, K. J. (2011). Religion and spirituality: Assessment and intervention. *Journal of Social Work in End-of-Life & Palliative Care*, 7, 99–109.

Dudley, J. (2014). From charity to social justice: An approach for churches and synagogues wanting to have more impact. Unpublished manuscript. Charlotte, NC: School of Social Work, University of North Carolina at Charlotte.

Dylan, A., & Coates, J. (2012). The spirituality of justice: Bringing together the eco and the social. *Journal of Religion & Spirituality in Social Work: Social Thought*, 31, 1–2.

Farnham, S. G., Gill, J. P., McLean, R. T., & Ward, S. M. (2011). *Listening hearts 20th anniversary edition: Discerning call in community*. Revised edition. Harrisburg, PA: Morehouse Publishing.

Fuller, R. C. (2006). *Wonder: From emotion to spirituality*. Chapel Hill: NC: University of North Carolina Press.

Gamble, D., & Weil, M. (2010). *Community practice skills: Local to global perspectives*. New York: Columbia University Press.

Harr, C. R., & Yancey, G. I. (2014). Social work collaboration with faith leaders and faith groups serving families in rural areas. *Journal of Religion and Spirituality in Social Work: Social Thought*, 33(2), 148–162.

Heschel, A. J. (1962). *The Prophets*. New York: HarperCollins.

Hick, S. F. (2009). *Mindfulness and social work*. Chicago: Lyceum Books.

Hill. A. J., & Donaldson, L. P. (2012). We shall overcome: Promoting an agenda for integrating spirituality and community practice. *Journal of Religion & Spirituality in Social Work: Social Thought*, 31(1–2), 67–84.

Hodge, D. R. (2004). Spirituality and people with mental illness: Developing spiritual competency in assessment and intervention. *Families in Society*, 85(1), 36–44.

Hugen, B., & Venema, R. (2009). The difference of faith: The influence of faith in human service programs. *Journal of Religion & Spirituality in Social Work: Social Thought*, 28(4), 405–429.

Hutchison, E. (2012). Spirituality, religion, and progressive social movements: Resources and motivation for social change. *Journal of Religion & Spirituality in Social Work: Social Thought*, 31(4), 105–127.

Kaseman, M., & Austin, M. J. (2005). Building a faith-based human service agency. *Journal of Religion & Spirituality in Social Work: Social Thought*, 24(3), 69–91.

Kennedy, S. S., & Bielefeld, W. (2002). Government shekels without government shackles? The administrative challenges of charitable choice. *Public Administration Review, 62*(1), 4–11.

King, M. L. (1986). *A testament of hope: The essential writings and speeches of Martin Luther King, Jr.* New York: HarperCollins.

King, M. L. (1990). I have a dream/Also letter From Birmingham jail. Logan IA: Perfection Learning.

Lee, E. O., & Barrett, B. (2007). Integrating spirituality, faith, and social justice in social work practice and education: A pilot study. *Journal of Religion & Spirituality in Social Work: Social Thought, 26*(2), 1–21.

Mullins, J. W. (2010). Spirituality and the twelve steps. *International Journal of Applied Psychoanalytic Studies, 7*(2), 152–160.

Netting, F. E., O'Connor, M. K., & Yancey, G. (2006). Belief systems in faith-based human service programs. *Journal of Religion & Spirituality in Social Work: Social Thought, 25*(3/4), 261–286.

Niedt, C., Ruiters, G., Wise, D., & Schoenberger, E. (1999). The effects of the living wage in Baltimore. Working Paper No. 119. Baltimore: Department of Geography and Environmental Engineering, Johns Hopkins University.

O'Connor, E. (1975). *Journey inward, journey outward.* New York: Harper & Row.

Seeber, J. J. (1990). (Ed.) *Spiritual maturity in the later years.* Binghamton, NY: Haworth Press.

Sheridan, M. (2012a). Introduction: Connecting spirituality and social justice within macropractice. *Journal of Religion & Spirituality in Social Work: Social Thought, 31*, 1–8.

Sheridan, M. (2012b). Spiritual activism: Grounding ourselves in the spirit. *Journal of Religion & Spirituality in Social Work: Social Thought, 31*, 193–208.

Svare, G. M., Hylton, M., & Albers, E. (2007). On our own: Social workers talk about spiritually sensitive practice within an organizational context. *Journal of Religion and Spirituality in Social Work: Social Thought, 26*(4), 95–113.

Tan, P. P. (2005). The importance of spirituality among gay and lesbian individuals. *Journal of Homosexuality, 49*(2), 135–144.

Thomas, M. L. (2009). Faith and collaboration: A qualitative analysis of faith-based social service programs in organizational relationships. *Administration in Social Work, 33*(1), 40–60.

Tonigan, J., Rynes, K. N., & McCrady, B. S. (2013). Spirituality as a change mechanism in 12-step programs: A replication, extension, and refinement. *Substance Use & Misuse, 48*(12), 1161–1173.

Williams, J. & Bond, J. (1987). *Eyes on the prize: American civil rights years, 1954 to 1965.* New York: Penguin Group.

Williams, M. J. (2003). *The prophet and his message: Reading Old Testament prophecy today.* Phillipsburg, NJ: P & R Publishing.

11

INFUSING SPIRITUALITY INTO EXISTING SOCIAL WORK APPROACHES

James Dudley and Heather Rikli Semmens

The best of modern therapy is much like a process of shared meditation, where therapist and client sit together, learning to pay close attention in those aspects and dimensions of the self that the client may be unable to touch on his or her own.

(Kornfield, 1993, p. 245)

We must create the climate in which clients can discover that they are worthwhile and have the rights and incentive – and in fact the obligation – to hope and stretch for something of value and to carry these beliefs into action.

(Saleebey, 2013, p. 34)

A spiritually sensitive practice approach cannot depend upon spiritual interventions alone. While this may be obvious, it's important to remember. The spiritual interventions covered in the previous two chapters are only a subgroup of available interventions for helping clients with spiritual issues. We must also find ways to integrate spirituality into the general approaches used by social workers. Social workers use numerous practice approaches to help their clients. They often develop their own eclectic style that combines aspects of several approaches in order to effectively address the individualized needs of each client system. The popular practice approaches, in most cases, do not explicitly focus on spiritual issues. A spiritually sensitive practice approach has to infuse spirituality into these general approaches. How we can do this is the focus of this chapter.

This chapter discusses ways to infuse spirituality into many of the popular practice approaches used by social workers. These approaches operate at different levels of practice—micro, mezzo, and macro. They include clinical practice approaches used in work primarily with individuals, families, and groups. In some instances these approaches also focus on macro concerns. Let's first recall that the spiritually sensitive approach described in the book is driven by 11 general principles introduced in chapter 5 and elaborated on throughout the rest of the book. The last principle, incorporating spirituality into existing social work practice approaches, is the focus of this chapter.

Principles of a Spiritually Sensitive Approach

1. It is an approach that works at all levels of client systems—micro, mezzo, and macro.

2. It is designed to meet core competencies of the Council of Social Work Education, the social work accreditation agency (CSWE, 2015).

3. The approach emphasizes being proactive in engaging the spiritual issues of clients.

4. The spirituality issues of clients and workers must always remain separate.

5. Spirituality is clearly defined and distinguished from religion.

6. Avoid underestimating the importance of religion to many clients.

7. The engagement phase is a critical one for identifying spiritual issues and setting the stage to discuss these issues.

8. The other three phases (assess, intervene, evaluate) also have critical functions in the helping process.

9. Worker preparation is important prior to each session.

10. Any ethical problems or other negative issues related to the clients' spirituality or religion are addressed.

11. Spiritual work can be integrated into several widely used general practice approaches.

Infusing Spirituality into General Practice Approaches

A spiritually sensitive practice approach can be fairly easily incorporated or embedded in several general practice approaches. The chapter attempts to do this by highlighting the links between seven commonly used practice approaches and eight general spiritual elements or "spiritual bridges" of a spiritually sensitive approach. Figure 11.1 lists eight spiritual bridges of a spiritually sensitive approach in the left column and seven of the general practice approaches frequently used in social work in the right column.

Eight Spiritual Bridges

First, let's examine what the eight spiritual bridges are, and then explore how some of them can be incorporated into each of the general approaches in different

Spiritual Bridges	Common Practice Approaches
1. Spiritual relationship building	A) Person-Centered Approach
2. Communicate spiritual empathy	B) Rational Emotive Behavioral Therapy
3. Identify and engage spiritual strengths	C) Narrative Approach
4. Cognitive messaging of spirituality	D) Motivational Interviewing
5. Facilitate spiritual development	E) DBT Approach
6. Assess the clients' spiritual issues	F) Meaning Therapy
7. Introduce spiritual interventions	G) Solution-Focused Approach
8. Utilize spiritual supports	

Figure 11.1   Lists of Spiritual Bridges of a Spiritually Sensitive Practice Approach and Seven Common Practice Approaches

ways. These spiritual bridges are distinct characteristics of the spiritually sensitive approach described in the book. While they are not the only elements that could be considered, they illustrate the process of incorporating spiritually sensitive practice into these general approaches. We begin by describing these eight bridges. These elements have been selected because they offer helpful "bridges" to infuse, embed, and sometimes simply add spiritual elements to existing general approaches that social workers use.

1.   Spiritual Relationship Building

There is broad consensus that little is likely to happen in helping clients unless we begin by developing a nurturing professional relationship with them during the initial engagement phase (Bein, 2008; Canda & Furman, 2010). This relationship is the portal to what will likely happen later in the helping relationship. When we meet with clients, we view them in a holistic way, including as spiritual beings. The clients' spiritual being is where we can tap into a need for finding deeper meaning in their lives as well as drawing on inspiration, motivation, and empowerment. We can do this by demonstrating curiosity about and interest in the clients' spirituality when they bring it up; further, we can encourage them to elaborate on their experiences with it when appropriate (Patterson, Hayworth, Turner, & Raskin, 2000). As we review several practice approaches in this chapter, we will look for ways to infuse spiritual relationship building into them. Most general approaches give emphasis to relationship building. The Person-Centered Approach, for example, is largely built around relationship building (Thorne, 2002). Motivational Interviewing and Ethnographic Interviewing develop the notion of relationship-building in other ways.

2. Communicate Spiritual Empathy

Empathy is always important to express to clients. Spiritual empathy refers to making special efforts to understand and affirm the clients' spirituality if it is expressed. The intent is to convey to them that you value them spiritually as well as in other ways (Bein, 2008). We foster relationships with clients by communicating in an empathic way, being in touch with our intuition as one source for understanding their issues. We also communicate empathy as a way of encouraging clients to feel welcomed, to openly be themselves as they participate, and to discover the helping relationship as an opportunity for them to engage anew in their self-determining capacities.

A caution to consider as we express spiritual empathy to our clients. We must be persistent in realizing that our focus is on the spirituality of the clients, and not our own (Gardner, 2011). A spark of interest in something the client says may evoke in us something that reminds us of our own spirituality. While this may help us grow closer to them, it is not an opportunity for us to share what we have in common unless the disclosure helps the clients. We also need to be aware of how our own personal religious and spiritual biases against some religious groups or beliefs need to be evident to us and kept under control. In addition, when a client wishes not to discuss these issues in any depth, we must respect this and refrain from attempting to bring them up (Hodge, 2004). This includes not communicating about such issues through our facial expressions or other non-verbal behaviors that may convey a special interest.

3. Identify and Engage Clients' Spiritual Strengths

Supporting the clients' spiritual strengths along with their other strengths is another bridge to infuse in general social work approaches. Social workers are usually tuned into emphasizing strengths or the positive attributes that clients may have, but we may overlook spiritual strengths in particular. Practitioners may even overlook that they are strengths because they have not been trained to look for them (Banerjee & Canda, 2009).

Saleebey (2013) has written extensively about the strengths of clients and the strengths perspective. He makes the important point that every individual, group, family, and community has strengths. Social workers should always operate from the assumption that we do not know the upper limits of a client's capacity to grow and change. Even when trauma and illness overwhelm clients, they can be overcome with hope and new opportunities. Strengths are defined broadly by Saleebey. Strengths are not only personal qualities, traits, talents, and virtues that are evident in clients. Strengths are also what they know about themselves and their world, and their personal stories, cultural wisdom, and worldview. Examples are an affiliation with a spiritual or religious organization; a spiritual discipline such as prayer, meditation, or chanting; a capacity to be intuitive or imaginative; feeling empowered spiritually; or a desire to know more about their spirituality.

Saleebey (2013) suggests de-emphasizing the clients' problems and what may be wrong about them. Instead, assessments should focus more on personal and environmental strengths. Assessment should be a joint activity between the worker and client and should lead to a discovery of the uniqueness of each client system. Preeminence is given to the client's understanding of the facts, believing what the client shares, and discovering what the client wants. Efforts should always be made to reach agreement on what is important and what has already been successfully completed.

Many of the concepts Saleebey uses have connections to spirituality and spiritually sensitive practice. Extensive use of self-determination in conducting assessments, for example, is emphasized in the book's approach. Emphasizing strengths and attempting to discover whatever can be beneficial to clients is also important to the book's approach, especially highlighting spirituality and spiritual resources whenever they can be empowering to clients. Optimistic views about what clients can do, even in dire circumstances, and the clients' capacity to be resilient are further examples of support for spiritual content. When it may be difficult for clients to readily identify their strengths, it is important to assist them in finding these attributes. In some cases it can be truly a strength that the individual has survived a traumatic event, or however downtrodden, they are brave enough to seek out help.

As we discussed in chapter 7, it is important to be keenly aware of the spiritual strengths of our clients during the engagement phase. These strengths could easily be different for each client system. They can also be obvious or subtle, overt or covert. Also, they are likely to be strengths relative to their own personal social circumstances. For example, someone who has lost a partner to death or divorce may be quite capable of coping with their situation and willing to probe deeper into the meaning it may have for them after the loss. Or they may be comfortable withholding their feelings in such a circumstance until their feelings have a chance to settle and become better understood. Both responses can be strengths that social workers must learn how to recognize as such.

As spirituality is explored with willing clients, observing what they share and how it is shared can reveal some strengths. For example, it is a strength when a client shares a well thought out description of their religious beliefs rather than simply reciting a familiar religious belief given by their religious group. Comfort with ambiguity and mystery in their lives can also be positive factors. Having an active spiritual practice, such as meditation or prayer, is a strength in itself as this takes conviction, motivation, and discipline to do. A person's spiritual practices also reveal how seriously they value their spirituality. How comfortably and freely they self-disclose the nature of their spirituality can also be an asset as spirituality is a complicated topic and for many, a personal and private matter. The more they share about who they are may suggest how important their spiritual self is to them (Rogers, 1977). The degree to which they are tolerant of other people's beliefs and practices is another strength to be valued as opposed to being closed or resistant to beliefs different from their own.

Some of the strengths mentioned in chapter 7 are also noteworthy examples. An affiliation with a spiritual friend or a spiritual or religious organization, for example, can be a strength as it takes good communication skills and an effort to maintain and develop such an affiliation. Group membership also takes a willingness to be able to listen to the thoughts of others and not to be totally self-absorbed. Self-awareness is also an important asset, including being able to identify one's own strengths and weaknesses and knowing what areas need more personal work. Being inquisitive about spirituality generally and being open to hearing about other people's spiritual practices are strengths as well.

Once these strengths are identified, it is good practice for social workers to mention that they observe them and suggest that it may be an asset that can help them in solving their problems. These positive attributes are also something to consider when preparing an action plan. How can each strength inform what needs to be done and how can it expedite positive outcomes for clients and their families?

4. Attend to Spiritual Messaging

Some of the general approaches used by clinicians focus on the importance of the clients' cognitive processes. They include Cognitive Behavioral Therapy and some of its offshoots such as Rational Emotive Behavioral Therapy (REBT). People tend to often be stuck in their thoughts without even being aware of what these thoughts are about. This is often a subconscious level of thinking that can be positive or negative. Unfortunately, these thoughts are more often negative. Further, these thoughts often have a major influence on how we view ourselves and how we respond to our problems. Familiar cognitive messages could be in the general order of "I am not ok," based largely on experiences we have had as children growing up, as discussed by Harris (1969). Examples of such thoughts are "I am a bad person." "I am not worthy of what I have." "I cannot succeed like other people." Spiritual and religious cognitive processes are often a part of these messages for many clients, particularly those who are religious or were raised in a religious family. Examples of negative religious messages are "God does not love me." "I have sinned and will go to hell." "God will never forgive me for what I have done." Or, "God favors others over me."

5. Facilitate the Clients' Spiritual Development

Spirituality is described as a developing phenomenon in people. Introduced in chapter 2, Fowler envisioned six stages of faith development varying from undifferentiated faith of young children to universalizing faith of mature adults. Erikson's eight psychosocial stages are also described and dovetail with Fowler's stages. Other developmental theories such as Oser's five stages are described in chapter 2 as well. Also, spiritual transformation, a developmental process that people can go through in finding themselves, is discussed in that chapter. In all of these theories it is assumed that people have the potential of moving forward through these stages, but it does not automatically happen. It depends almost entirely on each person and how they respond to their changing environment as they grow older.

Clients, like all of us, are spiritual beings that can be viewed as being at a particular spiritual stage of development in their lives depending upon the spiritual and psychosocial theories that are utilized. While we are likely to work with our clients on more immediate issues than spiritual development, we should always view our clients as developmental in nature with the potential to evolve mentally, psychologically, culturally, and spiritually as they grow biologically. It's true that clients, particularly in community agency settings, may not be in a relationship with a social worker long enough to significantly impact them developmentally. However, clients can grow and change in significant ways even during brief periods if they are in close, collaborative relationships with their social worker. Growth spurts can come in some of the most meaningful encounters. Social workers are encouraged to view their clients as people who have the potential to grow on a spiritual level, and this is likely to be influenced by how we engage them in the helping process. More is described about this engagement process in chapter 7.

6. Assess Clients' Spiritual Issues

Chapter 8 focuses on the assessment phase, when practitioners ask questions that are intended to bring a fuller understanding to the clients' presenting problem, any ramifications of their circumstances, and how they are functioning socially, psychologically, and spiritually. An effective spiritual assessment consists of asking spiritual and religious questions, general and specific, in a timely way, that are relevant to how the agency can help them. Usually, at least two or three carefully selected spiritual assessment questions need to be asked, and should be coupled with the practitioner's readiness to help clients elaborate on their responses if appropriate. The choice of which assessment questions the agency chooses to ask requires a thoughtful process of input from agency administrators, practitioners and, in some cases, client groups. Staff training also needs to be available to help practitioners know how to effectively respond to the answers clients give to these questions.

7. Introduce Spiritual Interventions

Chapters 9 and 10 introduce numerous spiritual interventions that can be introduced at different system levels of practice. Some of the general approaches used by social workers explicitly include spiritually friendly interventions. Two popular examples are Dialectical Behavior Therapy (DBT) and Meaning Therapy. In these instances, spiritual bridges have already been infused into their perspectives and strategies. With other approaches, a social worker will need to make a conscious effort to add spiritual interventions into the approaches they use.

Let's look at mindfulness as an example of a spiritual intervention. Mindfulness is viewed by most social workers as a non-religious spiritual approach that has the potential of being useful in virtually every client setting (Hick, 2009). It can be beneficial for staff members as well. Mindfulness is a basic spiritual practice that is easy to teach yet challenging for people to consistently implement over time. However, if it becomes a part of a person's routine, its positive impact usually becomes apparent. Its benefits include helping both clients and staff members slow down, experience greater inner peace, and be more fully present in the here and now. These qualities are especially valuable if they can be integrated into the helping process, where free-flowing discussions and attentive listening are so important. Mindfulness is especially relevant to teach and practice in client groups. Group members often readily participate in mindfulness exercises and recognize their benefits (Hick, 2009). Based on exchanges with other clients, they realize the rewards of learning about it. Clients of all different backgrounds and circumstances, including those with chronic mental health problems or addictions, and offenders, can benefit from experiencing mindfulness in their lives because their lives are likely to be filled with unproductive chatter and stress, which are not understood or managed. More information is provided about mindfulness in chapter 9.

Other spiritual interventions could also be pertinent for clients who identify either as religious or spiritual but not religious. Examples include using prayer or meditation. There are numerous ways that prayers and meditations could come up by clients as topics of interest. Most importantly, clients using these practices could be encouraged to describe and discuss how they are important to them and how they have helped. Different forms of prayer or meditation described in chapter 9 could be brought up as possible additional client resources. For example, clients who are on the go a lot and meditate as a regular practice could be asked if they have tried walking meditation. Similarly, the Medicine Wheel, a familiar spiritual intervention for many Native Americans, could be discussed for its value in the helping process as a problem-solving tool (Hoover, 2014).

8. *Utilize Spiritual Supports*

Spiritual and religious supports are one facet of social supports that can be very helpful to many clients. Social workers should become familiar with some of the types of clergy and their importance in different religious communities; this could be a part of professional preparation for helping religious clients. Many questions could be raised. When should clergy be considered for consultation and when can they be helpful in providing direct assistance to clients? What services can they provide? Clergy are usually referred to as pastors and ministers in Protestant Churches, priests in Catholic Churches, as imams in Mosques, rabbis in Synagogues, and shamans in Native American tribes and other spiritual groups. Many Hindu temples also use the term "priest" for their religious leaders. Clergy sometimes offer a wide range of services such as pastoral care to families when a loved one dies, hospital visits with members who are sick, officiating at funerals and memorial services, spiritual and religious counseling in times of crisis, officiating at weddings, premarital counseling, religious education offerings, and many other services. A clergy person's ability to offer such services depends upon many things, including their availability and their qualifications and credentials for conducting these services. Before making a referral, it is important to consult a clergy person to find out what they can offer, as their roles and work assignments vary widely.

Other religious resources are also available, including spiritual directors, pastoral counselors, parish nurses affiliated with churches, faith healers, spiritual or religious counselors, campus ministers, and hospital and university chaplains. Each of these spiritual supports and others have a particular role to play, and it is likely to vary from one religious community to the next. You might want to interview someone who is in one of these positions and ask them what they offer in services; also what kinds of background information would they need before accepting a referral. It can also be helpful to collaborate with other social workers in your agency and partner agencies in compiling a databank of spiritual and religious providers in the community who are readily available to assist clients.

Introduction to General Practice Approaches

A spiritually sensitive practice approach can be fairly easily incorporated in most general practice approaches used by many social workers. In an attempt to describe how this can be done, we describe possible links between each of the eight spiritual bridges described above and a variety of popular practice approaches used by social workers.

The practice approaches selected for this chapter are the Person-Centered Approach, Rational Emotive Behavioral Therapy, the Narrative Approach, Motivational Interviewing, DBT Approach, Meaning Therapy, and Solution-Focused Approach. A brief description of each of these seven approaches and how some of the spiritual elements can be incorporated into them follows next.

Person-Centered Approach

The Person-Centered Approach of Carl Rogers (Rogers, 1979, 1977; Rogers & Kramer, 1995; Thorne, 2002) is a popular humanistic approach of social workers. This approach meshes very well with a spiritually sensitive approach, especially two of the above bridges—spiritual relationship building and communicating

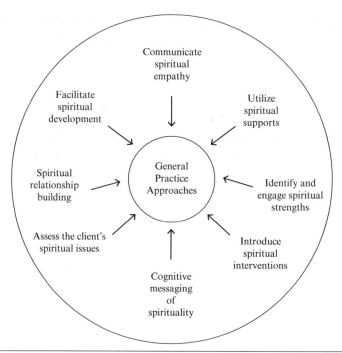

Figure 11.2   Spiritual Bridges to Several Social Work Approaches

spiritual empathy. Rogers stresses the importance of the person seeking help as the primary catalyst for changing themselves. Techniques are not emphasized in this approach, as the focus centers on the relationship between the client and the therapist (Thorne, 2002). The clients are central in addressing their problems by being open and honest. In return, the worker focuses on the client's subjective world and gaining a full understanding of how that person views life.

Spiritual Connections

Spiritual relationship building and spiritual empathy are two of the most obvious spiritual bridges to the Person-Centered Approach. Rogers stresses meeting clients where they are. If the clients' spirituality happens to be central to their self-worth and is ignored or played down, it could feel devaluing to them. Based on Rogers' perspective, the engagement phase is a critical time to look for overt or covert signs of client spirituality. It can be revealed in an off-handed expression such as "I couldn't do it by myself", or as a central concern, "I have lost all hope", or as a social support such as "I go to services on Fridays for prayer." During engagement, clients could easily open up or shut down based on how the worker responds to their spirituality or other aspects of their emotions. This is one of the reasons why building the relationship is so vital.

According to Rogers (Rogers & Kramer, 1995), empathetic understanding must be established at a level that goes far beyond basic sympathy. When the client shares their spirituality, we should not see this as a side issue or unimportant, particularly if the client places emphasis on it. The social worker should try to sense the very nature of the client's spirituality and any emotional areas, along with attempting to understand them. This is what we would call spiritual empathy. As clients are empathically heard, it becomes possible for them to be more attuned to the flow of their inner experiences, which is important to this approach. We should primarily listen but be prepared to ask the client for elaboration about a spiritual issue when it is volunteered only partially. Our primary intent is to listen for how any spiritual issue is important to the client especially in terms of its connections to the problem for which they are seeking help. This involves the social worker's full commitment to listening to their client's story and being totally present (Bein, 2008). Workers need to hear what is being said and not said, as well as feel it.

Genuineness or authenticity are also important to the Person-Centered Approach. This may be most challenging to workers when the client's spirituality is different from theirs. For example, we may feel uncomfortable with what a client says but it is important not to show judgment or lack of interest. According to Rogers (1979), acceptance or unconditional positive regard are important so that clients can say whatever is on their mind without fear of judgment. It is most likely through this accepting and non-judgmental approach that clients can openly share their utmost needs and desires.

Rational Emotive Behavioral Therapy (REBT)

This theoretical approach suggests that individuals are responsible for their own psychological issues because of the way they interpret life events and situations. REBT is a Person-Centered Approach that emphasizes being where the client is and encouraging the client to bring his/her strengths, issues, and problems up as early as possible. This approach connects very well with the spiritual elements of cognitive messaging of spiritual issues and promoting spiritual development. Clients will likely correct their faulty thinking when they learn to accept themselves as they are and leave behind the quest to be free from imperfections (Jones-Smith, 2011). A spiritually sensitive approach using REBT assumes that people are imperfect and hopefully always evolving to become more complete. Fowler's (1995) faith stages described in chapter 2 fit well with this developmental perspective about people's nature. Misguided thoughts about ourselves often surface when we tell ourselves that things *must, should, or ought* to be a certain way (Ellis, 1997) and sometimes strong religious beliefs are phrased in these ways (e.g. "You must believe . . . if you are to be a good person"). Using REBT, clients can be helped to become more relaxed and mindful about their thought patterns and to counter them with more positive self-messages. These internal cognitive messages, especially the more nagging ones, become more evident when we pay closer attention to our internal chatter and all of the "musts, shoulds, and oughts" that surface in chatter. According to Hodge (2004), traditional cognitive-behavioral approaches used in helping people with mental illness, for example, can succeed when modified to use positive beliefs derived from the client's spiritual belief system.

Spiritual Connections

Cognitive messaging of a client's spirituality and facilitating spiritual development are spiritual bridges to this approach. REBT's purpose is to correct this faulty thinking through the ABC Framework. "A" refers to the activating events, which trigger "B," irrational beliefs, which produce "C," the negative consequences (Overholser, 2003). Many times "B," or irrational cognitive messages are religious beliefs, as illustrated in Figure 11.3. This example describes what one student perceived as negative religious messaging for her; she was raised in a strict religious family but moved away from this belief system as she grew older.

In therapy, clients learn to dispute ("D") their irrational beliefs through forming a new "E," an effective manner of interpreting these events by asking reasonable questions. This is also referred to as cognitive restructuring. Here is where social workers can offer alternative religious beliefs to counter the negative ones.

O'Donohue and Fisher (2009) point out that REBT can be optimally used to offer alternative behaviors by asking reasonable questions about these behaviors. For example in Figure 11.3, several "B" or irrational messages were identified by one student. In Table 11.1, we offer questions, "E," that could be asked to help clients rethink these messages or behaviors. After reading all of them, attempt to identify an irrational religious or spiritual message or belief that you have and then offer a question or two to ask yourself in reinterpreting this message.

- Gay behavior is immoral.
- We must be kind to those who abuse or bully us.
- I must stay in a marriage with an abusive spouse to be accepted by my religious group.

Figure 11.3   Negative Religious Messaging of One Student

Table 11.1   Examples of Using "E" Responses

"B," OR IRRATIONAL BELIEFS AND BEHAVIORS	"E," OR REASONABLE QUESTIONS TO ASK FOR REINTERPRETING THESE BEHAVIORS
• Gay behavior is immoral.	• If two gay people love each other, are their expressions of affection for each other immoral?
• We must be kind to those who abuse or bully us.	• In what ways are you hurting yourself if you allow this type of behavior? Do you think your God would want you to do this to yourself?
• I must stay in a marriage with an abusive spouse to be accepted by my religious group.	• Do you think your God would want you to be abused by your spouse?

This re-interpretation of events leads to "F" which is new feelings about "A," the activating event that you began with. Using a spiritually sensitive approach, we will likely be regularly tuning in to how clients feel about themselves and others. We can periodically ask them to share how they are feeling about their reactions to these irrational beliefs and how this may be a change from before. We can also help them celebrate the positive changes in their feelings to a better "F," or re-interpretation. These interventions can in turn be helpful in promoting the spiritual development of our clients, among other things.

Narrative Approach

The Narrative Approach is also useful when thinking about cognitive messaging and spiritual issues. This approach relies on people's tendency to form and view reality through the telling and retelling of their stories (Combs & Freedman, 2012). Individuals possess the power to decide which narratives they will share and which ones they will ignore. In the therapy process the social worker and the client become partners who work together to re-author the client's life without imposing the worker's personal opinions on the process (Drewery & Winslade, 1997).

Narrative Therapy helps clients reveal how stories give meaning to their lives. In addition, family members, friends, and individuals in their community can serve as co-writers in the clients' narratives (Walsh, 2006). A person's reality is also constructed through interactions and language that conveys how individuals view topics such as race, age, income, and gender (Foucault, 1980). In addition, it conveys how people view spirituality, religion, culture, and related topics. Storytelling as part of the Narrative Approach involves listening at a deeper level, and helping the client discover hope, meaning, and inspiration.

Narrative Therapy views problems as external issues, so it is the task of the social worker to help the client rewrite their stories and separate themselves from the problem. They can help clients debunk negative thoughts or situations that people often accept without critically thinking about them (McKenzie & Monk, 1997). During the sessions the social worker helps individuals work through these tightly held beliefs and conceptualize them in a different light. To be free from these issues the person needs to understand that they do not inherently belong to them—they are external problems. This deconstructs the issue and makes way for reconstructing their reality in a healthier light.

Spiritual Connections

Cognitive messaging of spirituality and facilitating spiritual development are two of the spiritual bridges to this approach. Stories and characters in sacred writings are possible sources for rewriting our stories and reconstructing reality in a healthier light. The stories in the Hebrew and Christian Bibles provide examples. As an

---

Example of Storytelling in Spirituality and Religion

Storytelling is often evident in the sacred books of religions. In some in-stances, storytelling can help people identify with positive characters in these books. For example, the male spirituality movement has been searching for an authentic and revitalized masculinity. Arnold (1992) is one such author as he has written about masculine archetypes in the Bible as deeper reflections of who men authentically are to be. One archetype is the "warrior." Moses is described as a model warrior in the Hebrew Bible. Like Moses, warriors are not to physically dominate, control, and abuse others, but they are to "oppose evil, battle disease, attack problems, combat drugs, struggle with ignorance, fight fires, and make war on poverty." A good warrior also "attacks sick, evil, and weak men cloaked in a warrior archetype (dictators, sleazy politicians, and criminals)." Reading the stories of Moses over and over can be an effective way to cognitively teach young boys how to become healthy warriors in their societies.

---

illustration, the male spirituality movement sometimes has its roots in religious doctrine that gives special meaning to what masculinity is.

Motivational Interviewing

Motivational Interviewing fits very well as an approach that can help clients fur-ther develop their spirituality. Motivational Interviewing has been characterized as a conversation between a practitioner and client about change; it is also known to be client-centered and goal oriented (Matulich, 2013). This approach empow-ers clients and truly honors autonomy and self-determination. It helps clients develop their own arguments for making changes rather than the worker arguing for change. Using this approach, listening by the worker gives special attention to what the clients' messages mean to themselves, what clients are experiencing now, and what they are not saying.

Matulich (2013) focuses on six stages of change that clients can be at: pre-contemplation, contemplation, preparation for change, action, maintenance, and relapse. Motivational interviewing is especially helpful in describing the first three stages of practice. During stage one in pre-contemplation, clients share a problem they are having but do not show evidence that they are able to do something about it. An example could be, "I am aware that my addiction is hurting me in many ways but I have had it for years and have learned to accept it as part of my life." At this stage, effort is directed to helping clients move ahead to the next stage: contemplat-ing about the problem and possible ways to change it. According to Matulich, it's premature to move ahead any further than contemplation without getting too far ahead of a client. An example of a client in contemplation is, "Maybe I should consider joining an AA (Alcoholics Anonymous) group but when will I find time? I'm very busy." Stage three, preparation for change, comes next. Clients are at this stage of motivation when they are willing and ready to consider an action to address their problem. An example, "I need to find an AA group near my workplace so I can fit it in before I go home at night. Can you help me?"

It is important for a social worker to know the stage of motivation that clients are in to help them move to the next stage of motivation and not make the mistake of trying to help them far beyond where they are. Miller and Rollnick (2002) offer a set of questions to assess where a client is in terms of making changes in their life. They describe three dimensions of motivation for change—importance, confidence, and readiness. Do clients perceive the change that is being considered as important and if so, how important? Next, how confident are they that they can bring about this change? Finally, are they ready now to take action to bring about the change they are considering? Based on this approach, clients can also be asked these questions to address spiritual or religious issues:

1. **Assessing importance:** "On a scale from 0 to 10, with 0 representing none and 10 representing extremely high, how important is it for you to make these changes in your spiritual or religious life?"
2. **Assessing confidence:** "Using the same scale, if you decided you wanted to do something different in your spiritual or religious life, how confident are you that you could do it?"
3. **Assessing readiness:** "Is this something you want to discuss in counseling?"

Spiritual Connections

Motivational Interviewing fits well with a spiritually sensitive approach and some of the spiritual bridges. Spiritual relationship building and empathy, identifying spiritual strengths, facilitating spiritual development, and assessing the clients' spiritual issues are examples. First, this approach fits well with the philosophy of being spiritually sensitive since both approaches are empowering in intent, being client-centered, and emphasizing self-determination. Motivational Interviewing is particularly an effective approach to use in helping clients explore their spiritual issues in the engagement and assessment phases by helping them assess the stage of motivation they are in and the stages ahead of them to bring about changes in their lives. Most importantly, Motivational Interviewing can help clients focus on their spiritual issues, step by step, moving at their own pace.

Giordano and Cashwell (2014) recommend using Motivational Interviewing with clients when addressing spiritual and religious issues. One technique that they suggest relates to the ambivalence that many clients have about making changes. Being ambivalent about something can occur in many realms of people's lives, including the spiritual. Giordano and Cashwell offer several Motivational Interviewing techniques including "developing discrepancy." Often the values and behaviors of clients are in tension. This technique involves highlighting disconnects or discrepancies between the values that clients identify with and their current behaviors. These authors discuss how some clients may tend to avoid wanting to explore their spiritual issues but also periodically bringing up the need, often indirectly, to find more meaning or spiritual balance in their lives. In such an instance, a social worker can help these clients face this discrepancy, between hesitancy to make a spiritual change and realizing that this need is important. The worker can mention this quandary by stating both sides without taking a position. Hopefully, the client will then decide which side they wish to pursue next. Giordano and Cashwell (p. 73) share an example by summarizing the worker's comment about the client's quandary, "A part of you is afraid that God is mad at you and has stopped listening, but another part of you misses talking to God."

Dialectical Behavior Therapy (DBT)

DBT, a cognitive and behavioral therapy, draws on behaviorism, Zen Buddhism, and dialectical thinking (Koons, 2008). Behaviorism provides an approach to changing behavior, Zen contributes ways of learning to accept yourself, and dialectics contribute a worldview that strives for a balance between self-acceptance and change. DBT was created originally by Marsha Linehan in the late 1970s for use with individuals diagnosed with borderline personality disorder. Since that time this approach has also been used effectively with people who are emotionally vulnerable and have an inability to regulate their emotions, including chronically suicidal people, people with self-injurious behaviors, and severely disordered, multi-problem individuals (Bloom, Woodward, Susmaras, & Pantalone, 2012). The approach involves directing attention away from upsetting stimuli and regulating physiological arousal with Zen Buddhist techniques like deep breathing to reduce inner tension (Swales, Heard, & Williams, 2000). It also involves avoiding urges that result in mood-dependent behavior, such as shame for self-injurious behavior, and continuing to pursue goals unrelated to their current mood. This approach, among other things, actually implements spiritual interventions, including mindfulness skills.

Spiritual Connections

A spiritual bridge to this approach is actually using a spiritual intervention, mindfulness. Facilitating spiritual development is also a bridge. Zen Buddhism teaches many of the principles and skills of mindfulness (Koons, 2008). Skills are taught that are those of a "wise mind," like learning to observe and describe what is going on just as it is and without adding judgment. Focusing one's attention on one thing at a time rather than letting it wander is another skill that is taught. This skill helps a client to reduce excessive emotional arousal and to be more accepting of what is happening. Another skill is to learn to adopt a course of action for typical daily functioning that does what works, plays by the rules, and keeps the focus on the desired outcomes rather than allowing impulsive urges to interfere. This is intended to minimize the pain that a client may be experiencing based on their unhealthy arousals. All of these skills as they are learned facilitate the client's spiritual development.

Meaning Therapy

Meaning Therapy is another popular approach used by social workers (Wong, 2010). "Meaning" is exactly what it appears to be at first glance—its main focus is on the inner world of meanings of people's lives. Its complexity comes from a holistic perspective and the different ways people respond to their lives. Meaning Therapy is part of the new wave of therapies that can be best classified as existential, eclectic, and positive in orientation. Clients often need help in seeking meaning for what they are experiencing, especially when it involves a change or special event in their lives such as a personal loss, becoming unemployed, or experiencing a malaise of some sort. The roots of Meaning Therapy stretch back to Viktor Frankl's logotherapy (1986). It attempts to prepare individuals to deal with inevitable life stressors and troubles in a manner that allows them to find purpose and joy in life despite their struggles (Wong, 2010).

Spiritual Connections

This focus is very spiritual in itself—finding meaning in who we are and what our lives are all about. Building a spiritual relationship, assessing the clients' spiritual issues, and facilitating the clients' spiritual development are also bridges to this approach. Meaning is a central concept of spirituality, so this approach and its interventions overlap considerably with a spiritual approach. Meaning Therapy is a holistic and integrative approach that describes people as psychosocial-spiritual beings (Wong, 2010). Relationships are paramount in sessions as practitioners work to form a solid relationship with their clients, as well as work on strengthening client bonds outside of their therapeutic partnership. Social workers assist clients in reaching both their present and future goals, as well as in discovering their hope and happiness. This is accomplished by connecting strategies for handling current issues with long-term solutions, life goals, and their purpose for living as well (Cox & Klinger, 2011).

Several spiritual principles are evident in this approach. First, situational meaning is more important than an abstract sense of meaning about being human, according to Frankl, (1986). Another principle is that having meaning helps make suffering more bearable; without it suffering can lead to despair, depression and a loss of will (Wong, 2010). Also meaning is not just about what revolves around self-interest; more importantly, it requires that people transcend themselves to find their meaning related to others and the common good. According to Frankl (1986), a sense of meaninglessness pervades our society and explains in large part why so many people are unhappy. Without meaning, people tend to lack purpose, challenge, obligation, hope, and they experience boredom and pain. In response they tend to focus on material possessions, hedonic pursuits, addictions, and ambitions for power, wealth, and fame. Unfortunately, as popular as these pursuits are, none of them brings ultimate satisfaction. In contrast, reaching out beyond self-interests to contribute to the greater good can set one on a path to genuine and lasting meaning.

Meaning Therapy also claims that a practitioner's personal qualities are as important as their competencies in helping (Wong, 2010). A social worker must be genuine, compassionate, communicate empathy, have unconditional positive regard for the client, have a hopeful attitude toward life, and be personally secure to truly help someone. Further, according to Meaning Therapy, the worker is expected to pursue their own personal development to be effective using this approach. Meaning Therapy is also focused on the macro level and embraces many of the characteristics of multicultural counselling theory (Sue, Ivey, & Pederson, 1996). This approach seeks to understand and motivate clients at different levels, including the cultural context (Wong, 2010). Clients' cultural specific values and their

Component	Examples of Meaning Questions
1) Motivational Component (values, goals, aspirations)	What should I do with my life? What can I do best? What does life demand of me? What really matters in life? What do I value most?
2) Cognitive Component (making sense of self and situations)	What has happened? Why me? Why do all the prayers and hard work not get me anywhere? What does it mean? What kind of person am I?
3) Responsible Action (doing what is right, highest values)	What is my responsibility in this situation? What option is most consistent with my beliefs and values? Have I made amends for my mistakes?
4) Evaluation (levels of satisfaction/dissatisfaction)	How is my life unfolding? Have I achieved what I set out to do? Am I satisfied with how I have lived my life? What is the best thing I have done in my life?

Figure 11.4   Examples of Exploration of Meaning in Four Areas (Wong, 2010, p. 603)

social problems resulting from cultural barriers and discrimination are to be taken into account as well. Cultural barriers are to be replaced by bridges of cooperation as Meaning Therapy is about promoting both interpersonal and global peace.

Solution-Focused Approach

Solution-Focused Therapy highlights the client's strengths and their own power to find solutions to their current problems. This links this approach to a spiritually sensitive approach that highlights spiritual strengths. A Solution-Focused Approach suggests that it is more prudent to build upon what has been successful for individuals in the past, than what has gone wrong (Chevalier, 1995). The social worker also encourages clients to define their personal strengths and accept their view of reality (George, 2008). If the clients' solutions are beyond what is possible, they can always be modified to be more realistic. Meanwhile, prior solutions can be discussed in terms of what they may mean to clients. The process of discovering solutions is intertwined with the individual's strengths. "Solutions" are meant to serve a universal function to unlock the answers about what to do in a host of circumstances and issues.

Goals are important to the Solution-Focused Approach and become important in the initial session with a client. Goals often involve small measureable indicators of outcomes that are desired (Langdridge, 2006). In sessions that follow, the client is questioned about their progress in reaching these goals. These goals are intended to prompt an action that the client can take in reaching them (de Shazer, 1985) and can be directly tied to assigned homework. The assignment of homework is included in many cognitive or behavioral based approaches, including Solution-Focused Therapy, as it helps clients put into practice in the "real world" what they are working on in sessions. Homework can also be very appropriate when working on spiritual issues in day-to-day activities—for example, taking time each day to meditate.

The "miracle question" is a focal point of the Solution-Focused Approach (Freeman, 2007). Miracles may also be a relevant concept to some clients because of their spiritual beliefs (Metaxas, 2014). An exercise using the miracle question helps to unlock the client's wishes and hopes, even if they may be unrealistic. The worker asks clients to imagine that when they go to bed at night, a miracle occurs while they are sleeping. This miracle erases or rectifies the problem that brought them to therapy in the first place. Once the miracle is described in some detail, clients are asked to explain how they would know that it occurred by detailing how things would be different. This step encourages them to think about the future and envision it with hope (De Jong & Berg, 2008). It also allows them to start thinking about the possibility of overcoming their problem.

Evaluation is an important part of each session using the Solution-Focused Approach. With the focus being on a goal or "a solution," it is important to periodically check in to find out whether or not progress is being made toward this goal. Some evaluation questions that could be asked are:

- How will you know if the intervention you have selected has been helpful?
- Have we clarified the central issue that you want to address?
- What will the future look like without the problem?
- Have we achieved enough to end our work together?
- How is your spirituality developing?

Spiritual Connections

Spiritual bridges to this approach include identifying and engaging spiritual strengths, facilitating spiritual development, using spiritual interventions, and utilizing spiritual supports. Personal goals can have spiritual aspects to them and thus may have special meaning and purpose for clients. For example, a client may identify their goal to be finding a job that involves helping others or forgiving a partner for being mean or rude. If so, spiritual interventions may be important to consider, such as some of the interventions described in chapter 9. Building self-confidence, envisioning a future with hope and optimism, or possibly drawing on the help of a Higher Power can all be possibilities. For example, prayer or meditation may be relevant interventions for some clients in reaching their goals. A goal for some clients may even be a "calling" and thus something of importance coming from their God or Higher Power. A Solution-Focused Approach can be useful in helping clients sort out how realistic this "call" is for a client and discerning whether or not it is coming from their Higher Power or another source.

Conclusion

This chapter discusses how a spiritually sensitive practice approach can be integrated into many of the general practice approaches used by social workers. Eight spiritual elements are identified and described as "bridges" in connecting and infusing spirituality to each of these approaches. These bridges are spiritual relationship building, communicating spiritual empathy, engaging spiritual strengths, working with spiritual messaging, facilitating the spiritual development of clients, assessing the clients' spiritual issues, introducing spiritual interventions, and utilizing spiritual supports. While there are other spiritual elements that can also be considered, these eight were selected because they provide natural ways to build helpful bridges to many existing general approaches that social workers use. Seven general practice approaches are described and illustrate how these spiritual bridges can help these approaches become spiritually sensitive.

Discussion Questions and Exercises

1. Interview a clergy or lay person in your community who may be available to help people who are affiliated with a particular religious group. Ask him or her about the types of services they provide to their members in various circumstances of need (e.g. hospital visits, death in the family, counseling). Also ask them what kinds of information they would want to have before accepting a referral. Share what you have learned with the class and compile a resource manual of religious resources.

2. Which of the seven practice approaches highlighted in the chapter do you feel most comfortable using with clients? Explore how you could infuse some of the eight spiritual bridges into it. Which bridges are most helpful in integrating spirituality into the approach that you use? What difficulties, if any, do you see in integrating spirituality into this practice approach?

3. The REBT Approach described in the chapter discusses how some irrational spiritual or religious beliefs of clients may be obstacles for them in solving their problems. Asking clients questions that can help them reinterpret these beliefs in a more helpful way is one technique for overcoming these obstacles. As an exercise, identify an irrational spiritual or religious belief of a client and then come up with two or three questions that clients could be asked to help them reinterpret the belief in a more helpful way to their lives.

References

Arnold, P. M. (1992). *Wildmen, warriors, and kings: Masculine spirituality in the Bible.* New York: Crossroad.

Banerjee, M. M., & Canda, (2009). Spirituality as a strength of African-American women affected by welfare reform. *Journal of Religion and Spirituality in Social Work: Social Thought, 28*(3), 239–262.

Bein, A. W. (2008). *The Zen of helping: Spiritual principles for mindful and open-hearted practice.* Hoboken, NJ: John Wiley & Sons.

Bloom, J. M., Woodward, E. N., Susmaras, T., & Pantalone, D. W. (2012). Use of dialectical behavior therapy in inpatient treatment of borderline personality disorder: A systematic review. *Psychiatric Services, 63*(9), 881–888.

Canda, E. R., & Furman, L. D. (2010). *Spiritual diversity in social work practice: The heart of healing.* New York: Free Press.

Chevalier, A. J. (1995). *On the client's path: A manual for the practice of solution-focused therapy.* Oakland, CA: New Harbinger Publications.

Combs, G., & Freedman, J. (2012). Narrative, poststructuralism, and social justice: Current practices in narrative therapy. *The Counseling Psychologist, 40*(7), 1033–1060.

Cox, W. M., & Klinger, E. (2011). *Handbook of motivational counseling: Goal-based approaches to assessment and intervention with addiction and other problems.* Hoboken, NJ: John Wiley & Sons.

CSWE (Council on Social Work Education) (2015). *2015 Educational Policy and Accreditation Standards for Baccalaureate and Master's Social Work Programs.* Educational Policy Approved by the CSWE Board of Directors on March 20, 2015; Accreditation Standards approved by the CSWE Commission on Accreditation on June 11, 2015. Alexandria, VA: Author.

De Jong, P., & Berg, I. K. (2008). *Interviewing for solutions.* 3rd edition. Belmont, CA: Brooks/ Cole.

de Shazer, S. (1985). *Keys to solutions in brief therapy.* New York, NY: W. W. Norton.

Drewery, W., & Winslade, J. (1997). The theoretical story of narrative therapy. In G. Monk, J. Winslade, K. Crocket, & D. Epston (Eds.), *Narrative therapy in practice: The archaeology of hope.* San Francisco, CA: Jossey-Bass, 32–52.

Ellis, A. (1997). Must musturbation and demandingness lead to emotional disorders? *Psychotherapy: Theory, Research, Practice, Training, 34*(1), 95–98.

Foucault, M. (1980). *Power/knowledge: Selected interviews and other writings.* New York, NY: Pantheon.

Fowler, J. W. (1995). *Stages of faith: The psychology of human development and the quest for meaning.* New York: HarperCollins.

Frankl, V. E. (1986). *The doctor and the soul.* 2nd edition. New York: Random House.

Freeman, S. (2007). A focused solution to therapy. *Primary Health Care, 17*(7), 32–34.

Gardner, F. (2011). *Critical spirituality: A holistic approach to contemporary practice.* Burlington, VT: Ashgate.

George, C. M. (2008). Solution-focused therapy: Strength-based counseling for children with social phobia. *Journal of Humanistic Counseling, Education & Development, 47*(2), 144–156.

Giordano, A. L., & Cashwell, C. S. (2014). Entering the sacred: Using motivational interviewing to address spirituality in counseling. *Counseling and Values, 59*, 65–79.

Harris, T. (1969). *I'm ok – you're ok.* New York: HarperCollins.

Hick, S. F. (2009). *Mindfulness and social work.* Chicago: Lyceum Books.

Hodge, D. R. (2004). Spirituality and people with mental Illness: Developing spiritual competency in assessment and intervention. *Families in Society, 85*(1), 36–44.

Hoover, C. (2014). Presentation on Native Americans and the Spirit World, Charlotte, NC, May, 2014.

Jones-Smith, E. (2011). *Theories of counseling and psychotherapy: An integrative approach.* Thousand Oaks, CA: Sage Publications.

Koons, C. R., (2008). Dialectical behavior therapy. *Social Work in Mental Health, 6*(1/2), 109–132.

Kornfield, J. (1993). *A Path with heart: A guide through the perils and promises of spiritual life.* New York: Bantam Books.

Langdridge, D. (2006). Solution focused therapy. *Existential Analysis: Journal of the Society For Existential Analysis, 17*(2), 359–370.

Matulich, B. (2013). How to do motivational interviewing: A guidebook. 2nd edition. Available online at www.motivationalinterviewingonline.com.

McKenzie, W., & Monk, G. (1997). Learning and teaching narrative ideas. In G. Monk, J. Winslade, K., Crocket, & D. Epston (Eds.), *Narrative therapy in practice: The archaeology of hope.* San Fransico: Jossey-Bass, 82–117.

Metaxas, E. (2014). *Miracles: What they are, why they happen, and how they can change your life.* New York: Dutton.

Miller, W. R., & Rollnick, S. (2002). *Motivational interviewing: Preparing people for change.* 2nd edition. New York, NY: Guilford Press.

O'Donohue, W. T. & Fisher, J. E. (2009). *General principles and empirically supported techniques of cognitive behavior therapy.* Hoboken, NJ: Wiley & Sons.

Overholser, J. (2003). Rational-emotive behavior therapy: An interview with Albert Ellis. *Journal of Contemporary Psychotherapy, 33*(3), 187–204.

Patterson, J., Hayworth, M., Turner, C., & Raskin, M. (2000). Spiritual issues in family therapy: A graduate-level course. *Journal of Marital and Family Therapy, 26*(2), 199–210.

Rogers, C. R. (1977). *Carl Rogers on personal power: Inner strength and its revolutionary impact.* New York, NY: Delacorte Press.

Rogers, C. R. (1979). The foundations of the person-centered approach. *Education, 100*(2), 98.

Rogers, C. R. & Kramer, P. D. (1995). *On becoming a person: A therapist's view of psychotherapy.* New York: Houghton Mifflin.

Saleebey, D. (Ed.) (2013). *The strengths perspective in social work practice.* 6th edition. Upper Saddle, NJ: Pearson.

Sue, D. W., Ivey, A. E., & Pederson, P. B. (1996). *A theory of multicultural counseling & therapy.* Pacific Grove, CA: Brooks/Cole Publishing.

Swales, M., Heard, H. L., & Williams, J. G. (2000). Linehan's dialectical behaviour therapy (DBT) for borderline personality disorder: Overview and adaptation. *Journal of Mental Health, 9*(1), 7–23.

Thorne, B. (2002). Person-centered therapy. In W. Dryden (Ed.), *Handbook of individual therapy.* 4th edition. London: Sage, 131–157.

Walsh, J. (2006). *Theories for direct social work practice.* Belmont CA: Thomson Brooks/Cole.

Wong, P. T. P. (2010). Meaning therapy: An integrative and positive existential psychotherapy. *Journal of Contemporary Psychotherapy, 40*, 85–93.

12

EVALUATING SPIRITUALLY SENSITIVE PRACTICE

I am only one, but I am one. I cannot do everything, but I can do something. What I can do, I ought to do, and what I ought to do, by the Grace of God, I will do.

(Edward Everett Hale)

This we know. The earth does not belong to people. People belong to the earth. This we know. All things are connected. Whatever befalls the earth, befalls the people of the earth. We did not weave the web of life. We are but a mere strand in it. Whatever we do to the web, we do to ourselves.

(Chief Seattle)

Introduction to Evaluating Spirituality

Evaluation is the fourth component of a spiritually sensitive practice approach. It follows engagement, assessment, and interventions. Evaluation provides the means for determining many things important to spiritually sensitive practice. Overall, it provides accountability to clients, agency providers, funding sources, and others (Dudley, 2014). Evaluation tools can assist in addressing several issues, including determining the extent to which an agency is providing spiritually sensitive services. Evaluation tools can also assist in determining the extent to which social workers and other practitioners employed by the agency are adequately prepared to provide spiritually sensitive practice. Most importantly, evaluation tools can determine the impact of spiritually sensitive programs and practice on the clients it serves. Ultimately, evaluations are needed to provide evidence that spiritually sensitive interventions are effective in helping clients.

Challenges of Evaluating Spiritual Practice

Evaluations are perhaps the most challenging of the four practice components to develop and implement. There are several reasons for this. A prime reason is that there are a wide variety of research methods that are available and social workers may not know which methods are most appropriate in each situation (Bolin, Lee, Glenmaye, & Yoon, 2012; Harder, 2010). They may also not be skilled enough to analyze data and interpret it. Evaluations involve using research methods and many social work practitioners do not perceive their skills in this area to be particularly strong.

Evaluation consists of many different methods and strategies (Dudley, 2014). For example, it could use quantitative or qualitative methods or both. In this case it could, for example, measure how frequently clients attend religious services, a quantitative measure. Or it could measure a client's grieving process, which is likely to be captured qualitatively. Evaluation can focus on either a program (e.g. a grieving support group) or a practice intervention (e.g. teaching mindfulness to a client). Evaluation can involve measures at one time or several points in time. It could involve the client answering questions (e.g. a client satisfaction survey). Or it could be a behavioral measure of a client's progress over time (e.g. movement to a more developed stage of acceptance of a loss). In most cases, program evaluations use group designs (i.e., pre-experimental, quasi-experimental, or experimental designs) to evaluate the impact of a spiritually sensitive intervention on the recipients' progress.

Not only is conducting an evaluation challenging in a general sense, evaluation in the area of spiritually sensitive practice poses even greater challenges. A theme throughout the book has been that concepts like spirituality, spiritually sensitive practice, being religious or non-religious, spiritual development, and many other concepts are difficult to define and measure. Qualitative evaluation tools are primarily needed to measure these types of concepts. Consequently, social workers need skills in using qualitative methods and data analysis as well as quantitative ones to evaluate spiritually sensitive practice. As examples of the challenges of measuring these concepts, think about how you might answer the following questions if you were conducting an evaluation:

- How spiritual is a client?
- How religious is a client?
- What spiritual beliefs are important to a client?
- In what ways is a client's spiritual development changing for the better or worse?
- How aware are clients of their spirituality?
- What spiritual strengths do clients have?
- What are some beneficial client outcomes that can be anticipated from a spiritually based approach?
- How can/does a client's spirituality influence their grieving process after a loss?
- How can/does a client's spirituality influence how well they can forgive someone?
- How well prepared is an agency in offering spiritually sensitive practice to its clients?
- What skills of a spiritually sensitive approach does a social worker need to have when working with older adults, children, or other client groups?
- How can faith-based agencies offer a spiritually sensitive helping approach without imposing their own spiritual or religious biases?

- Can faith-based agencies empower clients to resolve their problems more effectively than secular agencies? If so, in what ways?

Evaluation and Empowering Clients and Communities

Canda and Furman (2010) offer a spiritually based perspective on evaluation. They recommend that evaluation be, at least in part, a process of discernment for clients; evaluation is important if it helps clients become aware of how helping strategies are beneficial to them. Canda and Furman also suggest that less attention be given to evaluations that measure how clients conform to the standards of the social worker or agency. Monitoring tools are especially helpful, from their perspective, that include reflection and dialogue with clients, focusing on exchanges about mutually agreed upon contracts, and consumer satisfaction inquiries and surveys (Hodge & Wolosin, 2012). In addition to monitoring, Canda and Furman (2010) suggest a process of transformation in which the clients and the helping system "mutually shape each other" (p. 232).

Fetterman, Kaftarian, and Wandersman (1996) and Zimmerman (2000) develop these ideas further as they argue for evaluation processes that are empowering people to develop skills they need to become independent problem solvers and decision makers. These processes, they believe, are critical in providing people with a particular stake in gaining control over their future, obtaining needed resources, and critically understanding their social environment. Fetterman and colleagues also discuss empowered outcomes of evaluations as the consequences that empowerment processes seek. Examples include creating or strengthening organizational networks, creating greater accessibility to community resources, and greater citizen control over community decision-making.

Participatory Action Research as a Resource

Participatory Action Research (PAR) is a comprehensive research approach known for empowering clients (DePoy, Hartman, & Haslett, 1999). Sometimes it is referred to as participant action research or critical action research as well. PAR is known for actively involving clients in all or most steps of the evaluation process. Some of the key PAR principles are:

- Collaborate with client systems affected by the problem to clearly articulate what the problem is, its scope, and all relevant parties.
- Articulate the purpose of the change that the evaluation is designed to accomplish for clients or a community.
- Have both professional and lay evaluators on the evaluation team.
- Train lay evaluators on how to design, conduct, and use appropriate research methods.

- Report findings in accessible formats for all interested parties including clients, their families, and communities.

Implementation of PAR in spiritually related practice can occur in all or at least some of the steps of an evaluation. For example, if involving clients or community stakeholders during every step is not realistic, they can be involved in particular steps. Client and community stakeholders can be particularly important in the first step of helping articulate issues that need to be evaluated. For example, how do a variety of clients view the relevance of their spirituality to the problems they are facing and the help that they need? Also, the last step of assisting in dissemination of the evaluation results to various community groups may be a helpful time to encourage other community groups to further develop their own spiritual and religious contributions. These PAR principles are definitely worth considering further as we continue exploring how to evaluate spiritually sensitive practice.

Important Evaluation Topics for Spiritually Sensitive Practice

Evaluations can focus on numerous topics related to spiritually related practice. Three important evaluation topics are highlighted in the chapter. This is not an exhaustive list of priorities but a place to begin. Evaluation activities in these three areas seems essential. First, evaluations are needed to determine how prepared agencies are in providing a spiritually sensitive approach. A second focus is to determine what practitioner competencies are needed for delivering a spiritually sensitive approach. Third, evaluations are important in determining the impact that a spirituality-sensitive approach has on clients. Examples of studies from the professional literature are presented to illustrate what research has been conducted.

Topic 1: The Agency's Role in Providing a Spiritually Sensitive Approach

Agency preparation is a macro concern. Without the agency committing itself to a spiritually sensitive approach and needed agency structures to support it, little may be possible from the practitioners delivering this practice area. Therefore, it is important to point out that work on this macro topic should ideally precede the work expected of preparing agency practitioners.

Doe (2004) points out that human service organizations should have their own spirituality-based organizational values or strategies that guide them. These organizational values can be manifested as organizational missions, goals, agendas, priorities, policies, or operational guidelines. Doe goes on to say that empowerment-focused organizational structures and management patterns are important macro places for infusing spirituality. Bolman and Deal (1995), in the business world, refer to this notion as "leading with soul," which encourages open discussions of ethical and spiritual issues. The essence of leadership goes deeper than analytical managerial skills to where courage, spirit, and hope are found and activated. Bolman and Deal also state that the heart of leadership must not lose touch with the leaders' own spiritual sources of vitality and energy. Further, Doe (2004) suggests that the spirituality of leadership means that leaders are committed to the possibilities of the human spirit that focus on the importance of relationships with others, non-authoritarian organizational power-sharing structures, and less hierarchical relationships within the organization.

The agency's role in offering spiritual and religious services can be reflected in its mission or vision and in a definition of what spirituality actually means in the context of the helping process. All of the stakeholders (e.g. administrators, board members, practitioners, community groups, and clients) can have input into these matters. The evaluation methods that can be used in addressing topic 1 include focus groups, questionnaires and interview studies, and other descriptive tools.

Mission and Vision Statements

Agency commitments can be evident in some instances in an agency's mission or vision statements. An example could be a phrase in the mission or vision statement such as a concern for the spiritual well-being of clients or a goal to promote or empower the clients' spiritually. Spiritual intervention provisions could also be mentioned in the overall description of the agency's services, such as providing meditation as one of several services to address substance abuse or offering forgiveness therapy in a family agency to address some marital issues.

While some agencies may communicate their commitments to spirituality and religion explicitly in mission statements, it is more likely for spirituality not to be mentioned in major introductions to an agency. An agency's commitments may be in several areas that include spirituality. For example, an agency could be committed to a holistic perspective that is concerned about many aspects of a person, including spirituality and religion. In other words, commitments can be implicit as well as explicit. Yet, because spiritually sensitive practice is relatively new to many agencies and sometimes controversial, the author recommends that some effort go into explaining whether an agency offers help in this area and how this help can be provided. This information could be included, for example, in the agency's brochures and community relations materials.

Defining What Spirituality Means

Another area of agency preparation that can be evaluated is how spirituality and religion are defined as client concerns needing services. In chapter 1, spirituality and religion are defined as broad and complex concepts. Also, many people do not distinguish between these two terms or perhaps they even understand them as largely the same. In this case, spirituality often may be seen as another descriptor of religion and these terms may be used interchangeably. Therefore, it is highly recommended that both concepts be defined and incorporated into the agency's policies and formal procedures. In addition, it is important that they be defined in ways that are meaningful to the spiritual and religious background of the clients and their communities. Based on the principles of Participatory Action Research (PAR) described above, this would be an opportunity for clients and community groups to assist in completing these tasks. Also, these concepts should be periodically updated and changed over time as experiences with the clients' spirituality evolves.

Spiritual Assessments and Interventions

A study by Svare, Hylton, and Albers (2007), described in chapter 5, focused on the elements of organizations that support or impede the implementation of spiritually sensitive practice and the views of staff members about these practices. They gathered data from a focus group of 11 social workers employed in a wide range of agency settings. The agencies represented in this study usually used an assessment form that included at least one spiritual or religious question, even though the type and depth of spiritual assessment varied widely. Findings revealed considerable variation in how workers in each agency responded to these questions; this seemed to indicate that agency policies and procedures be developed for why these questions were asked and how they were relevant to the agencies' purposes. They also found that the workers who were more religious tended to be more open to their clients' spiritual concerns while those who were not religious or did not view a place for spirituality in service provisions tended to view spirituality and religion as outside the scope of the agency (Larsen, 2011; Sheridan, 2009).

The author was part of a research team that conducted a pilot study of how local agencies in Charlotte addressed spirituality issues as an organization (Elmore, Davis, & Dudley, 2015). Phone interviews were conducted with nine agencies in the Charlotte area. These agencies were all current field internship agencies for social work students of an MSW program. Two of the nine agencies were faith-based and the others were either private nonprofit or for-profit. The initial findings of this study were similar to other studies in some ways. Many of the clients of these agencies do bring spiritual concerns with them. For example, four of these agencies indicated that clients frequently brought up spiritual concerns, while another three agencies said such concerns were raised occasionally. Two of the nine agencies indicated that spiritually was included in their mission statement. One said it is implicit in "honoring and helping a person reach full potential in all aspects of life." The other said the agency "strengthens and empowers individuals and families through professional counseling, programs and services inspired by Jewish values." However, only one agency reported having a definition of spirituality. This was the Jewish agency, and their definition was largely used to determine who qualified for particular services available only to Jewish clients. Some of the agencies not having a definition responded to the question of a definition with interesting alternatives as follows:

- "Religion is a specific faith system, while spirituality is much broader. Connection to nature, universe, etc. Always ask a client to define it for themselves."
- "Professionally and with our clients, everyone is able to practice whichever religion they choose."
- "We do not discuss our own views on religion. We allow families and volunteers to discuss the views they have to better make a match."
- "All work with clients is individualized to the specific client and families being served. If spirituality and religion are viewed as important to the client and/or families being served, aspects are incorporated into treatment."

Among other things, these comments suggest that a definition of spirituality might be better left up to the clients to define, and in most cases taking this position may be to prevent the introduction of any agency biases. On the other hand, there may be an inclination among these agencies to leave too much responsibility to the clients, including knowing that they can even bring up these concerns.

All but one of these nine agencies also reported that they ask initial spiritual assessment questions. These questions varied, but most of them simply asked the clients if they have a religious affiliation or attend a church. In addition, one agency asks clients "how spirituality looks in their life and how it may impact their treatment." This agency added that this may be something the agency surmises by context rather than directly asking, depending on the situation. Another agency provides adoption services and responded, "Adoptive parents are required to have a referral from a pastor or priest. They are also asked if they will take the adoptive child to church." These nine agencies were also asked if they offered any spiritual interventions to clients, and five said they did. All five of these agencies indicated that they provide mindfulness interventions, and one also offers yoga.

Faith-Based Agencies

Faith-based agencies have been investigated the most on how they introduce spirituality and religion as part of their program provisions. A model faith-based agency described in chapter 10 is one example. Kaseman and Austin (2005) describe a macro faith-based agency committed to both service and advocacy as a possible prototype for comprehensive faith-based human service organizations in the future. They identify several components of importance to their agency that are described in chapter 10, including the importance of staff members holding onto and sustaining the spiritual calling that undergirds their effort, remaining committed to their own personal spiritual renewal, seeking an interfaith and ecumenical mission, and a focus on their clients as the reason for their ministry.

A study of Hugen and Venema (2009) of 1,110 faith-based programs revealed that more than half of them viewed spirituality as central in their program. One-third of the programs communicated faith implicitly, mostly through acts of caring toward clients, and another one-fourth communicated their faith explicitly and indicated that the role of faith was critical to clients changing. Another focus was on the extent to which faith-related elements were incorporated into services for clients. The findings indicated that these agencies communicated faith implicitly more than explicitly, and they differed widely in terms of the intensity of their exposure of faith-related elements. Unfortunately, the nature of these faith-based elements was not shared in detail in the study. What was shared is reported in chapters 5 and 10.

While few studies beyond Hugen and Venema (2009) could be found that report on this, many faith-based agencies are likely to offer religious-based services by virtue of their identity as being faith-based. Perhaps these services are offered by someone who has specialized training, such as a hospital chaplain, pastoral counselor, or a spiritual director. In these cases, studies could focus on the explanations given by faith-based agencies for what these services are, who they can help, and how. Also if they tend to gravitate around particular religious beliefs this would be important to mention.

Research Questions Recommended for Topic 1

In conclusion, some studies have been conducted on how agencies introduce spirituality at the organizational level, but more are needed. Recommendations for questions that could be explored are:

- What kinds of spiritual or religious requests, problems, or issues come up in an agency's day-to-day experiences with clients?
- Are spirituality and religion identified as important to an agency's mission, vision, or overall purpose? Is it evident in any agency policies?
- If spirituality is not identified as being important, how are spirituality and religion supposed to be addressed if brought up by clients?
- How, if at all, do agencies define spirituality in the context of their services? How do they define religion in this context?
- What, if any, spiritual interventions does the agency provide to clients? What religious interventions? What kinds of client outcomes of a spiritual nature do agencies identify and evaluate, if any?

Topic 2: Defining Staff Competencies in Spiritually Sensitive Practice

Agencies should also assume some responsibility for preparing and training their staff members on how to respond to spiritual and religious issues of clients when they come up. This may involve formal or informal training and assistance. It can also involve having administrative and supervisory staff with expertise available to assist in this endeavor. Further, training can be available in opportunities for staff members to participate in workshops outside the agency.

Evaluation of the Worker Competence on Spiritual Matters

What does staff preparation entail? How do we know when this preparation is adequate? These are key questions to be addressed in this section. Chamiec-Case (2009) developed an instrument for exploring how practitioners' personal spirituality may be related to their commitment to a spiritually sensitive social work approach, and this is an important factor to consider. He designed and tested a preliminary instrument, referred to as the Integration of Spirituality in the Workplace Scale (ISWS), that determines the extent to which a social worker *perceives* that they integrate spirituality in the workplace. Chamiec-Case conducted focus groups and individual interviews and involved expert judges to create an instrument that measures practitioners' perceptions using a 7-point Likert scale (strongly disagree to strongly agree). Some of the key statements used in the instrument are:

- I believe that my work is part of my spiritual path or journey.
- My spirituality energizes my work.
- My spirituality influences my interactions with my clients and/or colleagues.
- I integrate my spiritual life with my work life.
- I believe that my work is an important way to live out my spiritual beliefs and values.

As these items suggest, practitioners may be more inclined to adopt a spiritually sensitive approach if they view it as connected in some way to their own spiritual path. However, these questions also raise questions about the need for boundaries to prevent the practitioner's personal spiritual issues from interfering with clients' spiritual issues. While Chamiec-Case (2009) offers a helpful framework, this framework does not directly address the large number of social workers unlikely to view their personal spirituality as important to the workplace. They will need preparation too (Larsen, 2011). Actually, preparation may be most important for social workers who resist or are indifferent to engaging their clients' spirituality.

Each social worker's practice consists of numerous interacting elements (engagement techniques, intuitive awareness, etc.). These interacting elements are dynamic and vary in how they are implemented from one client to another. That's what makes evaluating practice such a difficult concept to evaluate. For example, someone's practice can be observed and attempts could be made to decide if a checklist of behaviors are present. Or this evaluative approach could perhaps be carried out using a process recording that records all of the verbal and non-verbal communication of the worker in the context of an interview. Even in these evaluative approaches, however, much of what unfolds is not likely to be documented, such as the worker's knowledge and values that are relevant and the motivations for why workers do what they do at any point in an interview.

In most cases, professional practice is evaluated by beginning with a set of broad professional standards that are important to fulfill. In a somewhat similar way, professional standards are needed to define and evaluate spiritual competencies. The Society for Spirituality and Social Work (SSSW), at an earlier time in its history, developed a beginning set of spiritual competencies falling under three categories: knowledge, skills, and values (www.societyforspiritualityandsocialwork.com). These competencies are a good beginning foundation for setting helpful standards. This group referred to knowledge as a competency and they identified several areas of knowledge that are needed, such as knowledge of major faith traditions and the variety of spiritual experiences they support; also, the social context of spiritual experience and how culture interacts with spirituality. Another professional standard developed by SSSW refers to skills such as conducting and writing up a spiritual history and assessing a client's spiritual strengths and barriers as they support or impede a desired change. A third standard SSSW articulated is a values base in which a social worker is able to use a non-judgmental approach toward spiritual issues, value and respect diversity, and support client self-determination, among other specific indicators.

A beginning set of questions was asked of social work students in the author's Spirituality and Social Work course to help students know what would be expected of them by the time they completed the course. In brief, these questions also provide beginning standards for spiritually sensitive social work practice for that course. The questions are presented in the box on p. 303.

All of this discussion leads us back to the question of how we can evaluate whether social workers are prepared to practice in a spiritually sensitive way. Professional standards are needed that can be formulated by a representative group of professionals, particularly professionals who understand how to help clients with spiritual and religious issues, taking into account a diversity of clients and agencies. Hopefully, what the Society for Spirituality and Social Work began formulating in the past will be revisited.

Research Questions Recommended for Topic 2

Some efforts have been made to formulate social work competencies for spiritual practice but more effort is needed. Some authors have reviewed existing studies on this topic and have offered recommendations for future research (e.g. Oxhandler & Pargament, 2014). Evaluation questions recommended for topic 2 revolve around two overall questions: what are the most important spiritual

Student Expectations upon Completion of a Spirituality and Social Work Course

1. How well can you define and describe spirituality as a concept for practice? How well can you define religion as a practice concept and distinguish it from spirituality?

2. How well can you describe your own spirituality and religious orientation (if any)? Can you highlight the most important aspects of your spirituality?

3. How well can you learn the basic characteristics of the religious groups of your clients?

4. How well can you pick up on spiritual cues from your clients, especially during the initial engagement phase? How comfortable are you in incorporating these cues, when appropriate, into the work between you and your client?

5. What are some good general spiritual assessment questions that you could ask clients as part of the assessment phase?

6. What spiritual interventions are you comfortable offering to clients during the intervention phase?

7. How well can you critique the policies or lack of policies on spirituality and religion of an agency (such as where you are placed in a field internship)? How well can you assess the agency's efforts to prepare practitioners to work effectively with the spirituality of their clients? How can you help an agency develop new policies and assist with staff preparatory training if it is absent?

8. How well can you infuse spirituality into the general practice approaches you will use?

9. How well can you evaluate whether your spiritual interventions are effective?

competencies needed by a social worker and how can they be measured? Specific questions include:

- Which types of requests, problems, or issues are workers most comfortable addressing? Which types are they least comfortable addressing?
- How satisfied are social workers with their competencies in the spirituality and religion areas? What limitations in preparation do they perceive that they have?

- How well prepared are social workers in responding effectively to spiritual or religious requests, problems, or issues that come up from their clients?
- How do social work practitioners define spirituality in the context of their practice? How do they define religion?
- To what extent are social workers reading about and becoming more aware of evidence-based spiritual practices in their fields?
- Do Social Work and Spirituality courses provide enough preparation for spiritually sensitive practice? If not, what is missing?
- If social workers have not taken a Spirituality course, what are some helpful resources available for learning about spiritually sensitive practice?
- In what ways is the social worker's agency providing assistance and support for social workers in addressing spiritual and religious concerns of clients? Is training offered by the agency in workshops and/or supervision? Is this practice area discussed informally in staff workshops or other staff meetings? Are workers encouraged to attend available training outside the agency? Does the agency pay for any of the costs involved in attending these outside workshops? What is most helpful in all of these offerings? What is missing that social workers may want or need?
- If an agency does not offer its staff members any preparation, what do they expect of their staff members in this area of practice? Are they satisfied with how staff members currently address these issues? In what ways are they satisfied?

Topic 3: Evaluating the Effectiveness of Spiritually Based Interventions

Determining if an intervention is effective is perhaps the most central question of an evaluation (Campbell & Blunt, 2006). Is the intervention found to be responsible (or partially responsible) for bringing important gains for clients? Other types of evaluation, however, are also important (Dudley, 2014). Is the intervention that is selected based on evidence that it can be effective, are qualified staff members hired to implement it, and is the intervention implemented with quality standards? These are also important types of evaluations to consider.

Social workers should support evaluations that determine the effectiveness of their interventions. This includes developing measures of desired client outcomes that are valid and reliable. We also need to be able to describe our interventions as clearly as we can so that they can be replicated. Sometimes this becomes challenging with interventions like spiritual ones because we are working with elements that may be difficult to clearly define and measure (Thyer, 2006). For example, let's assume that intercessory prayer is an intervention implemented to help cancer patients during and after radiation therapy. Prayer has several interacting elements and most cannot be observed. Prayer involves people in communication with their God, but how this occurs for each person is largely beyond observation and measure. Also it is likely to vary considerably from person to person and attempts to measure it may interfere with how it occurs because of its often spontaneous nature.

The effectiveness of an intervention such as a spiritual intervention can be stated as a causal relationship existing between the intervention and the desired client outcome. The intervention causes an improvement to occur in the client's desired outcome. Let's say, for example, that a mental health program composed of several mindfulness exercises is provided to a group of teenagers who have ADHD (attention deficit hyperactivity disorder). The goal of this intervention could be to help the clients sit still for a 30-minute period at least twice during each day. The intent would be that sitting still will help them become more able to complete their schoolwork and homework.

Three Conditions for Causality

Three conditions must be met before concluding that a spiritual intervention brings about the desired client changes (Dudley, 2014). First, the intervention's implementation must precede any improvement in the client outcome. That seems to be an obvious condition, as an intervention should not be given credit for clients' improvement occurring before the intervention was actually introduced. Second, an association is to be found between the intervention and the client outcome; usually such an association is found using statistical tests. This means that as the intervention is introduced over time, desired changes in the client outcome become evident. In our above example, that would mean that the teenagers with ADHD, once attending the mindfulness series, would begin to be calmer and more comfortable sitting for longer periods. An evaluation design that has a measure of the client outcome both before (pretest) and after (posttest) the intervention is implemented will reveal whether such a change has occurred. The third condition for concluding the effectiveness of an intervention is the most difficult of the three to meet. It is a claim that the intervention, rather than something else, is responsible, at least in part, for improvements in the client outcome. This condition usually requires such things as adding a control group or a series of measures of the client outcome (time series design) to demonstrate that the intervention, not something else, made the difference. Unfortunately, when we talk about control groups, we get into ethical problems like determining who receives the intervention and who does not based on random selection and assignment to one group or the other. An ethical problem becomes apparent if someone who desperately needs the intervention ends up in the control group.

Thyer (2006) weighs in on these three conditions in an article that emphasizes the importance of faith-based agencies evaluating the effectiveness of their interventions. Thyer (2006, pp. 75–76) raises several helpful questions that agencies can ask when exploring how to evaluate an intervention's effectiveness. They are:

1. Do clients receiving the intervention seem to be getting better early on?
2. Do clients receiving the intervention demonstrate greater initial improvements, compared to those who did not receive the program or those who received standard care?

Thyer (2006) goes on to say that if the answers to the above questions are positive, then more complex inquiries may be warranted, such as:

3. Do the positive results endure for a long time?
4. Is the intervention effective across a diverse array of clients?
5. Is the intervention effective when applied in everyday practice settings?

Choosing an Evaluation Design

We have several evaluation designs that we can select from to determine the effectiveness of a program (Dudley, 2014). These designs have varying degrees of power in determining a causal relationship. Some designs are simpler to implement but can claim effectiveness with less confidence than others. For example, we can start with a design that simply measures what happens to clients after an intervention is introduced (one-group posttest-only design); this design can at least tell us if the intervention was unsuccessful. Based on this design, if the desired outcomes for clients are not evident after the intervention is complete, then the intervention seems to have failed to have had an impact and alternative interventions should be considered.

There are several choices of group designs that can be considered (Dudley, 2014). They begin with simpler ones and each succeeding design adds an additional element of complexity that strengthens the design's power to determine efficacy. The first two in the list below are pre-experimental designs, the third and fourth are quasi-experimental designs, and the fifth is an experimental design as follows:

1. a one-group posttest-only design (a basic "bare bones" design mentioned above);
2. a one-group pretest/posttest design (a pretest is added);
3. a one-group pretest/posttest design with a comparison group (comparison group added);
4. time-series design (in addition to the pretest and posttest measures, other measures of the desired outcome are added at different points in time);
5. an experimental design being a one-group pretest/posttest design with a control group (adds another feature, a control group).

Only experimental designs can claim that an intervention is effective with absolute confidence. In an experimental study, the clients are randomly selected from a larger pool of clients and then randomly assigned to either receive the intervention or the control group. In this way, each client is considered to have an equal chance of being in either group. However, using a random selection approach raises ethical concerns because those randomly assigned to a control group may need the intervention immediately or more than others assigned to the intervention group.

Spiritual Interventions and Client Outcomes

Many evaluation studies have already been conducted of programs using spiritual interventions. The results of these evaluations are important to know about so researchers can build on these studies in their own investigations. Smith and Teasley (2009) conducted an extensive literature search of evaluations of faith-based agencies that were conducted by social workers. They found and reported on 13 such studies. These studies had a variety of research designs. Some were only descriptive or focused only on program monitoring; others were outcome studies but without rigorous research methods. None of the research designs used an experimental design with random selection and assignment. The authors concluded from their review that rigorous outcome studies were lacking that clearly documented the evidence that the spiritual interventions were responsible for the changes in client outcomes.

Smith and Teasley (2009) went on to say that the basic theories undergirding these spiritual interventions that could pinpoint the theoretical mechanisms associated with changing clients were not given enough attention by researchers. In other words, these studies did not adequately identify the specific role that religion and faith played in impacting outcomes. For example, religious groups may offer a variety of faith-based interventions like Bible study, worship services, religious seminars and retreats, and fellowship gatherings that could vary widely across different denominations (Mears, Roman, Wolff, & Buck, 2006). While the services were usually identified, the role of religion within the context of these services was not adequately articulated and measured. They concluded by recommending that social work scholars should take on the challenges of assisting faith-based agencies in addressing these and other methodological limitations in evaluating their interventions.

Grettenberger, Bartkowski, and Smith (2006) also identified limitations in faith-based research. Self-selection of participants was one of them. Other limitations included a need for appropriate classification of the clients' levels of faith, obtaining an adequate sample size, and greater specification of outcome variables. They also identified the need for more tracking of clients over time, and a need for measurable definitions of spiritual transformation.

Smith and Teasley (2009) did summarize some helpful findings from these 13 empirical studies. These faith-based agencies seemed to be concentrated mostly in particular types of settings such as food relief, housing and shelter assistance, civil rights, youth, and recreation (Graddy, 2006). In addition, investigations of the outcomes of some spiritual or religious interventions revealed evidence of improvements in different client outcomes such as a decrease in addiction, decreases in HIV and STD risks, increased number of paid work days, less anxiety and depression, being hired for a job, regularly taking psychiatric medications, and increased self-image and self-assurance. Yet, this evidence, while important, was not documented to be the direct result of a spiritual intervention. A few of the programs also identified specific religious elements in their outcomes. Examples of such outcomes were frequency of expressing their faith more regularly (Christian), deepening ties with their existing faith practices (Hindu), and a deeper commitment to knowledge of their faith (Islamic). Other examples are increased levels of spiritual change, and levels of religiosity. Other studies' outcomes focused on increasing spiritual activities, beliefs, and rituals (e.g. Neff, Shorkey, & Windsor, 2006).

Examples of Evaluations of the Efficacy of Spiritual Interventions

Since efficacy studies are still limited in number and rigor in most fields, more such studies are needed. Extensive reviews have been conducted of existing efficacy studies in different fields. For example, Kaplar, Wachholtz, and O'Brien (2004) conducted a literature review of outcome studies that used spiritual and religious interventions to assist cancer patients. While the nature of the spiritual interventions were not explored in any depth, three types of outcomes were; they generally fell into specific biological, psychological, and spiritual areas. Overall, these authors found that these interventions had small to moderate effects on cancer patients. Another review article on spirituality, religion, and cancer suggests that spirituality in the field of oncology has growing importance (Peteet & Balboni, 2013). These authors point out that religious and spiritual beliefs have a significant influence on patients' decisions regarding complementary therapies and aggressive care at the end of life. They also point out that measures of spiritual well-being are positively associated with improved quality of life of cancer patients. While many professionals working with oncology patients claim that spiritual interventions are an appropriate aspect of their roles, their patients report that they provide it too infrequently.

In another extensive literature review, Yonker, Schnabelrauch, and DeHaan (2012) searched for studies investigating the association between indicators of spirituality and religiosity and psychological outcomes in adolescents and emerging adults. A variety of spiritual and religious variables were considered as independent variables for this review, such as:

- frequency of attending church or other religious services;
- observable spiritual and religious behaviors such as prayer and involvement in religious activities like youth groups and Bible studies;

- the importance of the adolescents' religious faith, evident in such things as a born again status; identification with a religious community or religious doctrines; connectedness with God or a Higher Power; and the importance of spirituality and religion as a source of refuge, coping or solace;
- evidence of spirituality and religion searching, such as being actively engaged in exploring questions about life's meaning; searching for the sacred; pursuing transcendent reality; and questioning the final causes and ultimate end of humankind.

Their review consisted of 75 studies encompassing 66,273 adolescents and examined the influence of these spirituality and religion variables on risk behavior, depression, well-being, self-esteem, and some personality factors. The results showed in many of these studies that spirituality and religion were positively associated with reducing risk behaviors and depression, and increasing self-esteem, well-being and personality traits like agreeableness and openness.

Another literature review of efficacy studies focused on the impact of Christian prayer on clients (Finney & Malony, 1985). The authors summarized the work they found into four categories: developmental studies of conceptions of prayer; research on motivations for praying; studies of the effects of verbal prayer; and the effects of contemplative prayer. Another literature review focused on the impact of Eastern arts (meditation, yoga, tai chi, qigong) on positive health and socioeconomic outcomes among maltreated youth (Waechter & Wekerle, 2015). All but one of the studies that Waechter and Wekerle reviewed showed some improvement for these Eastern arts intervention groups.

A particular area of research, the content of people's prayers, has also been cited as not being adequately studied. Ap Siôn and Nash (2013) conducted a study of the content of private prayers used in a health-related context. They investigated the prayer requests left on a prayer tree in a children's hospital in England. While most were prayers to God, some were made directly to a patient in the hospital. The types of most of these prayers were either intercessory or petitioning. The language employed by some of the prayers was highly religious while that of others was more secular. Beliefs were evident in some of the prayers, such as beliefs about God's direct physical interventions in the world and beliefs about angels. Many of the prayers also had elements of thanksgiving in them, with God viewed as accessible and listening to them. Most requests sought change in a patient's condition to the better or recovery from surgery. However, the nature of the help that was requested focused more on asking for such things as protection, strength, or guidance in contrast to seeking physical healing. One conclusion of this study is that these prayers provided the spiritual and religious staff of the hospital with helpful information about family members, such as the stages that they were in related to coping. Some were questioning why this happened, others were reflecting on it, and still others were accepting it.

Three Efficacy Studies

Let's look closely at three efficacy studies that evaluated the impact of different spiritual interventions on varied groups of clients. In each case they seem to provide examples of evidence-based practice. The spiritual intervention in each study is described in detail to provide the reader with information that might help you decide whether these interventions are possibly relevant to your clients.

Study 1: Mindfulness and CBT for People with Anxiety Disorders

The first study was a study of a multi-faith spiritual intervention intended to treat generalized anxiety disorder (Koszycki, Bilodeau, Raab-Mayo, & Bradwejn, 2014). This research design involved a randomized pilot trial of 23 participants, all of whom had at least moderate severe anxiety. These 23 people were randomly assigned, with 11 receiving the spiritual intervention and 12 receiving traditional supportive therapy. The spiritual intervention used a mindfulness approach drawn from Walsh (1999) and focused on core teachings found in many religious traditions rather than any one tradition. Cognitive Behavioral Therapy, combined with this mindfulness approach reported efficacy in reducing anxiety, excessive worry, depressive symptoms, and impaired role functioning. This intervention also produced greater changes in spiritual well-being that were maintained as of a three-month follow-up.

The intervention involved 12 weekly 50-minute sessions covering several spiritual themes in Walsh (1999) that could help people overcome anxiety disorders. Some of the spiritual themes were:

- contemplative practices to developing a calm and concentrated mind;
- understanding of the power of forgiveness in releasing emotional pain;
- making a connection between gratitude and positive emotions;
- being mindful;
- understanding the benefits of awareness and the costs of living mindlessly;
- recognizing the sacred in people, things, and ourselves;
- reducing and relinquishing attachments;
- cultivating generosity and service to others;
- seeking wisdom in nature, silence, and solitude.

Study 2: Spiritually-Oriented Group for Older Female Trauma Survivors

This study evaluated the effectiveness of a spiritually-oriented group intervention intended to lessen the physical and mental health symptoms of a group of older female trauma survivors (Bowland, Edmond, & Fallot, 2012). The study tested four hypotheses as follows: "a group intervention supporting the discussion of spiritual struggles and strengths and the development of new spiritual resources would reduce trauma-related post-traumatic stress, depression, anxiety, and somatic symptoms for older survivors of interpersonal trauma who indicated interest in such a group" (p. 74). The research design that the researchers used was an experiment using a control group. Three points in time were designated for measuring the four outcome variables: a pretest, 11 weeks later as a posttest, and three months beyond the time they completed the intervention. The ethics involved in assigning some of the women to a control group on a random basis was partially addressed by offering the opportunity for them to join the treatment group at a later time.

Their intervention consisted of an 11-session group offering spiritual interventions. Spiritual strengths were emphasized, including how spiritual strengths could help these older women. Also, the sessions focused on the difficulties that these women may have had growing up with backgrounds involving patriarchal Christianity and the burdens it may have imposed. The intervention was chosen because it has been used successfully before and is a manualized psychoeducational, cognitive-restructuring, and skill-building approach for addressing spiritual struggles in recovery from trauma.

Study 3: Forgiveness Psychoeducational Program for Seventh Day Adventists

The third study was a psychoeducational program that was designed to enhance a group of clients' forgiveness capabilities; it was run by social workers (Hernandez, Vonderfecht, Smith, Cress, Davis, & Bigger, 2012). Eighty-one clients participated in an eight-hour seminar over two days that presented forgiveness from a perspective of physical, spiritual, emotional, and relational wholeness. There was no control group. Their study investigated the impact of this program on 85 Christians who were almost entirely Seventh Day Adventists and mostly Caucasian. The program's curriculum included:

- an overview of forgiveness;
- mental health and physiological correlates of non-forgiveness;
- Biblical references and resources to enhance forgiveness capacity;
- a model describing the process of forgiveness based on Cognitive Behavioral, Reality Therapy, and Narrative Therapies;
- several dyadic exercises, which provided opportunities to practice forgiveness skills.

An underlying principle of this intervention was the belief that combining divine resources and human effort enables humans to perform cognitive and affective tasks needed for successful forgiveness of grievances. Several outcome measures were used to determine the program's impact on the participants. They included a forgiveness inventory, an anger index, a pain scale, and intensive interviews to evaluate how participants were affected. The results revealed some significant improvements in the forgiveness inventory, including significantly more forgiveness about their self-identified offenses and significantly improved overall cognitive responses to their forgiveness issue. They also reported a significant decrease in the amount of anger associated with the forgiveness issue as well as their verbalization of it. Feelings of pain associated with their forgiveness issues also significantly decreased. There were no significant differences reported in the behavioral aspects of their forgiveness.

Research Questions for Topic 3

While faith-based and other spiritually based programs are rapidly growing in number, the evidence that they are effective in helping clients reach their goals is not well documented. Evaluations of both faith-based and secular programs are important to conduct (Ragan, 2004). Among the research questions that need to be investigated are:

- What types of spiritual and religious interventions have been used and are currently available to be used? For each of these interventions, what evidence is available indicating that they have been effective in helping at least some client groups?
- What are the spiritual and religious elements in these interventions that are likely to be associated with changing client outcomes?
- What outcome measures have been used to determine the impact of a spiritual intervention on clients? What spiritually-related outcome measures in particular have been used and how have they been measured? Further, how valid and reliable are they?
- What impact does the context of a faith-based agency have on the spiritual interventions they provide and the client outcome measures they use? How are they different from the contextual influence of secular agencies?
- Overall, are faith-based programs effective? Are they more effective than secular programs in addressing the same problems?

Conclusion

Evaluation is the fourth component of a spiritually sensitive practice approach. Evaluation provides the means for determining many things important to spiritually sensitive practice. Evaluation tools can assist in defining what spirituality and spiritually sensitive practice are. Also, evaluation tools can help in determining if social workers are prepared to provide spiritually sensitive practice. Most importantly, evaluation tools can determine if spiritually sensitive interventions are effective in helping clients. An empowering perspective on evaluations is described to help clients gain the most benefits from such an evaluation. Extensive information is provided on how to conduct evaluations using quasi-experimental and experimental group designs. Finally, three efficacy studies are described, including the spiritual interventions and the group design that they used.

Discussion Questions and Exercises

1. As the chapter indicates, a client's spirituality can be difficult to define and measure. Both qualitative and quantitative question methods are usually needed. What questions would you ask clients to measure how spiritual and religious they are? What are some of the limitations of these questions?

2. If you were an administrator of an agency, how would you address the question of defining or not defining spirituality and religion? If you were to decide to define spirituality and religion for clients and staff members to have prior awareness of what they are and their importance, how would you define them in the context of your agency? If you were to decide not to define these terms, how would this be a possible problem for your staff members in addressing spiritual or religious concerns if they were brought up by clients?

3. Three efficacy studies are described in the chapter. Select the spiritual intervention used in one of these studies and explore whether it could be used with your clients, possibly with some modifications. Would the client outcomes identified in that study fit the needs of your clients?

References

ap Siôn, T., & Nash, P. (2013). Coping through prayer: An empirical study in implicit religion concerning prayers for children in hospital. *Mental Health, Religion & Culture, 16*(9), 936–952.

Bolin, B. B., Lee, K. H., Glenmaye, L. F., & Yoon, D. P. (2012). Impact of research orientation on attitudes toward research of social work students. *Journal of Social Work Education, 48*, 223–243.

Bolman, L. G., & Deal, T. E. (1995). *Leading with soul.* San Francisco: Jossey-Bass.

Bowland, S., Edmond, T., & Fallot R. D. (2012). Evaluation of a spiritually focused intervention with older trauma survivors. *Social Work, 57*, 73–82.

Campbell, D., & Blunt, E. (2006). Assessing the effectiveness of faith-based programs: A local network perspective. *Journal of Religion & Spirituality in Social Work: Social Thought, 25*(3–4), 241–259.

Canda, E. R., & Furman, L. D. (2010). *Spiritual diversity in social work practice.* 2nd edition. New York: Oxford University Press.

Chamiec-Case, R. (2009). Developing a scale to measure social workers' integration of spirituality in the workplace. *Journal of Religion and Spirituality in Social Work: Social Thought, 28*(3), 284–305.

DePoy, E., Hartman, A., & Haslett, D. (1999). Critical action research: A model for social work knowing. *Social Work, 44*(6), 560–569.

Doe, S. S. (2004). Spirituality-based social work values for empowering human service organizations. *Journal of Religion & Spirituality in Social Work: Social Thought, 23*(3), 45–65.

Dudley, J. (2014). *Social work evaluations: Enhancing what we do.* 2nd edition. Chicago: Lyceum Books.

Elmore, A., Davis, M., & Dudley, J. (2015). What community agencies say about their spirituality policies. Unpublished research report. University of North Carolina at Charlotte, Charlotte, NC.

Fetterman, D. M., Kaftarian, S. J., & Wandersman, A. (Eds.) (1996). *Empowerment evaluation: Knowledge and tools for self-assessment and accountability.* Thousand Oaks, CA: Sage Publications.

Finney, J. R., & Malony, H. N. (1985). Empirical studies of Christian prayer: A review of the literature. *Journal of Psychology and Theology, 13*(2), 104–115.

Graddy, E. A. (2006). How do they fit? Assessing the role of faith-based organizations in social service provision. *Journal of Religion & Spirituality in Social Work: Social Thought, 25*(3), 129–150.

Grettenberger, S. E., Bartkowski, J. P., Smith, S. R. (2006). Evaluating the effectiveness of faith-based welfare agencies: Methodological challenges and possibilities. *Journal of Religion & Spirituality in Social Work: Social Thought, 25*(3), 223–240.

Harder, J. (2010). Overcoming MSW students' reluctance to engage in research. *Journal of Teaching in Social Work, 30,* 195–209.

Hernandez, B. C., Vonderfecht, H., Smith, S. B., Cress, P. K., Davis, R., & Bigger, D. (2012). Development and evaluation of a faith-based psychoeducational approach to forgiveness for Christians. *Journal of Religion & Spirituality in Social Work: Social Thought, 31*(3), 263–284.

Hodge, D. R., & Wolosin, R. J. (2012). Addressing older adults' spiritual needs in health care settings: An analysis of inpatient hospital satisfaction data. *Journal of Social Service Research, 38*(2), 187–198.

Hugen, B., & Venema, R. (2009). The difference of faith: The influence of faith in human service programs. *Journal of Religion & Spirituality in Social Work: Social Thought, 28*(4), 405–429.

Kaplar, M. E., Wachholtz, A. B., & O'Brien, W. H. (2004). The effect of religious and spiritual interventions on the biological, psychological, and spiritual outcomes of oncology patients. *Journal of Psychosocial Oncology, 22*(1), 39–49.

Kaseman, M., & Austin, M. J. (2012). Building a faith-based human service agency. *Journal of Religion & Spirituality in Social Work: Social Thought, 24*(3), 69–91.

Koszycki, D., Bilodeau, C., Raab-Mayo, K., & Bradwejn, J. (2014). A multifaith spiritually based intervention versus supportive therapy for generalized anxiety disorder: A pilot randomized controlled trial. *Journal of Clinical Psychology, 70*(6), 489–509.

Larsen, K. M. (2011). How spiritual are social workers? An exploration of social work practitioners' personal spiritual beliefs, attitudes, and practices. *Journal of Religion & Spirituality in Social Work: Social Thought, 30*(1), 17–33.

Mears, D. P., Roman, C. G., Wolff, A., & Buck, J. (2006). Faith-based efforts to improve prisoner reentry: Assessing the logic and evidence. *Journal of Criminal Justice, 34,* 351–367.

Neff, J. A., Shorkey, C. T., & Windsor, L. C. (2006). Contrasting faith-based and traditional substance abuse treatment programs. *Journal of Substance Abuse Treatment, 30,* 49–61.

Oxhandler, H. K., & Pargament, K. L. (2014). Social work practitioners' integration of clients' religion and spirituality in practice: A literature review. *Social Work, 59*(3), 271–279.

Peteet, J. R., & Balboni, M. J. (2013). Spirituality and religion in oncology. *CA: A Cancer Journal for Clinicians, 63*(4), 280–289.

Ragan, M. (2004). *Faith-based vs. secular: Using administrative data to compare the per-formance of faith-affiliated and other social service providers*. Albany, NY: Rockefeller Institute of Government.

Sheridan, M. (2009). Ethical issues in the use of spiritually based interventions in social work practice: What we are doing and why. *Journal of Religion & Spirituality in Social Work: Social Thought, 28*(1/2), 99–126.

Smith, K. M., & Teasley. (2009). Social work research on faith-based programs: A movement towards evidence-based practice. *Journal of Religion & Spirituality in Social Work: Social Thought, 28*(3), 306–327.

Svare, G. M., Hylton, M., & Albers, E. (2007). On our own: Social workers talk about spiritually sensitive practice within an organizational context. *Journal of Religion and Spirituality in Social Work: Social Thought, 26*(4), 95–113.

Thyer, B. A. (2006). Faith-based programs and the role of empirical research. *Journal of Religion & Spirituality in Social Work: Social Thought, 25*(3–4), 63–82.

Waechter, R. L., & Wekerle, C. (2015). Promoting resilience among maltreated youth using meditation, yoga, tai chi and qigong: A scoping review of the literature. *Child and Adolescent Social Work Journal, 32*(1), 17–31.

Walsh, R. (1999). *Essential spirituality: The 7 central practices to awaken heart and mind*. New York: John Wiley & Sons.

Yonker, J. E., Schnabelrauch, C. A., & DeHaan, L. G. (2012). The relationship between spiri-tuality and religiosity on psychological outcomes in adolescents and emerging adults: A meta-analytic review. *Journal of Adolescence, 35*, 299–314.

Zimmerman, M. A. (2000). Empowerment theory: Psychological, organizational, and com-munity levels of analysis. In J. Rappaport & E. Seldman (Eds.), *Handbook of community psychology*. New York: Plenum, 43–63.

13

Tools for Your Journey

Don't you know yet? It is Your Light that lights the worlds.

(Rumi in Harvey, 1996)

You must be the change you want to see in the world.

(Mahatma Gandhi)

Our focus in this final chapter is on personal preparation for spiritually sensitive practice. In part it picks up on personal issues where chapter 2 left off. Chapter 2 assists the reader in exploring your own spirituality and religious or non-religious affiliations, an important initial step prior to engaging the spirituality of your clients. This chapter helps you take further steps in your journey to prepare yourself to become a more spiritually sensitive practitioner. The topics of preparation for this journey covered in the chapter are tools that you are encouraged to develop along the way. They are:

- Understand some of the challenges that practitioners face in the workplace.
- Claim self-care as a priority in your practice.
- Use spiritual tools to promote your self-care.
- Add tools to increase your happiness.
- Incorporate an awareness of joy into your practice.
- Learn from a variety of spiritual and religious perspectives.
- Explore a personal spiritual practice as a discipline.

As you take a closer look at these topics, you are also encouraged to explore more deeply who you are and are becoming personally and professionally. These topics are intended primarily for you, not your clients. Hopefully, they offer you a variety of ways of preparing to provide spiritually sensitive practice.

Understanding the Challenges for Practitioners

Preparation for work in the health and human service fields is important for numerous reasons. A growing number of concerns are evident in the workplace. Because these factors have a major impact on preparation for practice, we will begin with them. These concerns unfortunately are more often negative than positive and are evident both in work with clients and working within the context of an agency setting.

A pertinent mantra in many settings seems to be, "Do more with less." Funding restrictions have resulted in increased client workloads, stagnant wages, diminishing health and retirement benefits, too little appreciation of practitioners, increasing numbers of ethical problems, and less practitioner access to decision-making processes affecting client services (Skovholt & Trotter-Mathison, 2011; Laidag, 2007).

In addition, the multifaceted problems of growing numbers of clients sometimes can have an overwhelming impact on the human service system and its caregivers, and pose major challenges to problem solving. Clients are accessing services when they are already beset with multiple problems, and many of these problems, like chronic mental illness and obesity, have limited workable solutions. Also, a growing number of clients have involuntary or mandated status and appear, at least on the surface, less willing to engage the problems confronting them. Likely many clients feel they have little if any control over their lives and have lost faith and hope that their future will be any better. One overall effect of these and other developments is that too many practitioners are increasingly feeling frustrated and unhappy, and experiencing growing fatigue, cynicism, and eventually burnout (Cox & Steiner, 2013; Skovholt & Trotter-Mathison, 2011). Social work may be becoming a less desirable profession in the eyes of many practitioners because of all these challenges, diminishing positive supports, and forgotten reasons for why they joined the profession in the first place.

At the agency organizational level, the continued decline in funding for health and human service programs, growing competition for diminishing funds, and a greater presence of for-profit agencies and other new organizations are evident. Further, many of the newer providers often appear to be more interested in what's in it for them than what benefits their clients. In addition, consolidation and demands for increased efficiency are increasing and often can mean less actual assistance to clients. All of these factors are bringing further stress into the workplace. Along with these trends, funding sources are less likely to endorse many basic evidence-based practice principles such as being client-centered, being where the client is, and continuing client contact when it is needed. Instead, many agencies are giving emphasis to brief and often one-session contacts because of restrictive funding requirements.

Burnout can occur at many levels—physical, mental, emotional, and spiritual (Sheridan, 2012). It gradually develops with time and it often involves a deep devotion to helping a group of clients while minimizing or ignoring what it is doing to ourselves. Important areas of our self-care, such as getting adequate sleep, eating nutritiously, and regularly exercising become increasingly neglected. We find ourselves having less time set aside for fun, quality time with family and friends, and commitment to nurturing our spirit. Burnout can also take over when despair is more evident among our clients than hope. During current times, many of our social agencies are perceived as less and less a place where clients can make substantial improvements (Loeb, 2010; Maslach & Gomes, 2006; Sheridan, 2012).

Practitioners are also vulnerable to succumbing to vicarious trauma after continually witnessing clients and others who suffer from trauma, neglect, and basic social injustices (Cox & Steiner, 2013; Perlman & Saakvitne, 1995). This psychological and mental condition is most likely to occur when a worker exclusively or primarily helps clients who are experiencing trauma over a period of time. Examples include working exclusively with clients experiencing domestic abuse, HIV, or those who are dying. One way to minimize this effect could be to have more diversity of clients in a workload. For example, one social worker who works exclusively with AIDS clients every workday decided he was not going to continue to volunteer to work with the HIV community outside his job; this was his way of finding balance and improved coping.

A variety of terms, some more familiar than others, are evident in the literature for describing some of the problems faced by social workers and other human service workers personally. They include greater work stress, burnout, greater insecurity and risks of dangers, compassion fatigue, and secondary traumatic stress (Dane, 2002; Cox & Steiner, 2013; Figley, 1995). Definitions for some of these problems are described in the box below.

It's important to note that these negative descriptors are more evident in some agencies, and much less in others. There are many supportive and empowering workplaces across the country that are practicing exemplary evidence-based practice (Boudrias et al., 2011). Also, these models of exemplary practice are within reasonable reach for most other agencies.

Some Stress-Related Self-Care Problems

Stress—a process experienced by an individual when any environmental event is appraised as taxing or exceeding a person's resources and possibly endangering their well-being (Lazarus & Folkman, 1984).

Compassion fatigue—a pattern of exhausting emotions or behaviors that can occur when a social worker seeks to help traumatized or suffering people (Figley, 1995).

Vicarious traumatization—a psychological and mental condition that can occur when a social worker empathically engages with the trauma of clients continually over time. This problem can manifest itself as an over-identification with the clients' circumstances, reduced energy for client relationships, and less hope for success (Cox & Steiner, 2013; Perlman & Saakvitne, 1995).

Insecurities and potential dangers—client- and neighborhood-related exposures to threats, violence, potential harm, oppositional behavior, and related perceptions.

Burnout—the gradual draining of energy that can occur for social workers after they are persistently exhausted emotionally and physically from their jobs (Cox & Steiner, 2013).

Many of the problems cited above will not be easily solved. Examples include increasing wages and other benefits for practitioners, reducing caseloads, and placing greater emphasis on the needs of clients and less on cost efficiency and profit motives. Solving many of these problems will require commitments to new public policies, substantially more funding for health and human services, more innovative and early preventive interventions, and more organizational efforts to establish effective interventions. Many of these problems also clearly call for more advocacy and social justice efforts by social workers and others. In addition, more assistance is needed by many practitioners to become more fully prepared for effective practice.

Commit to Self-Care

Self-care for social workers and other human service workers is becoming more of a necessity at a time when greater attention is called for in addressing problems like greater work stress, compassion fatigue, and burnout. We all know, at some level of consciousness, that we cannot care for others and neglect or ignore our own needs. Yet, ironically that is what a lot of us drawn to social work have a tendency to do. We become great advocates for the people we serve but do not advocate very well for ourselves.

In response to these problems, recent literature on self-care and human services work is well worth considering (e.g. Collins, 2005; Cox & Steiner, 2013; Norcross & Guy, 2007; Skovholt & Trotter-Mathison, 2011). Most importantly, they suggest balancing empathy for clients with "standing apart" or having a healthy distance from them. Further, Cox and Steiner (2013) suggest that we can do more to discover the positive effects surrounding distressing events frequently faced by social workers. Among their specific suggestions for some are to be more fully present in work, find self-acceptance in just doing the best you can, and use free time more for gaining pleasure. Folkman (2008) among others found extensive evidence that positive emotions such as those reflected in the above suggestions can be important in coping and reducing stress processes. Some of this evidence indicates that positive emotions, when introduced in the workplace, can be important in coping and reducing stress processes.

What follows are several recommendations for helping practitioners in their preparation. These suggestions are not an exhaustive list, but they can help you develop a more positive and hopeful perspective, provide you with additional coping skills for combatting these problems, empower you, and in some cases contribute to bringing greater social justice to the health and human service enterprises. These suggestions are grouped into the following areas:

• spiritual tools and resources
• tools for greater happiness
• finding joy in your work.

Spiritual Tools for Self-Care

Studies exploring the relationship between health and stress have reported that spirituality and religion can play a key role in managing stressful events (Collins, 2005; Koenig & Spano, 2007). For example, Milano (1998) examined research on the relationship between religious commitment and a range of problems including depression, substance abuse, physical illness, mortality, coping with illness, and recovering from illness. The findings indicated that spiritual and religious involvement may be beneficial in preventing physical and mental illness, facilitating recovery from illness, and helping people cope with both physical and mental illness. Other researchers (Mackenzie, Rajagopal, Meibohm, & Lavizzo-Mourey, 2000; Musgrave et al., 2002) found that people with medical conditions like diabetes and arthritis reduced the anxiety and stress in their lives when they used spiritual rituals such as meditating, praying, reciting mantras, and reading from the Bible, Quran, or other holy works.

Self-care and spirituality are related to each other in numerous ways. The topic of spirituality comes to mind for many when we think about self-care. Both spirituality and self-care have similar objectives—taking time to pay attention to our personal needs, affirming and valuing what we do to help clients, learning from our experiences, and avoiding obstacles that can discourage us and impede healthy ways of helping others. Chapters 1 and 2 offer definitions of spirituality and religion. They also describe how some people view spirituality as one of several dimensions of a holistic perspective. Others view spirituality in a broader and more encompassing way that provides meaning, purpose, morality, well-being, and profundity in relationships with ourselves, others, and ultimate reality. Canda and Furman (2010, p. 87) describe their view of spirituality as a holistic model of spirituality. This model is displayed in a diagram as three concentric circles. The inner circle identifies spirituality as the center of the person. The next largest circle is divided into four aspects of a person's daily life—spiritual, biological, sociological, and psychological. The largest circle refers to "spirituality as the wholeness of the person in relation with all."

When we examine self-care as a problem to address, we will likely view it differently depending upon how we view spirituality. If we view spirituality as one of several dimensions of the person, we will likely treat it as one of many sources of resources to consider in helping practitioners. Some authors argue for this dimensional definition. Alkema, Linton, and Davies (2008) are an example of this in their study of hospice professionals. They asked their research participants what areas they depended on for self-care. Their list of results included the following sources, with examples of each:

1. physical self-care—e.g. eating well, exercising
2. psychological self-care—e.g. self-reflecting, journaling

3. emotional self-care—e.g. engaging in laughing and play
4. spiritual self-care—e.g. praying, meditating
5. professional self-care—e.g. taking breaks, balancing caseloads.

Body, Mind, and Spirit

In some contrast, those who view spirituality more broadly will likely view its role to have more influence in self-care. Perhaps they will have a view of body, mind, and spirit (BMS) as being interconnected entities (Leung, Chan, Ng, & Lee, 2009). From this unified perspective, for example, the mind would be replenished with mindful activities that help it to be more fully present to the body and spirit. The body would be an important source of understanding about pain, physical balance, and the need for exercise; it would also be more fully present in the here and now. Eating, for example, could place value on nutritious foods and mindful eating, and the time of eating would become a mindful and spiritual as well as a biological experience.

Leung et al. (2009) reframe this Eastern perspective of BMS so that it fits well with social work concepts. They propose that BMS be introduced as a way of promoting three goals in practice. First, BMS stresses the need to develop balance among the body, mind, and spirit. Second, BMS fosters highlighting the client's strengths. Third, this perspective gives emphasis to finding deeper meaning in the client's issues. As

---

Body Scan

Leung and associates (2009) suggest an exercise called a body scan. This is an exercise that a client can do. The client is asked to sit in a relaxed position, close her eyes, and concentrate on her breathing. Once the client is relaxed, she is asked to follow the rhythm of her breathing and begin paying attention to the various parts of the body. Beginning with her head, the client becomes totally focused on her head and notices any pain or discomfort. If pain is present there, she breathes healing energy into this area. Next, the neck is scanned and becomes a focus if there is any pain. Next moving through her body, she follows the same steps of stopping, noticing, and breathing healing energy into the next body part; the upper chest, the left arm and hand, right arm and hand, her stomach, until she reaches her feet and toes. Afterward, the client can share what she experienced, which can help her to explore the underlying meaning associated with any pain or discomfort, such as possible concerns or worries. People tend to manifest their stress, worries, and anxiety somewhere in their body without being aware that this is happening. The body scan brings insight and wisdom about the connections among body, mind, and spirit.

a practice perspective, these authors address the client domains of the physical, the mental and emotional, and the spiritual and existential. Changes in each of these domains is likely to induce change in the others. For example, breathing, awareness of the body, and movement are introduced in the physical domain to help elicit changes in the mental and emotional domains. Then, the mental/emotional and spiritual domains can help to reframe meaning and purposes in one's life.

Interventions in these three areas (body, mind, and spirit) are identified to help readers become more aware of each area and their connections (Leung et al., 2009). Examples of these interventions in the body include breathing, breathing meditation, therapeutic massage, tai chi/qigong exercises, and movement. The mental and emotional interventions include emotional validation, cognitive reframing, normalizing, and acceptance. Spiritual interventions include restructuring the meaning of pain and stress and focusing on transformation or moving to a place of deeper meaning.

Cox and Steiner (2013) discuss both personal and organizational strategies for promoting self-care. Many of their strategies are spiritual in nature or have spiritual implications. They view greater self-awareness as important in identifying physical pain and tension in our bodies caused by work stress. Self-awareness is also helpful to us in uncovering emotional symptoms of exhaustion, such as lapses in concentration and having difficulty making decisions. In addition, it helps us to come to grips with behavioral signs such as defensiveness, irritability, and greater use of alcohol or drugs. Self-awareness is also important to spiritual well-being in that we are encouraged to know who we really are at a deeper level and to be aware of and ward off a variety of stressors at our work sites that interfere with being effective in helping clients.

Self-care, according to some of the experts, also calls for helping professionals to practice mindfulness in combatting burnout (Cox & Steiner, 2013; Gockel, Cain, Malove, & James, 2013; McGarrigle & Walsh, 2012; Hicks, 2009; Skovholt et al., 2011). Being mindful in the present moment can produce a state of calm that can counteract many of the stressors of the work environment. When worries, anxieties, and self-deprecating thoughts come to mind, mindfulness can bring us back to reality as we concentrate on the present moment and our purpose in helping clients and collaborating with colleagues. Mindfulness can help us concentrate on what we can do to help clients without overdoing or unrealistically pursuing initiatives that we cannot realistically carry out. Compassion fatigue can result from going too far in expressing empathy with clients for our emotional well-being or being empathic with too many people without adequate rest and rejuvenation in between contacts. Cox and Steiner (2013) describe several mindfulness activities that practitioners can practice in and out of a work setting in three areas that reflect care of self. Visual practices could include such things as watching the movement of birds while walking in the woods, watching the fall of snow flakes, or noticing colors in the immediate surroundings. Audio practices of mindfulness could include listening to

Exercise on Mindfulness

Cox and Steiner (2013) suggest three different types of mindfulness practices—visual, audio, and tactile. Select one of them and practice what they propose or a variation of it for three consecutive days. Then discuss how the experience went with another person.

one instrument playing in a musical piece, noticing the sounds of children playing, or listening to the sounds of birds, animals, and insects in the woods. Tactile practices could be consciously giving attention to our breathing, periodically stretching our limbs to a place of comfort, or noticing the sensation of water over us during a shower or bath.

Spirituality, Self-Care, Organizational Strategies, and Workplace Wellness

Self-care authors also recommend organizational strategies to combat stress and burnout (Cox & Steiner, 2013; Norcross & Guy, 2007; Skovholt et al., 2011). They and others stress the importance of knowing the organizations in which we work, their overall purposes, and the extent to which they are compatible with who we are. Incompatibilities and overextending our personal boundaries can lead to greater stress. For example, are our job description and the assigned tasks realistic and in tune with our expertise, passions, and energy and comfort level? Knowing ourselves speaks volumes in being able to monitor how we are affected, moment by moment and over time, by what we do and with whom we work—clients, supervisors, administrators, and peers. How well do our passions and our skills fit with the clients with whom we work? How much respect and appreciation do we receive from the people to whom we report—supervisors, team leaders, and administrators—and how much do we need expressions of their appreciation? Also, within service organizations there can be many dysfunctional elements that can cause or exacerbate excessive stress and burnout. The list of organizational stressors can be almost limitless, such as overlooking the value of each staff member, indirect and faulty organizational communication, unnecessary competitiveness, both subtle and blatant unethical practices, unexplained expediencies that serve some and not others, a variety of informal ways of demeaning those who are less valued, a lack of clarity about what is expected, and demands by those in authority to deliver more than employees can reasonably do.

Workplace wellness is an important concept to consider when addressing problems in health and human service organizations (Cox & Steiner, 2013; Gantner, 2012; Skovholt et al., 2011). Workplace wellness involves implementing policies and practices that can effectively address stress, chronic fatigue, and burnout. Among efforts to promote psychological health are increasing employee involvement in the affairs of the organization (Grawitch, Gottschalk, & Munz, 2006). Examples include conducting employee opinion and satisfaction polls, offering forums on issues of importance to employees, and providing employees with a role in decision-making processes that affect their jobs.

Another proposed effort of workplace wellness is to encourage work-family balance. Agency policies are needed that promote a work-family balance, including offering family-supportive policies like family and medical time off, maternity and paternity leave, and a reasonable amount of vacation time. All of these initiatives also promote the spirituality of employees. Agencies wanting to help employees work out a balance in their lives can introduce them to the varied repertoire of spiritual practices described in this book.

Psychological health, a central concept of workplace wellness, refers to helping people feel peaceful, connected to others, relatively free of stress, free of harassment, and generally satisfied with their jobs (Boudrias et al., 2011). Psychological health clearly overlaps with spiritual health. All of these qualities are relevant to spirituality, as spirituality is also equated with being peaceful, in harmony with others, unencumbered by negative interferences in one's life, and being relatively content with oneself and one's circumstances.

Workplace wellness also has direct implications for implementing spiritually sensitive practice with clients. Agencies that offer spiritually sensitive practice hopefully have defined what spirituality and spiritual practices mean to them and they have delineated specific policies and procedures for implementing these policies. They have also prepared their staff members to be equipped to effectively assist their clients with such services. Good supervision is another way to combat many of the dysfunctional organizational practices mentioned earlier. First, there needs to be compatibility between supervisor and supervisee. Supervisors should be prepared to help with professional guidance as well as giving clarity about what the organization expects in terms of quantity and quality of practice. Good communication can create a trusting atmosphere for supervisees so that they can appropriately bring up any of these organizational problems and expect constructive ways for the supervisee and supervisor to jointly address them. In addition, the supervisors need to be considered when it comes to stress and burnout. They need to have knowledge about the problems of work stress, compassion fatigue, and burnout and the solutions available to overcome them. Supervisors also need to have enough time to meet with each of their supervisees.

Tools for Increasing Your Happiness

Some researchers have recently focused attention on two areas of positive emotion, happiness and joy. Both areas are important in preparing and sustaining healthy practices with clients. Happiness is an area of study pertinent to both personal well-being and preparation for spiritually sensitive social work. Several authors have recently investigated the topic of happiness as a mental health issue (e.g. Diener & Biswas-Diener, 2008; King, 2014; Lyubomirsky, 2007; Seligman, 2002). Happiness is positively associated with greater job satisfaction, greater productivity, and greater income (Seligman, 2002). People who are happy also endure pain better and more easily undo negative emotions.

The focus of Lyubomirsky's work, based on extensive research, is on how a person can increase their happiness. Lyubomirsky, Sheldon, and Schkade (2005) discovered a valuable finding about what determines happiness. They reported that 50 percent of the causes of happiness was found to result from heredity or genetic disposition; they suggest that this realm of causes was largely fixed and beyond significant change. In addition, only 10 percent was due to external circumstances such as the amount of money a person has (once people reached a reasonably adequate level of income), marital status, beauty, health, and other such factors.

These researchers claim that the remaining sources of influence, fully 40 percent of the causes of happiness, are determined by the intentional activities of people, their thoughts and behavior. Examples of this that Lyubomirsky and colleagues (2005) shared were the amount of quality time they chose to spend with family and friends, comfort with expressing gratitude for what they had, efforts to help others in need, optimism about their future, living in the present moment and savoring these moments, making physical exercise a regular habit, commitment to lifelong goals, and a capacity to cope well with their tragedies and crises. It's important to note that several of these perspectives and actions are also evident in being spiritual (Diener & Biswas-Diener, 2008). Enjoying a focus on others, desiring to help others, being comfortable expressing gratitude, and living in the moment are examples.

Based on these examples of behaviors associated with happiness, it's no surprise that Lyubomirsky and her colleagues (2005) go on to propose strategies that are similar to the above examples. Their recommended strategies for happiness are many. Among them are those listed next. These strategies also have spiritual aspects to them.

Expressing Gratitude

Expressing gratitude for what we have can become a regular routine of personal self-reflection as well as an important focus when talking with others (Lyubomirsky, 2007; Seligman, 2002). An important way to be mindful of gratitude in your life is to take time on a regular basis to reflect on what has recently happened for which you are grateful. So many big and small things can come to mind, such as a friendly smile from a colleague, a safe trip to and from a conference, a special meal prepared by your partner, a positive health checkup, being free of anxiety, relief from an allergy, a compliment, a chance to tell someone how much you appreciate them,

Strategies for Finding Happiness

1. expressing gratitude for what you have

2. avoiding overthinking and social comparisons

3. practicing acts of kindness

4. nurturing social relationships

5. learning to forgive

6. savoring life's joys

etc. Expressing gratitude on a regular basis can keep negative thoughts at bay or at least in balance. Examples of negative thoughts could be complaining about being alone or lonely, being angry about being unfairly criticized by a supervisor, and stewing on why you had to get the flu.

Avoiding Overthinking and Downplaying Social Comparisons

Avoiding overthinking and downplaying social comparisons are other helpful strategies for promoting self-care (Lyubomirsky, 2007). They can also be viewed as spiritual in nature. When we ruminate on a difficult work situation over and over, we may end up with a less productive and more pessimistic perspective on the outcome. In contrast, avoiding overthinking and drawing on mindfulness, meditation practices, and transcendence can lead us in a more productive direction. We can allow ourselves to be open to the unfolding process of the other people's views and the unknown from which we may be able to discover some unanticipated and creative solutions to the work assignment. Similarly, social comparisons can be a hindrance to our efforts when working with clients. Comparing our potential with that of a colleague may lead to less self-confidence and more unproductive distractions away from our primary intentions, to help clients. Such comparisons can fuel unhealthy competition with colleagues, while a spiritually motivated approach may emphasize bringing together what you and your colleagues can learn from each other and do together to benefit clients.

Practicing Acts of Kindness

Practicing acts of kindness is another strategy that social workers can consider almost any time, especially during their work hours (Lyubomirsky, 2007; Seligman, 2002). Each contact with a client can be viewed as a potential act of kindness, even though we may not always think of our contacts in this way. Having a conversation with a colleague or family member who needs someone to talk with can also be viewed in this light. Contacts with strangers and adversaries can also be viewed as an opportunity for kindness, and it often has to happen in a split second of opportunity. Just imagine the influence that a kind act can have on a chain of events of numerous people, first receiving a kind act and then passing it on in another way to someone else. Acts of kindness can be large or small, involve an enormous amount of our time and resources or they can be brief, simple, and expressed with a smile or word of appreciation. Kind acts can be viewed as giving ourselves away to others in some way. It may be listening to a colleague who has just lost a close friend, having a meal with someone who usually eats alone, giving money to a special cause, or just listening more deeply to what anyone says.

Nurturing Social Relationships

Another example of a set of strategies for promoting happiness and enhancing self-care involves nurturing social relationships. This can also be a strategy or a regular practice that serves self-care and spiritual expression. These relationships can be with colleagues, members of a social support network, clients, or others. Researchers (e.g. Diener & Biswas-Diener, 2008; Lyubomirsky, 2007) suggest that happiness and enhanced self-care can come from concentrating more on our relationships with others on the job and implementing steps that can strengthen these relationships in ways that benefit us, our colleagues, and ultimately our clients. Nurturing relationships with others outside work are also important, such as our partner or our children. We can do this in several ways. First, we can make more time to be in these relationships individually or in informal groups such as a get-together with neighbors. We can pursue these interactions by expressing more admiration, appreciation, and affection for others rather than what may be largely intellectual or small talk exchanges. With more fully developed and cooperative work relationships we can more easily address our differences and any conflicts that may arise in the future. Also, these relationships can be used to focus on ways to make the workplace more of a wellness enterprise and one that better serves clients (Diener & Biswas-Diener, 2008).

Learning to Forgive

Learning to forgive is also an important strategy, or more appropriately, a principle to live by (Lyubomirsky, 2007; McCullough, Pargament, & Thorensen, 2001;

Seligman, 2002). When someone treats us unfairly, ignores us, or does something to hurt us, the almost automatic response is to want to retaliate or to withdraw and pout about what took place. In neither case do we have an opportunity to convey how we may have been hurt, overlooked, or misunderstood. Nor do we open up to the possibility that this other person can better understand us and be given the opportunity to apologize. Forgiving someone takes courage and humility and it may make us feel vulnerable or weak. Yet, forgiving someone for something they have done against us can do more to help us and possibly help them. We can feel that the incident has been resolved, at least within us, and we can move on and avoid allowing this conflict to linger and distract us in the future. We can return to a comfortable emotional state and a sense of an internal resolution of what happened.

Savoring Life's Joys

Savoring life's joys is another strategy proposed to bring greater happiness and another sense of taking care of ourselves (Lyubomirsky, 2007; Seligman, 2002). Like gratitude, many positive things happen to us much of the time. Unfortunately, we may tend to downplay these positive experiences or overlook them. Or we may not view them as positive experiences unless we take time to reflect on them in our mind or with others and savor them as special. A breakthrough in a relationship with someone with whom we have had struggles is a moment to savor, whether it is with a family member, a colleague, or a casual acquaintance. Or a presentation that we have given or a helpful comment that we have made could be valuable or useful to others and deserves some savoring. So many positive things can happen to us if we reflect on them afterwards, and it helps to take time to relive them and enjoy and appreciate what they mean to us and possibly others.

Experiencing Joy in Your Practice

Being happy and feeling joy at the same time may occur often. Joy is a concept that is similar to happiness, as research in these two areas overlap in the field of positive psychology. Yet, joy is a concept that has meaning of its own. Buechner (1969) distinguishes happiness from joy by pointing out that we can create happiness in our lives while joy, in some contrast, comes from much more than what we do. Joy often appears unexpectedly as a gift for which we are not really responsible. It is a feeling with deep intensity whose source is less well known. Some would say it involves their Higher Power. Sometimes people are unexpectedly overcome with joy, such as when they see someone or something in a different light or with a renewed appreciation.

Happiness, on the other hand, is a more frequent state of mind and mood that can be achieved by taking on perspectives and actions such as those presented in the previous section. Buechner (1969) points out that we can create happiness

---

Joy

Joy seems to me a step beyond happiness. Happiness is a sort of atmosphere you can live in sometimes when you're lucky. Joy is a light that fills you with hope and faith and love.

(Adela Rogers St. Johns, 2010)

---

in our lives in several ways. For example, our choice of an intimate relationship with someone, a good job, or a wonderful vacation trip can bring happiness. Joy, in contrast, is more of a mystery that can happen anytime, anywhere, even in the midst of suffering or loss. Joy comes unexpectedly, sometimes suddenly, at a touching moment that is not repeatable. These moments can appear during a heart-felt exchange with a friend or a stranger, a glimpse of a sky full of beaming stars or the vibrant multicolored leaves of fall, or a realization that we are alive and have a world in front of us, for however long we do not care. It can also happen, for example, when progress is recognized and celebrated or a spontaneous exchange of appreciation occurs with a client or client group.

Pooler, Wolfer, and Freeman (2014a, 2014b) persuade us that joy is an important topic to consider in preventing burnout. They studied joy using a grounded theory approach, focusing on how research participants defined joy as it is expressed in social work. Their initial research questions ask, "As a social worker, in what do you find the most joy?" and "How do you find joy at work?" They do not provide a definition of joy but in their exploratory research encourage the respondents to introduce and develop their own definitions. Pooler and colleagues (2014a) followed up the responses of their participants' initial reflections on joy and the workplace with probes to learn more from the participants' own perspectives in their own words. Probes following expressions about joy were open-ended, like: What happened (when you found joy)? What effect did this experience have on you? On your work? On the way you see yourself as a social worker? Other probes went even further: How do you find joy at work? How would you tell a new social worker to find joy? What could you do to experience more joy at work?

Pooler and colleagues (2014a, 2014b) point out that most of the literature about the personal lives of social workers focuses on the negatives—depression, problem drinking, stress, and compassion fatigue. They found little information on the positives of being a social worker. They go on to say that this seems ironic since social workers attempt to give considerable emphasis to the strengths of their clients. Pooler and colleagues ask us why the profession is not looking at the strengths and other positive aspects in the lives of social workers. Positive psychology gives central attention to the positives in people (Fredrickson, 2001) and Pooler and colleagues' research is directly pertinent to this field of study. Positive psychology considers questions like: What makes life worth living? How do individuals find meaning in their lives? And how can organizations foster a positive climate for their staff members? Other social work researchers have pursued these issues as well, focusing proactively on compassion satisfaction, resilience, positive emotions, and optimism of social workers rather than just dwelling on the negativities (e.g. Collins, 2007; Radey & Figley, 2007).

The research interviews of Pooler, Wolfer, and Freeman (2014a, 2014b) were with social work students, a weakness of their study; investigating joy among practitioners with extensive experience would have been preferred. Their study was largely conversational form. They found that their responses reflected many themes about how and where joy was evident in the students' lives. Among the many interesting themes about joy expressed by various social work students in the sample are:

- Joy comes from making connections with some clients, being present with them and being heard by them. Joy also came from making positive connections with some colleagues.
- Joy comes from making a difference with clients, facilitating client changes, relieving client distress, and receiving gratitude. It also comes from affecting macro-level issues and creating innovative interventions.
- Joy also comes from making meaning in their jobs by finding a fit with their specific job and their identification with the social work profession and by finding pleasure and satisfaction in helping others.
- Joy came from making a life or gaining a perspective on what's important, being realistic about what to expect of oneself, and finding satisfaction and joy in little things. Joy was also gained by developing a perspective that you can always learn new things, gain self-confidence, and mature over time.

These sources of joy overlap considerably with spiritual notions. Joy involves finding meaning in what you do as a social worker, a spiritual notion. Spirituality is

---

Where Do You Find Joy in Social Work?

Take a few moments and ask yourself these questions:

- What does joy mean to you personally?
- Where do you find joy especially as a social worker? Can you identify three or four ways?
- Considering the above four themes found by Pooler and his colleagues, how are your ways of finding joy similar or different?
- What effect has your experience with joy had on you? On your work?

also closely tied to helping others and finding the joy in these contacts and in what happens as the helping process unfolds. Think about how these themes might be your themes as well and reflect on how they may bring joy to you by responding to the exercise on p. 331.

Nhat Hanh (2013) has suggestions for how to experience joy in the workplace and beyond through a Buddhist way of working. His ideas are also useful for non-Buddhists in the workplace. In his writings generally, Nhat Hanh usually offers very specific and practical things that people can do. He creatively does this in the work context in his book. Among his gems he discusses mindful ways of sitting, walking, answering the phone, a restroom meditation, handling strong emotions and anger, a peace treaty with fellow employees, loving speech, and mindful meetings among other things. Possibly by incorporating some of these activities into your work at your agency, you will be more sensitized to the presence of joy all around you.

Learn from a Variety of Religious and Spiritual Perspectives

There is a broad consensus within the human services community that preparation for professional practice is essential. In social work, the accreditation standards of the Council of Social Work (http://www.cswe.org/) articulate broadly what professional practice entails. Yet, we know that most social work students and graduates are not adequately prepared to work with the spiritual and religious needs of their clients (Canda & Furman, 2010; Furman & Chandy, 1994; Rothman, 2009; Sheridan, 2009). This is the case even though spirituality and religion are required content areas to cover in social work programs based on accreditation (CSWE, 2015). Among the ways that we can become more prepared to provide spiritually sensitive practice include taking courses and other professional programs on spirituality in social work, receiving supervision and consultation from professionals knowledgeable about spirituality, attending pertinent continuing education workshops, and other ways.

Ellor, Netting, and Thibault (1999) make the point that as human service workers we have an obligation to understand the role that spirituality and religion play in our own lives as well as the lives of clients. This is a position supported by two important social work principles. First, practitioners are expected to have self-awareness, including awareness of themselves as spiritual beings. Second, practitioners are to assume a holistic perspective that engages the biological, psychological, social, cultural, and spiritual dimensions of a client. As part of preparation for spiritually sensitive practice, Ellor and colleagues suggest that practitioners explore several questions to find out more about their knowledge, beliefs, attitudes, feelings, and practices pertaining to spirituality and religion. Many of these questions are similar to the ones described in chapter 2, while some go beyond these questions and explore potential areas of contention between the clients' and practitioners' spirituality that can pose obstacles to a spiritually sensitive approach. Some of the questions that can raise contentious issues in our work with clients are shared briefly as follows.

1. To what extent do I feel that my religious or spiritual beliefs or practices are the "best," or "better" or "preferred" way?
2. How do I feel working with clients with religious or spiritual views opposed or in conflict with my own?
3. To what extent am I open to learning about the religious or spiritual views of clients when they are different from my own?
4. To what extent am I willing to consult other professionals with expertise in religion or spirituality, especially in areas in which I do not have expertise?
5. How comfortable am I in self-disclosing my own thoughts about religion or spirituality to clients when it can be appropriate and helpful to my clients?
6. To what extent can I attempt to help clients who wish to explore transcendence or a Higher Power when I do not believe in either?

As an exercise, take another look at the spirituality and religion questions described in chapter 2. Then review the questions listed above. Afterward, find a colleague and discuss how each of you responds to these questions. In particular, discuss your responses to the questions that may seem most challenging for you in practicing spiritually sensitive social work.

Our Spiritual and Religious Motives for Becoming Social Workers

Some studies of social work students have uncovered an important reality that has been largely overlooked in many social work education programs. Many students at both the BSW and MSW levels have chosen to become social workers for spiritual and/or religious reasons (Canda & Furman, 2010; Rice & Dudley, 1997). This is not a surprise as people from religious backgrounds have pursued social work careers going all the way back to the early social work days of the settlement movement and charity organization societies. Most of these early agencies had church sponsors and church members as volunteers. Because the motives for choosing a social work career are important, we can not only encourage students to share their motives for wanting to become a social worker on admission applications; they can also be encouraged to openly share their spiritual and religious backgrounds in courses and in student meetings and exchanges where important socialization occurs.

These discussions can help students gain greater insight into the importance of their spirituality for themselves as well as the discovery of a wide range of spiritual expressions from other students. As examples, several African American students talked about the strong messages that they heard in the Black Church about "giving back to the community" (Rice & Dudley, 1997). Others talked about mission trips they went on with their churches. One said, "We ministered to the poor and elderly. During that time in my life I realized my desire to help and the gift that I had been given, a kind heart. When I considered a career and higher education I always came back to memories of these summers and the satisfaction I felt then." Most existing Spirituality and Social Work courses also encourage such discussions, but unfortunately the vast majority of social work students do not have access to such courses. A recommendation of the book is that a crucial part of preparing students to practice in a spiritually sensitive way includes having these discussions. Chapter 2 identifies several types of questions that can be explored in spirituality courses.

How Religious Groups Can Offer Help with Preparation

How do we live our lives? What do the different religions emphasize? Is there a prescribed or ideal way to live? If so, how do people know when they are following that way or drifting from it? What happens when they no longer follow such a path? Or what if a religious group does not explicitly prescribe how a member or follower should live their life? What gives a person's life its form and direction? Most religious and spiritual groups have much to offer on these questions. Religious groups often hold out an ideal self to which they strive. However, the many religious groups are far from agreement on all that that ideal self should be. Yet, they do remind us, among other things, that we are creatures who are always changing or in flux, whether for the better or worse. According to Walsh (1999), the great religions of the world help us in at least three important ways: 1) reducing painful feelings such as fear and anger; 2) fostering helpful attitudes like gratitude and generosity; and 3) cultivating positive emotions like love and compassion.

Religious groups like Buddhism can help us examine where we are in our development professionally and personally as we prepare ourselves for a spiritually sensitive practice approach. We have already discussed the importance of finding our true self in chapter 2. In contrast, our outer self is largely a product of our past and present—our childhood and later experiences, our current social roles and circumstances, and other societal influences. Many of us can be urged to review our existing lives, reflect on what parts of us could be improved or need changing, and work on developing a healthier sense of who we are. The Buddha described meditation as a means of cultivating healthy qualities of heart and character that are natural to us (Kornfield, 1993). Various Christian, Jewish, and Muslim prayer forms can help us develop these qualities as well. Some of these qualities are restraints from causing harm, kindness, perseverance, wakefulness, and compassion. Also spiritual qualities like steadiness, wisdom, faith, and mindfulness are encouraged.

Social workers' preparation for practice is important and has many dimensions to it. Kornfield (1993), a Buddhist therapist and monk, introduces an exercise titled "Who am I?" It is an exercise involving two people in which one asks the question "Who are you?" of the other person. The question is asked over and over and the other person responds with whatever comes to mind. In the beginning their responses may include general things such as I am a man or woman, a father or mother, a social worker or nurse. But as we are asked over and over, we are likely to go deeper and share reflections that may get at more of who we really are or want to be. This may include latent or undeveloped characteristics that have not been fully conscious before, insights into how our past lives have influenced who we are becoming, or evolving images of who we imagine becoming but haven't yet expressed or developed. Please consider finding another colleague with whom to participate in this exercise and see if it can be helpful to you.

The Buddha, when asked what he believed, replied, "I am awake." By being "awake" he was referring to what is happening in life in the here and now. Being awake means being free to fully see, hear, feel, and experience what is here now. Being awake also means being free of attachments, cravings, and other distractions (Walsh, 1999). Some of the most obvious attachments we have in our culture are possessions such as a fancy home and a sporty car, having power, having sex on our terms, high status, using drugs, and other culturally valued things. According to the Buddha, these attachments never seem to satisfy our appetites. We always seem to want more after an initial excitement and contentment and we never seem to get enough. Our lives can be quite easily distracted by our need for attachments or cravings that consume us and our time.

You might ask what this awakening concept has to do with living your life in a worthwhile way. Attachments are different from desires in that we feel we must have them, while desires can be freely pursued or ignored. According to the Buddha, the time and energy that goes into seeking and maintaining our attachments are likely to be costly and they will likely bring more suffering than pleasure (Walsh, 1999). For example, you may be dissatisfied with your physical surroundings where you live and feel compelled to go out and buy something new (e.g. new furniture

---

Exercise: Discovering Ourselves the Buddha Way (Walsh, 1999)

1. How awake do you think you are to what is happening in your daily life?

2. What attachments or cravings do you have? How powerful or compelling are they? To what extent do they distract you from being fully present?

3. Reflect on the costs of these attachments to you. How content are you with what you desire or crave?

4. To what extent can you fully participate in your present world free of attachments and cravings?

5. Being relatively free of attachments, what do you think would be the most satisfying thing you could do that would reflect your essence?

or granite countertops) or add some decorations (e.g. painting, new sofa, hanging new pictures). There is nothing wrong with these possessions in themselves as long as they are not expected to meet deeper inner needs. This may lead to contentment for a short while before the need arises again to do something more, and the cycle may continue all over again without any lasting contentment. Similarly, an attachment could be an uncontrolled desire to look more attractive or appear more dignified in public. Whatever the extent of the attachment, large or small, it can lead to a time-consuming effort that may bring more frustration and anxiety. As an alternative, we can try to stop always looking for satisfactions outside ourselves that may only temporarily reduce cravings.

As attachments become less and less attractive, people can devote more of their lives to discovering their essence and the type of work that naturally fits with who they are, and meditative exercises may help us discover our deeper yearnings. Deeper, long lasting satisfactions can only ultimately come from within. Among other things social workers can explore whether their desired future naturally fits who they want to be or are. Questions they could ask themselves include (Walsh, 1999):

- What makes me most satisfied?
- What is the most valuable thing(s) I have learned over time?

After answering such questions another set of questions could be asked:

- To reach these aspirations, what strengths and skills do I need to recognize in myself?
- What are some beginning steps I can take in achieving these aspirations?

Explore Your Own Spiritual Practice

Sheridan (2012) describes a spiritual approach for macro practitioners that addresses problems of burnout, unproductive competitiveness, adversarial relationships, and aggression. She describes seven themes of an evolving spiritual activism that are inherent in a growing number of macro-practitioners. These seven characteristics are described in their entirety in chapter 10. While all of these themes are in one way or another relevant to all of social work practice, the final two are especially intriguing and relevant to mention here. Sheridan suggests that for practitioners to change on the outside, they will need to commit to inner work. This makes good sense in that if we are to help clients explore their spirituality concepts, we undoubtedly will want to more fully engage our own spirituality. The inner work and outer work that we do needs to be consistent with each other if we are to be truly authentic and effective. The other theme identified by Sheridan (2012) that naturally follows the first one is that practitioners are encouraged to commit to a personal spiritual practice. This recommendation is based on what various macro practitioners have reported needing and doing. She stresses that such a practice be in keeping with each person's own personal faith journey, which offers them motivation for their involvement, inspiration, and centering. For example, if a practitioner is an atheist or describes their journey as a humanist, they might want to follow a practice using mindfulness, while a Christian might follow a practice of daily Bible study, traditional prayer, or centering prayer.

Several steps are suggested for developing such a spiritual practice. These steps can be compatible with virtually all religious groups and with those who are non-religious. First, it is important to find a **regular time** for such a practice. This time should not conflict with family time or work or other important activities. It should be a natural time for you to get the most out of this experience. It may involve, for example, getting up a half hour earlier if you are a morning person. The afternoon or evening may be better for someone who is more alert at these times. It would probably be most helpful to write a very specific time into your schedule that will not easily be overlooked. Begin with 10 minutes or more of time and see how easy it is to experience that much quiet time. Gradually you can expand the time to 20 minutes, then 30 minutes or more.

Second, find a **location** that is comfortable for you, preferably away from noises and traffic. A corner of a room that is usually not used or a spare bedroom may work best. Or a back porch or maybe even walking around your neighborhood may work. Sometimes a place at a work site may work, such as a quiet time in your office or a walk to a park during lunch as possibilities. One particular place that you can always go is preferred so that you can view this as a special place for your spiritual practice and that alone. Being away from noise created by others in your home or apartment and away from areas that are heavily trafficked such as a dining room or TV area are also important. However, just because you will want to minimize noise, doesn't mean it won't happen. Noise is also possible and it is one interference to learn to manage and ignore if possible.

As a third step, plan to have an **altar** at your location. If it could be interfered with when not in use, it can always be taken down between the times it is used. Altars are described in chapter 9 as an existing spiritual practice of some clients or a possible spiritual intervention offered by a social worker. Your altar is intended only for you and should be created to bring optimum meaning to your spiritual practice. It could be a candle or burning incense. Or an icon or painting. It could be some photos, possibly of family members, friends, or other loved ones. Religious symbols will likely be important for some, such as a cross, prayer beads, a Bible or Quran, or Hindu deities. For others, a non-religious set of items will be chosen. Whatever has the most meaning to you spiritually is what you should choose.

Another important step is to decide on **activities** or how you will spend the time in your practice. A spiritual practice of some sort is to be chosen—something that works best for you. Many will choose to read sacred scriptures, devotions, or poetry while others will choose to mostly pray or meditate. Some may choose to chant. Some may want to have enough room in their space for yoga poses or dance. In many cases more than one activity is likely to be chosen during each time of practice. It is important to choose activities that work for you. Your spiritual practice can change every time you do it or it can remain the same. What is most important is to not force yourself to practice any particular activity or to expect the same activity to work every time. Try not to let boredom or sleepiness set in. Conversely, the goal, if there is one, is to develop such a meaningful practice that you will look forward to getting to it when that time comes each day. One indication of this is that you will feel something is missing in your day when you don't take time to practice.

To have a deeper personal impact, it is important to practice on a **regular basis**. Yet, there will be times that you miss your practice. You may be away from home, forget, be very sick, or have a required work assignment in conflict with your practice time. This is normal and all you can do is be aware that you missed it and get back to your schedule as quickly as you can. However, when beginning a new spiritual practice, anticipate some ups and downs. You may easily be meditating and find yourself thinking about what you have to do and this may compel you to stop meditating abruptly. That's why it is important to start small. Start by sitting for 10 or 15 minutes. Don't add to that time until you feel you are becoming comfortable with practicing for these 10 to 15 minutes. It's wise to have no major expectations. Just practice sitting or reading a special reading. Begin to notice how you are feeling while you are sitting. Stay in touch with your breathing. Maybe you are beginning to feel relaxed and relieved to just sit and have no expectations. Sitting can be very restful if you are someone who is always on the go. Just take in this restful state and enjoy it.

Along with a regular daily spiritual practice, it can be helpful to occasionally have longer experiences of spiritual practice to replenish your body, mind, and spirit from fatigue. **Retreats** are one popular way to do this. Instead of taking 10 to 20 minutes for your practice, retreats offer a half-day, an entire day, or a weekend if you can afford to get away. You may be able to do this every month or maybe only once a year. If you have a car, you may be able to travel from your area to the mountains, into a wooded area, or to a lake or ocean shore point. If you do not have the financial resources to go away, try to find a quiet, welcoming place nearby, like a chapel or sanctuary of a church, synagogue, or mosque open to the public for prayer and meditation. Alternative places are a nearby park, an empty classroom or other unused room, or a public garden. Use your imagination in searching out possible respite places you can visit that will help you to settle in and be still.

Your **activities during a retreat** are much like that of your daily practice—to "be" and not to "do." Whatever you can do to unwind, relax, and transcend your busy life should be your focus. If you are religious, take your sacred books or devotions. Also take the items that make up your altar so that you can set up an altar wherever you are. Prayer and meditation may be central to what you do. You can review a wide range of types of prayer and meditation in chapter 9. Non-religious people can take poetry or inspirational reading material that is important to you. Everyone is encouraged to consider taking and using a journal too, so that you can write things down that happen to you in your experiences that are important. They may be new insights about your daily routine, a nagging pain from a difficult relationship, or spiritual matters of some sort, such as what it feels like to experience

---

A Meditative Bike Ride

(Patrick Swan)

I was able to spend a few hours today on what I would definitely describe as a spiritual retreat. I took my bicycle out on a journey around town to find the perfect spot to spend some time escaping. . . . I started my trip by taking about ten minutes to stretch and plan my route. I was sure to breathe properly while I was stretching, being more mindful of this practice lately. I started to imagine the areas I could explore. I knew of a nice trail and greenway that passed by a lake, forest, and creek that would probably be perfect. . . . Once I made it to the trail I was going to take I decided to slow down and be sure to enjoy more of the natural scenery. There were several new birds I hadn't seen in the area before. One seemed like a crane, which I couldn't remember seeing in the city before. I also saw a few geese. I wondered about their migration patterns as I passed them several times. It occurred to me how amazing it was this animal, like many others, had developed the ability to migrate such as they did, almost as a single symbiotic entity. . . . The spot I picked to meditate was a huge open lot, several acres large, that was surrounded by a neighborhood next to the greenway I was riding along. . . . The experience I had there on a swing was probably the most relaxing I'd had in a long time, and very thought provoking. I opened my eyes at times and stared at the earth moving beneath me. It made me feel very large as I looked at the worn grass and dirt drift under my feet. I looked at the old knotted tree, and wondered how many others had been in this same position. When I closed my eyes I imagined and felt myself floating on water somewhere, perhaps in an ocean. I realize now that I was picturing the ocean at night, with very few waves. . . . Most of all I just felt calm, without thinking; feeling the breeze and the sensation of moving with it. It was extremely relaxing, and looking back the swing was a perfect location for what I wanted to do. There was a slight enough breeze that would swing me around every few minutes, and also cooled me. I don't think I could've picked a better spot. I realized once I started coming back to my original mindset that I'd really been able to block out so much, such as the construction that was going on, thoughts that had been plaguing me earlier in the day, and just normal chatter. I spent about 30 minutes on the swing before I started coming back more "to reality", and deciding to head back home.

this practice. Or possibly you will want to journal about pressing difficulties that you have been tending to ignore and insights about ways you can more deeply discover or face them while minimizing their impact on the future.

Collins (2005) suggests several types of spiritual practices based on a Christian perspective. Many of her suggestions are relevant, with slight modifications, to non-Christians as well. She points out that these practices can help you embody more strength and love within as well as reduce the stress and anxiety of your work and other factors in your environment. She describes several themes that can be emphasized during a spiritual time. Some of these themes have already been mentioned; others have not and are highlighted below with examples.

- **Sabbath Keeping** is a practice of setting aside time each week to stop the usual routines, rest, and simply be in the moment. Sabbath time can be used to express a sacred ritual, visit with family and friends, visit youth or seniors in your community, nap, or take a long leisurely walk.
- **Finding Holy Silence** is a time to experience the quiet and stillness of the moment. This can happen for an hour or more or for smaller time periods such as five minutes of each hour while doing computer work. Set aside times not to talk, drive, work, or eat. Meditation is a good way to use this time as it involves mostly concentrating on your breath and emptying yourself of your thoughts, worries, or other chatter.
- **Expressing Your Spiritual Essence** is a time to re-connect with your true deeper nature to help it become more of who you want to become. This can be implemented in many ways that promote a deeper divine or mystical awareness in you such as participating in special spiritual rituals, ceremonies, support groups, and worship experiences.
- **Embracing a Principle of Stewardship** involves actions that give back to and serve others. It involves caring for the earth in our daily practices and long term plans, and keeping our environmental footprint small while expanding the contributions that we leave behind.

St. Ignatius of Loyola, who lived in France in the 16th century, developed many spiritual exercises still popular today (Hermes, 2001). He was also the founder of the Jesuit Order of Catholic priests, the order with which Pope Francis is affiliated. Ignatius' exercises emphasized guided imagery, discussed more fully as a spiritual intervention in chapter 9. Ignatius suggested that one way to pray is to focus on a passage or story in a sacred reading like the Bible or Quran. In a somewhat modified version, imagine yourself in this scene smelling the air, feeling objects or nature nearby, etc. As you feel this scene, imagine with whom you identify or are repulsed, possible fears and joys, attractions and distractions. Let things happen in this scene that may go well beyond the sacred writings you began with. Then imagine Jesus, Moses, Muhammad, or a revered contemporary spiritual leader coming to you and asking a very personal and important question. What would the question be? Try to answer the question in this spiritual figure's presence and stay there as long as it feels nourishing. One set of exercises that St. Ignatius developed had to do with the consolations and desolations in our daily lives.

Tree of Contemplative Practices

Another set of spiritual practices, more secular in nature, has been developed by the Center for the Contemplative Mind in Society (Center for Contemplative Mind in Society, n.d.). This Center has as its mission to transform higher education by encouraging contemplative perspectives to create more active learning and research investigations that are based on discovering a more just and compassionate society for all people. One of the resources created by this Center is the Tree of Contemplative Practices (http://www.contemplativemind.org/practices/tree). The Tree of Contemplative Practices describes contemplative practices that are either currently in use or could be used in secular organizational and academic settings.

The Tree of Contemplative Practices offers a number of practices that can enhance the quality of a person's life and strengthen their actions taken to promote a more just and compassionate society for all people. In the diagram on this

---

Exercise

Collins (2005) offers four different themes and types of spiritual practice described above. Select one of them and experience this practice for yourself for a few days. Afterward, share your experience with another person.

Exercise: Reflecting on Our Consolations and Desolations

(O'Brien, 2011)

One helpful way to be in touch with yourself each day is to reflect on your day after it's over. First, you can reflect back on times you have been consoled, possibly by your Higher Power, spirit, or other sources. Times of consolation are when we feel energized, drawn more deeply into community, and able to look beyond our experience to take in the joys and sorrows of others. We also need to reflect on when we have times of desolation in our daily routine, such as when we turn away from hope, get caught in a cycle of negative emotions, and feel drained of energy. By examining periodically when we feel consolation and desolation, we receive clues as to where our spirit may be present in our daily lives as well as learn more about changes we may want to make to walk more closely with our spirit.

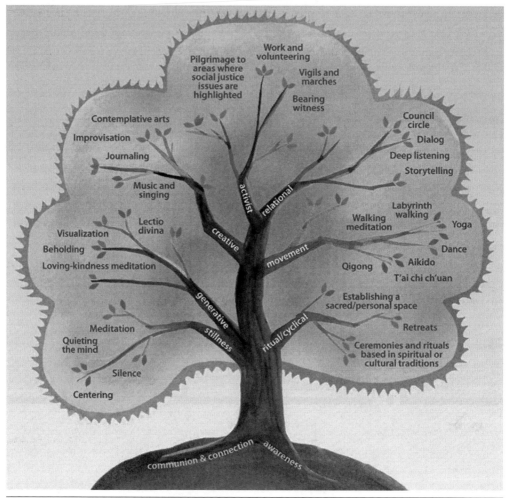

Figure 13.1   Tree of Contemplative Practices

Source: www.contemplativemind.org

group's website, you will find links to descriptions of many of these practices in the branches of the tree. They include:

- stillness (practices include centering, silence, and meditation);
- generative (practices include beholding, loving-kindness meditation, and Lectio Divina);
- creativity (practices of contemplative arts, improvisations, and journaling);
- activism (practice of pilgrimages);
- relational (practices of deep listening, dialogues, Council Circles, and storytelling);
- movement (practices of walking meditation, labyrinth walking, yoga, qigong, aikido, and tai chi);
- ritual (practice of retreats).

An unusual intent of this tree and its spiritual practices is that it is to be used in learning environments such as university and college classes as well as research investigations. While some of these spiritual practices derive from religious groups, they are presented in non-religious ways so they can be applicable to the work and educational worlds.

Conclusion

This chapter focuses on how social workers can prepare for spiritually sensitive professional practice. Preparation includes paying attention to and understanding some of the major challenges that we face in our jobs including being aware of how our clients and colleagues affect us and how the agency itself can have both positive and negative influences on us. The chapter covers several ways that we can prepare, including taking care of ourselves, using spiritual self-care tools, finding happiness and joy in our lives, and learning from a variety of spiritual and religious groups. Readers are also encouraged to develop your own personal spiritual practice to promote your wellness. This personal practice can also help you slow down and become better prepared to give each client the quality care they deserve.

Closing Thought

Nothing can dim the light which shines from within you.

(Maya Angelou)

Discussion Questions and Exercises

1. Walsh (1999), in this chapter, asks us to reflect on some key questions as we pursue our aspirations. They include the following:
   - What makes me most satisfied?
   - What have been my most satisfying relationships and what were they like?
   - What is the most valuable thing(s) I have learned over time?
   - To reach these aspirations, what strengths and skills do I need to recognize in myself?
   - What are some beginning steps I can take in achieving these aspirations?

Journal some reflections on how you would answer these questions for yourself. Or find a friend and explore these questions with each other.

2. Social workers' preparation for practice is important and has many dimensions to it. Kornfield (1993), a Buddhist therapist and monk, introduces an exercise titled "Who am I?" It is an exercise involving two people in which one asks the question "Who are you?" of the other person. The

question is asked over and over and the other person responds with whatever comes to mind. In the beginning their responses may include general things such as I am a man or woman, a father or mother, a social worker or nurse. But as we are asked over and over, we are likely to go deeper and share reflections that may get at more of who we really are or want to be. This may include latent or undeveloped characteristics that have not been fully conscious before, insights into how our past lives have influenced who we are becoming, or evolving images of who we imagine becoming but haven't yet expressed or developed. Consider finding another colleague with whom to participate in this exercise and see if it can be helpful to you.

3. As mentioned earlier, another set of spiritual practices, more secular in nature, has been developed by the Center for the Contemplative Mind in Society (The Contemplative Mind in Society, n. d.). Investigate their website where the Tree of Contemplative Practices is displayed (http://www. contemplativemind.org/practices/tree). As an exercise, pick one of the practices on this tree and become acquainted with this practice by using it for a few days. Then step back and reflect on how this practice has been or can be useful to you in your work as a social worker.

References

Alkema, K., Linton, J., & Davies, R. (2008). A study of the relationship between self-care, compassion satisfaction, compassion fatigue, and burnout among hospice professionals. *Journal of Social Work in End-of-Life & Palliative Care, 4*, 101–119.

Boudrias, J., Desrumauz, P., Gaudreau, P., Nelson, K., Brunet, L., & Savoie, A. (2011). Modeling the experience of psychological health at work: The role of personal resources, socio-organizational resources, and job demands. *International Journal of Stress Management, 18*, 372–395.

Buechner, F. (1969). *The hungering dark*. New York: HarperCollins.

Canda, E. R., & Furman, L. D. (2010). *Spiritual diversity in social work practice*. 2nd edition. New York: Oxford University Press.

Center for Contemplative Mind in Society (n.d.). The tree of contemplative practices. Available online at www.contemplativemind.org/practices/tree.html.

Collins, S. (2007). Social workers, resilience, positive emotions and optimism. *Practice: Social Work in Action, 19*(4), 255–269.

Collins, W. L. (2005). Embracing spirituality as an element of professional self-care. *Social Work & Christianity: Journal of the North American Association of Christians in Social Work, 32*(3), 263–274.

Cox, K., & Steiner, S. (2013). *Self-care and social work: A guide for practitioners, supervisors, and administrators*. Washington, DC: NASW Press.

CSWE (Council on Social Work Education) (2015). *2015 Educational Policy and Accreditation Standards for Baccalaureate and Master's Social Work Programs*. Educational Policy Approved by the CSWE Board of Directors on March 20, 2015; Accreditation Standards approved by the CSWE Commission on Accreditation on June 11, 2015. Alexandria, VA: Author.

Dane, B. (2002). Duty to inform: Preparing social work students to understand vicarious traumatization. *Journal of Teaching in Social Work, 22*(3–4), 3–20.

Diener, E., & Biswas-Diener, R. (2008). *Happiness: Unlocking the mysteries of psychological wealth.* Malden, MA: Blackwell Publishing.

Ellor, J. W., Netting, F. E., & Thibault, J. M. (1999). *Understanding religious and spiritual aspects of human service practice.* Columbia, SC: University of South Carolina Press.

Figley, C. R. (1995). Compassion fatigue: Toward a new understanding of the costs of caring. In B. H. Stamm (Ed.), *Secondary traumatic stress: Self-care issues for clinicians, researchers and educators.* Baltimore: Sidran Press, 3–28.

Folkman, S. (2008). The case for positive emotions in the stress process. *Anxiety, Stress, & Coping,* 21, 3–14.

Fredrickson, B. L. (2001). The role of positive emotions in positive psychology: The broaden-and-build theory of positive emotions. *American Psychologist, 56*(3), 218–226.

Furman, L. D., & Chandy, L. M. (1994). Religion and spirituality: A long neglected cultural component of rural social work practice. *Human Services in the Rural Environment, 17*(3/4), 21–26.

Gantner, R. K. (2012). *Workplace wellness: Performance with a purpose.* Moon Township, PA: Well Works Publishing.

Gockel, A., Cain, T., Malove, S., & James, S. (2013). Mindfulness as clinical training: Student perspectives on the utility of mindfulness training in fostering clinical intervention skills. *Journal of Religion & Spirituality in Social Work: Social Thought, 32,* 36–59.

Grawitch, M. J., Gottschalk, M., & Munz, D. C. (2006). The path to a healthy workplace: A critical review linking healthy workplace practices, employee wellbeing, and organizational improvements. *Consulting Psychology Journal: Practice and Research, 58,* 129–147.

Harvey, A. (1996). *Light upon light: Inspirations from Rumi.* Berkeley, CA: North Atlantic Books.

Hermes, K. J. (2001). *Beginning contemplative prayer: Out of chaos into quiet.* Ann Arbor, MI: Charis Books.

Hicks, S. F. (2009). *Mindfulness and social work.* Chicago: Lyceum Books.

King, B. E. (2014). *The habits of happy people.* Presentation sponsored by Institute for Brain Potential, Los Banos, CA.

Koenig, T., & Spano, R. (2007). The cultivation of social workers' hope in personal life and professional practice. *Journal of Religion & Spirituality in Social Work: Social Thought, 26*(3), 45–61.

Kornfield, J. (1993). *A path with heart: A guide through the perils and promises of spiritual life.* New York: Bantam Books.

Laidag, J. (2007). Recognizing the hazards. In J. Norcross & J. Guy. *Leaving it at the office: A guide to psychotherapist self-care.* New York: Guilford Press, 35–63.

Lazarus, R. S., & Folkman, S. (1984). *Stress, appraisal, and coping.* New York: Springer.

Leung, P. P., Chan, C. L., Ng, S., & Lee, M. (2009). Towards body-mind–spirit integration: East meets West. *Clinical Social Work Journal, 37,* 303–311.

Loeb, P. R. (2010). *Soul of a citizen: Living with conviction in challenging times.* 2nd edition. New York: St. Martin's Press.

Lyubomirsky, S. (2007). *The how of happiness: A new approach to getting the life you want.* New York: Penguin Books.

Lyubomirsky, S., Sheldon, K. M., & Schkade, D. (2005). Pursuing happiness: The architecture of sustainable change. *Review of General Psychology, 9,* 111–131.

McCullough, M. E., Pargament, K. I., & Thorensen, C. E. (Eds.) (2001). *Forgiveness: Theory, research, and practice.* New York: New York, Guilford Press.

McGarrigle, T., & Walsh, C. A. (2012). Mindfulness, self-care, and wellness in social work: Effects of contemplative training. *Journal of Religion & Spirituality in Social Work: Social Thought, 30*(3), 212–233.

Mackenzie, E. R., Rajagopal, D. E., Meibohm, M., & Lavizzo-Mourey R. (2000). Spiritual support and psychological well-being: Older adults' perceptions of the religion and health connection. *Alternative Therapies in Health and Medicine, 6*(6), 37–45.

Maslach, C., & Gomes, M. E. (2006). Overcoming burnout. In R. M. McNair (Ed.), *Working for peace: A handbook of practical psychology and others tools.* Atascadero, CA: Impact Publishers, 43–49.

Milano, M. G. (1998). Religious commitment and health status: A review of the research and implications for family medicine. *Archives of Family Medicine, 7*(20), 118–124.

Musgrave, C. F., Allen, C. E., & Allen, G. J. (2002). Spirituality and health for women of color. *American Journal of Public Health, 92*(4), 557–560.

Nhat Hanh, T. (2013). *Work: How to find joy and meaning in each hour of the day.* Berkley CA: Parallax Press.

Norcross, J. C., & Guy, J. D. (2007). *Leaving it at the office: A guide to psychotherapist self-care.* New York: Guilford Press.

O'Brien, K. (2011). *The Ignatian adventure: Experiencing the spiritual exercises of St. Ignatius in daily life.* Chicago: Loyola press.

Perlman, L. A. & Saakvitne, K. W. (1995). *Trauma and the therapist: Countertransference and vicarious traumatization in psychotherapy with incest survivors.* New York: Norton & Co.

Pooler, D. K., Wolfer, T., & Freeman, M. (2014a). Finding joy in social work: Interpersonal sources. *Families in Society, 95*(1), 34–42.

Pooler, D. K., Wolfer, T., & Freeman, M. (2014b). Finding joy in social work II: Intrapersonal sources. *Social Work, 59*(3), 213–221.

Radey, M., & Figley, C. R. (2007). The social psychology of compassion. *Clinical Social Work Journal, 35*, 207–214.

Rice, D., & Dudley, J. (1997). Preparing students for the spiritual issues of their clients through a self-assessment exercise. *Journal of Baccalaureate Social Work, 3*(1), 85–95.

Rothman, J. (2009). Spirituality: What we can teach and how we can teach it. *Journal of Religion and Spirituality in Social Work: Social Thought, 28*(1–2), 161–184.

St. Johns, A. R. (2010). *Happily grateful.* Seattle: Compendium.

Seligman, M. E. (2002). *Authentic happiness: Using the new positive psychology to realize your potential for lasting fulfillment.* New York: Free Press.

Sheridan, M. (2009). Ethical issues in the use of spiritually based interventions in social work practice: What we are doing and why. *Journal of Religion and Spirituality in Social Work: Social Thought, 28*(1/2), 99–126.

Sheridan, M. (2012). Introduction: Connecting spirituality and social justice within macro-practice. *Journal of Religion & Spirituality in Social Work: Social Thought, 31*, 1–8.

Skovholt, T. M., & Trotter-Mathison, M. (2011). *The resilient practitioner: Burnout prevention and self-care strategies for counselors, therapists, teachers, and health professionals.* New York: Routledge.

Walsh, R. (1999). *Essential spirituality: The 7 central practices to awaken heart and mind.* New York: John Wiley & Sons.

Index

Note: Page numbers in **bold** type refer to **figures**
Page numbers in *italic* type refer to *tables*